DAMN FINE SOLDIERS

DAMN FINE SOLDIERS

The Epic Story of Task Force 2-7 Infantry and the 21-Day Attack to Baghdad That Changed Modern Warfare

LT. COL. SCOTT RUTTER (USA, RET.) AND MATTHEW PAUL

FOREWORD BY #1 *NEW YORK TIMES* BESTSELLING AUTHOR BRIAN KILMEADE

STACKPOLE BOOKS

Essex, Connecticut

STACKPOLE BOOKS
An imprint of The Globe Pequot Publishing Group, Inc.
64 South Main Street
Essex, CT 06426
www.globepequot.com

British Library Cataloguing in Publication Information available

Library of Congress Cataloging-in-Publication Data
Names: Rutter, Scott author | Paul, Matthew, author
Title: Damn fine soldiers : on the road Baghdad with the Army Task-Force 2-7 / Lt. Col. Scott Rutter and Matthew Paul.
Description: Essex, Connecticut : Stackpole Books, [2026] | Includes bibliographical references | Summary: "A frontline account of the battles, the brotherhood, and the grit that defined the opening drive of Operation Iraqi Freedom. Visceral and reflective, Damn Fine Soldiers is an unfiltered account of modern war, told from the tip of the spear that drove deep into Iraq in March and April 2003. More than a memoir by two commanders who led from the front, it is testimony and tribute to the fighting spirit of the American soldier"-- Provided by publisher.
Identifiers: LCCN 2025049661 (print) | LCCN 2025049662 (ebook) | ISBN 9781493096992 paperback | ISBN 9781493097005 ebook
Subjects: LCSH: Iraq War, 2003-2011--Personal narratives, American | United States. Army. Task Force 2-7 | United States. Army. Infantry Regiment, 7th. Battalion, 2nd | Iraq War, 2003-2011--Regimental histories--United States
Classification: LCC DS79.765.U6 R88 2026 (print) | LCC DS79.765.U6 (ebook)
LC record available at https://lccn.loc.gov/2025049661
LC ebook record available at https://lccn.loc.gov/2025049662

The views expressed in this publication are those of the author and do not necessarily reflect the official policy or position of the Department of Defense or the U.S. government. The public release clearance of this publication by the Department of Defense does not imply Department of Defense endorsement or factual accuracy of the material. Some of the names identified in the book have been changed to protect privacy.

For our fellow service members and their families, a portion of the proceeds from this book supports TAPS.

T★A★P★S
Tragedy Assistance Program for Survivors

CONTENTS

FOREWORD

BRIAN KILMEADE, FOX NEWS, COHOST OF *FOX & FRIENDS* AND HOST OF *ONE NATION WITH BRIAN KILMEADE*

It's a great honor for me to write this foreword for Lieutenant Colonel Scott Rutter, though I am fully aware that I did not fight in this war—I only covered it every day on *Fox News*. I was there on the air as our troops crossed the Kuwaiti border into Iraq live on *Fox & Friends*, carrying the invasion to the American people in real time. But what truly gave me insight and understanding was what I witnessed in Kuwait one week before the invasion—watching and reporting on our troops as they prepared for what lay ahead. I saw men and women in every base camp before any enemy engagement, and I could not have been more impressed. The dedication, professionalism, and patriotic pride were everywhere.

It was in Kuwait that I first met and reported on Lieutenant Colonel Rutter and his unit. I saw firsthand how deeply he cared for his troops and how meticulously he prepared them for the mechanics and adjustments needed to win a war whose full scope no one could yet comprehend. I also knew, painfully, that some of the soldiers I was getting to know would not make it home—a reality I have never forgotten.

What Scott and his cowriter Matt Paul accomplish in *Damn Fine Soldiers* is to bring readers into the war itself. They reveal the constant adaptation required to succeed, the trust the Pentagon placed in its battlefield commanders, and the unrelenting demands of modern combat. Before drawing any conclusions about this war, one should read this book—and others like it—to understand how our professional fighting force evolved as the fight itself changed, learning from mistakes and forging new ways to prevail.

Perhaps most impressive is how Rutter's Task Force 2-7 shaped the battlefield and excelled in one of warfare's most challenging environments—urban combat. They fought in cities where the enemy lived, in places we had never set foot before. The fighting was literally house to house. The task force faced fierce resistance at key waterways, particularly at strategic crossing points fortified by Republican Guard units. The book vividly details the complex coordination of combined arms operations that enabled successful bridging maneuvers under fire, showcasing the tactical innovations that emerged amid the chaos of battle.

What I believe readers will value most about *Damn Fine Soldiers* is its human element. Beyond the strategy and tactics, this book captures the humanity at the heart of modern warfare. Yes, we have the best equipment and technology—but what you will come to understand is that we also have the best soldiers. And through these pages, you will come to know some of their names.

History often remembers wars through the lens of generals, presidents, and defense secretaries. This book shifts that focus to the men and women who fought the Iraq War—their decisions, their courage, and their will to survive when survival itself was victory.

I have immense respect for every generation of America's warfighters, but I have always believed that this generation stands equal to, if not above, them all. *Damn Fine Soldiers* will show you why—and remind you what true service, sacrifice, and leadership look like.

ENDORSEMENT BLURB FROM MAJOR GENERAL BUFORD BLOUNT US ARMY RETIRED, CG 3ID (M) OIF1

As the commanding general of the 3rd Infantry Division during the invasion of Iraq, I had the privilege of witnessing firsthand the exceptional performance of Task Force 2-7 Infantry throughout our lightning advance to Baghdad. In *Damn Fine Soldiers*, Lieutenant Colonel Scott Rutter and Matt Paul have masterfully captured the ground truth of modern combat operations through the eyes of those who executed them at the most crucial moments.

The book's unflinching account of the intense engagements faced by Task Force 2-7 Infantry during the march to Baghdad—the ferocious battles at Objective Raiders, the harrowing urban fighting in Samawah, and the lightning assault across the Euphrates—reveals the extraordinary challenges overcome by American soldiers operating at the limit of their endurance.

The battle for Baghdad International Airport stands as the decisive engagement of the invasion. There Task Force 2-7 Infantry encountered layered, sophisticated defenses including entrenched Republican Guard positions, reinforced bunkers, and presighted artillery. Rutter's tactical acumen shone as he rapidly established critical blocking positions along the eastern approaches, effectively cutting off Iraqi reinforcement routes. When intelligence indicated a large mechanized Republican Guard counterattack forming to strike the airport proper, Task Force 2-7 didn't merely hold their ground—they launched a preemptive assault. I watched as their combined arms teams methodically destroyed this threat through synchronized tank-infantry operations, neutralizing a force that could have significantly delayed our timeline for securing Baghdad. The sight of Task Force 2-7's Bradleys and Abrams tanks maneuvering under fire while dismounted infantry cleared complex terrain demonstrated combined arms mastery at its finest.

During these intense firefights, I witnessed extraordinary acts of heroism—tank commanders exposing themselves to direct fire to better direct their gunners, infantry squads assaulting fortified positions with unrelenting courage, medics rushing through active kill zones to reach wounded comrades.

Perhaps most impressive was the task force's rapid redeployment from the airport when I ordered them to reinforce 2nd Brigade during our attack from the south of Baghdad. I made the decision to personally travel with Task Force 2-7 during this decisive action—a testament to both the operation's critical importance and my complete confidence in Rutter's leadership. Watching these already battle-weary soldiers move with precision and purpose to destroy enemy forces at Objective Curley was nothing short of inspirational. Their heroic efforts gave the 2 BDE commander the combat power necessary to continue the attack from the south and enter Baghdad while destroying enemy forces. This rapid reinforcement operation exemplified the division's agility and Task Force 2-7's unwavering commitment to whatever mission they were assigned.

Scott Rutter's command presence throughout these engagements was remarkable—always positioned where he could best influence the fight, maintaining clear-eyed focus even under the most chaotic conditions. His partnership with Matt Paul in creating this definitive account ensures that both the tactical brilliance and human dimensions of these operations are preserved for future generations.

Damn Fine Soldiers stands as essential reading for military professionals seeking to understand combined arms maneuver against determined conventional forces, and for all Americans who want to comprehend the extraordinary sacrifices their fellow citizens made during those historic twenty-one days in 2003. The speed, violence of action, and tactical excellence demonstrated by Task Force 2-7 Infantry represents the finest traditions of the American combat arms. Their story deserves to be told, studied, and remembered.

ACKNOWLEDGMENTS

We wish to extend our deepest gratitude to the soldiers who shared their stories, experiences, and reflections with us. This book exists because of their courage, honesty, and willingness to relive difficult moments so that others might learn and remember. Their voices breathe life into these pages.

This work is dedicated not only to them, but also to their families—those who stood steadfastly behind them through long deployments, sleepless nights, and the many sacrifices that military life demands. Their strength and support are inseparable from the achievements we recount here.

As coauthors, we recognize that while these pages reflect our own experiences, they also carry the voices of many. The true authors of this story are the soldiers who lived it alongside us, and the loved ones who carried them through.

—Lieutenant Colonel (Retired) Scott Rutter and Matthew Paul

PREFACE

Every infantry officer dreams of commanding a battalion. No soldier who has witnessed combat wishes for conflict, but leading troops at that level represents the pinnacle of one's professional development and the culmination of years of preparation and perseverance. Infantry battalions are large enough to fight independently but small enough that their leaders still know all their soldiers by name. Battalion command represents the last chance for an officer to lead from the field, shoulder to shoulder with soldiers. The generals fight from a distance; I was in the turret with my gunner and with the soldiers when they dismounted and fought. Not only was I given the opportunity to command, but I was assigned to one of the heaviest, most lethal units in the United States Armed Forces: 2nd Battalion, 7th Infantry. It belonged to the 1st Brigade, 3rd Infantry Division headquartered in Fort Stewart, Georgia.

In every generation, there are warriors who stand at the edge of history and push forward. 2-7 Infantry "Cottonbalers" did just that in the spring of 2003. This is not just a story of tanks and tactics, of maps and maneuvers. It's also a story of ordinary men who became extraordinary under the weight of war.

From the breach at the Iraqi border to the gates of Baghdad, these soldiers endured the longest nights, the harshest terrain, and combat more intense than the Army had seen since Vietnam. They didn't fight for glory or recognition. They fought for each other. They led from the front, adapted under fire, and held the line when the enemy surged. Their legacy isn't just written in medals and citations; it lives in the memory of every soldier who survived those twenty-one days of hell.

This book is a tribute to their grit, their sacrifice, and their brotherhood. It's a reminder that leadership isn't about rank—it's about presence.

That courage isn't the absence of fear—it's the will to act in spite of it. And the legacy of 2-7 Infantry isn't confined to history. It continues in every soldier who trains, fights, and leads today. On March 20, 2003, a combined force consisting of Army, Air Force, Navy, Marines, and coalition allies launched Operation Iraqi Freedom, aimed at toppling Iraq's regime. Our objective required a swift and violent thrust to the capital. It was a modern-day *blitzkrieg* aimed at the Iraqi regime's base of legitimacy and power. That is exactly what we did.

This is a true account of my battalion's actions during Operation Iraqi Freedom. It offers multiple perspectives from the war, focusing on the human cost and on the decisions that weighed on those in command.

The march was long, hard, and dangerous. Just as in Vietnam, the enemy was everywhere; some wore uniforms and some did not. Commanders had to make critical decisions with limited information, adapting constantly to the "fog of war." This reality shaped every move and underscored the principle that the enemy always gets a vote. Danger and death waited around every bend in the road and behind every building. The only things you could trust were your own judgment, your equipment, and the soldiers to your left and right. We were cut off—cut off from our supply lines, our homes, our friends, and our families. There was only one direction in which we could travel, and that was north. The only way home was forward . . . through Baghdad.

2-7 Infantry fought eight decisive engagements over twenty-one days against the Iraqi enemy force of elite special operators, the Republican Guard, regular Iraqi Army, and irregular militia. We were truly the "Tip of the Spear." In many instances, 2-7 was the first ground force to break through enemy defenses, absorb the initial shock of combat, and force the fight forward. Our battalion helped pave the way for the 3rd Infantry Division's capture of Baghdad. The Army awarded my soldiers countless medals for valor, including the Medal of Honor, posthumously awarded to Sergeant First Class Paul Smith for his incredible actions at Saddam International Airport on April 4, 2003.

March to April 2003 marked the last time the US Army conducted a large-scale combat operation. Although this book is not intended as a "how-to" on leadership or a handbook for conducting combat operations, the hard-fought lessons still matter and resonate today. Our goal is to share the thoughts, feelings, and decisions we experienced during that time and describe firsthand the sights, smells, and sounds of war, up close and personal.

We have also attempted to provide the reader with some background on Iraq and the build-up to war. We describe the uncertain period after the regime collapsed, and our introduction to a new kind of enemy—one that mined the roads, fired mortars and RPGs, and then disappeared into the shadows.

We discuss strategy and how our mission fit within the broader coalition effort in Iraq. We also tried to provide some insight and perspective on the greater Global War on Terror by illustrating the post-9/11 battlefield at the tactical level. We share many vivid accounts of small unit actions exemplifying how our soldiers and leaders performed under fire while navigating a strange place, a different people, and while suffering the most savage conditions that pushed them to their breaking point. The courage, discipline, ingenuity, and endurance they demonstrated time and again will stay with us forever.

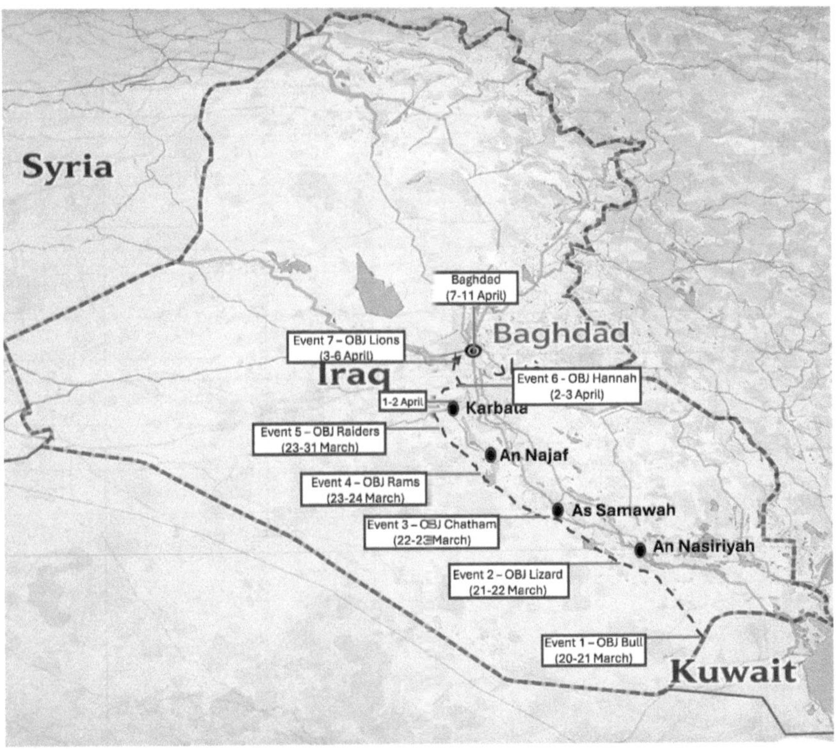

Task Force 2-7 events 1-7 campaign map with dates.
Source: Author's image.

MARCHING ORDERS

Only one military organization can hold and gain ground in war—a ground army supported by tactical aviation with supply lines guarded by the navy.

—*General Omar N. Bradley, A Soldier's Story (1951)*

The desert was still black when we rolled out, engines growling low in the darkness. The air smelled of oil and dust, thick in my throat. My soldiers were silent, each lost in their own thoughts, checking weapons by touch more than sight. Somewhere out there, beyond the horizon, waited the border of Iraq and a war whose shape and cost none of us could see. I remember gripping the radio handset and thinking that in a few hours, I will be asking these soldiers to risk everything. Am I ready? Are they?

On the eve of war, we sat there in the desert sand thinking about the past, present, and future. It was a strange place—seven thousand miles from home. But in a strange way, it also felt close to home. The sand reminded me of the popular beaches of Hilton Head or Tybee Island, less than an hour's drive from my home at Fort Stewart, Georgia. I could close my eyes and run my fingers through the sand, imagining myself seated peacefully on the soft earth surrounded by hundreds of happy men, women, and children. You could almost hear the hypnotic crash of the surf as it slammed against the shallow ocean floor. The relaxation, the serenity, and the joy of watching children play could all be felt with the scoop of a hand and the feeling and the vision one gets when the small stones cascade through the fingers like a waterfall. In my mind it was last summer, my last pleasant memory of life before the inevitability of war in Iraq. But I wasn't surrounded by children at play. No one around me was laughing. Nothing here was funny.

I was surrounded by heavy metal instruments of destruction and hundreds of anxious young Americans waiting impatiently for the word to go north. The soldiers of 2-7 Infantry wondered what the next few days and months ahead would bring. They reflected on the loved ones they'd left behind—our curious children, our caring wives and sweethearts, and what they must have been thinking at that very same moment. Many of us reflected on the mission and our awesome responsibilities to it. Our success or failure would determine the fate of the war and the greater Global War on Terror would be held in the balance. The star-lit sky was as clear as it had been the last two months we were here in this desolate country, training and readying ourselves for the harsh realities of combat. The weather was on our side this night—the unforgiving sand and wind would give us a brief respite during our fateful leap into enemy territory—the first step of many throughout our audacious drive north . . . into the breach and onward to Baghdad.

I knew from the beginning that the march into Iraq would be more than a mission. It was a gamble with lives, reputations, and history. For my soldiers, the stakes were brutally simple: survival. For me, it was the crushing weight of leadership. Every order I gave could decide whether a soldier lived or died. And for the Army, the outcome of our fight would either validate a decade of preparation or it would expose our flaws. We weren't just driving north into the desert—we were driving into the unknown, with the eyes of the nation fixed on us. Regardless of the outcome, things would never be the same again.

None of us could have guessed how fast this war would unfold, or how quickly the desert would turn into fire and steel. Within weeks, we would be charging down the streets of Baghdad, fighting block by block against a desperate enemy. But on that night, all we had was the silence of the desert, the weight of our gear, and the unspoken knowledge that history was about to test us.

The last year and a half was a prelude to this moment—the poignant sentiments still frozen in my mind. Perhaps the epic story of Task Force 2-7 Infantry began on September 11, 2001—a day that would begin like any other in the US Army. The typical American soldier conducted morning physical training, qualified with his assigned weapon on the rifle range, stood guard at a checkpoint in Bosnia or Kosovo, or scanned the horizon for illegal military activity along the desert sands of Sinai, Egypt. The 2nd Battalion, 7th Infantry Regiment of the 3rd Infantry Division had an ordinary morning, mundane by Army standards. It was the beginning of my unit's lifecycle, where we were in the process of "standing up"—filling our ranks with new soldiers and noncommissioned officers (NCOs) right before we could transition into a comprehensive training regimen that would later culminate with a training center rotation or a deployment anywhere in the world.

During the period between the close of the Persian Gulf War and 2001, the Army's operational tempo increased by 300 percent. At the same time, the Army shrunk to 70 percent of its size during the 1991 Persian Gulf War. Our commitments abroad in the 1990s were deemed "Operations Other Than War," or OOTW for short. Consequently, the US Army's focus shifted from warfighting to nation building. During the 1990s, the bulk of our troops was deployed in a peacekeeping role in the Balkans—during the tumultuous period following the Soviet Union's collapse, resulting in the destabilization of the Communist politico-economic franchise in eastern Europe.

Because all our deployments abroad were not of a combat nature, the training focus at the time was less on maneuvering large formations of infantry and armor on the same scale analogous to the 1991 war in Iraq. Over the course of a decade, we lost some of our warfighting skills. By the summer of 2001, we were a paradox—an Army constantly in motion yet less ready for the kind of sustained, high-intensity fight that would come after the towers fell. We had the will, the professionalism, and the pride. What we lacked was the depth, the funding, and the strategic focus to match the scale of the challenges that were about to confront us.

On 9/11, the battalion was at the tail end of a very long and tedious training support cycle, which is typically characterized by individual and unit taskings designed to support various activities throughout the division. This is conducted while other units in the division conduct real-world missions or are training and preparing for those types of missions. In our case, the other two battalions of our brigade were on deployment to Kosovo, "KFOR Rotation-3A," as part of a multinational peacekeeping force under NATO command. We were left behind holding down the fort, so to speak. Our primary responsibility was to act as the brigade's rear headquarters, with myself as the acting brigade commander. Every tasking that would normally flow from division to brigade was routed directly to my battalion. Every task that our brigade's three battalions could accomplish would now have to be completed by mine alone. As a result, our training was slighted and consequently the morale within the battalion was at an all-time low . . . the calm before the storm.

September 11, 2001. This day should have been as ordinary as the last. Tragedy struck during the typical American's morning—waking up, preparing for work, driving to work, drinking that first cup of coffee. The day would have progressed, where we would have spent the next eight to twelve hours slaving over a desk or working with our hands and standing on our tired, blistering feet. Finally, around dusk, we hardworking Americans would have driven home and talked with our families about our days over dinner, perhaps a dish of meat and potatoes topped off with a slice of hot apple pie. The early morning hours of 9/11 were shaping up to be just as routine as those of 9/10. It would take a significant event to break the cycle of this mundane yet picturesque illustration of American life.

Terrorists put a damper on our plans for this seemingly ordinary day—a day that should have been as ordinary as the last. Nineteen radical terrorists dubbed "Al Qaeda" took control of four planes, crashing two into the World Trade Center's Twin Towers and one into the Pentagon; the fourth was forced into the Pennsylvania ground by its passengers. Three thousand innocent American citizens were killed as a result. 9/11 changed everything and everyone. It changed how we thought about humanity and our values, how we thought about our security, and it rallied the country for war. In my lifetime, I never saw America more united than on 9/12. If you owned an American flag, you flew it. If you didn't own one, you bought one.

September 11, 2001, was a day that would forever live in infamy. It was to be only the second time in the past century a foreign enemy launched a significant attack on American soil. The fabric of our freedom was ripped out of our very souls—we were all New Yorkers that day. It was clear that America would rise from the ashes like a phoenix and strike down those responsible. With our heads bowed while observing a moment of silence, I made a commitment to myself to never waste an opportunity to train and prepare for the possibility to fight this emerging battle and its new diabolical enemy—a capable adversary who not only kills mercilessly but also embraces and memorializes the prospects of his own death in the process. Our lives and, infinitely more important, our freedom and way of life hinged on our ability to keep our fighting skills sharp. Our sacrifices and our accomplishments would write our nation's history in this new generation of warfare. The fighting will of the American soldier would have to endure the future hardships that lay ahead—our strength, perseverance, and stamina in this war would decide nothing less than the fate of the world.

We heard stories from eyewitnesses in New York City, illustrating the experience while describing the emotions during each of the events that unfolded on September 11, 2001. One lady in particular recounted feeling overcome by fear after viewing the second plane impale itself into the Twin Towers. She said that when they heard the sound of a third plane in the sky, panic erupted on the streets until they looked up and finally saw the sun sparkle off the American fighter jet soaring through the sky, intent on intercepting additional terrorist-controlled planes and protecting the city from further attacks. The lady recalls feeling an overwhelming sigh of relief. She felt safe again. Her experience was an ominous symbol of what was yet to come. The US military would avenge those lost on this tragic day and would make things right again. Since the events of 9/11, our battalion, and perhaps the entire Army, renewed our focus on our wartime mission—to close with and destroy the enemy.

Shortly after the September 11 terrorist attacks, President George Bush addressed the nation and declared war on terror. Our country's new mission was to root out terrorists and their support structure across the globe. We would attack terror on many fronts. If other countries did not support our efforts, they would be deemed to be "with the terrorists." America's first target was Al Qaeda. This terrorist organization was seeking refuge within the borders of Afghanistan and was afforded protection and safe haven by the Taliban regime. The president closed his address with a simple order to his military: "Be ready."

Captain Matt Paul's perspective on September 11, 2001:

> My father's generation remembers where they were when President Kennedy was shot. My generation remembers where they were on the morning of 9/11.
>
> We were out in the woods at Fort Stewart on the morning of September 11, 2001, just me and my mortar platoon conducting a live-fire exercise. Ours was the only platoon from 2-7 Infantry in the field that week, which in hindsight felt almost prescient. For the past year I had dragged these young soldiers into the field every month—rain or shine—to shoot live rounds and refine our field craft. They were tired of me by then. To them, I was the fun police, the guy keeping them from the club, from Nintendo, from girls. Until that morning, I was the enemy.
>
> We had an old television rigged up in the Fire Direction Center, a little thirteen-inch screen with rabbit ears pulling in static-ridden channels. The set played in the background while we fired missions, its faint glow almost lost in the daylight. When the first plane struck the Twin Towers, we barely paused. We thought it was some freak accident and kept shooting. But when the second plane hit, everything

> stopped. All thirty of my soldiers huddled shoulder to shoulder around that tiny screen, watching in silence as the country we swore to defend came under attack.
>
> I wrestled with whether to send us home or stay in the field. The decision came quickly—this meant war, and we needed to train. No further explanation was required; the soldiers understood it without me saying a word. Every round we fired after that wasn't just another mission—it was aimed at Osama bin Laden. I was the only one with a cell phone in 2001, so I passed it around and let each soldier call home to reassure their families that they were safe. That night, the joking stopped. The air was tense, serious, focused. My platoon had finally found its purpose, and in that moment they stopped seeing me as the enemy.

The 7th Infantry Regiment has a long and honorable lineage of defending America, "being ready" for the country as far back as 1798. It was mustered out of service only two years later in 1800. On May 3, 1808, the regiment was reorganized and has been in honored service ever since. Former president Zachary Taylor was one of the first officers to serve in the newly formed regiment. Andrew Jackson—another former president—commanded the regiment as part of a larger force fighting the British during the War of 1812.

The 7th distinguished itself during the battle of New Orleans in 1815 when they sought cover behind bales of cotton, affording them protection against the advancing hail of British musket fire. They held their ground and sent the British Army into full retreat, leading to the eventual withdrawal of the British Army from American soil forever. As a result of their actions during the battle of New Orleans, the regiment coined its eternal nickname, "The Cottonbalers." Over time, its soldiers earned a reputation as "damn fine soldiers."

> Before you stands a damn fine soldier . . . a COTTONBALER . . . by God! I can be counted on to accomplish any mission . . . any task . . . any job. I have been in the arena. My face is covered with dust, sweat, and blood. I have known the sweet fragrance of freedom for I have paid the price. I am a damn fine soldier . . . a COTTONBALER . . . by God!

The Cottonbaler Regiment has been called upon for action during every major conflict since its formation in 1798, earning seventy-eight battle streamers during its participation in the Civil War, the Spanish American

War, the Philippine Insurrection, the Mexican War, World Wars I and II, the Korean and Vietnam Wars, and the Persian Gulf War. It is considered the Army's top regiment for its date of inception, campaign participation, and awards and decorations. No infantry regiment in the history of our Army has seen more combat than the 7th. Every new Cottonbaler officer learns the history; every new lieutenant lugs around a bale of cotton during long runs and ruck marches to feel the history. They don't forget it.

I was privileged to command the 2nd Battalion, 7th Infantry Regiment, the "Willing and Able" Battalion. For the most part, the regimental formation is gone in today's Army structure, but the title remains for historical reasons. And as the lowest numbered Cottonbaler battalion still in active service, I had the honor of safeguarding the original regimental colors (battle flag) dating all the way back to the War of 1812—the same colors that dominated the New Orleans battlefield. As in previous conflicts that determined our nation's destiny, the Willing and Able Battalion and its Cottonbaler Regiment would be committed to one more fight, the Global War on Terror.

Iraq was not Afghanistan, and in 2003, it still had a capable military. It could fight on the ground and in mechanized formations. It never fully recovered from Desert Storm in 1991, but it could still fight if properly motivated. It could shoot, move, and communicate. It had some of the best equipment the Russians could provide, including T-72 tanks, attack helicopters, and long-range artillery and missiles. Whether the Iraqis could orchestrate all their combat assets to mount a stubborn defense was still an open question. It was a question we would keep asking ourselves from the Iraqi border to Baghdad. To win decisively in Iraq meant that the US Army needed a formation like ours. My unit, part of the 3rd Infantry Division, was perfect for such a mission.

The 3rd Infantry Division is a mechanized infantry division consisting of four primary combat systems—the M2A2 ODS (Operation Desert Storm) Bradley Fighting Vehicle, the M1A1 Abrams Main Battle Tank, the AH-64 Apache Gunship, and the M109A3 Paladin. The combined effects from these weapon systems can produce a devastating effect on any enemy. The systems comprise the phalanx of the division, but only with an infantryman's boots on the ground can an army declare total victory in war. A major emphasis within any infantry division is the effective employment of its dismounted infantrymen. Their ability to seize and hold terrain is the decisive factor and is of paramount importance in battle. Our division had three maneuver brigades with three maneuver battalions each, equipped with either tanks or Bradleys. My unit had the Bradleys—designated a mechanized infantry battalion.

The infantry fighting vehicle is called the "Bradley," in recognition of General Omar Bradley, the prominent World War II field commander who was considered by many as "The Soldier's General." Throughout the war, his efforts and command philosophy clearly demonstrated his care and concern for his soldiers' well-being. This same care and concern for the infantry soldier would be considered while designing the Bradley Fighting Vehicle. Billions were spent and careers were sacrificed to make the Bradley the best infantry fighting vehicle in the world.

In the late 1980s, the Bradley replaced the M113 Armored Personnel Carrier as the Army's primary armored infantry transport system. The M113 lacked sufficient armor, armament, or speed to be successful in the Cold War battlefield. The Bradley would compensate for all these shortcomings, enabling the soldier in combat to effectively kill and survive on this new, emerging battlefield. For the soldiers inside it, the Bradley was more than a vehicle—it was transportation, protection, firepower, and sometimes the only thing standing between life and death.

The US Army upgraded the Bradley Fighting Vehicle in both speed and armor several times. All Bradley variants were battle-tested during Operation Desert Storm in 1991. Shortly after the war, Bradley crewmen were surveyed on the efficiency, durability, lethality, and survivability of the various systems on the vehicle. The Army reviewed the crewmen's answers and recommendations and developed five upgrades to the Bradley. The new Bradley would be equipped with a laser range finder that automatically directs the precise aim of the weapon systems on to the target, a target identification system designed to minimize fratricide, troop benches in the rear troop compartment as opposed to individual seats—facilitating the rapid dismount of infantry—an improved ammunition upload system, and a water heater designed to cook Meals-Ready-to-Eat (MREs). These improvements resulted in the official upgrade of the Bradley system and the classification was subsequently modified from the M2A2 to the M2A2 (ODS).

Prior to Operation Iraqi Freedom, our mechanized infantry battalion consisted of about nine hundred soldiers, broken down into three rifle companies—Alpha, Bravo, and Charlie Companies—and a Headquarters Company composed of the task force mortar, medical, maintenance, and scout platoons, the headquarters' staff, and support personnel. Our companies were nicknamed Rage, Bushmaster, Rock, and Headhunter, respectively. Each rifle company fielded fourteen Bradley Fighting Vehicles and nine infantry squads. A single rifle company was extremely lethal, possessing the capability to attack and destroy an entrenched enemy force while still preserving enough combat power to continue their attack elsewhere.

My battalion's mortar platoon, known as "Thunder," consisted of four carrier-mounted 120mm mortars responsible for providing immediate and responsive indirect fire support to the battalion. Mortars are a battalion commander's "hip pocket artillery." If a commander couldn't get bombs or artillery on to a target, he had his mortars right there with him, with guns laid on the target, and with ready gun crews simply waiting for the order to "FIRE." Each thirty-four-pound, high-explosive mortar round is designed to inflict maximum destruction in a large area, capable of annihilating troops in open ground, collapsing buildings, and demolishing bunkers.

"Sabre," as the scout platoon was referred, employs ten armored high-mobility multipurpose wheeled vehicles (HMMWVs) to accomplish their unique mission, to provide the battalion commander with on-site battlefield intelligence. They are referred to as the "eyes" of the battalion. With their advanced long-range optical devices, they can see the enemy deeper than the rest of us, well beyond the battalion's front lines. Scout teams can provide the battalion with early warning, classify bridges, gather intelligence on enemy obstacles and dispositions, and even fight the enemy directly to test their capabilities, strengths, and weaknesses. In training and in war, I often used my scouts for route reconnaissance—to find the best path for the rest of my battalion to travel.

Our battalion was not called upon for the war in Afghanistan. Our nation would not adopt the same strategy as the Soviets in the 1980s, of blanketing the country with entire divisions of tanks and armored personnel carriers. The large military footprint was the very cause of alienation from the Soviets and a major source of popular support for the *Mujahadeen*, the Islamic resistance group born out of the Soviet-Afghan War. Its roots grew strong there and inspired decades-long holy war throughout the Middle East, the Balkans, Europe, and the United States. Over the course of ten bloody years, the *Mujahadeen* skillfully picked apart the cumbersome Soviet military a piece at a time as they lumbered laboriously and clumsily through the isolated villages and tight mountain passes characteristic of their new and unfamiliar battlefield. In a sense, the Soviets brought a hammer to fix Afghanistan, when they should have brought a Phillips-head screwdriver.

Throughout Operation Enduring Freedom, we sat idly by and watched intently our brothers in the 101st Airborne and 10th Mountain Divisions conduct combat operations on the mountains and in the many caves of Afghanistan. The soldiers and leaders in 2-7 Infantry were chomping at the bit, eager to participate in this new conflict, and their eagerness quickly developed into impatience. I was resilient; I continued to assure my soldiers that their time was near and soon they would answer their nation's call. I would tell them that the Army is saving their best for last. As a result, their focus never wavered. We plunged into field training exercises, honing our fundamental skills in marksmanship, Bradley Gunnery, and basic fire and maneuver. My mortar platoon deployed to the field every month to shoot live rounds—when they hit their marks on accuracy, they then worked on speed.

Every brigade within the 3rd Infantry Division placed a great deal of time and resources into training for their biannual, month-long rotation to the National Training Center (NTC) at Fort Irwin, California. In July and August 2002, our brigade conducted a field training exercise designed to develop each of their infantry, armor, and engineer companies. Every company was put through a series of maneuver training lanes designed to hone their collective skills in fire and maneuver, communication, breaching obstacles, and seizing and defending terrain. Conducted in the swampy, restrictive terrain typical of Fort Stewart, Georgia, our training under these conditions didn't seem especially valuable at the time. Only later did we realize how well it prepared us for operations in Iraq—along the same kind of narrow, muddy roads winding through the Tigris-Euphrates River Valley.

Our brigade called this exercise "Raider Focus." After each company met the necessary training objectives, the entire battalion conducted a "force-on-force" exercise with an opposing force unit, in this case, our sister battalion—Task Force 3-7 Infantry would serve as our new enemy. A force-on-force training exercise is nothing more than a mock battle between maneuver units, lasting anywhere from twenty-four to seventy-two hours.

Our division, known as the Marne Division, certified each battalion deploying to NTC in a variety of tasks, and the two primary tasks evaluated were attack and defend. Not choreographed and with particular advantages and disadvantages granted to both sides, it is the objective of the attacker to close with and destroy the defender. The defender's objective is to fight back and hold its ground. Both sides do everything they can to win. It is a fair, no-holds-barred approach to preparing a unit for both the integrity of the battlefield and the realities of combat. The 3rd Infantry Division's moniker for this exercise is "Marne Focus."

In October 2002, our training culminated with our thirty-day training rotation to NTC. Located in the middle of the Mojave Desert at Fort Irwin,

California, this piece of real estate is ideal for maneuvering large formations of armored vehicles of up to a brigade in size. The terrain resembles a cross between that of Iraq and Afghanistan, with flat, open desert, surrounded by rocky mountain sprawl arrayed intermittently throughout the training area. Nearly as big as Rhode Island, NTC is the largest land-based maneuver training area in the world. It was the Army's crucible—a place that broke units down and built them back up. The desert was merciless, the enemy adaptable, and the lessons unforgiving. The training area is defined doctrinally as a Maneuver Box but nicknamed simply as "the Box." Every unit entered the Box thinking it was ready for war. Every unit left humbled, smarter, and, if lucky, still intact.

While in the Box, a brigade combat team, the BLUEFOR (the friendly unit), along with their subordinate units conduct mock engagements with an indigenous enemy. The enemy consists of American soldiers permanently assigned to the NTC and are organized into an opposing force unit, or simply OPFOR (a dedicated enemy force played by US soldiers). The clash between the OPFOR and BLUEFOR can be considered a fair fight, with both sides evenly matched in firepower. However, the advantage will almost always reside with the home team on their home turf—the 11th Armored Cavalry Regiment (ACR) serving as our enemy OPFOR.

The Indigenous almost always hold the advantage in war, no matter the century. The Greeks at Thermopylae used their rugged terrain and local knowledge to blunt the vast Persian army. Centuries later, Spanish partisans bled Napoleon's veterans dry with relentless ambushes in their own villages and hills. The Vietnamese turned their jungles into a weapon, first against the French at Dien Bien Phu and later against anyone who tried to impose control from the outside. And in the mountains of Afghanistan, the *Mujahadeen* made Soviet armor and aircraft irrelevant, striking and fading into terrain they knew like home. Again and again, history reminds us that invaders may bring numbers, technology, and firepower, but the defender fights with the land, the people, and time itself. NTC would be no different.

Leaders and soldiers of the 11th ACR are trained experts in enemy tactics, techniques, and procedures, and they are given carte blanche to determine when, how, and where they will fight the unit on rotation. The Box is their home turf, and they know the terrain like they know their own backyard. Friends of mine that served in the 11th ACR told me that after a couple of rotations, they no longer needed to use maps or navigation tools. The 11th ACR is also very flexible, adapting their tactics based on current threats abroad operating in the streets, deserts, and caves. They are free to experiment and try different approaches—anything necessary to win. The enemy at NTC definitely has a vote.

The training exercises are meant to simulate the same conditions a unit will encounter and must condition itself to in combat. The unpredictable desert terrain and climate, a lack of sleep, a high operational tempo, and, not to mention, a flexible enemy that can think for itself are the principal factors that affect the participating unit at NTC.

For obvious reasons, no matter how proficient rotating units may claim to be before a rotation, most are humbled by the OPFOR within only minutes after their initial engagement. At every opportunity, the OPFOR will capitalize on our failures and shortcomings, and before the rotating unit leaves the Box, those lessons learned are captured and presented to the unit by trained and competent officers and NCOs in the form of an after action review (AAR)—a phased and interactive approach to highlight what should have happened according to the original plan, what actually did happen when the bullets started flying, what the unit should do next time in order to be more successful, and finally develop a collective strategy for improvement.

While training at NTC, we focused on attacking along narrow corridors, clearing large trench networks, crossing rivers and canals, and operating in a biologically or chemically contaminated environment for extended periods of time. The simplest tasks or missions become difficult while wearing all the protective gear and navigating around or through contaminated areas. The missions that we performed were closely tailored to the ones that we would later conduct in Iraq.

The missions at NTC were well designed. For example, a trench system was constructed with exact dimensions mirroring those of an Iraqi trench measured from commercial satellite photos. It took engineers over a month to construct this elaborate trench network, comprising over three kilometers of reinforced bunker complexes and six-foot-deep communications trenches connecting them. It looked like something out of a World War I movie.

We were charged with clearing the trench of all enemy soldiers defending inside. A single two-lane road was the only practical route leading into the trench, requiring the entire brigade to travel in a tight file formation for most of the distance. You could imagine that a formation this large concentrated on a single road would present quite an easy target to one's enemy, especially to a unit as well trained and prepared as the OPFOR.

We attacked with brute force and with, what we perceived at the time, superior firepower. Over 75 percent of my battalion was destroyed before we were even within a mile of the trench. Most of us couldn't even see it before we were killed. We performed so poorly on the first attempt that we were made to readjust our tactics—really our entire way of thinking—and perform the mission once again. The results were much better on the second attempt. We managed to get about a company's worth of infantry into the trench and kill most of the bad guys. Despite significant losses to men and equipment, we were still able to accomplish our mission. We couldn't get too overjoyed with our victory—we lost over half of the battalion in the process of achieving it. In training, those losses meant bruised pride; in war, the same mistakes would have meant many letters home to grieving families. A single casualty is unacceptable in my book, and we would need to take a closer look at our strategy and tactics if we were to ever conduct this type of mission for real in the future.

Every mission was of an offensive nature at NTC, each with its own unique objective. By day fourteen in the Box, we conducted a total of seven attack missions, with the first five being force-on-force missions against the OPFOR. The last two attack missions were executed using live ammunition against thousands of prearranged targets of varying shape and size while integrating every weapon system in the brigade, to include fixed wing aircraft, compliments of the US Air Force and Navy. If our battalion failed to meet the training objectives for a particular mission, the mission was subsequently repeated until the objectives were successfully met.

We forged a tight relationship with the NTC staff—the "Observer/Controllers." By 2002, the NTC staff started to evolve into more of a coaching or partnership role with the rotating units like mine. They would still grade us, to be sure, but they would also collaborate with us before, during, and after each mission. My counterpart, Lieutenant Colonel Edge Gibbons, was great. He would always ask me what I wanted to improve as the battalion commander, or what specific battlefield operating systems his team should focus on during the next mission. I asked Edge to help me refine our ability to shoot, move, and communicate. We needed to work on maintaining our offensive tempo. Stalling out in the enemy's backyard would have disastrous consequences at NTC and in the real fight ahead.

Destroying the enemy in combat is important, but so is taking care of our own soldiers, especially our wounded soldiers. I asked Edge to also keep an eye on my medical platoon and my entire unit's ability to care for its wounded quickly and effectively. I knew we would be going off to war, and casualties were inevitable. We couldn't brush off casualty care or casualty evacuation in training. If we missed the opportunity here at NTC, my soldiers would die of their wounds in combat. It would have a devastating effect on morale and on our ability to sustain our offensive tempo.

Our experiences at the NTC tested our ability to plan and prepare our units while operating in a time-constrained environment. We learned how to use our time wisely by prioritizing our preparations and by delegating various tasks to subordinates. We also learned that there is no substitute for full-force rehearsals—to rehearse the specific tasks as planned using the same personnel and equipment and at the same speed that we would later perform in combat. The rehearsal brings the plan to life for the soldier by illustrating the sequential tasks that must be performed throughout the depth of the operation for the mission to be a success. As a result, the soldier gains a better understanding of his tasks and how they fit within the overall framework of his unit's mission.

My entire battalion gained proficiency on conducting detailed planning and preparations for combat operations. This training experience proved invaluable to the commanders, staff, and soldiers while conducting operations in Iraq shortly thereafter. The rotation, essentially, served as a valuable, large-scale rehearsal for the upcoming campaign—unknown to us at the time, less than only few months away. The lessons we learned at NTC saved lives in Iraq. I attribute our success in Iraq to three things: good soldiers, good leaders, and NTC.

As valuable as the NTC rotation was, it fell short in a couple of key areas. First, it provided few opportunities to fully stress test our logistics under extended combat conditions. Logistics wins wars. We trained to fight but not to sustain the fight for expanded periods and long distances. Every mission at NTC, we were fully armed, fueled, fed, and hydrated. Later, in Iraq, this gap became apparent—our supply chains strained under the weight of dispersed operations, long lines of communication (LOC), and unpredictable demands. Additionally, NTC fell short in transitioning from combat to stability operations; once the bullets stopped flying, we would need to be proficient at securing populations and reestablishing local governance.

During our AAR following our last mission in the Box, the boss, Major General Buford Blount, presented us with some recommendations and a proposed strategy for working on those areas most in need of improvement. He made the point that most units, in the past, would have around six months or so to make these fixes, but in our case, we would need to improve immediately. More so than in any other organization in the world, different rumors circulate throughout the army about as frequently as the sun rises and sets. It is one of the few norms in the US Army, next to change. Before the rotation, rumors spread that our division was earmarked to take part in the looming military campaign to disarm Iraq and remove Saddam Hussein from power. The commanding general's guidance did not confirm or deny those rumors, but it was certainly prescient and enough to keep the battalion ready and poised for war.

Throughout our prior field training exercises and Kuwait deployment, our battalion was organized into an infantry battalion "task force." In early January, we had given our brigade's tank battalion, 3-69 Armor, our Charlie Company and received their Bravo Tank Company in return. Bravo Tank Company, nicknamed Knight, consisted of fourteen M1A1 Tanks. We also received Bravo Company of the 11th Engineer Battalion, named Bulldog. Bulldog was equipped with Armored Combat Earthmovers, dismounted engineer squads, and rocket-propelled line charges used to breach wire obstacles and minefields. Their primary mission was to enhance the mobility of the task force's movement—traveling north to Baghdad as quickly and as quietly as possible was paramount to our success.

Other attachments to the task force included a fire support cell from our direct support 1-41 Field Artillery Battalion—capable of placing artillery fire on to fortified enemy positions with pinpoint accuracy. An Air Force Enlisted Terminal Attack Controller team, or ETAC, was added to the task force—responsible for coordinating and directing tactical air support. A Psychological Operations and a Civil Affairs Detachment were integrated into the task force in late February—together they were configured and trained to influence or coopt the civilian population during both peacetime and during combat conditions.

Days before we crossed the border into Iraq, our task force was fortunate to have received two embedded news reporters. Carolyn Glick wrote for the *Jerusalem Post* and Michael Corkery wrote for the *Providence Journal.* In Iraq, information would become more powerful than bombs and bullets. Enabling transparency in how we prosecute war had risks, but the benefits outweighed the risks. The American people, Iraqis, and other potential friends and foes would watch and read about our actions during our twenty-one-day march to Baghdad. I did everything I could to make Carolyn and Michael part of the team while respecting their objectivity and independence at the same time. They were exceptional reporters, and they were fearless.

Task Force 2-7 Infantry became a self-sustaining and mutually supporting team, a lethal force capable of accomplishing any mission. I couldn't have asked for a better team to lead into combat.

September 11, 2001, had a drastic effect on foreign policy and how our nation deals with terrorist-harboring countries as well as belligerent regimes amassing weapons of mass destruction. Our foreign policy subscribed to the ancient proverb, "The enemy of my enemy is my friend." Iraq fit the bill. It is logical to believe that international terrorists needed a country like Iraq to extend their operational reach and expand their organizations' capabilities—with suitcase nukes, shipping containers ferrying poison gases, mail laden with weapons-grade anthrax spores, or a food supply contaminated with undetectable toxins or biological agents. Iraq could certainly marry their resources with a terrorist's unconventional tactics and capabilities to achieve a significant, strategic objective. With ample intelligence, international terrorist organizations and Iraq could deal a knockout blow to the economic infrastructure of any freedom-loving country in the West or in Europe.

The post-9/11 America was prepared for a regime change in Iraq. The conditions were ripe, and in the fall of 2002, President Bush presented a resolution to the United Nations taking a hard line against Saddam Hussein and his regime. UN Resolution 1441 called for unconditional inspections of all suspected weapons of mass destruction storage sites and research facilities. This began the political-diplomatic tug-of-war that lasted for a couple of months preceding our deployment.

Meanwhile, at the unit level, we continued to plan and prepare for war. We worked on those areas the division commander pointed out in that cold AAR review trailer back at NTC only a couple of weeks prior. We were quickly back at the business of training and now preparing for war. My staff deployed to the field and worked on their ability to command and control (C2) the task force while "on the move." C2 on the move proved challenging using the systems and methods available at the time, especially while on the ground and working inside large, static tents (it would improve later). During our NTC rotation, I needed my Tactical Operation Center (or TOC)— also referred to as a "main command post," run by a small group of specialized or hand-picked staff officers and NCOs—to remain operational and in the fight especially during the decisive moments. However, my battalion was too spread out, and it moved too fast for the static TOC to keep up and stay in communication range of my forward elements. My TOC had the best staff officers and NCOs—I needed them to know what was happening at any given moment to help me keep the battalion on the right tasks, to prevent fratricide, to fuse intelligence, and to make recommendations to me on how to adjust the plan as the conditions changed. But they could not do that while on the move at NTC because they never trained on it. The training gap was evident there and needed to be addressed.

Imagine trying to run a private company while riding inside a moving truck, unable to see outside, shouting over engine noise, with phones cutting in and out, and knowing every wrong decision could get someone killed. Now, I expected my staff to do something similar—to perfect C2 while operating inside the tight, loud, and bumpy troop compartment characterizing the Army's M577—a Vietnam-era Command Post Vehicle resembling a giant shoebox with tank treads on the bottom. These unfortunate staff officers and NCOs were responsible for tracking the battle from start to finish while on the move. Not only did they have to track unit locations and status updates, I required them to send clear and accurate reports to our higher headquarters. Any erroneous or distorted message could result in a failed mission or dead soldiers. The staff coordinated the actions of every one of our maneuver formations and supporting assets within the task force while barely able to see or hear and while expending most of their energy simply trying to keep their balance inside their moving track. Imagine a surfer surfing while trying to read, write, talk, and watch television at the same time. Our staff would not wipe out in the open ocean. Rather, they would bang into each other or against the tight metal confines of the M577. Cuts, scrapes, breaks, bruises, motion sickness, and physical exhaustion were unavoidable.

In January 2003, the 3rd Infantry Division received their order to deploy. We were to deploy by air and sea to Kuwait to prepare for a possible war in Iraq. Making these preparations are referred to in the Army as "building combat power." Deploying a mechanized formation like the 3rd Infantry Division across the globe is no small undertaking. It is why it often signals a major political shift and commitment to escalate hostilities. The 3rd Infantry Division is designed to win wars—the ability to transport it to a combat zone quickly can mean the difference between victory or defeat.

The days leading up to our deployment were long and tiresome. Captain Matt Paul served as my mortar platoon leader as his primary function, but in times like this, he also served as my unit movement officer. He spent long days working with division movement officers, logisticians, the Air Force, commercial transport companies, and about a dozen other organizations to determine what equipment we needed to bring and how to transport it. He worked with forward liaisons in Kuwait to identify the prepositioned equipment we could draw once we arrived in theater. Matt had great attention to detail, and that was needed at times like this. A month ago, his wife told him that she was pregnant with their first child. Instead of celebrating and spending his final days with her, he was preparing the battalion for war.

We prepared our designated tracked vehicles for rail movement. It was necessary to transport them by train to the Port of Savannah, where we would then load them on to large naval or merchant marine vessels for their seaborne journey to Kuwait. Our wheeled vehicles were organized and prepared for convoy movements to the port, where they would rejoin the tracked vehicles and undergo the same waterborne transportation process.

Each infantry and armor battalion received around fifteen twenty-foot shipping containers to load and transport their mission-essential equipment from Fort Stewart, like tools, spare parts, and individual gear. If it fit, we loaded personal items too, like coffee and tobacco products—essential to some that needed them to function during long missions and sleepless nights. We packed everything that could fit into our assigned containers, everything but the kitchen sink. At the time, we believed we might deploy for a year or perhaps longer. It was fear of the unknown—we had shipped more equipment than we could even load on the vehicles we would later receive in Kuwait. We would try to find the space. Our rule of thumb was "better to have and not need, than to need and not have."

Soldiers brought their assigned weapons to the rifle range to confirm their accuracy settings (zeros) and subsequently qualify with them. "Qualification" is the Army's measure of a soldier's proficiency with his weapon, and it is a requirement that must be completed to the appropriate Army standard either semiannually or just prior to a deployment. My objective was to ensure that each weapon system was not only accurate and fully functional but that each soldier had confidence in his ability to acquire and engage targets with the same weapon he would later take into combat.

We issued every soldier in the battalion the new Joint Service Lightweight Integrated Suit Technology (JSList) Nuclear, Biological, and Chemical Overgarments. These were designed to be less cumbersome and more durable to the soldier in combat. The suits had a demonstrated ability to last longer while worn. We also received the new "Interceptor" Body Armor. Replacing the old Vietnam-era flak vests, the new armor was engineered to be less cumbersome to the soldiers yet strong enough to stop a small caliber bullet from penetrating. Receiving this important equipment not only increased the soldiers' chances for survival, but it also increased confidence in their ability to survive on the battlefield. This proved to be a valuable combat multiplier while conducting combat operations in the sands and cities of Iraq only two months later.

About two weeks before our departure, my battalion conducted what's known as soldier readiness checks, or SRC. This is the process where soldiers conduct individual administrative and physical preparations prior to a deployment. Soldiers were afforded the opportunity to make out a will, get glasses, receive their anthrax and smallpox vaccinations, and update their life insurance. It took a couple of days to process every soldier in the battalion task force.

The Family Readiness Group, or FRG, held meetings and updated phone rosters known as the FRG "Chain of Concern." The battalion's chaplain and I briefed the family members about the deployment and gave them guidance on sending mail. The battalion's internet website was updated and was used as a resource for the families to receive updated information on where their soldier was and what he was doing. The family members were well prepared and, as a result, the majority elected to remain in the Fort Stewart area in lieu of relocating closer to friends or family, a historical trend before major military deployments. They felt supported. There was the feeling that they were all in this together.

On January 23, 2003, Task Force 2-7 Infantry made the fateful trip to Kuwait. All the soldiers said their goodbyes at Fort Stewart the evening before our midnight bus ride to Hunter Army Airfield in Savannah, Georgia. Wives said goodbye to "Honey," girlfriends to "Baby," and confused yet teary-eyed children said goodbye to "Daddy." Is there a right way to bid farewell to the ones you love and may never see again? Many tears were shed that night. The ones we left behind were the true heroes, they deserved better.

After forty hours in transit, with over twenty hours in the air, the bulk of Task Force 2-7 Infantry was on the tarmac at the Kuwaiti International Airport (ironically, the same airport seized by the Iraqi Army in 1990, precipitating the first war with Iraq in 1991). We were later bussed from the airport to Camp Arifjan, the major port installation where we would inventory, inspect, and sign for our vehicles and equipment. Civilian contactors operated this camp. Since the Persian Gulf War, these civilians have been contracted with our military and were charged with the responsibility of managing and maintaining a permanent fleet of vehicles and equipment issued to rotating units on deployment.

Since the cease fire with Iraq in 1991, battalions and entire brigades have taken part in a continuous rotation of forces through Kuwait. Over the years, the rotation evolved into a four-month training rotation, like an enhanced version of NTC. Units conducted world-class training in both live-fire and force-on-force exercises. Commanders rotating in Kuwait over the last decade enjoyed quite a bit of freedom to train their units, limited only by their own imagination. In addition to the training value, our forces in northern Kuwait bolstered our containment policy and deterrence against Saddam Hussein's regime.

Short of Iraq's southern border, Camp Arifjan, Doha, and the forward border camps served as an intermediate staging base for new forces flowing into theater. It had enough infrastructure to receive additional forces and quickly push them through the Reception, Staging, Onward movement, and Integration (RSOI) processes. Trained to some extent at the National Training Center, RSOI is a lock step process designed to prepare a unit for combat operations. It is the final step of any combat deployment, where a unit "builds combat power"—organizing and positioning personnel, equipment, and logistics before initiating hostilities with the enemy.

Two weeks before our arrival, our equipment, to include combat vehicles, was offloaded from three separate naval vessels and subsequently staged inside Camp Arifjan's motorpool. The ships carried enough equipment to outfit an entire brigade combat team. This includes not only the one tank and two infantry battalions but the engineer, field artillery, and support battalions as well. These vehicles and equipment were not shipped from Fort Stewart. Rather, they came from the "Army Propositioned Stocks" housed in these three vessels floating in and around the Persian Gulf. The vehicles and equipment we previously deployed from Fort Stewart would fill gaps and augment what we drew from prepositioned stocks at Arifjan. Our newly formed task force had special needs and more people, requiring more stuff.

As a lesson learned from the Persian Gulf War, our Army must possess the ability to rapidly deploy to any contingency area in the world in order to overcome a mounting enemy threat. Initially during Operation Desert Shield, the defensive phase leading up to the war, only light infantry forces defended the Saudi Arabian border. Heavy forces were necessary to transition the coalition to the offense in order to decisively crush the Iraqi Army and rout their occupying forces from neighboring Kuwait. Getting heavy mechanized forces into the theater of operations quickly proved to be of critical, strategic importance. But it took a long time back then.

The 2nd Brigade and elements of the 3rd Brigade had already been stationed in Kuwait between four and twelve months prior to our 1st Brigade's deployment. The 3rd Brigade, in country the longest, was allowed to return to Fort Stewart for the holidays, between late November and until the order to deploy the entire division was given in early January. Both 2nd and 3rd Brigades received equipment and vehicles permanently assigned to Camp Arifjan. Their Bradley Fighting Vehicles were an older model, equipped with a less advanced target acquisition system. They would fight the war with 1991 Persian Gulf War technology. Nevertheless, the older Bradleys were still superior to the Iraqi's BMP-1 or BMP-2 infantry fighting vehicles.

Our brigade's equipment was in good condition. Fortunately, our brigade signed for M2A2 (ODS) Bradley Fighting Vehicles, the newer model and the one we owned and trained with back at Fort Stewart for over five years. Most of the other vehicles were brand new with under a hundred miles logged on their odometers. Some of these vehicles were untouched but were older models and obsolete by the active duty Army standards. For example, we took possession of M577 armored command post vehicles built in 1977, inferior to the later 1990s version. They still had steering sticks instead of a steering wheel. We also received 2.5-ton trucks, nicknamed "Deuce and a Half"—a vehicle that has been around since World War II. The Army's new light medium tactical vehicle, or LMTV, replaced the Deuce and a Half in the late 1990s. Notwithstanding, all the equipment was fully functional and would serve its purpose, regardless of age or maturity.

It took us about six hours to upload our vehicles and equipment on heavy equipment trailers and prepare them for their cross-country journey to our border camp to begin the next day. We would get settled into our border camp first, in time to receive everything within a few days. We deployed an advanced party to Kuwait a few weeks before our arrival to pave the way for the main body and ease the reception and integration process for the rest of the task force. It helped. Major Cooney, my battalion XO, along with all the company XOs, oversaw the offloading of the fleet and ensured the breakdown of vehicles was appropriate and accurate. It went smoothly, and they were even able to fulfill requests for additional HMMWVs, trucks, and trailers. Recognizing the mission's scope and scale in advance, we secured the extra stowage space to meet our expected operational demands. We also expected battlefield attrition and would need some redundancy.

Our bus ride to our border camp took almost the entire night to complete. Most of the route took us through the open desert, traversing highways of compacted sand. Roads did not look like roads. The Kuwaiti buses gave us a bumpy ride, and consequently sleep was out of the question for most of us light sleepers. During the ride, I learned that the bus drivers ferrying soldiers to the border camps were contracted civilians from other countries, mostly poor countries. Third-country nationals performed many jobs inside Kuwait, and the actual Kuwaiti citizens served as either managers or owners who may or may not even reside in the country. Many of the wealthy oil business owners maintained a permanent residence in Kuwait but also spent most of their time in either Europe or America.

Before September 11, 2001, the three main Army camps along the Kuwait-Iraq border were named "kabuls," Arabic for "camp." The kabuls were numbered one through three. As a commemoration of the states most impacted by the tragedy of 9/11, the kabuls were subsequently renamed. The three major camps were renamed Camps Pennsylvania, New York, and New Jersey. Our brigade was garrisoned in Camp Pennsylvania. It was smaller than Camp New York and about equal in size to Camp New Jersey. Originally, each camp was designed to support one battalion task force. Now three task forces plus all the brigade's supporting units were consolidated here. Before our arrival, we were told that additional facilities were installed in the camps to accommodate the increasing number of soldiers. We had no specifics, but we assumed or hoped the accommodations would suffice. We expected more dining facilities, phones, and Port-a-Jons.

We arrived at Camp Pennsylvania during the early morning hours of January 26, 2003, and quickly staked our claims on a few of the many temperature-controlled tents inside the camp. The younger soldiers reacted quizzically to the many reinforced concrete blast shelters positioned throughout the camp. "What is that for?" they must have been asking themselves. The older and more experienced NCOs took them under their wings and explained that the shelters are needed when Saddam decides to launch missiles at us. They would provide us some protection and sanctuary from the lethal effects. Now war was starting to look and feel very real for all of us. But the soldiers cared more about the accommodations, or lack thereof. Whoever masterminded Camp Pennsylvania's support infrastructure for our brigade clearly did not understand math. Every soldier had to wait in long lines to take a shower, to make a telephone call, to eat, and to take a piss. Maybe the camp's mastermind knew we wouldn't be staying here long.

Within days, our prepositioned equipment from Camp Arifjan and our twenty-foot containers shipped from Georgia would catch up to us here. This began the tiresome two-month process of configuring our vehicles for combat. We had to marry our equipment with our vehicles in practical ways—in ways to enable some comfort while maximizing our ability to fight and kill the enemy. It was a challenge to find the space to load all our equipment, especially for those who would ride in different vehicles than they used back at Fort Stewart.

The task force developed a routine of maintenance, nightly training meetings, and regular planning sessions for our upcoming campaign. The companies as well as the mortar and scout platoons began an intensive training regimen focused specifically on the type of terrain and enemy they could expect to encounter in Iraq. A task was trained repeatedly until the appropriate standards were met, then it was trained again for good measure. The soldiers' confidence in their own capabilities grew as a result. Initially, we focused on individual skills. These are the skills the soldiers will remember and will be forced to rely upon in combat. After the soldiers achieved a high level of competence on their individual skills, we transitioned into squad-, platoon-, and then finally company-level training exercises. Within only a few weeks, Task Force 2-7 Infantry was at the top of their game.

In just a few of short weeks, the entire 3rd Infantry Division was on the ground in Kuwait. Shortly after our arrival, the Army issued a "Stop Loss/Stop Movement" Order. This primarily affected those soldiers operating within central command's (CENTCOM's) area of responsibility whose enlistments were nearing their completion or on orders to permanently change station, or PCS, to another unit. It meant no one was leaving—no transfers, no end-of-service departures. This meant that the same team who trained and deployed together would also fight together in the ensuing months ahead. The order would remain in effect for the duration of the war or for as long as the CENTCOM commander and the Department of Defense deemed necessary. The order came at the appropriate time because our task force was due to lose many key personnel—the same personnel who were instrumental to our success during our NTC rotation only two months earlier. We had a good team then and we would keep the same lineup for whatever future road lay ahead.

We spent our time in Camp Pennsylvania during the early weeks of February performing maintenance on our vehicles, zeroing and test firing all our weapon systems, and continuing to train on the tasks necessary for success in the upcoming campaign. Our division received useful instruction and training on advanced rifle marksmanship techniques and military operations in urban terrain, or MOUT. A MOUT live-fire facility was constructed for units to train in, and a program of instruction was created and facilitated by retired special operations soldiers, now working for private military corporations contracted by the DoD. The facility comprised about five blocks, with four narrow streets and twelve buildings of varying size and shape.

Not much to look at, but very similar to the small villages we would soon encounter inside Iraq.

The training program initially focused on individual short-range marksmanship otherwise known as quick or reflexive fire, then transitioned into team-, squad-, and platoon-level MOUT operations. The soldiers learned the fundamentals of moving as an individual and as a member of a team within a built-up area, becoming experts on how to move between and inside of buildings and structures as a single, fluid unit, with each soldier mutually supporting the other. The training culminated with a platoon-level live-fire exercise, executed while integrating tanks, Bradleys, and psychological operations teams. Nearly every infantryman in the division received similar blocks of instruction, and this training later proved necessary.

Coalition commanders and the Kuwaiti government made many arrangements to enhance our protection. Certain restrictions were placed on traveling outside of the camp, and soldiers were ordered to lock and load ammunition in their weapons once they left the gate. I tasked my scout platoon to escort vehicle convoys, ideally suited for such a mission given their armored HMMWVs with machine guns and automatic grenade launchers. This was a practical measure and it also had training value for my scouts.

Kuwaiti Bedouins occupied much of the surrounding area prior to the US and UK military buildup in late January. Nomadic Bedouins migrated through the open desert, living off of the land and off of the animals they shepherded. They were simple people who rejected a contemporary lifestyle, either by birth or by choice. Most were noncitizens shunned by the Kuwaiti government, but they still had the right to migrate through training areas, including live-fire ranges. American Army forces had to shut training down to accommodate these Bedouins and their normal activities. Some Bedouins would perform this distraction as a clever attempt to trade their noninterference with a case of MREs.

Just prior to the division's arrival, the Kuwaiti government removed the Bedouins from the entire northwest region of Kuwait. Apparently the threat level increased because of our deployment. The Iraqi secret service could have easily infiltrated and blended in with the surrounding Bedouin populations. Skirting around the border through Saudi Arabia and into Kuwait was not impossible or beyond conception. We had to protect ourselves. While preparing for war, we needed to maximize the element of surprise and deny the enemy the ability to gather intelligence on our disposition, composition, and strength.

The political climate changed drastically from January to February 2003. The prospects for war, at least in the eyes of our enemies abroad, became more of an inevitability with every passing day. Terrorist incidents increased throughout Kuwait before we completed our deployment to our forward base camps. Soldiers were harassed along supply routes between Camps New York, New Jersey, Pennsylvania, and Doha, housing the Coalition Forces Land Component Headquarters. American civilian contactors were even targeted in the south, in and around Kuwait City. Specific threats were reported inside the camps as well. As terrorists normally do, they could target soldiers and civilians when they were at their weakest and most vulnerable.

On February 12, 2003, Osama bin Laden issued another call for all Muslims to rise up to meet the growing American threat. He was quoted as saying, "Anyone who helps America, from the Iraqi hypocrites or Arab rulers . . . whoever fights with them or offers them bases or administrative assistance, or any kind of support or help, even if only with words, to kill Muslims in Iraq, should know that he is an apostate." He added, "Fight the Devil, because the Devil will be overcome and defeated. God will give us victory." "It is going to be a great battle and we are going to defeat the enemy." Shortly thereafter, the United States, Great Britain, and Spain submitted a resolution to the UN Security Council stating that "Iraq has failed to take the final opportunity afforded to it in Resolution 1441." Tensions were escalating.

As the war drum beat louder, Brian Kilmeade from Fox & Friends arrived at Camp Pennsylvania and embedded with Task Force 2-7 for several days, determined to capture our soldiers' stories. His reporting mixed the humorous with the serious, giving America a window into both the grit and the spirit of our battalion task force. We showed him live training exercises, and he immersed himself fully, building camaraderie with the troops. His crew, lighthearted and genuinely funny, injected much-needed humor and calm into an environment that was otherwise growing tense as the war drew near. The experience of hosting them was unforgettable—one of those rare moments when the outside world truly connected with our unit on the ground.

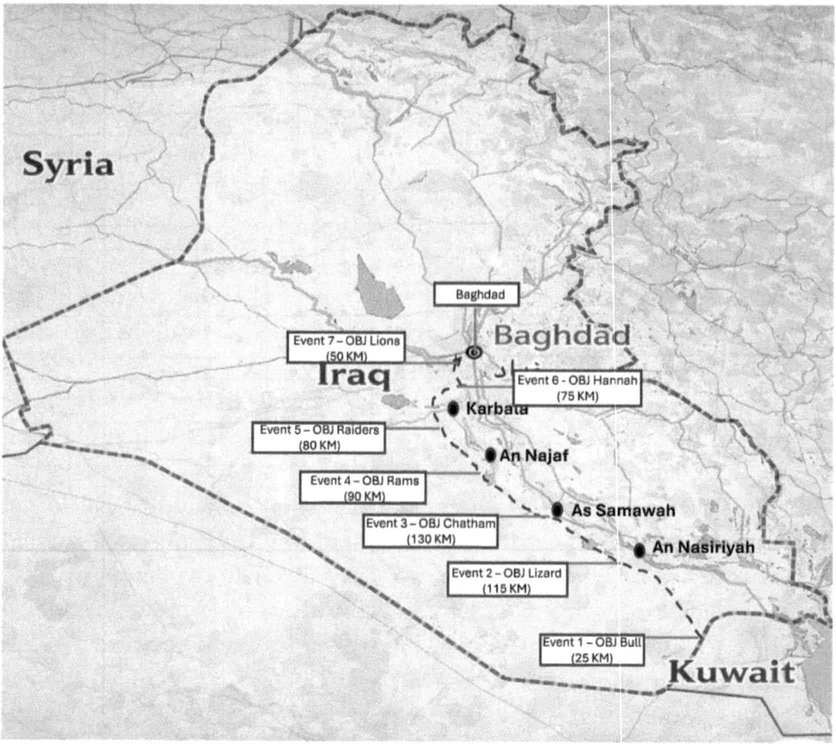

Task Force 2-7 battle plan from Kuwait to Baghdad.
Source: Author's image.

TROOP LEADING PROCEDURES

"A pint of sweat will save a gallon of blood."

—General George S. Patton Jr., training address (1942), quoted in The Patton Papers, *Vol. 2, ed. Martin Blumenson (1972)*

By late February, the 3rd Infantry Division moved out of their camps and into assembly areas in the open desert. This was necessary to make room for follow-on units of the 101st and 82nd Airborne Divisions and, later, the 4th Infantry Division. The living conditions were bleak compared to those of Camp Pennsylvania; it didn't take long for us to miss the long lines and crowded conditions. Dubbed "Camp Nowhere" by many soldiers in the task force, the surrounding environment was barren, with sands of open desert as far as the eyes could see. This was "camping out" at its worst. We slept in portable tents or inside our uncomfortable vehicles. The food we ate here could not compare to the quantity or quality we enjoyed back at Camp Pennsylvania. Above all else, we were now completely isolated.

Each company, to include the mortar and scout platoons, and combat support trains occupied their own perimeters. The only interaction soldiers in these formations had now was with each other. A blessing in disguise, the time we spent together in the desert forced the soldiers to talk to each other on a whole new level. The topics of conversation became personal, and when this happens, typically, the bonds between soldiers will become stronger. Talk turned to families back home, personal problems, and even fears. They leaned on one another for their moral support and emotional comfort. The outcome became a combat multiplier—while isolated here, all nine hundred souls of Task Force 2-7 Infantry became a family and would now fight even harder so their brothers-in-arms could make it home alive and back to their loved ones they left behind. Never underestimate the power of esprit de corps and brotherhood in an infantry unit in combat.

Leaders did everything in their power to make the conditions a little more bearable for their soldiers. Soldiers made a few trips to the AAFES stores located in Camps Pennsylvania and New York. They purchased magazines, soda, and candy and distributed these items evenly among themselves. We built showers out of crates, pickets, and ponchos. We even organized a couple of trips to the brigade support area, giving our soldiers an opportunity to make phone calls home.

As soon as we were settled in our new desert oasis, my staff and I immediately began in-depth mission planning and wargaming for our upcoming campaign. This is known as the military decision-making process, or simply MDMP. MDMP is the process where the staff analyzes the mission assigned to it and then, using a structured process, develops a viable course of action to accomplish it. In other words, it is how the Army plans a fight: it allows commanders to weigh risks and turn uncertainty into action. A course of action—a plan—is only viable if it fully accomplishes the mission with the least amount of harm. It defines winning. Plans are unacceptable when they could result in high casualties or collateral damage or simply outstretch available resources like logistics.

My staff was seasoned on MDMP, especially after countless field training exercises and an NTC rotation. They knew how to thread the needle, finding ways to win with few losses and within the limited resources we had. No staff was better at MDMP than at Task Force 2-7 Infantry. Nevertheless, every good plan that will succeed in the end depended on timely and accurate intelligence—one thing we really lacked at the time. We had smart intelligence officers making educated guesses about the disposition, composition, and strength of the enemy. But we really didn't know because, at our tactical level, intelligence was incomplete and evolving, and this created risks and unknowns we would need to grapple with the entire march to Baghdad.

Detailed operational plans and then later "warning orders" were issued regularly to each of the key leaders throughout the task force. A warning order is a heads up, of sorts. It's telling your formation that something is coming up soon and here is what we know so far so you can start getting ready. It doesn't have all the final details yet, but it gives people enough information to begin planning, preparing equipment, and getting mentally ready. My staff churned out a new warning order almost every day at Camp Nowhere. It became routine. I wanted to keep my subordinate units informed so they could do their own planning and preparation in parallel.

Warning orders are not quite "operation orders," but they are an update to the operational (basic) plan, providing more details on how the unit intends to conduct the operation. Knowing we could be called forward into Iraq at any time, it was important to keep the leaders as well as their soldiers focused and prepared to accomplish any of their prospective missions in the days ahead.

The staff's immersion into the developing plan and the accelerated distribution of warning orders to the task force initiated our final troop leading procedures. This is the process that begins when commanders disseminate the plan to their subordinate leaders and then these subordinate leaders in turn develop their own, unique plan within the framework of their commander's guidance and intent. Ground and aerial reconnaissance are typically used as tools to confirm or revise the plan—tools that we did not possess at the time. I was frustrated because I knew firsthand the potential impacts if we did not have a fully fleshed out, intel-driven plan. We would become vulnerable if we attacked the wrong targets or seized the wrong terrain. If we were given the green light to go tomorrow, we might be attacking blind.

In the absence of good intel, we had to prepare for anything. Every night, I could see allied jets flying over top of me at Camp Nowhere and crossing into Iraq to enforce the no-fly zones, but no intel from those missions ever made it down to my level on the ground. There was a disconnect somewhere. The US military made many improvements in functioning as a joint force since Desert Storm 1991, but we still had a ways to go, especially in places like interoperability. Confirming what was and was not on the other side of the border would have been helpful to me and my task force.

Planning for Operation Iraqi Freedom involved a lot of moving parts. The three biggest factors we had to think about were the enemy, the terrain, and how much time we had to get the job done. The terrain was tricky. In the west, it was mostly flat desert. But in central Iraq, it changed quickly around the Tigris and Euphrates rivers. There were marshes, cities, farmland, and even rice paddies. Time was tight and the goal was clear: remove Saddam Hussein and his regime as quickly as possible. Speed mattered. But the biggest challenge was figuring out the enemy—who they were, how they might fight, and whether they would fight at all. Most of our planning focused on trying to think like the enemy commander. We would imagine how he might respond to our moves, and then how we would counter his response—like a game of chess, or even a tug-of-war between two evenly matched teams. And no matter what, we had to be ready for the worst in every possible scenario.

Prior to Operation Iraqi Freedom, intelligence sources estimated the Regular Iraqi Army's combat power to consist of approximately 2,300 tanks, 4,500 armored personnel carriers, and 2,100 pieces of artillery. It totaled five corps and were headquartered throughout the country. The Iraqi corps our command was concerned with in the south was III Corps, and within this corps, the 11th Light Division and the 51st Mechanized Division.

The 11th Light Division was the main force occupying Kuwait City during Operation Desert Shield in 1990 and was later routed by Marines and Saudi Arabian Forces during Desert Storm in 1991. The 11th was headquartered in An Nasiryah, with the bulk of the force occupying blocking positions in and around the city. Reinforced by a tank regiment, their presence created a barrier along two major highways leading north to Baghdad. They also occupied defensive positions around Tallil Airfield, a strategically important airfield marked for seizure by the coalition. We would need the tarmac to launch helicopters, fixed-winged aircraft, and unmanned drones—necessary for the next phase of the attack farther north against the Iraqi Republican Guard.

The 51st Mechanized Division (Regular Army) was headquartered near Al Basra, Iraq's second-largest city, merely a stone's throw away from neighboring Kuwait and Iran. We believed the 51st was responsible for defending Basra and, quite possibly, dispatching forces to seize or destroy the southern Rumilyah oil fields. In terms of Iraqi strategy, the 11th Light defended the country's southern front and the 51st Mech protected their eastern flank. Saddam needed each division to halt the coalition advance and create what the press and politicians could spin as a quagmire. If they could not prevent a penetration, he could at least hope they would achieve enough success to inspire his Republican Guard to fight and hold the inner-ring defense around Baghdad. The martyrdom of his Regular Army and the deaths of a few Americans in the south could have all been part of a grander scheme to win a propaganda war.

Prior to the onset of Operation Iraqi Freedom, the Republican Guard Forces Command consisted of two corps, totaling three armored divisions, two mechanized divisions, and one light infantry division. The Republican Guard would commit themselves again for one more battle, one last battle. They would serve as the main effort, or "decisive operation," within the framework of the Iraqi military's defense of Baghdad. Saddam would shape his regular and irregular military's defense of the country around the strategic employment of the Republican Guard.

All regular, special, and irregular military forces would be utilized in a subservient role, directly supporting the Republican Guard or reinforcing its success. All six of the Republican Guard divisions would be committed against coalition forces during Operation Iraqi Freedom: the al-Nida, Baghdad, Medina, Nebuchadnezzar, Adnan, and Hammurabi Divisions. Most of the Republican Guard forces were positioned along the outer rim of Baghdad's perimeter defense, with most units digging in within fifty miles of the capital city. Every major approach into Baghdad would be blocked by an element of the Republican Guard.

The US Army's 3rd Infantry Division set its sights on one Iraqi Republican Guard division. The Medina al-Munawarah Division, translated "Medina the Luminous," blocked the southwestern approaches into the capital city along our axis of advance. The Medina was an armored division consisting of three armored brigades, the 10th, 2nd, and the 17th, and one mechanized infantry brigade, the 14th. They were committed in the Iran-Iraq War, the Persian Gulf War, repelled Kurdish and Shia uprisings, and would be employed one more time during OIF.

The Medina Division was a battle-tested unit. They clashed with the US Army's 1st Armored Division during the Persian Gulf War of 1991. The Medina lost sixty-one tanks, thirty-four armored personnel carriers, eleven artillery pieces, forty-eight trucks, and seventy-two of their soldiers were captured. Despite heavy losses, they fought with a stubbornness and resilience, refusing to accept outright defeat or surrender. Instead they conducted a fighting withdrawal to the east. With a brigade's worth of personnel and materiel completely destroyed, the Medina managed to consolidate, reorganize, and reposition to survive and fight another day. This is what professional armies do, and it was something we trained on time and again at NTC. Following the ceasefire in 1991, the Medina was instrumental in quelling political revolts throughout the country. The Medina Division was considered by many as the showcase of the Republican Guard—the best trained, most competently led, and best funded Republican Guard unit in Iraq.

The Special Republican Guard (SRG), known as the "Golden Division," served as Saddam's Praetorian Guard and, like the Republican Guard, was headed by Qusay Hussein, Saddam's youngest son. Created by Saddam himself in 1992, the SRG was responsible for preserving and protecting the integrity of the regime in Baghdad, and until the onset of Operation Iraqi Freedom, the SRG was the only uniformed military force authorized to enter and operate within the confines of the capital city, just like Rome in ancient times where its legions were strictly forbidden to enter the city gates for fear of an armed coup d'état. The SRG guarded symbolic and strategic locations in and around Baghdad.

The SRG force consisted of four brigades. Brigades one through three consisted mainly of infantry and security forces, with the fourth brigade consisting of two tank regiments equipped with T-72 main battle tanks. The SRG fielded a substantial air defense capability in addition to their ground maneuver and security forces. The SRG operated primarily as independent battalions, permanently posted in and around Baghdad with detachments scattered throughout the Sunni Triangle, extending as far north as Tikrit and as far west as Ramadi. The battalions were charged with guarding the regime's critical assets and structures, to include WMD storage sites (so we thought). They also guarded Saddam Hussein himself and his inner circle, performing similar duties to the American Secret Service.

By virtue of their special mission, these SRG soldiers were the most trained, resourced, and financed in the whole Iraqi military, bar none. They were a cut above the Republican Guard, even the Medina Division. Moreover, their standards of living and quality of life were significantly greater than those of their Republican Guard or Regular Army counterparts. If one unit was going to fight to the last man, it would be the SRG. We believed the SRG would rally the remnants of the retreating Republican Guard and Regular Army forces in Baghdad and would organize and orchestrate a final, bloody defense of the capital city . . . "Fortress Baghdad," as it came to be known.

Saddam Hussein didn't just rely on his regular army—he also leaned heavily on paramilitary and reserve forces. One of the most controversial and unpredictable groups we faced during planning was the Fedayeen Saddam, or simply "Fedayeen." These fighters were more like personal enforcers than soldiers. They were fiercely loyal, aggressive, and feared. After the US invasion, many of them didn't surrender. Instead they disappeared into the population and reemerged as insurgents, using guerrilla tactics like ambushes and roadside bombs to attack coalition forces.

We knew they existed, but we didn't fully understand what they were capable of or how they planned to fight. During our planning sessions, we discussed these irregular forces and developed general countermeasures. But we didn't spend endless hours chasing hypothetical scenarios. We could have played the "what-if" game forever, but the truth was that we wouldn't know what we were up against until we were on the ground. I didn't want to waste valuable planning time preparing for a ghost enemy. Instead we focused on the threats we could see and anticipate. That said, we still gave some attention to the Fedayeen, the Ba'ath Party Militia, and the Al Quds forces—just enough to be ready if they showed up.

Our planning assumed that the Saddam Fedayeen would bolster Saddam's defenses by suppressing the civilian population, ambushing coalition supply lines, and coercing the Regular Army to fight the coalition head on. The Republican Guardsmen and SRG trained the Fedayeen. Many represented the inner circle of Saddam Hussein. In addition to conventional military tactics, these irregulars were proficient in the conduct of sabotage and terrorism, to include suicide bombing. Intelligence predicted this force to number over forty thousand strong, with most of the force operating in civilian clothing—making the job of coalition forces exponentially more difficult. Overall command and control of these forces was placed in the hands of Saddam's eldest son, Uday. As a fighting force, the Fedayeen would prove second rate, but as a disruption force, the Fedayeen were ideal for infiltrating the civilian populations and disrupting the coalition's success during the rebuilding phase that would follow the military campaign. It was rumored that these forces operated in strength in every major city and town between Kuwait and Baghdad.

About a decade after the Ba'ath Party took power in Iraq, Saddam created a militia force to preserve the integrity and security of the party. Similar to the American National Guard, this reserve force protected the integrity of the Iraqi government and their internal interests while serving as a backup to the regular armed forces during times of war. The militia received annual training on weapons and basic soldier skills with funds provided by the Ba'ath Party. After its formation, membership quickly swelled to upward of fifty thousand strong, and many of those militiamen fought for the Palestinian insurgency during the Lebanon civil war from 1975 to 1976. It was an effort to unofficially promote the Ba'ath Party while allowing Saddam to claim that he did not have direct or official involvement in the conflict. By 1987, the Ba'ath Party Militia boasted some 650,000 members and came to be known as the "People's Army."

The People's Army mission during the Iran-Iraq war was twofold: defend key installations, towns, and cities within Iraq and suppress the Shia populations in the south and the Kurdish in the North. Akin to the Confederacy's "Home Guard" during the American Civil War, the Ba'ath Party Militia hunted down and executed deserters of the Iraqi military, imposing loyalty to the party with an iron fist. During Operation Iraqi Freedom over a decade later, the Ba'ath Party Militia remained a threat to the coalition. Before the war, we knew they would impede our efforts to win over the noncombatant population, but whether they would directly oppose our forces on the battlefield would remain an open question until we had boots on the ground. Some of the militia force would work in tandem with Saddam's Fedayeen, disrupting the coalition along its march to Baghdad and supporting the insurgency after the regime's downfall.

Following the onset of the Israeli-Palestinian conflict in 2000, Saddam Hussein formed a paramilitary organization called "Al Quds," translated as "Army of Jerusalem." The object of this organization was to support the Palestinian's Intifada and remove all non-Arabs from Israel. However, this was mainly just a propaganda move intent on rallying support from the Iraqi people and the remainder of the Arab international community. Saddam was simply making a statement that Iraq supports the Palestinian cause. The strength of this new force was claimed to possess over one million soldiers. Organized into brigades, the Al Quds forces were recruited mainly from schools and colleges and were obligated to "volunteer" for service. With no true intent on employing this paramilitary force to march on Jerusalem, they became another reserve component complementing Iraq's standing army. Like the Fedayeen, an Al Quds presence existed in every major city and town in Iraq; however, intelligence sources believed the force existed merely on paper and did not pose a true threat to the coalition.

Military plans are based more on fact than assumption. We made a few assumptions, but we developed our tactical plans based on the facts as we knew them prior to the start of the war. We predicted that an irregular militia force of some sort would resist, but we knew that, above all else, the Republican Guard and SRG would put up an orchestrated and organized defense of their capital. By February, we received credible intelligence that uniformed Iraqi soldiers and equipment had moved out of their base areas to strategic locations and were beginning to dig in vehicles and entrenchments along key avenues and choke points within the outer ring of Baghdad. They were going to fight, and we had to develop a feasible and executable plan to defeat those forces before we could effect control over the city and the rest of the country.

The 3rd Infantry Division's mission was to encircle and destroy the Medina Division of the Republican Guard, then seize Saddam International Airport and the intersection of Highways 1 and 8. The destruction of the Medina Division would disable the Iraqi military's power base while enabling the 3rd Infantry Division to isolate Baghdad from the south and southwest, setting conditions for regime change. If it were necessary to make incursions or an all-out assault into Baghdad to force regime change, this would be accomplished with the support of lighter elements of the 101st and 82nd Airborne Divisions—ideal for fighting in urban areas.

Our 1st Brigade's mission was a supporting operation for the 2nd Brigade. Our mission was designed to support the main attack against the enemy's center of gravity—the critical hub where the enemy draws its strength and power. We identified the Iraqi Medina Division's 2nd Armored Brigade as its center of gravity. Consequently, this is where our 3rd Infantry Division's 2nd Brigade would focus its main attack.

Initially, my 1st Brigade would attack the 14th Mechanized Brigade and hold it in place long enough to secure a bridgehead over the Euphrates River, isolating the Medina Division from the north. The bridgehead would serve as my division's point of penetration into enemy territory—the rear of the Medina and inside of the SRG's inner-ring defense of Baghdad. Exploiting this penetration afforded us a clear path to Saddam International Airport. Isolating the Medina from the north would allow our 2nd Brigade to close with and destroy the Medina Division's 2nd Armored Brigade from north to south. Our 2nd Brigade's attack route would resemble a fishhook. Once they destroyed the Medina's 2nd Armored Brigade, my 1st Brigade could finish off the rest of the Medina Division and then pivot north to Saddam International Airport in southwest Baghdad. There were several moving parts and dependencies. There were risks and unknowns. But it was actually a simple plan for our division, one that we trained for. Simplicity is key in times of uncertainty and the fog of war.

The movement north would be long and contested and would stretch our logistics. We would need to get to Baghdad with enough combat power to threaten Baghdad. If successful, our 1st and 2nd Brigades would end this operation with a stranglehold around Baghdad's neck in the south. The Marines would perform similar actions on similar Iraqi formations in eastern Iraq. They would move abreast of us along our march to Baghdad.

Task Force 2-7 Infantry's main task was to "fix" the 14th Mechanized Brigade of the Medina Republican Guard Division near the city of Al Musayyib, thirty miles southwest of Baghdad. We were to hold the enemy in place long enough for our sister battalions to establish and secure the bridgehead over the Euphrates. Our mission was paramount to 1st Brigade's success. For any river crossing to be successful, it is necessary to create diversionary crossings at different points along the river. A successful deception could inhibit enemy forces from concentrating at the actual crossing site. Tactically, we would fix a brigade from the Medina, but on a larger scale, we would achieve a "feint"—a supporting diversionary attack aimed at deceiving the enemy as to the actual location of the main attack. A reconsolidated 1st Brigade would then advance northeast and seize Saddam International Airport, located within the southwestern outskirts of Baghdad. The 1st Brigade's seizure of this important objective would result in the successful isolation of the city from the southwest, creating the conditions for Saddam Hussein's regime to collapse.

To bog our force down and be drawn into a city fight was the enemy's objective. The enemy perceived the city fight to be our Achilles's heel—it would negate the advantages of our weapon systems and place us into a position of vulnerability, easily exploitable by guerrilla hit-and-run tactics. Saddam Hussein believed that significant American casualties could be sustained from within the southern Iraqi cities and towns. If these casualties mounted, he believed America's political leadership would lack the stomach to continue the attack north, the rest of the way to Baghdad. What Saddam failed to grasp was that the American psyche had changed a lot since 9/11. We would fight on, no matter the consequences.

The enemy adopted this campaign of resistance after lessons learned from the Battle of Mogadishu in 1993. It was even rumored that Saddam distributed the movie *Blackhawk Down* to all his regular and irregular military commanders. We were not going to play by his rules. We would defy conventional wisdom and assume risk where required. In this case, our main supply route, otherwise known as our LOC, would be at risk. We planned to bypass the enemy-held cities and towns in the south to preserve our combat power for the Republican Guard and SRG forces in and around Baghdad. But this left our LOC—our lifeline—vulnerable. While stretched thin, our logisticians would be susceptible to attack from bypassed regular and irregular forces. Our flanks would remain completely unsecure until those cities and towns could be pacified. It was a risk our division had to take in order to facilitate shock and awe and overwhelm the regime into submission as rapidly as possible.

I think a lot about our campaign in Iraq and draw many similarities to Patton in Europe. General Patton would have loved Operation Iraqi Freedom. It was right out of the Patton playbook. On the night of July 31, 1944, as his 3rd Army was pushing through France mauling the Germans, Patton gave this pep talk to his staff. It was as if he foresaw our drive to Baghdad.

> There's another thing I want you to remember. Forget this goddamn business of worrying about our flanks, but not to the extent we don't do anything else. Some Goddamned fool once said that flanks must be secured and since then sons of bitches all over the world have been going crazy guarding their flanks.

> We don't want any of that in the Third Army. Flanks are something for the enemy to worry about, not us. I don't want to get any messages saying that, "We are holding our position." We're not holding anything! Let the Hun do that. We are advancing constantly and we're not interested in holding on to anything except the enemy. We're going to hold on to him by the nose and we're going to kick him in the ass; we're going to kick the hell out of him all the time and we're going to go through him like crap through a goose. . . . We have one motto, "L'audace, l'audace, toujours, l'audace!" Remember that gentlemen.
>
> —*General George S. Patton Jr., speech to the 3rd Army, 1944 (collected in* War As I Knew It, *1947, and* The Patton Papers, *1972)*

On the battlefield, the Iraqis would present an extremely diverse set of enemy forces—a very unusual order of battle comprising myriad combatants ranging from extremists with explosives strapped to their chests to the most professional and well-trained Iraqi soldier. My task force focused on the Republican Guard's Medina Division and the SRG. The Medina was responsible for defending the southern and southwestern approaches into Baghdad. Most of their equipment was "non-NATO," Warsaw Pact manufactured and imported equipment Most of it was outdated, befitting only the early days of the Cold War. They were outmatched by our technology in virtually every class of aircraft, armor, artillery, and infantry combat systems. They were capable of inflicting harm on us and disrupting our plans, but they were outmatched nonetheless.

We knew the SRG was near the Saddam International Airport with an equivalent of about two small brigades composed of infantry and armor. The SRG had the most capable T-72 main battle tanks in Saddam's Army. The Iraqis assigned the 8th Battalion of the 1st SRG Brigade as the permanent security force for the airport. They were quartered there and would surely defend their home base if attacked. The 1st Regiment of the 4th Armored SRG Brigade was headquartered just north and within striking distance of the airport—we assumed it would reinforce the SRG's 8th Battalion. These SRG formations could concentrate in and around the airport to mount a strong defense or a possible counterattack. Saddam Hussein was smart enough to know that the airport was decisive terrain—we could use it to reinforce our forces with more equipment and combat power to continue our attack into the heart of Baghdad. The significance the airport would play within our broader campaign strategy could not be understated. Saddam would likely do everything in his power to blunt our offensive at the airport, before we could turn east to seize Baghdad and effect regime change.

Before we could engage the SRG, we would have to go through the 14th Mechanized Brigade of the Medina Division first. Recognizing this, we spent most of our planning time on the latter. We could focus more attention on the SRG after we defeated the 14th Mech. For all we knew, the SRG could have relocated, retreated, or have even been destroyed from the air by the time we arrived at the airport. The 14th Mechanized Brigade consisted of three mechanized infantry battalions equipped with T-72 main battle tanks and BMP-1 armored infantry personnel carriers. At 100 percent strength, each battalion would defend with eleven T-72s and thirty-three BMP-1s. We estimated the 14th Mech's forces to be reduced to 66 percent strength by the time we made contact with them. We predicted that our Air Force, Navy, AH-64 Apache Gunships, and artillery would have significantly reduced their numbers before launching our ground attack.

Our intelligence predicted that the 14th Mechanized Brigade's objective was to block Highway 9 to protect the western flank of their sister unit, the 2nd Armored Brigade. The Iraqis' 2nd Armored Brigade was believed to be the Medina Division's main effort, the "decisive operation." Their mission was to establish defensive positions in and around the intersection of Highways 1 and 8, just south of Baghdad, thereby protecting the southern approaches into the city.

The 14th Mechanized Brigade would defend with two battalions forward, positioned in two areas approximately five to ten kilometers northwest and southwest of Al Musayyib. It would retain one battalion behind the other two, serving as the decisive operation in and around Al Musayyib. It would use the city, its Highway 9 Bridge, and the Euphrates River as a natural barrier to our approach. The 14th Mech would maintain a mobile reserve force east of the Euphrates River, consisting of six T-72 main battle tanks. Their commitment of armor would likely focus on reinforcing their decisive operation in the city—to either force us out of the city or to plug any gaps we may have created during our attack.

The 14th Mech would integrate additional measures to disrupt our plans. We assumed it would emplace antitank and antipersonnel mines in key choke points west of the city to halt our attack along our avenues of approach. If we got bogged down long enough, the 14th Mech could hit us with artillery, mortars, and chemical agents. The combined effects could halt our advance or even force us to withdraw. Our fate could become even more dire if the 14th Mech rallied any substantial reserves from within the city to counterattack our exposed flank or rear while we were stopped and disorganized. This was our worst-case scenario, and it was one that played out time and again at NTC. We would be ready for it.

If the Iraqis lost a significant number of their forces during any phase of the battle, they would likely withdraw to the east of the Euphrates to Iskandariyah. There they could regroup for a counterattack to either reinforce the eastern defenses of the Highway 9 bridge or, if emboldened, to attempt to retake lost ground on the western side of the river. Another possibility we had to consider was that the 14th Mech could withdraw across the river and blow the bridge, eliminating the option for us to pursue the retreating enemy forces and continue our attack north to the airport or Baghdad itself.

Crossing the river was a chance I did not want to take. It was not part of my mission, but plans always change in war. The coalition might have needed us to secure it as a crossing site. If the Iraqis did blow the bridge, my lead formations on the other side could be cut off from our main force and could be destroyed. I neither had amphibious capability for my infantry to cross the river nor did I possess engineering assets to lay a hasty pontoon bridge. Those capabilities were elsewhere in the brigade and division. My soldiers on the other side would be stuck. They would have had to find a way to escape and evade, or fight for their survival long enough for us to rescue them.

Our job to fix the 14th Mech in Al Musayyib was intended to achieve two outcomes: prevent them from counterattacking the rest of my brigade north of us and deceiving them into believing that we were attempting to use the city's Highway 9 bridge as a crossing point. The actual crossing point over the Euphrates was several miles to our north—my brigade planned to concentrate its remaining battalion task forces there to take it while we were operating to their south, in and around Al Musayyib. Task Force 2-7 Infantry was on its own, and I had the autonomy to deploy my task force in ways I deemed necessary to support or enable the rest of my brigade.

There was the worst-case enemy scenario and then there was the most likely scenario that we needed to consider in our planning. We believed the 14th Mech would likely fight from static positions and would remain in a defensive posture for the duration of the battle. Soldiers from the 14th Mech would likely die in their holes or they would throw up their hands and give up just before we could fire the first shot. Decision making is centralized at the upper echelons of command in the Iraqi Army, and it was not uncommon for a general to issue orders down to a single platoon. After any Iraqi unit sustained casualties, their reaction time was usually too slow to have any real effect. During the 1991 Gulf War, US Army formations destroyed Iraqi brigades and battalions only moments after making first contact. Once battered and beaten, the 14th

Mech would probably surrender or capitulate before our first tank came close to the Highway 9 bridge. At best, the 14th Mech might organize a slow and fragmented withdrawal to the east across the bridge. Maybe then they could regroup to mount limited, small-scale counterattacks to harass our advance north.

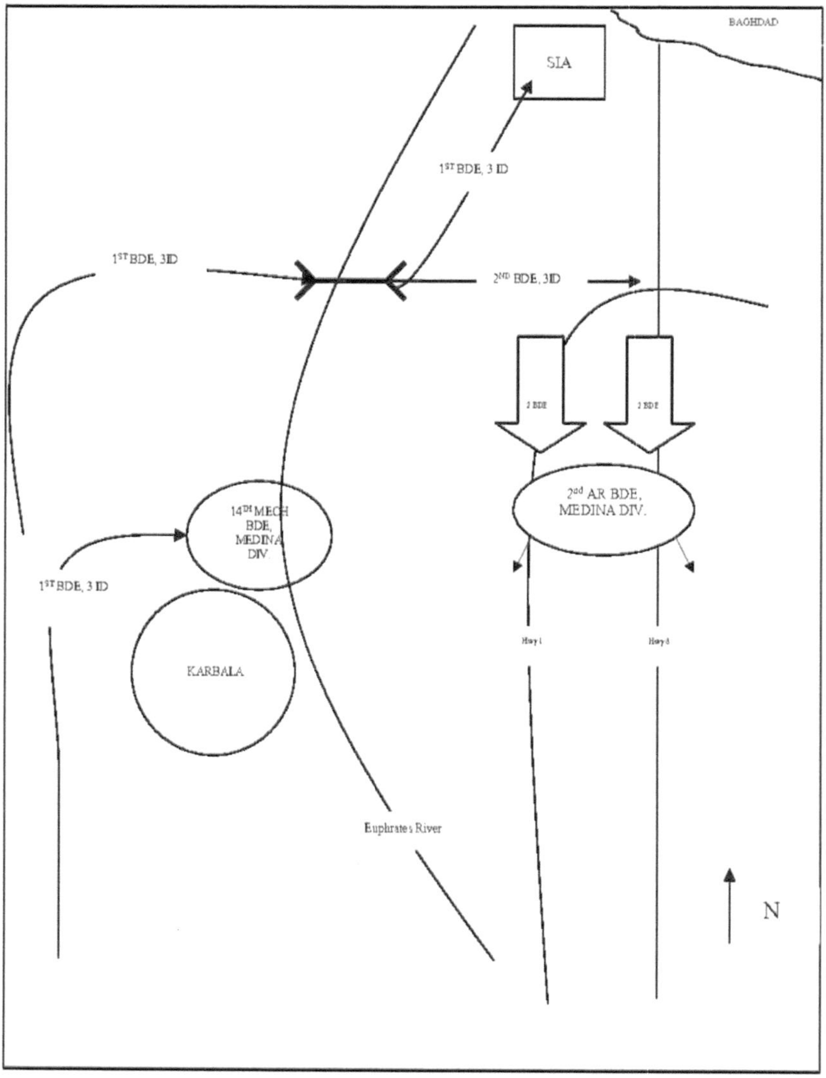

3rd Infantry Division battle plan for the Medina Division of Republican Guard.
Source: Author's image.

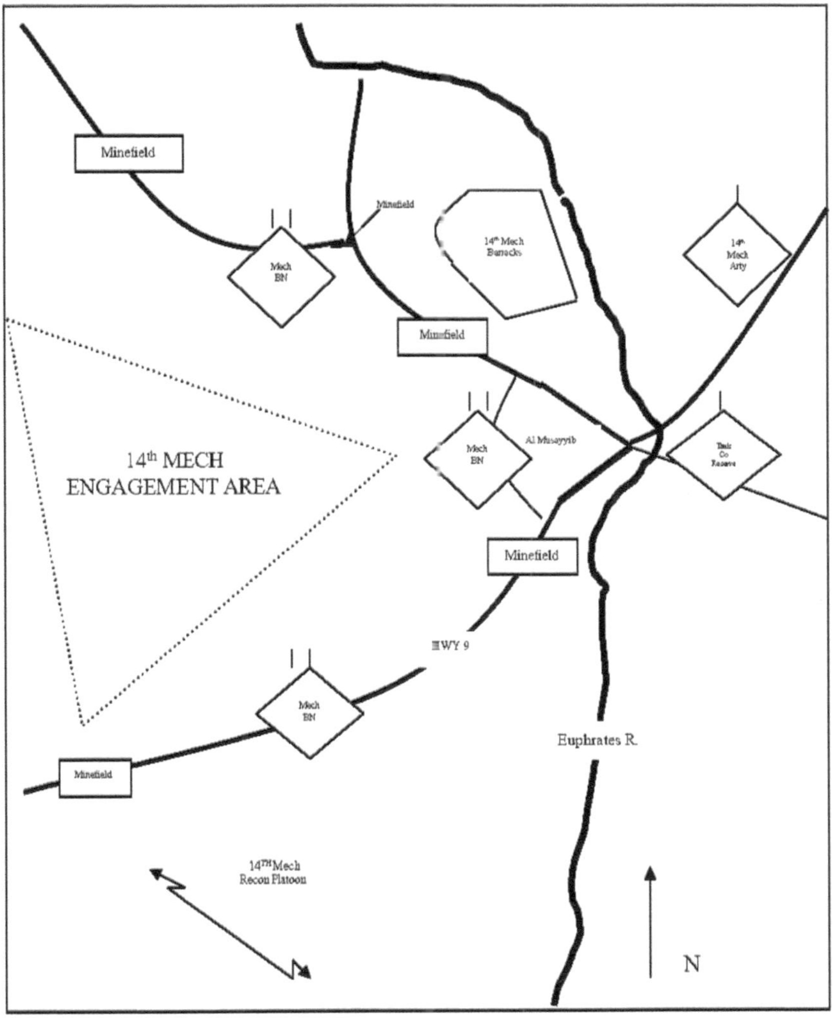

Task Force 2-7 battle plan for the 14th Mechanized Brigade of the Medina Division, Republican Guard.
Source: Author's image.

Our brigade, known as the "raider" brigade, decomposed its battle plan into seven significant and distinct events. These events encompassed the entire operation, from the Kuwait-Iraq border crossing to the occupation of Saddam International Airport in Baghdad. All the events began and ended with the accomplishment of a specific objective along our axis of advance. Objectives in the southern half were not largely focused on the enemy. Rather, my brigade planned combat support-related activities including tactical refueling, recovery, maintenance, and resupply. This operation would be the longest near-continuous mechanized attack in history—vehicle breakdowns, logistical challenges, and fatigue needed to be factored in and mitigated before reaching the brigade's northern objectives. My brigade focused the northern objectives on seizing terrain or destroying enemy formations.

The key to our success was speed—to advance to Baghdad as rapidly as possible. My brigade shaped its entire operation to facilitate this fast operational tempo. Our goal was to avoid decisive engagements in the south, bypassing the enemy in built-up towns and cities along the route to Baghdad. This was a necessary component of the broader campaign's "shock and awe" strategy. CENTCOM identified Baghdad as the regime's center of gravity. It was a symbol that must be seized and controlled to effect regime change. The seven events led to this objective.

Event 1 consisted of the breach through the Iraq-Kuwait obstacles and the destruction of the Iraqi border outposts. The Iraqis built a string of concrete towers overlooking their border with each of their neighboring countries. Along the Kuwaiti border, the Iraqis reinforced their outposts with an elaborate obstacle belt, consisting primarily of deep tank ditches and tall, sand-packed berms. This combination of early warning and disruptive obstacles could provide the Iraqi military with enough time to alert, mobilize, and deploy their forces to defensive positions throughout the country. Each of the outposts along the Kuwaiti border were designated with a letter. Task Force 2-7 Infantry was responsible for the initial penetration into Iraq, to include the breach itself and the destruction of Command Outpost B, or "Bravo." We would conclude Event 1 once we occupied Objective Bull. Bull was nothing more than an empty patch of real estate twenty-five kilometers deep into Iraq. Here each of the battalions and support units would catch their breath while organizing for the long movement that would quickly follow.

Event 2 consisted of a 115-kilometer movement to Objective Lizard, southwest of An Nasiryah. We would traverse open and unpopulated desert, at least sixty miles from the nearest Iraqi military installation. Given our distance from populated areas and expected enemy formations, we did not anticipate any resistance along the route. While at Lizard, we would refuel and regroup before our next push to Objective Chatham.

Our task force had a "be prepared to" mission to reinforce our division's 3rd Brigade attack against the 11th Iraqi Regular Army Division northwest of An Nasiriyah. The 3rd Brigade was assigned the mission to seize Tallil Airfield southwest of the city, an important airfield to the

Iraqi Air Force. It would be used by coalition forces as a forward operating base later in the operation. Additionally, our 3rd Brigade would seize a bridgehead north of the city for the Marines to pass through and attack north, abreast of our division. 3rd Brigade's mission was not only tactically necessary but also had strategic importance to the coalition: to attack Baghdad along multiple fronts. Additionally, achieving control over the south with our division and the Marine Expeditionary Force could degrade Iraqi morale and their will to fight before we reached our northern objectives.

My brigade planned for an optimistic contingency if the regime collapsed following our initial incursion into southern Iraq. Saddam and his henchmen could flee the country. Lower-level Iraqi military leaders or government officials could assume control over the government and surrender to coalition forces. If this happened, we would find the nearest main highway leading north to Baghdad and conduct a mad dash to the capital. We would need to get there quickly to secure the population and provide governance. Our focus would immediately transition from combat to stability and support operations. This was the best-case scenario.

The next three events, Events Three through Five, were focused solely on movement north. They were essentially march objectives and our actions there would enable us to maintain our continued momentum. If we were hit by chemical or biological weapons in the south, we would take an alternate route to Baghdad. We would swing wide to the west, in the middle of the empty, arid Iraqi desert, as an effort to conceal our movement and elude the deadly effects. This would certainly be our brigade's worst-case scenario in this phase of the operation. It was important to have a contingency against WMD because at the time we really believed that Saddam would use what he had as a desperate attempt at survival. Notwithstanding, nothing short of an act of God would stop our advance.

Event 3 consisted of a 130-kilometer movement to Objective Chatham southeast of As Samawah. We were a little uneasy about the route, most of which was to be conducted on populated highway roads. It was here that we anticipated initial resistance—our first encounter with Iraqi paramilitary forces.

Event 4 would take us on a ninety-kilometer movement to Objective Rams, where we would make our final preparations prior to our first suspected contact with the Republican Guard.

Event 5 would take us on an eighty-kilometer movement through the An Najaf Escarpment and into Objective Raiders just south of the Karbala Gap. At Raiders, we expected first contact with reconnaissance elements from the regular Iraqi Army or Republican Guard forces. We expected to reach Objective Raiders within two to two and a half days after crossing over into Iraq. This was roughly the 250-mile mark, a point where our logisticians needed the attack north to stop long enough for resupply to catch up.

Event 6 marked our major transition from movement to maneuver. Here we would deploy into our attack posture and stand toe to toe with Iraq's elite forces defending Baghdad's outer ring. Most of our training at NTC would pay off here, during Event 6. The event began with our passage through the Karbala Gap and ended with our attack into the 14th Mechanized Brigade of the Medina Republican Guard Division at Objective Hannah, just west of Al Musayyib. We would also be prepared to reinforce the rest of my brigade on Objective Peach if they should need our additional forces.

Event 7 began with our attack beyond the Euphrates River and ended with our seizure of Saddam International Airport, dubbed Objective Lions. Saddam International Airport was only a few miles from center city Baghdad, a symbol of the regime's power, and an ideal springboard to launch future operations into the city. The airport's seizure would serve as a catalyst toward regime change—a domino-like collapse of the government—beginning with the Special and Regular Republican Guard forces, followed by the paramilitary Ba'athist diehards. Eventually—after recognizing their insignificance and lack of control—the government itself would quickly tumble.

Events One through Seven would enable us to topple the regime. The sight of our Bradleys and tanks parked inside of Saddam's airport—just outside of the Iraqi capital—would render the regime inconsequential enough to quit and make way for the coalition and a new future. Maybe. If the Iraqis continued to resist, we would have no choice but to root them out and continue to destroy them from the air and from the ground.

We had a "be prepared to" mission of repositioning north of the airport as an effort to block a potential Iraqi counterattack. At the time, the Hammurabi Republican Guard Division was positioned along Baghdad's northwestern line of defense, with forces tied into the rest of the city's outer ring of protection. Less than fifteen kilometers north of the airport, they were certainly within striking distance and could disrupt my brigade's southwestern cordon of Baghdad. A bold maneuver along our western flank could isolate my brigade from the rest of the coalition's ground forces. We could reposition to block and hold the Hammurabi in place long enough for a follow-on force—perhaps the US Army's 4th Infantry Division—to complete its destruction and continue the attack north to Tikrit, or even as far north as Mosul.

My task force's main focus and the majority of our planning went into our fight with the 14th Mechanized Brigade of the Medina Division at Objective Hannah. My specified task from my brigade was to "fix" the 14th Mechanized Brigade in order to provide freedom of maneuver to Task Force 3-69 Armor as they seize a bridgehead over the Euphrates River, called Objective Peach. Ours was a supporting mission. My brigade designated Task Force 3-69 as its main effort. They would seize the bridgehead and pave the way for the rest of the division to follow.

Author of *On War* Carl von Clausewitz asserts that to achieve one's objectives in war, one must impose his will on the enemy. He emphasizes that the most effective way to accomplish this is by killing him. Anything else is of a secondary order of importance. My staff and I were Clausewitz's subscribers and we very effectively put his theory into practice throughout the campaign. One of Clausewitz's Principles of War is "Simplicity." I believe that Clausewitz would agree that our battle plan against the 14th Mech at Objective Hannah was a simple one.

Our simple plan called for me to position all three of my companies in the best locations to inflict maximum destruction on the enemy while minimizing their own—making good use of our advantages in weapons' range and lethality. The scout platoon would conduct wide-area reconnaissance, screening the task force's flanks while providing us with targeting data using their long-range thermal optics. They had the potential to spot targets before anyone else. The mortar platoon's role was to provide immediate suppression against suitable targets as they appeared on the battlefield. Field artillery, attack aviation, and tactical air support would prepare or shape the battlefield for us by attacking and destroying preplanned targets throughout the objective area. The entire plan was shaped around killing the enemy. By killing the enemy, we negate any possibilities of future enemy conflict. Our enemy could not interfere with my brigade's Euphrates River crossing if it was destroyed. It was a very simple plan, one that we were trained and ready for.

The planning process encompasses most of the initial steps within the troop leading procedures. Receiving the mission, initiating movement, planning and wargaming, conducting reconnaissance of the objectives, and issuing the plan in the form of warning orders and operation orders are all inclusive within the first seven of eight steps in the troop leading procedures. Once we completed the mission planning and issued the orders down to the lowest level, all task force leaders conducted the last and arguably the most important troop leading steps—inspections and realistic rehearsals—necessary for the plan's execution to result in success. No plan survives first contact with the enemy. So it is important to have the right tools necessary and the flexibility gained through rehearsals to adapt to the enemy and to the situation. Learned adaptability through rehearsals leads to mission accomplishment no matter how the circumstances may change on the ground.

Troop leading procedures are an ongoing process that should begin when a unit perceives the next mission; they do not need to wait to receive the final plan. Troop leading procedures began for us way back at NTC and later at Camp Pennsylvania with our mission-focused training. All we had to do now was to ensure we had all the tools necessary to be successful. We needed to ensure that we had the correct amount and types of supplies. Additionally, we rehearsed tasks specifically tailored to our upcoming mission and inspected our weapons, special equipment, and vehicles both inside and out.

After we occupied our assembly area, we spent a great deal of time refining and testing out our vehicle load plans. Not a trivial thing—our vehicles would serve as our homes, our weapons, our offices, and our refuge over the next twenty-one days. The drive north would push us and our vehicles to the limit, and beyond. Efficient load plans would enable us to carry all our needed equipment through the torturous desert climate and diverse terrain across the country. It was important for each vehicle to be loaded up in a safe, accessible, and uniform manner. If one soldier transferred to another vehicle, he would not need to search for a piece of equipment; it would be loaded in the same place and in the exact manner as the one before. A good load plan was not only important, it was also necessary. It was life or death.

We had almost double the normal load of equipment than we were normally accustomed to. For redundancy purposes, we deployed nearly all our equipment from Fort Stewart. This was in addition to the full complement we received back at Camp Arifjan, Kuwait. Rather than haphazardly pile the tools, bags, ammunition, and weapons, we needed to have a plan to load the excess equipment to ensure that the soldiers were safe and that the proper functioning of the weapon systems on board were not obstructed in any way. Every bag, weapon, and piece of equipment was either tied or strapped down to the inside or outside of the vehicle to avoid a shift, because any shift could result in damage to the equipment or bodily harm to the soldiers inside. Our goal was to load enough supplies, ammunition, and food and water to last for at least ten days—longer than normal. All of us knew we would be moving so far and so fast that our logisticians would find it challenging to be able to keep pace and adequately resupply our forward elements.

We knew the desert sands would take their toll on our weapons and our vehicle engines. This was one of our biggest concerns. When presented with an opportunity to kill or be killed, our weapons would have to be able to shoot. When ordered to drive, our vehicles would have to be able to drive. Many of us mailed requests home for small paintbrushes and pairs of extra-large pantyhose. The brushes would be issued to each soldier to clean his assigned weapon of sand and dust, with the pantyhose to be placed around each of the vehicle air filters to minimize the amount of sand entering the engine. This would reduce the overall strain on the engine throughout the 350-mile drive. The barrier created by the pantyhose would enhance the engine's performance while increasing its overall lifespan. Within two weeks, we received scores of packages containing the brushes and panty hose we requested. After we crossed the border, these items were worth their weight in gold.

We calculated the distance the battalion would travel from the border to Baghdad at well over three hundred miles. Without a major pause, this is the farthest a single mechanized unit would attack in the history of mechanized warfare. The distance would take its toll on the vehicles, especially traveling within a desert environment. Precautions and considerations must be made to facilitate a movement of this scale. We loaded extra repair parts, fuel cans, oil, grease, and other lubricants. We loaded additional track and tires. We also loaded up tow bars and tow cables in the event of a vehicle breakdown. Self-recovery was the task force's standard operating procedure. If a vehicle broke down, it was the crew's responsibility to hook up to another vehicle and tow to the next checkpoint or even to the next objective, if practical. There, responsibility for the recovery and repair of the vehicle would transfer over to the maintenance team.

The task force rehearsed recovery operations and other combat support functions like casualty evacuation and tactical refueling. Mass casualty situations would require every unit to make contingency plans to use their own combat lifesavers and their own vehicles to transport the wounded to the nearest casualty collection point. Unlike in training, the nearest collection point might be forward or in another direction that was not behind us—there would likely be no "rear area." Tactical refueling would need to happen quickly. Every vehicle in the battalion task force would need to be refueled at nearly the same time at each objective. At NTC we could stagger refueling operations, and there we didn't need to worry about real enemy bombs, mortars, or RPGs igniting 2,500 gallons of fuel. We also planned to conduct a dozen other maintenance and support actions while waiting to be refueled. We would not be stopping for long and there was not a moment to waste at each objective. Every crew had the processes down to a battle drill.

Commanders identified and planned for the obvious contingencies, even considering going to the bathroom during the long legs of the journey. One might think this would be an easy thing to consider. Well, nothing was going to stop the forward progression of the task force, not the enemy and not even our bodily functions. My formation would definitely not stop for pee breaks. Every vehicle crew stockpiled their empty water bottles to be used for number one. Soldiers were extremely creative while planning for number two—soldiers and leaders did some creative things with toilet seat covers, string, and garbage bags purchased from Camp Doha, Kuwait. Some of the soldiers loaded up on Pepto-Bismol tablets, Imodium, and Kaopectate to plug their intestines long enough to make it the whole way to Objective Raiders, where they could enjoy the time and the privacy to do their business properly.

We planned and rehearsed for combat contingencies—equally important to planning for the long movement—because once we got from point A to point B, we would have to be ready to fight. Our rehearsals were built on those lessons learned at the NTC. Because our plan was of an offensive nature, my battalion and company-level rehearsals consisted mainly of occupying firing positions, assaulting while mounted and dismounted, and breaching obstacles. In other words, closing with and destroying the enemy.

My special platoons did similar training for their unique missions. The mortar platoon rehearsed crew drills and firing position occupation techniques tailored to the task force's offensive mission. They had to move, stop, and shoot quickly. They called it "hip shooting." They needed to be responsive. The scout platoon rehearsed long-distance mounted and dismounted reconnaissance and reconnaissance while on the move. Many of the rehearsals focused on operating in linear and nonlinear (360-degree) battle space.

In addition to combat training, the battalion task force received additional training on enemy prisoner of war handling, processing capitulating Iraqi military units, and searching civilian vehicles. We would be interacting with the Iraqis in ways that did not always involve shooting our guns at them. Everything we did before we crossed the border was intended to build our depth, breadth, and confidence.

While in the assembly area, company commanders and platoon leaders constantly reassured their men that they would be successful. It was necessary for the soldiers not to just think they will accomplish their mission and win but to absolutely believe it beyond the shadow of doubt. To survive the lengthy and potentially dangerous drive and to preserve enough energy and resolve to kill the enemy would require nothing less than 100 percent determination from the leaders and the soldiers they led.

Task Force 2-7 leaders built confidence in their soldiers through the detailed understanding and comprehension of the mission through training and rehearsals. The more they studied the maps and rehearsed the routes and the tasks, the more confident they became. Leaders kept the soldiers busy focusing on the mission but also found time for important distractions. They found time for humor. Task Force 2-7 soldiers and leaders knew how to make each other laugh and make light of any situation. Alpha Company held regular skit sessions, each harmlessly poking fun at the officers and NCOs throughout the task force.

Soldiers were kept at ease as much as possible and were constantly reminded by their leaders as well as their families about how important their mission was and that they have the unwavering support of the American people. This support was reflected in the letters and care packages sent to us by various schools, hospitals, and youth organizations. This gesture of support was a true combat multiplier. It fueled every one of my soldiers with a sense of duty, and it gave them the strength to endure the hardships they would soon face. The people with whom they were about to fight for now had names, faces, and stories of their own. Task Force 2-7 soldiers would now give all they had to defend these people, and they would certainly make them all proud to be Americans.

Soldiers of the task force could hear the countdown to war. The war drums were beating loud and clear. 1st Brigade issued its final operation's order to my task force on March 9. Five days later, on March 14, 2003, V Corps key personnel rehearsed the breaching operation into Iraq. From corps level down to each of the companies, commanders and staffs up and down participated in this important exercise. It was a mounted, full-dress rehearsal, with each leader traveling in his own vehicle and while operating inside a ten-square-kilometer space. With each of these vehicles lojacked from a satellite-based battle tracking system, key personnel were able to see each other as blue icons on their systems' display screens. The rehearsal afforded every command echelon an opportunity to practice moving their pieces around on the battlefield, while also providing them with an opportunity to see how their unit's mission fit within the larger framework of the corps' breaching operation.

The rest of the corps made final preparations for combat—from opening the vacuum-sealed chemical suits and trying them on for size to distributing and uploading our ammunition into our weapon systems. I estimated the quantities of ammunition we received were just enough to accomplish our mission. This was a major concern of mine. Urban warfare and elusive tactics would turn ammunition into our most precious resource. If the situation took a turn for the worst and the Iraqis put up a stubborn defense, how would we have enough ammunition to continue our attack? We would have to stop and wait to be resupplied by trucks traveling over one hundred kilometers through hostile territory.

Breaking the seal of our chemical suit containers was a significant milestone because while exposed to oxygen, the suits were mission capable for only forty-five days after we broke the seal—the countdown was on. We did not have spare sets, so if there was contamination, we might need to halt operations and wait for resupply. I am not sure if that was a known logistical gap or if there was a bigger plan to abandon the mission or avoid fighting through contamination if it happened. Around the same time, our assistant division commander for maneuver, Brigadier General Lloyd Austin (future SECDEF), met with the task force and gave us a pep talk. He told us that our mission was right and just and when we were called upon to cross into Iraq to make the march with resilience and aggression. He told us to keep moving forward while never looking back. We knew we were going to cross the border soon.

The last few days leading up to the war were focused on minutia. "The devil is in the details," some say. There were quite a few little things that needed to be accomplished before the war. Ankle biters. For example, leaders had to organize and put together over twenty map sheets, depicting the terrain between Kuwait and Baghdad. Countless operational graphics and over three hundred checkpoints had to be drawn on or over the maps on clear plastic sheets. The same checkpoints and other key grid coordinates had to be inputted into our global positioning systems to aid in navigation to our objectives. We are fortunate to have had the extra days to complete these small yet important tasks.

While listening intently to our portable short-wave radios on March 17, members of the task force heard President Bush's speech granting Saddam Hussein and his sons forty-eight hours to leave Iraq or else face military action. Following the news, many soldiers quickly wrote a letter home, perhaps the last letter they would ever write. We were told earlier that the flow of mail would cease during our march to Baghdad and would not resume until after the fighting had stopped and the supply lines were secure. Most of the letters reminded families what we as soldiers were fighting for and how motivated and ready we all were.

Two days later, on March 19, 2003, we relocated to Attack Position Dawson, our forward springboard within five kilometers of the Iraqi border and within striking distance from the border outposts. We were directed to line up in column formation, like ducks in a row, directly behind our assigned breach lanes, with no defensive perimeter and without the typical measures taken to enhance our protection in the field. The enemy land-based threat was minimal, and I predicted we would not remain here for very long. Kuwaiti contractors had already disabled the electric fence and began the reduction of each border obstacle on the Kuwaiti side. It was obvious to everyone that we would be making our crossing soon, probably within the next twenty-four hours. Given all the activity we could see around the border area, it was down to only a matter of hours, not days. Anticipation of the upcoming attack was consuming all of us. We were ready to go.

On the early evening of March 20, we learned that attempts to resolve the Iraqi conflict peacefully had failed. We huddled around short-wave radios, listening intently to President Bush's address to the world, signifying the beginning of the war and learning for the first time the operation's name—Operation Iraqi Freedom. Pinpoint coalition air strikes had been directed on high-value targets inside Baghdad to decapitate the regime with one single blow.

My junior leaders under me informed their soldiers of the recent developments. The war was on. Expecting to hear cries of bravado, the soldiers remained stoic and focused on the many tasks before them, the quiet professionals they were. They were numb, stone cold, and focused on the mission. They thought about their responsibilities to themselves, to each other, and to the task force. They thought about bigger things too, like what it takes to be a good soldier in war. And they wondered whether they would measure up. Leaders gave Task Force 2-7 soldiers the time and the space to reflect.

Even though we spent a lot of time training and preparing for war, many of us, deep down, thought this day would never come. Bloody, close combat was only a remote possibility until now—an intangible. For most of the soldiers, it was like waking up from a dream. Now, at the foot of the Iraqi border, the uncertain prospects of war quickly morphed into a hard, sober reality. The only way home was through the Iraqi berms that lay before us. The stage was set. Task Force 2-7 Infantry and its damn fine soldiers were ready for war.

EVENT 1

The Breach

"The eyes of the world are upon you. The hopes and prayers of liberty-loving people everywhere march with you."

—General Dwight D. Eisenhower, Order of the Day, June 6, 1944

Armies often defend to rest and prepare. The Romans built Hadrian's Wall, Byzantines fortified Constantinople for a millennium, and France relied on the Maginot Line. All worked for a time, until they were eventually breached or bypassed. Breaking through prepared defenses remains one of war's most dangerous tasks. The British learned as it tried and failed at New Orleans in 1815; Task Force 2-7 Infantry learned it at NTC, where nearly every mission involved a breach and OPFOR made us earn it. Before each breach, I recalled Desert Storm's lesson, that great battalions are built on great platoons. Tanks and engineers mattered, but success hinged on squads and platoons executing under pressure. I watched them at Fort Stewart—tight, disciplined, ready. Fire support and mine-clearing helped, but none of it mattered if the platoons weren't solid. They were.

On the evening of March 20, 2003, Bravo Company, 2-7 Infantry, under the command of Captain Steve Szymanski, successfully penetrated the Iraqi Border along the 3rd Infantry Division's Passage Lane's 6 and 8A and completed the destruction of the enemy's Command Outpost Bravo.

CP Bravo was a reinforced concrete observation tower overlooking the Kuwaiti-Iraqi border and was garrisoned by a platoon of regular Iraqi Army soldiers. Their mission was to provide early warning to the Baghdad regime in the event of a coalition attack. Each command post along the border was equipped with a fiber optic cable that ran from their location all the way to the Iraqi Ministry of Defense Headquartered in Baghdad. It was imperative that we take the enemy by surprise before he had an opportunity to alert the regime of our attack. The goal was to race north as far and as fast as possible before the Iraqi military could prepare and stage their chemical or biological weapons for employment.

A distinguished West Point graduate, Steve would command his company brilliantly during the breach, and he would certainly live up to the same standard of excellence as other popular West Pointers like Grant, Patton, and MacArthur, to name a few. Grant at Vicksburg faced Confederate earthworks that seemed unbreakable, yet through tenacity and maneuver he cracked them open and split a nation in two. MacArthur at Inchon chose audacity and shock, striking where the enemy least suspected and turning the tide of the Korean War. Patton's breakout from Normandy exploited momentum with rapid maneuver—it became the beginning of the end for the Germans. Steve's breach into Iraq was more than just a passage through dirt and obstacles; it was a continuation of an American tradition using surprise, violence of action, and speed to change the course of a campaign. It changed history.

I selected Steve for this important mission because his talent for multitasking was second to none. He had the ability to analyze and think clearly while under pressure. I placed several assets of mine under his control because I knew the situation would be dynamic and unpredictable. I always subscribed to Murphy's law: what could go wrong would go wrong. Steve's assigned assets included engineering capabilities, smoke obscuration, and priority for fire support. As the frontline commander on the ground, he had a better sense of the situation than I did. Therefore he could employ these assets better and faster than I could. We needed to solve problems at the breach quickly because an entire Army behind us could bottleneck and become lucrative targets for long-range missiles.

Like Desert Storm 1991, our breach was preceded by a "Battery Six"—thirty-six rounds of 155mm high-explosive artillery shells concentrated on each Iraqi command post along the Iraqi Border. Our division's AH-64 Apache helicopter battalion followed the artillery salvo with aerial strafing runs, battle damage assessments (BDA), and real-time intelligence reporting back to the ground units waiting to breach and cross the border. The Apache helicopters combined with the artillery could do the job—whatever remained after the artillery, they finished off with Hellfire missile strikes and bursts of 30mm cannon fire.

The light show presented by the artillery was truly amazing. Task Force 2-7 Infantry soldiers stared into space and enjoyed viewing these illuminated messengers of destruction ascend high into the sky and then descend into a horizon of darkness. In a way, it was a comforting feeling to see so many shells and rockets delivered on to the enemy. It gave us a sense of invincibility.

The Iraqis reinforced their border defenses with an electric fence, followed by multiple tank ditches and berms extending ten kilometers deep into Iraq. In addition to engineering assets, I also augmented Bravo Company (Bushmaster) with a section from the medical platoon and a PSYOPS detachment. The medics were in place to treat enemy and friendly casualties at the breach. They operated under strict rules forbidding the evacuation of Iraqi wounded back to the Kuwaiti side of the border. PSYOPS would play messages on their loudspeaker to convince any Iraqi survivors to capitulate to coalition forces. We would evacuate these survivors forward, north of the border. This was a new paradigm for us because we always trained to evacuate enemy casualties or prisoners of war to our rear area, not to move them forward. Our big dilemma here was that our PSYOPS loudspeakers could not outrange some of our guns. We could shoot the enemy at safe distances, before they could be close enough to hear the PSYOPS messages. So we had to position PSYOPS as far forward as possible. Yet still every one of my soldiers with a gun would need to make hard life or death decisions. We would need to give the Iraqis every opportunity to surrender or capitulate, but I could not put my soldiers in grave danger. There are no perfect options in war.

Our engineer company, Bulldog, provided the critical assets our task force's success relied on at the border. Their job was to work in tandem with Bushmaster to create two major causeways into Iraq. The rest of the division and follow-on forces could then flow through. With Bushmaster in overwatch, Bulldog was less concerned with enemy bullets. They were more concerned with minefields and making the route trafficable for both light and heavy-wheeled vehicles and myriad tracked vehicles. Bulldog would need to bridge and cut lanes through the berms and ditches, likely reinforced with antipersonnel and antitank minefields, a deliberate and difficult task to perform, especially in total darkness—I conducted my breach in Desert Storm 1991 in broad daylight.

Captain Szymanski divided Bushmaster evenly among both passage lanes. He personally commanded the reduction of Lane 6 and confirmed the BDA of Iraqi Command Outpost Bravo. He collocated with his 1st and 3rd Platoons commanded by Lieutenants Jones and Padien, respectively.

2nd Platoon, under Lieutenant Myslviwic, comprised the main force of Bushmaster's Lane 8A team. The company XO, Lieutenant Hoyseth, joined 2nd Platoon to help oversee the work and maintain communications with Captain Szymanski. Typically, commanders and their XOs split up, especially if the platoons perform complex tasks and are dispersed. Steve followed the playbook during the breach.

Steve organized his two elements into small, combined arms teams capable of breaching and reducing the border obstacles and destroying enemy forces along the way. Bulldog's commander, Captain Mike Bliss, would position himself forward to inspect his engineers' technical work, to provide quality control, and to call additional resources forward should the situation require it. I was forward too, just behind Bushmaster. This breach was a complex mission, and it required seasoned experts and leaders to be as far forward as possible. But there was certainly a risk that too many leaders in the same place could become dangerous or counterproductive. This was a complex mission, and conflicting orders could cause friction, confusion, and delays. So I made it clear that Bushmaster owned the breach, and everybody supported Bushmaster until we were across and out of danger. The mission would fail without unity of command.

Other commanders might have placed the engineer officer in command of the breach. However, I believed that in a contested breach, overall command should be given to the maneuver commander, typically an infantryman or a tanker. The breach itself is only a means to an end. Engineers should focus on technical tasks, and maneuver commanders own the tactical tasks. Maneuver commanders typically have a broader view of the mission and are more adept at orchestrating resources to accomplish it, including engineers, artillery, or air support. They are integrators by trade. We trained this way during Marne Focus back at Fort Stewart and during our NTC rotation only a few months prior.

I committed every asset at my disposal to the breach. Redundancy is arguably the single most important tenet during any breaching operation; at NTC, we lost many assets due to enemy fire and real or simulated breakdowns. We employed both light and heavy engineering assets including armored vehicle launched bridges, or AVLBs. The old M-60 tank chassis would launch the AVLB sixty feet to bridge tank ditches. Armored combat earthmovers (ACE) accompanied the AVLBs to fill trenches with dirt and to cut through sand berms. Complementing the AVLB and ACE were the mine clearing line charges, or MICLICs. MICLICs launched from 1.5-ton trailers pulled by M113 armored personnel carriers. They used rockets with line charges and blast overpressure to blow the mines and clear a one-hundred-meter lane roughly ten meters wide. Engineering assets were positioned to support both lanes during the breach.

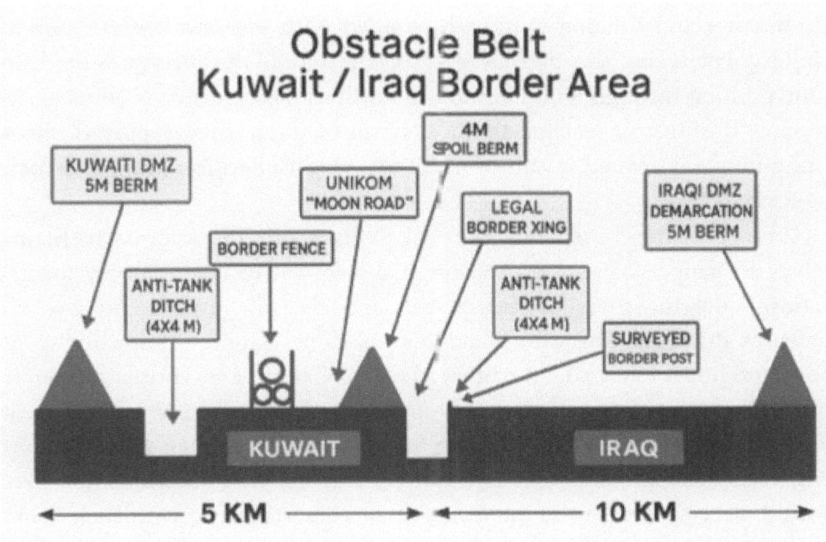

Kuwait/Iraqi Border, March 20, 2003.
Source: Author's image.

Lanes 6 and 8A were situated in the middle of an Iraqi vehicle graveyard, left over from Desert Storm 1991. A junkyard of burned-out tank hulks and armored personnel carriers disrupted our breach. They cluttered our battlespace and created unnecessary white noise to the whole breaching operation. It was hard to tell the difference between an old target and a real target. Many anxious Bradley gunners filled these old targets full of holes. Intelligence reported Iraqi vehicle movements along the border days prior and it suggested the Iraqis might attempt to hide inside the graveyard to harass our initial breach or follow-on forces. The chilly night air cooled the old Iraqi armor just enough to register a signature on their Bradley's hi-tech thermal sights. Bushmaster exercised tactical prudence and engaged.

Minutes after initial penetration into Iraqi territory, contact reports flooded the radio net, "Able 6, this is Bushmaster 6, we're identifying two BMP's, we're going to engage." BOOM! . . . BOOM! BOOM! BOOM! . . . BOOM! BOOM! BOOM! I could hear the Bradleys' cannon fire over the radio and I could see tracers in the distance. They lit up the sky. The engagements between Bushmaster and the Iraqi armor along the border caused the Bulldog engineers to slow their breach tempo.

Despite the delays, the reduction of these obstacles was textbook. Bushmaster and Bulldog worked in concert with one another. As soon as Bulldog cut a lane through a berm or tank ditch, Bushmaster wasted no time pushing through it and bounding north to the next major obstacle. As soon as Bushmaster reached the next berm or ditch, they deployed into a firing line and created a wall of steel, covering Bulldog's advance to their next obstacle.

For centuries, engineers like Mike's have proudly referred to themselves as "sappers" because their original role was to "sap" enemy fortifications—digging trenches and tunnels and clearing obstacles to weaken defenses during sieges. Mike and his engineer "sapper" company spent countless hours rehearsing the breach back in Camp Pennsylvania and while they were camped out in assembly areas near the border. Even earlier, at Fort Stewart and at NTC, Bulldog honed its skills through repetition. Its engineers were as competent as they were fearless. Without hesitation, they would place themselves at the front, often vulnerable and with their backs turned to the enemy. They performed acts of heroism time and again during the breach and later, along the march to Baghdad. Several of these brave souls would sacrifice life and limb.

Once the breach and reduction of the border obstacles were complete, around 2300 hours, our division's 3rd Brigade conducted a forward passage through Bushmaster and began its attack into the 11th Iraqi Light Division northwest of An Nasiriyah in and around Tallil Airfield. I predicted the passage would take a couple of hours, but due to limited visibility conditions, it lasted all night and even well into the morning.

Bushmaster wasn't the only ones that saw action that night. As the rest of the battalion task force waited for its turn to cross over into Iraq, a Patriot missile launched directly over the border. Captain Matt Paul, my mortar platoon leader was one of those stuck on the south side of the border, waiting for his turn to cross.

> *Captain Paul:* The site of the missile and its sonic boom sent a chill down my spine. "What the hell was that?" I heard soldiers shout out loud. It then occurred to me, the Iraqis were launching missiles at us! We were not mentally prepared for this. "How dare they shoot at us . . . we're Americans, the good guys!" many soldiers thought to themselves—at the time still innocent and ignorant to the realities of war—the enemy gets a vote. "Gas, gas, gas!" I heard soldiers scream. Soldiers raced into their vehicles and thrusted on their

> chemical suits and masks, achieving a mission oriented protective posture, or MOPP level 4. "MOPP level 4 is not in effect" I heard the Battalion Tactical Operations Center exclaim over the radio. "Who the hell gave the order to go to MOPP 4?" questioned Major Kevin Cooney, the battalion executive officer. The frightened soldiers took their masks off as quickly as they put them on.

The XO and I did not want to panic the soldiers unnecessarily just prior to combat operations. Systems were in place to track missile impacts, chemical detection, and contamination by analyzing wind patterns. If we were going to be contaminated, we would have plenty of time to react. In this case, our Patriot successfully intercepted and destroyed the enemy missile overhead. As a result of the missile exchange, we were ordered to remain in MOPP level 1, wearing our overgarment top and bottoms. We were to remain in this posture for the next fifteen days. The missile attack was sobering for me. The Iraqis would fight after all, and now Iraqi leaders and their military high command clearly knew we were coming. Our march to Baghdad would not be easy and it would not be fast.

By 1000 hours on March 21, 2003, the remainder of Task Force 2-7 Infantry crossed over into enemy territory along our two assigned passage lanes, beginning the first leg of our long journey to Baghdad. We had effectively "crossed the Rubicon" in Iraq and there was no turning back now. The task force advanced in two file formations, both moving abreast of one another along our two assigned passage lanes. Rage, Thunder, Bulldog, and the combat support trains moved through Lane 8A. Everyone else moved through Lane 6.

The Rage commander, Captain Rob Smith, had a bit of bad luck only seconds before his Bradley lurched forward into Iraqi territory. Less than two kilometers from the border, Rob's Bradley engine quit, leaving him stranded in the middle of the Kuwaiti desert. He ordered his XO, First Lieutenant Cuevas, to drive to him and surrender his Bradley until he could get his own Bradley fixed. Cuevas would literally take a backseat to his commander for the next three hundred miles. Other follow-on forces drove by the defeated Smith and cracked jokes as they sped by, while spraying Smith and his crew with dirt and debris from their spinning tracks. Many Bradley crewmen view their Bradley as an extension or reflection of themselves and place a great deal of pride in its care and maintenance. Most crews even name their Bradley, like it was an actual member of the crew or even their own family. Even though Smith and his crew were not to blame, their predicament was still embarrassing and would be hard to live down.

About five kilometers to the east, Knight, our attached Patriot battery, the TOC, and the scouts crossed via Lane 6. Most obstacles had two passage points, one constructed for the tracks and one for the wheels. Bulldog's sappers had cut open berms and filled in ditches with sand. They dropped AVLB bridges over top of ditches they could not fill. The tracks plowed over the sand, while the wheeled vehicles drove over the bridges. Wheeled vehicles could have gotten stuck in soft sand and risked bottlenecking the entire crossing. It took a little while for my entire formation to navigate through the entire depth of the Iraqi border defenses. Once I received word that everyone was across, I was relieved. Relief eventually turned to anxiety when I realized that the border breach would be one of the easiest parts of the war.

The movement to Objective Bull was uneventful and lasted approximately 1.5 hours. The task force traveled in a diamond formation with Thunder (mortars) and my medical platoon directly behind the lead company.

The trip across the border could only have been described as ominous. The terrain across the border quickly changed from a hard-packed sand to a soft, quicksand-like surface with patches of grass cultivating much of the southern Iraqi landscape. Only a few miles north of the border transported us to different world—a world of darkness and despair. The sight and stench of death served as the front door into Iraq. Our route took us through the massive graveyard of decaying Iraqi tanks, artillery, and armored personnel carriers destroyed during the Battle for the Wadi Al Batin in 1991. Here Republican Guard forces locked horns with the VII Armored Corps of the US-led coalition against Iraq. The VII Corps drove over this elite Iraqi formation as if they were merely a speed bump along their road to the Euphrates. The metal coffins littering the battlefield comprised a giant metaphorical tombstone that read, "This is what happens when you awake the sleeping giant."

I assumed the Iraqis never sterilized the battlefield because making this defeat public knowledge could have undermined and destabilized the Iraqi government. Shortly after the Iraqi Army's defeat and withdrawal, they were forced to quell Shia and Kurdish uprisings throughout most of the country. If the public learned just how inferior or vulnerable their army was, the unrest could have escalated into a full-blown civil war and regime change.

It was a confidence builder for Task Force 2-7 soldiers to see what their Army was capable of as they passed countless formations of dead enemy tanks. It was also a reality check. The soldiers realized they were about to carry out the same horrid task, to close with and destroy the enemy. Or very simply, to kill. This was no longer merely words on a piece of paper or icons depicted on a map—this was not a video game—this game was for real, and it would soon become very personal. Success or failure would now be measured in blood. I wondered if the Iraqi soldiers lucky enough to escape this slaughter twelve years ago could appreciate the futility of another confrontation.

We occupied Objective Bull at 1400 hours and proceeded to conduct our priorities of work. We wasted no time refueling our vehicles, cleaning our air filters of dust and sand, checking our tracks' tension and fluid levels, and, most importantly, cleaning our weapon systems of all the dust and grime littering the arid landscape. The desert condition's diminishing effects on Army equipment were laid bare at Bull. Sand covered every square inch of our equipment, including our vehicles and weapon systems. NTC and the Mojave Desert provided a more forgiving type of sand than here, in southern Iraq. These conditions really take their toll—weapons and equipment will break or malfunction. We dedicated every free moment at Bull cleaning and maintaining our equipment for it to survive the next leg and to function properly in combat. In fact, we followed a prioritized checklist at every leg of our journey to Baghdad.

One significant event did occur shortly after our occupation of Objective Bull. Our PSYOPS team, call sign "Chaos," broadcasted a message to a nearby Bedouin camp. Using their HMMWV-mounted loudspeakers, the message was supposed to direct the civilians to keep their distance and not to interfere. So it was a complete surprise to see Bedouins exiting their homes with their hands in the air and begging for mercy. "Chaos 92, this is Able X-ray, what's going on with the civilians?" "No, that's the wrong tape," Staff Sergeant Vongsvirates, the PSYOPS team leader, scorned his young soldiers sitting next to him. He then replied to the TOC over the radio, "Ahh, we played the wrong message Able X-ray, standby," Vongsvirates reported back, embarrassment evident in his voice. The first message played directed the Iraqis to surrender or else they would be shot. Once the PSYOPS team played the correct message, the civilians returned to their homes, a little shaken up and confused.

Feeling bad about the incident, the PSYOPS soldiers offered the Iraqi children candy and gum as an effort to make amends. PSYOPS soldiers like to joke about their slogan, "We mess with people's heads." Here the joke turned into a reality—the Bedouins' heads were thoroughly messed with during our chance encounter, and I had hoped the same mistake would not be made later. We would encounter more Iraqis the further north we would travel. Baghdad was a metropolis, roughly the size of Detroit, with every building, street, and alleyway flooded with densely packed mobs of nervous civilians. Baghdad had a larger population density than Los Angeles, California. It had a diverse population with regime loyalists and regime haters. It had Shia, Sunni, and Kurdish Arabs—and none of them really got along with each other. Baghdad also had Turkmen, Christians, and more. Playing the wrong PSYOPS message there could mean the difference between mission success or mission failure. We could get it wrong here with five Iraqis, but not five million in Baghdad.

The task force had some time leftover at Bull, so the soldiers took the opportunity to eat and to relax. We left Objective Bull for Objective Lizard at 1630 hours.

We encountered very little resistance while breaching and penetrating into Iraq's borders. Some might say that the breach was largely unopposed. Some even referred to it simply as a border crossing. It was a bit more complicated than crossing a street. No one will ever know if any of the armor we shot up had enemy soldiers inside. We did not have the time to stop and confirm BDA. This was a new kind of war. We were a lot less concerned with body counts than our counterparts in Afghanistan or in past conflicts like Vietnam. The march to Baghdad was a unique mission, different from rooting out terrorists or communists in jungles, caves, or cities. Killing bad guys was part of our tactics but it was not the strategy—removing Saddam was the sole object of our coalition's strategy. If we could remove Saddam without a single loss of life, we could still accomplish our mission. Killing and destroying the enemy's equipment were merely a means to an end.

The breach during OIF was different from my experience during Desert Storm 1991. The scale of the conflict was much bigger in 1991 than 2003. We had a bigger coalition and the Iraqis had a bigger army. The entire 1st Infantry Division penetrated the Iraqi Army's outer defenses. The regular Iraqi Army mounted a more stubborn and elaborate defense, including an intricate obstacle system tied in with tanks, artillery, and infantry designed to disrupt or block our advance east to the Republican Guard. In 2003, the Iraqis chose not to mass their forces directly in front of ours on open ground. That would have been a gift to the coalition.

It was obvious to me that the Iraqis applied lessons from 1991. They would not meet us head on and on our own terms. Rather, they would seek advantages in built-up and populated urban areas along the march to Baghdad. The coalition could not deal the Iraqis defeat in a single engagement. We would have to keep moving north and fight where the Iraqis chose to fight, without slowing our momentum. It meant that Operation Iraqi Freedom would be won in pieces, through the combined effects of smaller units. Divisions, corps, and theater armies were almost irrelevant . . . brigades, and especially battalions and their soldiers, at the tactical edge would decide the outcome.

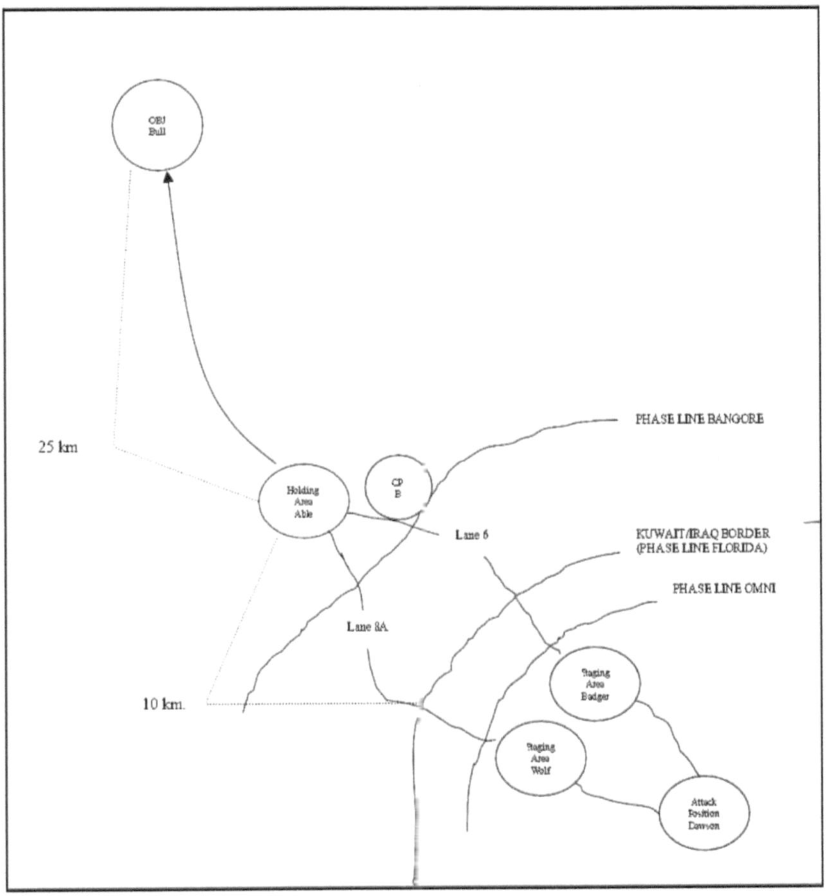

Event 1 Task Force 2-7 in breach and crossing the Kuwait-Iraq border, March 20–21, 2003.
Source: Author's image.

Trail 2-7 Infantry Units crossing the Iraqi border. Courtesy of Task Force 2-7 History.
Source: Bill Thompson.

EVENT 2

The Drive from Hell

"Just drive down that road, until you get blown up."

—Attributed to General George S. Patton Jr., remarks to reconnaissance troops

The task force resumed its march from Objective Bull to Objective Lizard in a diamond-shaped formation, with the scouts leading the march. The mortar and medical platoons traveled in their usual spot, tucked behind the lead formation.

Daylight left us around 1900, and it would take some time for the moon to make its appearance. Until then, visibility was poor. The trace amounts of ambient light from the stars would not be enough to make our night vision goggles effective. Speed was of the essence. Consequently, I ordered every vehicle in my formation to turn their headlights on. It was a tactical risk, but it was an acceptable one. I was not expecting enemy contact and there were many Bedouin tribes dispersed throughout our axis of advance. It was an effort to maximize speed while minimizing accidents. I think it was a wise move.

The order to turn our headlights on was a big shock to most of my soldiers. They thought I was joking. Hesitating at first, they eventually complied. My scout platoon leader, First Lieutenant Gleason, felt uneasy about moving in hostile territory with no light discipline. The scouts are lightly armored, and their safety is in their ability to remain unseen. Gleason was a West Pointer and New Jersey farm boy, with an imposing stature of six foot five and about 225 pounds. In any other life, he could have played lineman for the NFL, an awkward sight for a scout, whose job is to see without being seen. Introverted, yet a confident and sound leader, he was the best scout platoon leader I ever served with. He always found creative ways to find solutions to complex problems. And I never gave him easy missions. I knew he didn't like these conditions, but I also knew he would make the best of it. I had to trust the intelligence that the enemy would not operate in force this far to the west. And the border breach indicated to me that the Iraqis were not looking for direct conflict on open ground.

Traveling with headlights on was almost never done while training back at Fort Stewart and especially at the NTC. Despite the many accidental deaths and injuries sustained while training in total darkness, conventional US Army wisdom strictly affirms that "we own the night." Our inventory of night vision devices was more than adequate to see and navigate through the dark of night. Turning our headlights on, or any light for that matter, is to surrender our technological advantage. However, leaders in war need to be adaptable and must apply common sense to every situation. The enemy's disposition and our firepower advantage would mitigate any risk. Additionally, I thought speed would act as a form of security—getting to our next objective before the enemy could organize a defense or counterattack. From the sky, we must have looked like a Christmas tree. Adaptability at all levels really characterized the "shock and awe" campaign. It was instrumental to our success.

The movement itself went well. Some of the vehicles, unable to keep up the pace, gradually fell back to the rear of the formation. Some of the older model tracks and wheels were beginning to show signs of fatigue, overheating periodically throughout the movement. At speeds up to forty miles per hour, M577 commanders dumped water on their engines to cool them down. The soldier would have to surf atop the vehicle—while in motion—and dump bottle after bottle until the engine moved out of the red. This would work for an hour or so, and then the soldier would have to do it all over again.

The maintenance support during the initial push to Objective Lizard can be characterized as an NCO success story. Seconds after a vehicle breakdown was reported over the radio, the NCOs did not waste a single moment while assessing the situation and quickly determining the proper course of action. The downed vehicles were either repaired on the spot or hooked up for a tow to the next objective. Command Sergeant Major Fox and Battalion Motor Sergeant Master Sergeant Kelly aggressively executed this mission. They spent all night playing whack-a-mole with issue after issue. They bloodied their hands changing tires, repairing track, Jerry-rigging engines and transmissions, and doing whatever it took to keep the task force rolling forward. Every vehicle in the battalion task force made it to Objective Lizard because of their tireless efforts. Many of our vehicles were sitting on ships or in motorpools for years. Consequently, we assumed we would see issues during the first leg of our journey, and we were prepared for them. The push to Lizard was the stress test.

Our trip to Objective Lizard was historically the longest and fastest our battalion has ever moved without a single pause, surpassing all other campaigns throughout the 7th Infantry's history: ninety-four kilometers in less than eight hours, with most of the distance covered at night and in the dark. My attached Patriot Missile Battery was the last formation in my task force to arrive at Objective Lizard.

The Patriot unit was designated Alpha Battery, 2nd Battalion, 43rd Air Defense Artillery Regiment (Patriot) and was based out of Fort Bliss, Texas. They were under our tactical control for the march up to Lizard. They traveled with us for their added protection, but it was not a part of our task force or under our operational control. Our job was to escort the Battery to Objective Lizard where they would place their missiles into operation to cover our division's movement through Objective Chatham. Chatham was situated inside a natural chokepoint sandwiched between Highway 8 and the city of As Samawah, a likely target for enemy missiles.

The Iraqis possessed Scuds, Al-Samouds, and Frog-7 missiles—capable of delivering conventional, nuclear, biological, or chemical agents over one hundred miles. Not far from Baghdad's outer ring defense—nicknamed the "Red Zone"—Objective Chatham was within effective range of every missile in the Iraqi arsenal. Intelligence assessed it likely the Iraqis would try to hit us with chemical or biological agents while we passed through this significant objective. The Patriots were the only countermeasure.

During Desert Shield/Desert Storm, the Army discovered that the Patriot missile, originally intended to shoot down enemy aircraft during the Cold War, was also effective against large enemy missiles flying at high altitudes. The Patriot intercepted many Iraqi Scud missiles bound for strategic targets in Israel and Saudi Arabia. The US Army upgraded the Patriot several times since Desert Storm, increasing its versatility and effectiveness each time. Over a decade since the first Iraq war, the coalition would deploy the improved Patriots again, but in novel ways.

The Patriots in Iraq would pioneer new doctrine. Instead of operating for long periods at secure sites, they would now fight alongside ground forces in hostile territory. They had to meet challenging demands—to cover ground forces while moving only short distances, then reposition as the conditions changed. They no longer had days to adjust, they only had hours or minutes to set up. Their equipment was heavy. Their transport vehicles were meant for roads, not sand—they were wheeled, and they weighed more than our tanks. But they were now expected to operate like a field artillery battery—move, stop, set up and shoot, then move again. They were well rehearsed. They did a great job despite all the challenges. The terrain was unforgiving. I dedicated an M88 to the Patriot formation—a large armor recovery vehicle, called a "wrecker"—to move with them in case they got bogged down. That happened more than once, but we persevered quickly and continued mission.

As we inched closer to Objective Lizard, the Patriot battery fell behind and got stuck—really stuck. I tasked my scout platoon to find a suitable route from the Patriot's stalled position to Objective Lizard. While the rest of the task force occupied Lizard to rest, rearm, refuel, and repair, the scouts were hard at work finding a lifeline for the Patriots. The old motto "scouts out" was an earned one. Scouts were almost always overworked and often underappreciated. They operated on the front lines or behind enemy lines, and they often worked while others rested or played.

Lieutenant Gleason dispatched two scout sections in two different directions to recon potential routes, a task our scouts have mastered through experience and training. After three hours of driving and looking, the scouts finally found a route of enough hard packed sand to carry the Patriots to Objective Lizard. By then, the Patriot vehicles got themselves unstuck and postured to move again. Major Cooney took charge of their movement and, with the aid of the scouts, shepherded the battery the rest of the way to Objective Lizard.

Surprisingly, most of the task force formation, including the Patriot Battery, occupied Objective Lizard under their own power. The task force's plan required all broken vehicles to be towed to Objective Raiders where the mechanics had more time to conduct the needed repairs properly. At Lizard, we were one step closer.

The task force executed its priorities of work in record time while at Objective Lizard. One by one, companies began to initiate their own security and rest plans. The Patriots, along with the scouts, played catchup upon their arrival. The drivers would rest first and would rest longer than the other crewmen. It was imperative they had enough energy to make the next major push to Objective Raiders—the next opportunity for a real break.

Task Force 2-7 soldiers were on autopilot at Objective Lizard. They did not have to wait to be told by their leaders to conduct their priorities of work. They took the initiative and performed their required tasks on their own. They appreciated consequences of complacency. They knew that the mission and their lives were at stake. They forced each other to complete these tasks to a high standard. They checked each other's work and motivated each other to keep going. "Clean your weapon, jackass," we heard some soldiers say. Soldiers accepting responsibility for their own performance and that of each other is every combat leader's dream. It was soldiering at its best. Hollywood likes to highlight and sensationalize individual acts of bravery. But the real test of a good soldier is the endurance and the discipline to do the mundane things while he or she is tired, scared, hungry, or even bored. Those things matter in war.

Shortly after we were all settled in Objective Lizard, the adrenaline began to wear off and the fatigue of driving straight through the night and day was beginning to set in. The initial rush we all had experienced after breaching the border had faded. It felt like stepping off a rollercoaster ride—a big ride filled with drops, loops, and twists. But we still had to do our duty with a clear head and while in control. I looked to my Bradley gunner, Staff Sergeant Jason Trombly, as a source of strength and energy. His value extended far beyond his gunner skills—he understood that combat effectiveness demanded more than weaponry. He was the epitome of the professional soldier and NCO. We set an example for each other. It was a silent, unspoken competition. It kept me going.

Bradley and tank commanders almost always have a special relationship with their gunners. Typically, commanders like me get to hand-pick the best gunners in the unit. Often the best gunners are also the best soldiers in the unit. Staff Sergeant Trombly was both. I was privileged to serve alongside Staff Sergeant Trombly in the crucible of combat. He was, without question, the finest Bradley gunner not only in our battalion task force but arguably across the entire Army. Positioned directly beside me in the turret, Jason became my right arm during the invasion. Our relationship transcended the typical crew dynamic; we formed an unbreakable combat partnership where mutual trust meant survival.

Jason's technical mastery of the Bradley weapons systems was matched only by his situational awareness and tactical instinct. Even during the most intense firefights and grueling operational tempo, he maintained unwavering focus. Yet his value extended far beyond his gunner skills. He understood that combat effectiveness demanded more than weaponry.

When exhaustion clouded my judgment, Jason recognized the danger and intervened. He would insist I catch precious moments of sleep between operations, ensure I maintained nutrition when adrenaline suppressed hunger, and share the crushing weight of command decisions without overstepping his role. In the chaos of war, Jason created pockets of sustainability that preserved our fighting edge when it mattered most.

We remained at Lizard for about eight hours and were required to remain there to give 3rd Brigade the time necessary to complete their mission. They were executing their plan to destroy the 11th Iraqi Light Division, seize Tallil Airfield, and secure a critical crossing site over the Euphrates River. This would comprise a foothold along the coalition's axis of advance. We also remained at Objective Lizard as their reserve force, if they required us. As a combined arms reserve force, we could have been committed to reinforce their attack, recover lost ground, or cover a withdrawal.

Information operations would be critical to the success of our shock and awe campaign. Months prior to the ground war, the coalition contacted several senior Iraqi officers, promising them a future in the new Iraq. We preferred the Iraqis' Regular Army to remain intact to help us secure the country following the removal of Saddam's regime. Back in February, we received credible intelligence claiming that two of the three brigade commanders from the 11th Light Division would refuse to fight and would willingly capitulate to coalition forces. As a result, we did not anticipate that 3rd Brigade would need our support but were prepared in either case.

The Iraqi Army commanders were given explicit instructions about how to capitulate to coalition forces—in an unambiguous and nonthreatening manner and using an approach easily identifiable by our soldiers. We would need to avoid unnecessary killing early in the war if there was any hope of turning the Regular Army to our side. As it turned out on the night of March 21, the Iraqi Army did put up a fight, and consequently our 3rd Brigade held nothing back. They seized all their objectives without our help, with minimal casualties, and were ahead of schedule. The coalition was now on its own . . . the Iraqi Army would neither join us nor play by our rules, and a fait accompli was not going to happen.

The next event in the attack marked a shift in our tactics. We were now going to drive on paved and populated highway roads. I altered our formation from a dispersed, diamond-shaped formation into a close file formation.

An armored column of thirty and sixty-ton killing machines resembling ducks in a row. Much of our route at this point took us near and, in some cases, through a few small cities and towns lining the highway roads. We referred to these places as strip areas. Despite our plans to avoid populated strip areas, we really had no choice. The division had to keep the length of the formation as compact as possible. As a result, both 1st and 2nd Brigades moved abreast of one another with my task force on the extreme eastern flank. Our position meant we would move through the outskirts of these cities and towns. It was not going to be an easy drive. We covered the division's eastern flank. We would act as its phalanx should the Iraqis choose to attack.

I moved the task force out of Objective Lizard at 1000 hours on March 22. We measured the move to Objective Chatham at 130 kilometers long, with 95 percent of the distance composed of paved roads and strip areas. The trip began with a forward passage of lines through 3rd Brigade, south of An Nasiryah.

The last element of the 3rd Brigade we needed to pass through was an explosive ordnance disposal (EOD) team. They had rigged demolition charges to a large enemy weapons cache and had already lit the five-minute fuse to blow them in place. My scout platoon was the first in the task force to encounter this EOD unit. We had to quickly pass through 3rd Brigade and continue the attack as the lead attacking element for the division. Time was a factor. The pressure for us to rapidly advance north was upon us.

> FIRST LIEUTENANT GLEASON: "Able 6, this is Sabre 1, EOD is blocking the road, they say they are about to blow a weapons cache."
>
> LIEUTENANT COLONEL RUTTER: "How much time?"
>
> FIRST LIEUTENANT GLEASON: "Five minutes."
>
> LIEUTENANT COLONEL RUTTER: "Tell them to cut the fuse, tell them we are now the lead task force in the division, we have to keep moving."
>
> FIRST LIEUTENANT GLEASON: "Able 6, this is Sabre 1, he says he can't stop the demo."
>
> LIEUTENANT COLONEL RUTTER: "Ask him if we can go around."
>
> FIRST LIEUTENANT GLEASON: "He says it's too dangerous."
>
> LIEUTENANT COLONEL RUTTER: "Tell him we're going anyway."

The entire task force darted passed the EOD site and all the vehicle commanders ducked their heads down within the protection of their armored vehicles. BOOM! The C-4 plastic explosives wired to the weapons cache exploded about fifteen seconds after our trail vehicle bypassed the EOD site. I looked back and could see the mushroom cloud billowing in the sky. After we completed our passage, we became the tip of the spear, the lead attacking element within the entire coalition ground force in Iraq.

We took Highway 1 for only a few miles, then turned northwest on Highway 8 for the rest of the movement, marked Alternate Supply Route Jackson on our maps issued to us back in Kuwait. After Chatham, we would then turn northwest (again) on to Highway 28, Route Rovers, for the rest of the way to Objective Raiders. I felt like a tourist. Operation Iraqi Freedom in 2003 was before Google Maps. The analog maps we had were not great, and we were in unfamiliar territory. Most street signage was in Arabic, if there was any signage at all. Everything looked the same.

The first half of our movement to Objective Chatham could be characterized as euphoric. We were humbled by the warm greeting we received by thousands of civilians along the route, predominately from Iraq's largest Shia population in the south. Children waved, men saluted, and women expressed tears of joy at our arrival. We all felt like our grandfathers must have felt while liberating France during World War II. It was just like a scene out of *Band of Brothers* during the famed unit's liberation of a Belgium town, previously occupied by the Nazis.

The surge of elation ended abruptly, giving way to sharp disillusionment at the small city of Al Kindr, one of many desolate strip areas about sixty kilometers into the march to Objective Chatham. Al Kindr was probably more of a town than a city. It was difficult to tell. In Iraq, the distinction between town and a city was never as clear-cut as it is in America. Al Kindr had characteristics of both—clusters of shops, garages, and markets along the main strip that gave it the bustle of a small city, yet the size, services, and infrastructure more resembled a rural town. To us, it looked like a halfway place, caught between modernity and neglect, difficult to categorize by American standards. Any populated area near the Euphrates had ancient origins, evolving out of necessity or survival. Just a couple of specks barely visible on our 1:100,000 scale topographic maps, this small city was virtually irrelevant to us at the time. City blocks with buildings two to three stories high lay to our immediate north, with small rural houses and farmland to our south.

Our delightful greeting from the Iraqi civilians just a few miles ago lured us into a false sense of security. To the passerby, Al Kindr went from bustle to ghost town, akin to a typical western movie before a gunfight. The streets cleared out only seconds prior to the impending showdown. The city was to become our "OK Corral." The lack of curious bystanders lining the highway here should have tipped us off to the presence of the enemy. Knight spotted an abandoned weapons cache lying on the ground, near a small bridge at the edge of town. Something was definitely up.

While leading the task force, Scout Section Leader Staff Sergeant Gains discovered what appeared to be a BRDM perched on the edge of town. The BRDM is an enemy scout vehicle mounting a turreted 14.5mm cannon. It appeared to Gains to be old or burned out, perhaps knocked out previously from the air. Before he could fully develop the emerging situation, the BRDM came to life and darted north into the city.

The enemy situation unfolded at the very moment my medical platoon observed a press vehicle with "TV" clearly marked on its hood and doors. It had rolled over onto its side and fallen into a drainage ditch lining the road. The driver, later identified as a photographer on the news team, lay dead from either the crash or from enemy fire. A frightened reporter was curled up next to his damaged vehicle and screamed for our help. "GOD HELP MEEEE!!!!!" he repeated over and over again until finally my medical platoon leader, First Lieutenant Jesse Delgado, hoisted him into his HMMWV and calmed him down. The reporter identified himself as a *Newsweek* reporter but was not embedded with coalition forces at the time. Earlier in the day, he and his partner drove well ahead of our formation, intending to get breaking footage of our column on its march to Baghdad. The Iraqis in Al Kindr tried to kill them both. The reporters were either very brave or very stupid.

Before I learned what had happened with the reporter, panic erupted over my battalion command radio net. "Able 6, this is Sabre 1, I was just shot at with an RPG from the town!" The scout platoon leader, First Lieutenant Gleason, came to within a hair's breadth of his life as he trotted passed this seemingly quiet town. The town was about to get thunderously loud. Multiple contact reports flooded the radio. "Able 6, this is Able 8, I saw a BRDM take a shot then duck back into the town," the medical platoon leader confidently reported. Knight 7, First Sergeant Rodriguez, reported seeing a mortar pit with RPG gunners taking up positions on the outskirts of town. Reports of civilian trucks repositioning troops throughout the town caught my attention.

My command radio net was blowing up with different reports. Initial contact in the fog of war always results in inaccurate reporting. Maybe we all saw the same thing or perhaps our minds were playing tricks on us. Adrenaline has a powerful effect on one's perception of reality. Or maybe all of the contact reports were correct. In any event, I had to filter out the noise, assess what was happening, and determine how to react accordingly. If this was a bigger force, we would probably have to stay and fight until we destroyed it or until it withdrew or surrendered. As the division's lead formation, we could not leave the enemy here intact to harass the formations behind us. This would be our first significant contact with the enemy—the first of many along the route to Baghdad.

My commander's guidance to me was clear: neutralize any enemy threats along the way. Bypassing was not an option. We would have to make a stand in Al Kindr to keep the route open for follow-on forces. However, we could not get bogged down here in urban combat. There was no time to go house to house to root out the enemy. The town would eventually need to be cleared out, but for now we just needed to shut the enemy down long enough for coalition forces behind us to drive through. We had to do something, and we had to act now—hesitation almost always leads to failure in combat. I took charge of the situation and ordered the task force into action. I initially ordered the mortars to quickly set up their guns.

"Thunder 6, this is Able 6, a little help here." "Able 6, this is Thunder 6, roger." Captain Matt Paul and his mortar platoon veered off the road and positioned their guns on a small patch of mud adjacent to the highway. Their firepower may have been necessary. I directed Rage 6 to move one of his Alpha Company platoons into the outskirts of town to develop the situation and engage the enemy. I needed more information about the threat in the town. I needed to know how big and how dangerous it was.

Knight reoriented and deployed closer to the town to support Rage. Knight's Bradley platoon destroyed six enemy mortar positions about one hundred meters northwest of the highway. Over forty Iraqi soldiers emerged from their fortified mortar pits with their hands held high, surrendering. A masonry wall lined Al Kindr's southern boundary, paralleling the highway. There were only a few gated entrances and exits into and out of the town. Rage executed a flanking maneuver, swinging around Knight's left and skirting the wall with its 2nd Platoon, under First Lieutenant Gallo, on the extreme northwestern edge of town. Bushmaster performed a similar action to the southeast. Within a few minutes, we isolated the enemy from three sides.

The enemy found themselves in a pincer, with Knight at their front, Rage on the left, and Bushmaster on the right. Bradleys, tanks, and infantrymen on the ground were fully deployed at this point. Our show of force and the speed at which we deployed overwhelmed the Iraqis. About twenty Iraqi soldiers approached First Lieutenant Gallo's platoon with their hands up and tears in their eyes. One couldn't tell if they were tears of joy or tears of fear. The Iraqis were subsequently taken prisoner, and we deduced that they might have been Regular Army, perhaps remnants of the Iraqi 11th Light Division who escaped defeat in An Nasiryah. They could have also been irregular militia, judging by the looks of their torn clothing and ragged physical appearance.

After the prisoners were processed and loaded up, the task force postured itself to resume its movement. At this point in the engagement, it was around 1900 on March 22. The sun had set and the small crescent moon offered us little visibility while we wrapped things up in Al Kindr. Soldiers prepared their night vision devices for the rest of the drive to Objective Chatham. Just after all our vehicles were set back on the road and were preparing to move again, suddenly the city lights went dark. The enemy pulled the plug.

Lieutenant Gleason reported six enemy combatants attempting to crawl toward our formation, a distance of one hundred meters on open ground. Through his night vision goggles, Gleason could clearly see the RPGs slung over their backs.

> FIRST LIEUTENANT GLEASON: "Able 6, this is Sabre 1, six dismounts are low crawling up to the aid station!"
>
> LIEUTENANT COLONEL RUTTER: "Sabre 1, this is Able 6, can you clear fires with Knight?"
>
> FIRST LIEUTENANT GLEASON: "Able 6, this is Sabre 1, roger."
>
> CAPTAIN LEE: "Able 6, this is Knight 6, we are clear."
>
> LIEUTENANT COLONEL RUTTER: "Sabre 1, this is Able 6, engage and report."

KAKKAKKAK!! Three bursts of .50 caliber machine gun fire and the enemy dismounts were toast. "Able 6, this is Sabre 1, engaged and destroyed six enemy dismounts." The next thing we knew, waves of dismounted Iraqi infantry poured out of the town and attempted to do the very same thing their comrades attempted only moments prior. The Iraqis were attacking us using tactics unseen since the Vietnam War. It was strange. They must have been reinforcements from the east of the Euphrates. There was a bridge nearby and they could have easily crossed over while we were dealing with the prisoners and preparing to resume our movement north.

Knight 6, Captain Jimmy Lee, was caught off guard. At the time, he was on the ground processing prisoners and checking up on his soldiers when the enemy launched their assault. Captain Lee's tank broke away to refuel during the lull, but his crew raced back once the shooting started. When the fireworks began, Lee leapt back onto his tank with all the finesse of an Olympic athlete. He knew he had to quickly assess the situation and figure out what was happening, and fast. Lee knew I would need him in his tank and in command of his formation.

At this point in the engagement, half of my Bradleys and tanks were deployed along a line, orienting their guns at the town. An eruption of .50 caliber, 40mm, 25mm, and 7.62mm machine gun fire devastated the Iraqi attackers. Bradleys fired their machine guns in a "Z pattern" formation—a preferred technique while engaging an infantry formation in depth. The tracers from each of the Bradleys criss-crossed several times—it looked like a laser light show. All the gunfire created a wall of light and lead, and any combatant that stood in its path was hacked to pieces.

The Iraqis clearly underestimated our capabilities to fight at night. Nobody must have briefed them about our technology. One more wave of Iraqi dismounts attacked. They only made it a few steps before they were cut down by massed machine gun and cannon fire. Rage launched a barrage of 25mm high-explosive ammunition at another group of combatants seeking cover behind a berm. The 25mm shrapnel was the only way to neutralize them.

Lieutenant Gleason could see the engagement unfold from his position at a high point south of the town. He observed one brave combatant rise to his feet preparing to assault only to be cut down by a barrage of Knight's gunfire seconds later. The combatants kept coming, and Knight kept shooting. After a few minutes into the fusillade, Lieutenant Gleason prompted the end of the engagement: "Knight 6, this is Sabre 1, stop shooting, they're all dead."

I recommended First Lieutenant Gleason for a Silver Star for his actions under fire. His clever positioning and his combat reporting were decisive, resulting in our rapid response and effective deployment against a determined enemy at Al Kindr. If we responded differently, or slower, the outcome may have been different. We could have taken casualties, or we could have impeded the coalition's advance. Gleason helped me thread the needle at Al Kindr—neutralize the threat, keep them from harassing the follow-on forces, preserve our speed and momentum, and minimize any collateral damage. Here is an excerpt from the recommendation:

> *First Lieutenant Gleason's mission was to move forward of the Task Force in order to screen and to identify enemy forces in zone to protect and provide early warning to the Task Force. Near the village of AL KINDR, a large enemy force using small arms, machine gun, mortar and rocket propelled grenades (RPGs). The enemy was positioned in a camouflaged bunker and trench complex, when they engaged 1LT Gleason's Scout Platoon with an intense fusillade of small arms, machinegun, and rocket propelled grenade fire. 1LT Gleason's timely and accurate reporting prevented the Task Force from maneuvering into the Enemy kill sack and allowed the Task Force to plan and execute a hasty attack with coordinated close air support. With total disregard for himself, First Lieutenant Gleason alerted the Task Force and cross-talked with the Task Force Commander and Commander of Team B in order to direct and focus the Task Force's direct and indirect fires. Throughout the enemy assault, First Lieutenant Gleason maneuvered to maintain observation and direct contact with the enemy in order to accurately direct maneuver elements to enemy locations. Braving the enemy fusillade, he directed Team B to the enemy, allowing Team B to destroy a large enemy force in fortified in bunkers complex and a series of trench lines. 1LT Gleason's reporting allowed the integrated direct and indirect synchronization necessary to bring overwhelming combat power against the enemy. The Task Force was able to locate, fix and destroy the enemy with zero casualties. First Lieutenant Gleason's personal bravery to maintain direct and observational contact was critical in the identification of all enemy units.*

While securing the area, about fifteen minutes after the engagement, Iraqis were seen transporting guns from one building to another deeper into the city. Due to the rules of engagement (ROE) I interpreted at the time, we were obligated to treat these persons as noncombatants. It was a gray area. At the time, their actions of merely carrying guns did not display hostile intent. Guns were everywhere in Iraq. Had the Iraqis pointed the guns at us or displayed a threat in any way, we could engage them as combatants. Our soldiers observing these Iraqis discriminated these targets and demonstrated commendable restraint while discerning friend from foe. Our object of this war was to overthrow the regime and our goal was to kill only where absolutely necessary in order to achieve that objective.

In any event, Al Kindr went quiet and would not pose a threat to follow-on forces. How long that would last was an open question. Nearby, across the Euphrates was an Iraqi safe haven—the enemy could move freely, regroup, reinforce, and posture for a serious counterattack. If they had the will, they could do it, but not any time soon. I probably bought the coalition a few hours. Whatever the Iraqi force was at Al Kindr was no more and would need time to reconstitute to pose a serious threat.

The Iraqis' attack was an exercise of futility. They had no chance. Whether they knew this or not, we will never know. Task Force 2-7 yielded twenty-three enemy confirmed killed in action (KIA) and destroyed four technical trucks mounting machine guns in Al Kindr. This was our first major engagement with the enemy. Our baptism by fire was a big success. Most importantly, not a single Task Force 2-7 soldier was killed or wounded in the exchange. It was a tactical victory, but I couldn't get too excited because, strategically, it meant the Iraqis were going to fight. The Iraqis at Al Kindr displayed tremendous zeal against overwhelming odds, and that was a little unnerving to me. It meant the campaign to topple Saddam's regime would not be easy. More people would die, and destruction and violence would come to characterize the rest of our journey to Baghdad.

Initiative in battle is defined as the ability to set the terms of battle—to keep the enemy on the ropes and to continue to force him to react. I felt like our success at Al Kindr gave us the initiative and the momentum to continue our attack the rest of the way to Baghdad. It was our first big test in combat since the border, and we passed.

Intelligence suggested that the Fedayeen may have compelled the combatants at Al Kindr to attack us. They infiltrated many Iraqi cities and towns, recruiting locals into their service. Some of the locals were enticed by money and others compelled into service. We found money rolls hidden inside of pockets or boots of the dead and wounded. Saddam withdrew millions of dollars prior to the war, and our intelligence believed that some of the money went to recruit and fund the irregular resistance. One by one, the coalition would discover these bastions of resistance in virtually every major Iraqi city north, south, east, and west.

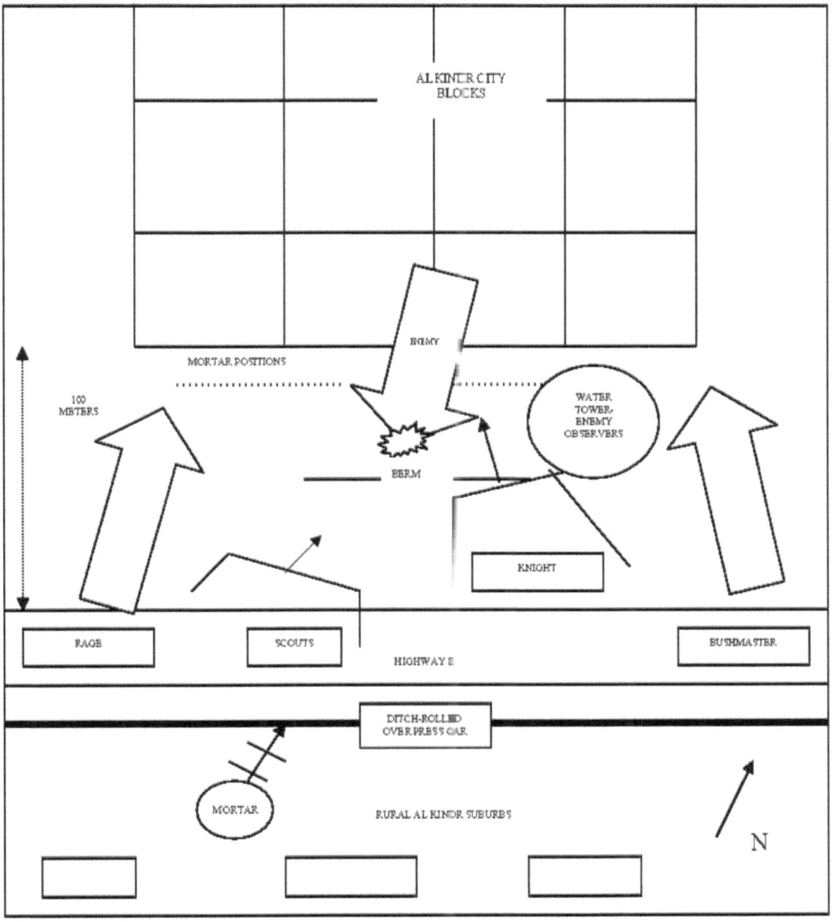

"First Contact": Task Force 2-7 reaction to a prepared ambush on Highway 8 by a platoon of Saddam Fedayeen, March 22, 2003.
Source: Author's image.

EVENTS 3–5

The Drive from Hell, Part 2

"Go forward until the last round is fired and the last drop of gas is expended . . . then go forward on foot!"

—*General George S. Patton Jr, quoted in* The Patton Papers, *Vol. 2, ed. Martin Blumenson (1972)*

It was now 2200 hours on March 22 and it was time to continue our movement north. I ordered Captain Rob Smith's Rage Company to stay behind and contain the enemy inside the town. This would allow safe passage for follow-on forces trailing the task force. Al Kindr was one of many small cities and towns along our route to Baghdad. I had hoped that this hotspot in Al Kindr was an anomaly. Maybe the rest of the march would be quiet. I probably would not be able to commit any additional forces if the Iraqis put up stiff resistance anywhere else along our route of attack. We would be stretched too thin. I could spare one company for a short period, and that was it. If I overcommitted my task force to route security, we could not accomplish our mission to destroy the Republican Guard farther north.

The rest of the division was also stretched and could not divert additional resources to route security. If the Iraqis chose to fight from multiple cities and towns, every division soldier would have to fight through it, even those not meant for direct combat. Truck drivers, doctors, supply specialists, and more would need to literally shoot their way through the gauntlet. These specialists were in short supply, and we needed them alive and focused on their special tasks—not trading fire with Iraqis. We needed these specialists to fix trucks, treat patients, and perform dozens of other tasks to sustain our combat troops on the front lines. They could provide the coalition the depth it needed in case of a prolonged conflict in or around Baghdad and whatever mission that followed.

Captain Smith was a team player but also exceled as an independent operator. He enjoyed the autonomy, and I knew he could operate within a very general set of guidelines and still meet my intent—to protect follow-on forces, protect his own company, hand off responsibility of securing the town to a follow-on unit (whoever that may be), then reconsolidate with the rest of the task force as quickly as possible. I still felt uneasy about leaving them behind, for their sake and for the task force. We needed Rage for the Republican Guard. At full strength, we were still outnumbered. And the Iraqis would enjoy any natural advantages of fighting on their home turf.

The remainder of the task force departed Al Kindr. Because we spent more time there than planned, the rest of 1st Brigade bypassed us and pressed north. Lieutenant Colonel Terry Ferrell's 3-7 Cavalry (CAV) Squadron—a division asset—sped by as well, to get to their next objective. That was expected because the CAV usually operates on the division's front lines, often isolated and in constant contact with the enemy. We had to catch up. We had over fifty kilometers to go to reach Objective Chatham. For this next night movement, I ordered the task force to keep their headlights off. Although I remained hopeful of little resistance, we now had to expect it. Limited visibility might slow us down a little, but we would be too exposed and vulnerable if we were lit up. We needed the tactical advantage that our night vision technology provided us. Nevertheless, we still moved at record speeds without the headlights, at times hitting fifty miles per hour. When we reached Chatham, we immediately began our priorities of work.

Objective Chatham was just a march objective, a spot on the ground a unit must reach. My task force needed Chatham to stop and refuel our vehicles before continuing our advance through As Samawah and onward to Objective Rams. My logistics officer, Captain Scott Knight, nicknamed Chatham the "blazing inferno." Our refueling trucks were massive, unarmored, and vulnerable. If the Iraqi combatants were smart, they would target us there. That is exactly what I would do if I was on the other side. Knocking out one or two refueling trucks would have stopped our entire attack cold. So we needed to refuel the task force quickly—our success depended on it.

While at Chatham, we received intelligence from our brigade headquarters that the Brigade Reconnaissance Troop and the division's 3-7 Cavalry Squadron encountered significant enemy resistance within the city that lay directly ahead, As Samawah. The CAV sent a HMMWV back through our formation, carrying a wounded soldier to be treated and evacuated further to the rear. This sounded worse than our encounter at Al Kindr.

From my vantage point, the As Samawah streetlights outlined the silhouette of the city. From a distance, it looked nice and peaceful. But it would not be peaceful for us. The illuminated metropolis would act like a gauntlet of fire we would need to fight through. Once we exited the city we could return to the open desert and be out of harm's way. We needed to drive through part of the city, then turn west on Highway 28, a one-lane road leading us to Objective Raiders. It would be like driving through the gates of hell. As Samawah was bigger and more densely populated than Al Kindr. It would be harder for our armor to maneuver and to engage targets around tight corners and at higher elevations shooting down at us. It would be a tougher fight. But at least now we were prepared for it.

I positioned my scouts and Knight in the lead, followed by mortars and Bushmaster. I told Bushmaster to secure the battalion combat trains' support elements in the rear. The support vehicles were too vulnerable to travel alone and unprotected. Most of them pulled trailers and could not easily back up or turn on a dime. I dispersed my firepower as evenly as I could throughout my formation. The task force needed to push through the city as rapidly as possible, using speed as a form of security. In this scenario I did not know if we would be predator or prey. We had some advantages in speed, technology, and firepower. But this was the enemy's home turf and fighting them deep inside cities would degrade some of our advantages.

The brigade's reconnaissance troop sent us an eight-digit grid coordinate to an enemy bunker. An enemy BMP armored personnel carrier reinforced the bunker and overlooked the highway we would soon travel. It was a prepared position, occupied by a squad-sized force equipped with one recoilless rifle and two heavy machine guns. Their weapons were trained on our approach, in a textbook location to ambush our formation. I guess this was the As Samawah welcoming committee.

The moment the target was identified and pushed across the fire support channel, the net erupted—fire supporters from every corner chiming in, ready to unleash steel. As the commander, I felt like a trader on the floor of the New York Stock Exchange—surrounded by a frenzy of voices, each fire support element shouting for priority, trying to get their strike in before the window closed. Task Force 2-7 hadn't directed air, artillery, or mortar support yet at this point in the war. So now everyone wanted the mission—my Air Force ETAC and their pilots circling overhead, 1-10 Field Artillery Battalion trailing the task force, and Captain Paul with his 120mm mortars all debated over who was a better shooter to engage the target. This was one of the first real opportunities to engage the enemy with heavy fire support assets, and each of them wanted to get into the fight. It was always better to kill from a distance than to put soldiers at risk in a close fight. Air, artillery, or mortars could have destroyed the bunker. Air was probably overkill and, to be honest, I trusted my own mortars and artillery more. I trained with them, and I knew the people in charge. My mortar platoon leader worked for me. The Air Force is great, but I didn't want them to drop a bomb on us by mistake. Fratricide was unlikely, but why take the chance with the Air Force when an Army asset could suffice, I thought to myself. I needed my mortars to preserve their ammunition for the bigger fight with the Republican Guard. I decided to go with artillery. It would do the job, and the artillery battalion did not have the same logistical or supply challenges my mortars had.

I directed my fire support officer, Captain Jason Happe, to work up the fire mission, and he promptly sent it to 1-10. They shot the fire mission as we began our charge to the foot of the city, covering us as we moved. First Lieutenant Simmons, the Knight Company FSO, would observe and control the fire mission. He sent over fifteen rounds of 155mm artillery precisely on to the target. They set each round with a delayed fuse, exploding after they penetrated the bunker. First Lieutenant Simmons reported the battle damage to Jason: the bunker was destroyed and the BMP was in flames. I drove through the overpass and could see the concrete rubble and the twisted, smoking metal. Anyone inside was incinerated or in pieces. The fiery gates into the city were now open.

While attacking through the city along Highway 8, Knight left their infantry platoon behind, commanded by First Lieutenant Johnson. His job was to secure the overpass south of the city. It was key terrain, overlooking the entire city and dominating all southern approaches. They would have to hold the overpass long enough for 1-10 Field Artillery and the remainder of the division's supporting assets to safely pass through. Their four Bradleys deployed in a square formation surrounding the overpass, with their dismounted infantry occupying positions in the center. Some infantrymen were on the bottom and others on top of the overpass.

We did what I did not want to do. It was a repeat of Rage in Al Kindr, leaving more of my formation behind to secure the route. I did not like stretching the task force further, but we really had no choice. What made this riskier than Al Kindr was that now we were only leaving a platoon behind to fend for itself. Platoons can only do limited things and have no means to sustain themselves over long periods. Consequently, I ensured that Knight 6, Captain Jimmy Lee, knew that this was to be only temporary and that First Lieutenant Johnson's platoon should not get too comfortable. If the enemy chose to counterattack it in force, they could be in real trouble. This was not an easy decision.

The rest of the task force darted past First Lieutenant Johnson's platoon and started to snake through the outskirts of the city. At this point along the route, we had to conduct a forward passage of lines through 3-7 CAV. The division charged 3-7 CAV to secure key parts of the city to allow the rest of us to pass through unmolested. I did not have a strong feel for how they were dispersed throughout the city, and at the time my staff was unable to establish radio contact with their TOC. My Blue Force Tracking system told me they were right on top of me now, only I couldn't see them with my naked eye or on my Bradley thermals. At times, my Blue Force Tracker screen showed ghost units—icons of friendly forces that weren't there. The phenomenon was likely the result of satellite latency or a software hiccup in the still new system we were given just weeks before we crossed the border.

Unknown to me at the time, lead elements of 3-7 CAV were ambushed by massed enemy artillery as they made their incursion into the city a couple of hours earlier, while we were tied up with the enemy at Al Kindr. The CAV relocated approximately six kilometers southeast of the town and intended to conduct a deliberate attack into the city at daybreak the next morning. The level of resistance was much larger than they had anticipated. With better intelligence, artillery and close air support, and a more detailed plan, their attack would prove successful. But with or without them, we were going through the city. We could not wait for their attack; we had to get past the city now and on to our next objective.

While passing through the outskirts of As Samawah, my ETAC, call sign "Advance," received numerous reports of suspicious vehicle revetments and activity along our route. They received initial reports from joint surveillance and target attack radar system, or JSTARS, equipped aircraft.

Only moments later, two A-10 Warthogs orbiting low above the city confirmed the JSTARS reports.

The A-10 is a ground trooper's best friend and has proven its worth in combat time and again over thirty years. Endeared to the Army as the "Tank-Buster," or the "Flying Tank," it is extremely effective while operating in an air-to-ground support role. Army soldiers revere the Air Force–owned aircraft not only for its ability to sustain multiple hits from armor-piercing ground fire but also for its ability to inflict severe damage to enemy tanks and infantry with their precision guided bombs and their infamous 30mm machine cannon firing up to 3,900 rounds per minute. The cannon is so powerful that, when fired, the recoil will actually slow the velocity of the aircraft. Soldiers nickname that sound "Puff the Magic Dragon." The reverberating "BURP" sound is so unique and memorable that a soldier never forgets it. The cannon didn't sound like gunfire—it was more like a giant chainsaw tearing through the air. It sounded and felt unnatural. It was a deep metallic growl, almost like a dragon clearing its throat, before everything in its path disappeared. A-10 pilots are also known to be fearless. They are good at getting in the middle of firefights and they don't mind taking hits when they need to.

The A-10s on station dropped over a dozen parachute flares over suspected enemy targets along the highway, less than a kilometer ahead of us. The illumination would help the pilot discriminate the target as friend or foe. Unfortunately, the flares were dropped so close to friendly forces, they illuminated our column of tanks and Bradleys enough for any ambitious enemy combatant nearby to acquire and target us with a well-aimed RPG.

It was curious: If the A-10 and JSTARS are spotting targets that close, why couldn't we see them? Our thermals would have surely been able to identify the heat signatures, unless the enemy shut his vehicles down—making their temperatures the same as the ambient air. Maybe the Iraqis were getting smarter, keen on what our weapons could do and how to protect themselves accordingly. Maybe the enemy positions the pilots reported on were ours or a friendly unit close by, conceivably 3-7 CAV to our southeast. Operating from the air is very different from operating from the ground. And these pilots are moving at hundreds of miles per hour—a very different perspective than ours. I knew that the 3-7 CAV commander, Lieutenant Colonel Terry Ferrell, was a great CAV commander, so I deduced two things if he was nearby: (1) He would have found a way to make contact with me already, and (2) He would have already made contact with the A-10 pilot and directed him onto the enemy targets. But CAV scouts are also good at hiding and avoiding exposure as part of their tradecraft. I wasn't sure what to make of the situation. The potential for fratricide was looming with every passing moment. It just didn't feel right.

> ADVANCE 11: "Able 6, this is Advance 11, JSTARS reports dozens of vehicle revetments along the highway and most of them are occupied by what appears to be trucks." I'm talking to an A-10 on station and he confirms it.
>
> ABLE 6: "Advance 11, I have no contact with Brigade or 3-7 CAV. I have no idea where 3-7 CAV is located. FBCB2 [Blue Force Tracker] is telling me that they are where JSTARS is reporting enemy trucks."
>
> ADVANCE 11: "The A-10 pilot wants you to clear him to drop some ordnance on those revetments, over."
>
> ABLE 6: "Negative, tell the pilot to take an appetite suppressant. I won't clear him to fire until I can gain contact with 3-7 CAV."

That was that. I exercised prudence and decided against air support. Desert Storm 1991 taught me the risks as well as the horrible and irreversible consequences of fratricide. There is nothing friendly about friendly fire. We would not engage targets we could not positively identify as enemy. I owned the decisions and the outcomes on the ground, and the pilots would have to obey.

The task force slowed its movement but continued to advance into the gauntlet. BOOM!! The high-pitched explosion heard for miles and even through our combat vehicle crewman, or CVC, radio helmets could only have originated from the 120mm main gun of an M1A1 Abrams tank. While cresting a subtle rise in elevation, Knight's lead tank spotted a technical (gun) truck mounting a heavy antiaircraft machine gun on the reverse slope of the hill. It was clearly lying in ambush, coiled up like a snake while waiting for the precise moment to strike. More technical trucks appeared in our sights, hastily converging on our formation's flanks, but were quickly cut down by a steady volume of 25mm Bradley fire.

These must not have been regular Iraqi Army. My assessment was that these combatants were unskilled irregulars, perhaps Fedayeen. I believed that professional Iraqi soldiers would not attempt to attack our tanks and Bradleys head-on with such inferior weapons—commercial trucks mounting machine guns is not a fair fight against our armor. In the US Army, we train our soldiers to hit the right targets with the right weapons as early as basic training. I assumed the Iraqi Army trained its soldiers to do the same thing. The unfortunate Iraqis packed inside these gun trucks paid the price for their lack of intelligence or training about our capabilities. Prisoner interrogations later revealed that the Iraqis were told that our tanks were made of wood. And early in the conflict, they did not realize we could see at night. It is no wonder that many of these misguided Iraqis stood toe to toe with our armor, arguably the best armor in the world. I wouldn't call it courage . . . it was ignorance.

The first technical destroyed by our lead tank was now enveloped in fire, and it straddled a critical crossroads. It was a fork in the road. One turn of this junction would lead to our next objective and the other to more combat and potential disaster. We only needed to transit through part of the city to get to our next objective. That was the plan. Our movement through the city was going well until our tank company, Knight, took a wrong turn directly into the heart of the city. Instead of turning left to Highway 28, Knight turned right, remaining on Highway 8. Running the full length of As Samawah, Highway 8 connected the city's southern outskirts to its northern limits. Navigating under fire is not easy, and the burning hulk at the critical turn created some confusion for Knight's lead elements.

After only a few moments into the wrong turn, the city awakened. Less than a kilometer in, the enemy initiated a well-prepared ambush along the lead elements of our convoy. WHYZZZZ!!! Sergeant Greenwood, commanding bumper number "B12," was the first to feel the effects of an RPG impacting his tank's top armor. It startled the tank crew but did little damage to the tank. RPG fire opened the ambush. The Iraqis fired from elevated positions in the city, on building rooftops and upper floors—places where it was difficult for our weapons to reach. We fired back with what we could. Soon there was so much fire that it looked like night turned to day. There were more fireworks here than in any fourth of July fireworks demonstration I had ever witnessed.

The entire city opened fire on Knight, the lead element in the task force formation. A brilliant demonstration of tracer fire filled the air. The enemy's glowing green bullets colliding with our red tracer rounds. This looked like a laser light show from a distance. A steady hail of enemy AK-47 and RPG fire ricocheted off Knight's tanks.

So many thoughts rush into a commander's head after making contact with the enemy. As a battalion task force commander, I had to trust that my company commanders and platoon leaders would deal with the immediate threats. My value was in coordinating reinforcing assets like artillery, air support, and reserve forces from the ground, if needed. My role was to see the bigger picture—to understand our situation and its impact on my brigade and division. I had to assess impacts to future follow-on missions.

At As Samawah, I was intent on getting past the city as quickly as possible. I thought about how this engagement could impact our future plans for the Republican Guard. I thought about how it could change all our planning assumptions. In a minute or less, I had to assess and understand what was happening, why it mattered, and how I, as the task force commander, should respond. The first thought that came to mind was that we needed to break contact with the enemy and continue our movement northwest to our next objective. But what I didn't know was whether breaking contact would be easy or hard. The two choices before me, in this moment, were to stay and fight or to disengage and get back on course.

At As Samawah, I also thought about logistics. Logistics wins wars. It occurred to me that the Iraqis must have limitless amounts of ammunition, and they would not hesitate to use it when the conditions favored it. The Iraqis did not run out of ammunition in As Samawah. I was starting to get concerned. It was becoming obvious that we would need to fight the Iraqis in cities to win, but we might not have enough ammunition to finish the job. We did not move stockpiles of ammunition with us along the march, and I knew transporting it north from Kuwait would be a real challenge for our logisticians. Transporting it through contested cities would be impossible. My commanders above me assumed that we would collapse the regime before we exhausted our logistics. Maybe that assumption was wrong. I was beginning to question it anyway.

This scene in As Samawah would replay in every city between here and Baghdad. If the enemy put up such a stiff resistance here, Baghdad would be no cakewalk. My fears grew. Knight 6, Captain Jimmy Lee, described the scene in As Samawah as "Bakara Market with tanks," referring to the US Army Rangers' costly raid into the Bakara Market, Somalia, in 1993. As in the Bakara Market, fire erupted from every direction and every dimension: inside buildings, on top of buildings, around corners, under the ground, and from moving vehicles. Noncombatants mixed with combatants. In March 2003, over 100,000 Iraqi civilians called As Samawah home.

Knight's situation was the epitome of the fog of war—ambiguous, opaque, and confusing. Everything moving was a potential threat. But we were well trained and disciplined soldiers; we just couldn't shoot everything. We followed our ROE, and when the ROE was ambiguous or did not apply to our situation, we fell back on the Geneva Convention and the Law of Land Warfare. Even in war, we follow rules. My gunners and commanders in As Samawah had milliseconds to discriminate between friend, foe, and noncombatant.

Captain Lee led his company through the gauntlet of over two hundred enemy fighters, along three kilometers of unwelcoming enemy territory. The crossroads and the turns into and out of the city were very difficult to decipher clearly on our small 1:100,000 scale maps. I was behind Knight company, and once I realized the formation had taken the wrong road, I quickly tried to undo the mistake. "Knight 6, back up and turn around, you made a wrong turn!" I informed my tank company commander, Captain Jimmy Lee. Turning around was a bad option, but pressing the march through the rest of this hostile city on the wrong road was a worse option. Attempting to trade fire with every Iraqi combatant in the city until they were all dead was the worst option. I considered all three options, but simplicity and common sense quickly prevailed—we were off mission, and we needed to get back on mission.

Being disoriented in the middle of an enemy held city while under fire is just about the worst situation any combat leader or soldier could find themselves in. It quickly became an unpleasant experience for everybody, to say the least. Knight, traveling the most distance, had to turn around and fight through the same gauntlet as before. Speed would be their security, moving and shooting as quickly and as accurately as they could. If a tank threw a track, it would mean certain death for the crew once dismounted and exposed. Getting out of the tank was not an option. Any broken or disabled vehicle would have to be pushed until it was out of danger.

Our task force returned the enemy's fire with every weapon system at our disposal. It was difficult to see the enemy. We aimed each rifle, machine gun, and cannon at the bright flashes to our left, right, front, and rear. The enemy's muzzle flashes were the only objects within the gauntlet we could aim at. The enemy was elusive. They would engage, run and hide, then reengage. There were so many that the fire never really stopped. The lead tank commander aimed his 120mm main gun into the top floor of a three-story building—a fortified building the Iraqis used to rain fire down on top of our column. He pulled the trigger, unleashing the devastating effects of fifty pounds of high-explosive ammunition. Fifteen enemy fighters flew out, lifeless, dismembered, and mixed in with the broken rubble. The image was surreal and morbid. The charred debris became an obstacle along our escape route. Knight had to navigate around it, slowing them down.

Captain Jimmy Lee's (Knight Company Commander) perspective on As Samawah:

> I did not expect the volume of enemy contact that we experienced in As Samawah. Charlie Troop, 1st Cavalry (Brigade Reconnaissance Troop), had a section in front of the task force. They made first contact there, sustained an injury, and fell back within the protection of 2-7 to execute a CASEVAC (casualty evacuation). My impression was there was probably a small team who felt bold enough to take on a couple of scout HMMWVs and got off a lucky shot. The contact was reported to come from the overpass at the entrance of the town. Lieutenant Colonel Rutter made available all assets to neutralize the enemy so that the task force could continue their attack north unimpeded. We planned an artillery barrage on the overpass. We were tied to the roads; even during the approach to the town the fields were potentially "no-go" terrain due to recent rains.
>
> Our "causeway fight" at the National Training Center during our November 2002 rotation brought with it lessons learned that I applied here. Typically I would lead with a tank platoon. During the causeway fight, I learned that when restricted to a route, if the tanks go down, they impede the infantry platoon's ability to get to the front and rapidly deploy. I rearranged the order of march and placed the infantry platoon in the front. Because the dismounted contact was at the overpass, their task was to seize the overpass in order to facilitate the passage of the company, and ultimately the task force, through the area unimpeded.
>
> I was short four tanks at the time. During our move from Objective Lizard that morning, two tanks went down due to maintenance (from separate platoons), therefore forcing two additional tanks to stop and tow them to our next objective. I pulled the two tanks remaining from my 3rd platoon and placed them under the command and control of 1st Tank Platoon and their two tanks. My combat power was six tanks, four Bradley fighting vehicles, two Air Defense Linebacker Bradleys, and three solid infantry squads. Additionally, my FBCB2 (Force XXI Battle Command, Brigade-and-Below) was down at the time, leaving me to navigate with a red lens flashlight and a 1:100,000 scale map . . . in a city . . . at night, and my thermal night-sights were also down on my tank. I felt like a blind man with both hands tied behind my back going into a tough-man contest.

Following the artillery mission, the infantry platoon seized the overpass with minimum contact. The company passed through and continued the attack. What appeared to be a major intersection on the map ended up being a dirt road that we failed to identify. Once we passed the intersection, we encountered an ADA piece that the A-10 pilots reported as being active earlier. Sergeant Height, a young tank commander with the skills and courage of the most experienced tank commanders, destroyed the vehicle. At this point, A-10s began dropping flares in an attempt to identify enemy positions in the town. We were not there for a fight, but to get the task force through safely . . . a fight had to happen. During the move into the town, I begin receiving reports from my company about personnel moving through the city with weapons. When a tank would scan their turrets, the people basically froze in place . . . as if to think we would not see them if they stopped. Based on the reports prior to the war, that many soldiers would capitulate as well as the thought that many would bear arms to protect themselves from a ruthless regime that may attempt to destroy the families of soldiers refusing to fight, seeing people in a town with weapons was not unexpected. It was only about a minute into this quick thought process that we sensed it was more than innocent people trying to protect themselves.

The reports increased to a point that we suspected there were over two hundred to three hundred people in the town with weapons . . . and the reports came from several locations so we ruled out "double reporting." My lead tank then took an RPG from the top floor of one of the buildings. The RPG hit the bore evacuator on the gun tube. As we discovered later, it barely left a scratch, but at the time, it was a tense moment. Once the RPG launched, we began to receive heavy volumes of small arms and RPG fire from both sides of the four-lane road. The Iraqi Army/militia was fighting from the various buildings and earthwork locations in the town. It immediately reminded me of the movie *Black Hawk Down*. It so closely resembled the movie that I even quoted lines from the movie over the radio when applicable in answering/transmitting radio messages. When I watched that movie, I always tried to think what I would have done differently if I were there with a mechanized force; well, I was there . . . in As Samawah. The fighting was so close that Lieutenant Colonel Rutter's Bradley was engaging the enemy as he located the turn I missed. Reports continued to come in about vehicles maneuvering behind buildings and what appeared to be more personnel entering the town in an attempt to reinforce, or perhaps the enemy was repositioning. The company performed exceptionally well during this first major engagement. I was immediately impressed

> with the quality of the junior leaders in the company and felt proud they were fighting with me and not against me. They exuded initiative throughout the fight, cross-talking to each other, making recommendations to me, identifying enemy targets for other tanks while they were in their own fight. It was a beautiful event in terms of what we accomplished in the environment we were in. If we were not so hurried to continue our fight with the division to the north, the task force could have cleared out the town that night. We had the ability, determination, and initiative, but there was a more pressing need for us to continue on, leaving the town for elements of 1-41 Infantry and 101st Air Assault to clean up later. The task force made it through safely with all its assets/attachments as a result of the fighting and also due to my infantry platoon, known as the Outlaws, who remained at the turning point that night, fighting back multiple counterattacks, and then falling in to the rear of the task force formation.
>
> My analysis of the enemy that evening is as follows: The enemy personnel in the vicinity of the overpass when the Charlie Troop scout section entered town was essentially a robust observation post. We stopped on the outskirts of town to conduct refueling operations. I believe the composition of our mechanized force was identified or called in from towns we previously passed, triggering the OP to fall back into the town, warn of our approach/composition, and prepare a deliberate ambush. I feel certain that the Iraqis encountered losses to fratricide since the ambushes were placed on both sides of the road; therefore they were essentially shooting toward each other. The road curved to the right in the town where another ambush was set to fire at vehicles traveling down the road . . . thus creating a semblance of a U-shaped ambush. I am not certain as to the enemy BDA, but I am confident we destroyed/injured over 80 percent of the personnel fighting. Those that survived uninjured were the ones who attempted to destroy my infantry platoon with multiple counterattacks as they were protecting the task force during its passage for the duration of the evening.

The task force eventually turned around and quickly proceeded to the next major objective, Objective Rams. The scouts established a traffic control point at the troublesome crossroads, pointing the remainder of the task force in the right direction, toward Highway 28—also called Route Rovers. This duty was then handed over to First Lieutenant Johnson from Knight Company; he detached one of his Bradley sections from the overpass to relieve the scouts and secure the crossroads.

Between the overpass and the crossroads, First Lieutenant Johnson remained in As Samawah for almost six hours, securing safe passage for follow-on forces while absorbing a constant barrage of machine gun and mortar fire from within the city. The enemy's actions were unabated. All Johnson could do was dig in as best he could and shoot back if he had a good opportunity. He even attempted some limited maneuver to attempt to scare the enemy and push them back into the city—like a leashed watchdog trying to scare away a potential burglar.

The enemy's defense of their city was well rehearsed, and they certainly anticipated our arrival. Perhaps the Iraqis at Al Kindr gave them early warning. We estimated at least one hundred combatants killed in the exchange. Based on the reporting alone, twenty-two enemy fighters were confirmed KIA. Additionally, fourteen enemy antiaircraft artillery pieces and two technical trucks were reported destroyed in As Samawah. Given the close exchange in the congested city and the limited visibility, civilian deaths or injuries were also likely. I hoped not. We took every precaution and followed the rules we had at the time.

Captain Lee was awarded the Silver Star for his courageous leadership under fire. Here is the recommendation:

> *Captain James Lee distinguished himself by exceptionally valorous actions in the evening of 22 March 2003 as the Commander of Team B of Task Force 2nd Battalion, 7th Infantry Regiment, 3rd Infantry Division (Mechanized) during a Task Force attack against an entrenched enemy along Highway 8 in the town of As Samawah in Iraq. While maneuvering his Tank-Heavy Company Team under the hours of darkness as the advance guard for the Task Force Captain Lee accurately emplaced indirect fires against an initial enemy ambush positioned over a railroad overpass at the entrance to the city proper. While maneuvering his team through the city to clear the way for the rest of the Task Force Captain Lee and his team entered a carefully planned ambush defended and over-watched by an overwhelming enemy force using automatic weapons, machine guns, mortars and rocket propelled grenades (RPGs). Upon initial contact and while his tank was engaged by small arms and armor piercing rocket propelled grenades Captain Lee engaged through and maneuvered his team to destroy the overwhelming ambush force. Throughout the engagement Captain Lee accurately employed direct and indirect fire weapon systems in order to destroy a numerically superior enemy force. This extraordinary event allowed his Team and the Task Force to complete its mission by allowing the Task Force that included attached Patriot Missile Systems to move through the town unimpeded and protected from enemy forces. Captain Lee's extraordinary heroism without regard for his own life in order to protect others are in keeping with the highest traditions of the military service and reflect great credit upon himself, his unit, and the United States Army.*

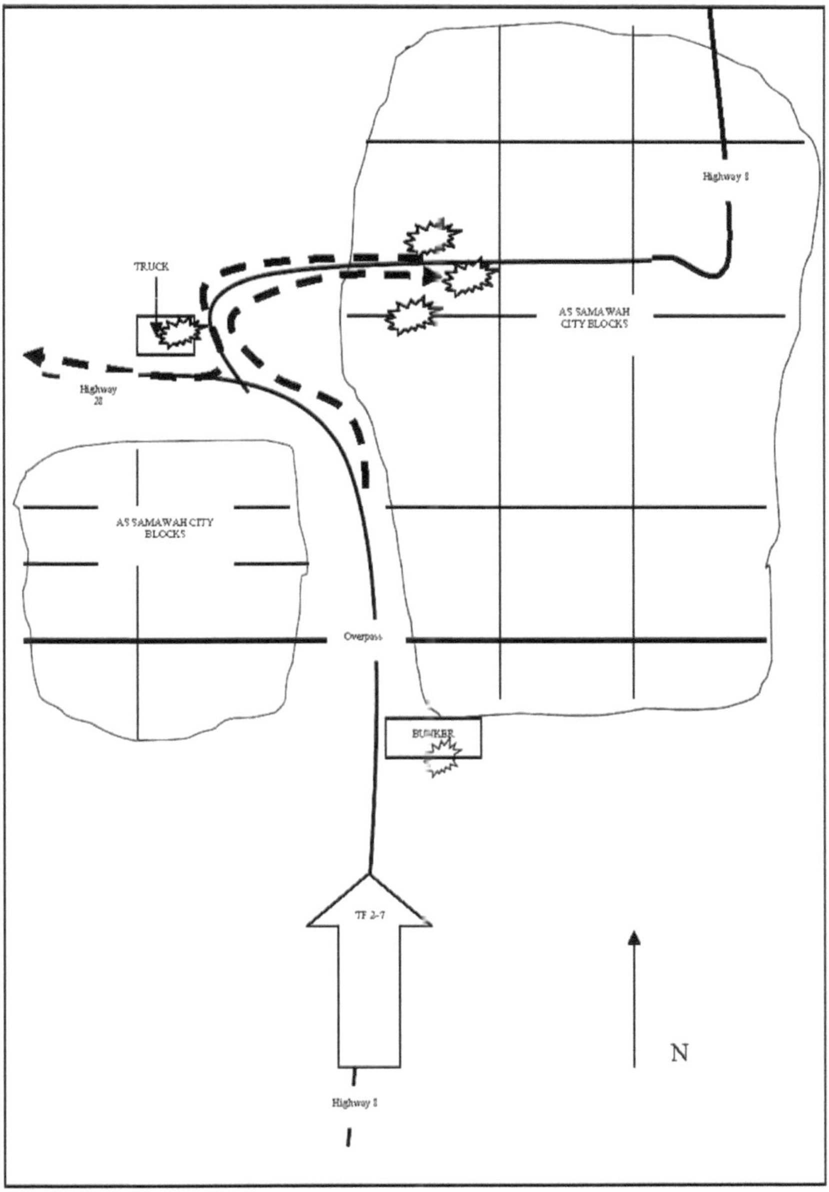

Task Force 2-7 ambush at As Samawah Highway 8 by Saddam Fedayeen irregular militia, March 22, 2003.
Source: Author's image.

Task Force 2-7 Infantry was the first coalition unit to transit through As Samawah. It would also be one of the last. The city was too hot. Eventually, the coalition rerouted most follow-on forces to the south, detouring around the city, causing traffic to bottleneck. It delayed the flow of supplies to us in the north in the days ahead.

Our actions within As Samawah spanned the remainder of March 22 and into early March 23. Time was a factor. 2nd Brigade pushed north around my task force and the rest of my 1st Brigade while we were tied up with the enemy in As Samawah. Objective Rams was located ninety kilometers north along Highway 28, adjacent to a main oil pipeline extending from northern to southern Iraq. 2nd Brigade made unexpected contact with a large, irregular force near Rams shortly after we resumed our march. Consequently, my brigade ordered my task force to stop short of Rams by about fifty kilometers because 2nd Brigade needed us out of their way to eliminate the threat. They needed space to fire and maneuver. So we made good use of the time. We conducted tactical refueling operations, conducted maintenance, ate, and stole as much rest as we could.

Just before our departure, First Lieutenant Johnson from Knight Company managed to catch up to us and rejoin the formation, just in time for our next major thrust north to Objective Raiders. Like a stray bird trying to catch up to the flock, Johnson's platoon, alone and isolated, drove for five straight hours at top speed in a desperate attempt to reconsolidate with the task force. They did not want to be left behind and miss the big show. I was relieved to have them back under our wing. I was worried they would become a lost platoon.

Our next objective after Rams, Objective Raiders, lay 130 kilometers ahead. Partway through the movement, we would have to pass over the An Najaf escarpment. This significant piece of terrain consists of a large sand dune with a thirty-degree inclining slope. The escarpment rises sharply from the surrounding plain, with an elevation change of roughly fifty meters over a short horizontal distance. What began to threaten us more than enemy fire was sustainment. Fuel, ammunition, recovery assets, and repair capability were all finite, and every kilometer north magnified the strain. Speed kept us alive, but it also punished our logistics. From that point forward, every decision carried a second calculation: not just could we win the next fight, but could we support it afterward. I was concerned about the long drive ahead and the long climb to the top of the escarpment, and what it might do to our mobility. Our vehicles have been moving for days now, and they were weighed down like pack mules, carrying all our ammunition and extra equipment.

The An Najaf escarpment began in the city of An Najaf and extended westward for over thirty miles. During the planning phase of the operation, there was some doubt about whether or not some of our vehicles could even make it over the dune, but these concerns were put to rest once we arrived—all of our wheeled and tracked vehicles could make the climb. Not only did we anticipate stalled vehicles along the escarpment, we also expected enemy contact. Intelligence estimated Iraqi corps or division-level reconnaissance, at a minimum. We expected to see recon units operating in BRDM vehicles or even civilian trucks or motorcycles. If we were vulnerable, they could trigger a ground attack or an attack from a distance using rockets, artillery, or missiles.

My soldiers could not be more ready to cross over the escarpment. We made all our final precombat and preexecution checks and proceeded to advance through the escarpment and onward to Raiders. We received word earlier that our brigade's tank battalion, 3-69 Armor, made contact with a battalion of irregular militia ahead of us, near the escarpment. The coalition pounded the escarpment with long-range artillery and A-10 Warthogs prior to our brigade's crossing. Approaching the large dune, we spotted up to one hundred spent artillery and mortar shell casings littering the desert floor. Task Force 3-69 Armor clearly hit something big here, and I wondered if they left any fight for us. At the helm was Lieutenant Colonel Ernest "Rock" Marcone—my old battle buddy from Desert Storm. Rock wasn't just a commander, he was a force of nature. With his warrior instincts and iron resolve, any resistance in his path didn't stand a chance. Just prior to our crossing, I heard over the radio that he was successful in neutralizing the threat, but I was warned that there may be pockets of enemy resistance retreating north of the escarpment. We would have to keep an eye out for them.

Crossing over the escarpment felt like we were on a rollercoaster ride, climbing gradually in altitude just before the big drop. If the enemy attacked, it would be impossible for us to maneuver or shoot back during the climb. It was a twenty- to thirty-minute period of vulnerability for my combat units: Sabre (scouts), Knight, Bushmaster, and Thunder (mortars). I left my combat supply trains on the south side of the escarpment until my combat formations could clear the north side. I wanted to keep my vulnerable supply vehicles safe. I also wasn't sure if they could make it up the escarpment. I didn't want them to break down or stall out halfway up, creating a bottleneck for the rest of the task force. I needed to test out the slope with our combat formations first.

Our crossing over the escarpment was successful—my combat formations made it over the dune under their own power with ease. We scanned left and right for any signs of enemy, but it looked quiet. All we could spot were lifeless Iraqi bodies and charred machine gun–mounted trucks. My supporting combat supply train formations would cross later with no issue.

Upon crossing over the escarpment, my brigade ordered me to seize a suspected WMD storage facility north of the escarpment. The coalition identified the compound as an SSE, or sensitive site for exploitation. The facility was a large, rectangular-shaped compound. Comprising over one hundred acres in real estate, its silhouette was clearly depicted on our topographic maps. It was a very large facility about the size Fort Stewart's main post area, housing over fifty buildings including storage warehouses. Many of the buildings were modular, similar to an American mobile home or trailer. They garrisoned soldiers, office space, and stockpiles full of weapons and ammunition. The compound was isolated, about three miles from the nearest population center. There was a reason for its isolation. I surmised that this place must have been a facility on the United Nations Monitoring, Verification, and Inspection Commission's (UNMOVIC's) inspection list.

The scout platoon split up and occupied observation points roughly five kilometers north and south of the compound as an effort to isolate our attack and provide early warning to the task force in the event of an Iraqi counterattack. Soon after the scouts were set in their positions, Bushmaster and Knight quickly deployed online with one another. Knight established a cordon around the northeastern portion of the compound as an effort to further isolate Bushmaster's assault.

The mortar platoon occupied a firing position just northeast of Knight, within two kilometers of the compound. They laid their guns on the heart of the compound; their rounds were prepped and were just waiting for the order to fire.

Before the assault, my scouts provided Bushmaster real-time intelligence on the disposition of the compound and its defending Iraqi soldiers. Scout Staff Sergeant Dow observed enemy activity inside the compound from his assigned observation point about five kilometers to the south, near the escarpment. He reported the enemy massing their forces in the northern portion of the compound. Bushmaster now knew the best place and method to begin their attack, from the south. Always best to breach the enemy's defenses where they are weakest, not where they are strongest.

Bushmaster penetrated into their objective by charging a Bradley directly through the chain-linked fence surrounding the compound, opening a door for the rest of the company to flood through and begin their sweep of the facility. Bushmaster's infantrymen dismounted from their Bradleys and, with precision, began to systematically clear each building and structure within the compound. It took Bushmaster's infantrymen on foot two hours to search just five buildings. It was exhausting work, and they had scores of buildings left to search. Iraqi uniformed soldiers scattered about frantically from building to building. I heard two loud explosions—BOOM! . . . BOOM! While busting open doors, Bushmaster activated a few booby traps wired to explosives. In both instances, the blast blew inward and upward, not outward toward the soldiers, and miraculously not a single soldier was killed or wounded by the explosions.

Clearing rooms and buildings is slow, violent work for an infantry unit. While we held some advantages in this isolated compound, the danger and slow pace made it clear that this was not a tactic I wanted to repeat in cities. In urban terrain, this kind of operation would bleed us dry. Shock and awe would become something else entirely: a war of corners, casualties, and chaos. It would strip away momentum and replace it with a grinding, costly fight. Our fight would devolve into attrition and bloodshed. It would be the fight the Iraqis wanted. While clearing the compound, Bushmaster received only sporadic enemy gunfire and encountered many Iraqi soldiers willing to surrender. The bulk of the Iraqi defense was situated in the north and was oriented primarily to the southeast. Bushmaster attacked the compound from the southwest initially but then deployed across multiple axes. It confused the Iraqi defenders, and eventually they found themselves surrounded by Bushmaster's Bradleys maneuvering to their east and dismounted infantrymen advancing from the north, south, and west. Once the Iraqis knew that they were beaten, they promptly surrendered by the masses.

During our search and interrogation of the prisoners, we found the bulk of the defenders to be support soldiers who supplied spare parts, ammunition, and weapons to the Republican Guard—their red triangle patch sewn and clearly visible on the shoulders of their uniforms. They were not frontline Republican Guard infantrymen, and it was clear that they knew they were outmatched. A few desperate Iraqi soldiers attempted to jump in their cars and flee to the open desert but were subsequently chased down and surrounded by Bushmaster's Bradleys, whose tracks and six-hundred-horsepower engines could traverse the soft desert sand at a much quicker pace than an Iraqi automobile.

During the clearing operation, we heard a THUMP, THUMP, THUMP in the distance. "Able 6, this is Able 4, we're taking incoming fire, were going to conduct a survivability move," a situation report

Captain Knight, my battalion logistics officer, offered me in a quizzically calm and composed tone of voice. There were incoming enemy mortar rounds targeted at my task force's supply trains, located on the south side of the escarpment. They received incoming 82mm mortar rounds from within the city of An Najaf, only three kilometers away. Fortunately, all the enemy's mortar rounds landed short and missed Captain Knight's formation. His formation was vulnerable, out in the open and operating in light armor and soft skin supply trucks.

I kept Captain Knight's supply trains on the south side of the escarpment because I felt that would be the safest place for them to operate during the engagement at the suspected WMD compound on the north side. I was concerned about their survivability given their lack of protection. They were vulnerable to all forms of direct and indirect fire. Our engagement at the escarpment taught me that one spot was as good as the next in this war. This was not Desert Storm 1991. So I tried not to overthink location and positioning during the rest of the war.

Iraq was now a 360-degree, multidimensional battlefield. There was no safe haven and definitely no "rear area." The enemy was everywhere, and it came in many forms—from mortars or rockets launched from a distance, to suicide bombers blending in with the civilians, to the guerrilla employing hit-and-run ambush tactics, or to the uniformed soldier on patrol or defending a pillbox along a highway intersection. Every Task Force 2-7 soldier, regardless of job or rank, must be prepared to react to enemy contact in all forms and to fight back if necessary. We needed to take risks, but risk taking still needed to be calculated. I would not put my support assets in needless danger or act recklessly, but I wasn't going to overanalyze it at this point.

An Najaf emerged as one of several strongholds of resistance encountered along our advance, occupied by Fedayeen fighters and other paramilitary groups. It fell to other elements of my division to isolate and contain the city, holding the perimeter long enough for follow-on units to execute a deliberate incursion and systematic clearing operations. These efforts were essential to setting the conditions for regime change, followed by stability and support operations aimed at restoring law and order, initiating reconstruction, and delivering humanitarian aid.

Iraqi resistance came to an abrupt halt when Bushmaster's 2nd Platoon seized the headquarters building situated in the heart of the compound. An Iraqi general officer commanding the defense from inside was quickly subdued and taken prisoner. At the time of his capture, he was found frantically operating his wire and radio communications linked to fighting positions along the perimeter of the compound and elsewhere, perhaps to Baghdad. He quickly informed his captors that this compound was so important that if it fell to the coalition, his army would target and destroy it with a missile attack. That didn't sit well with me. We were well within range of Iraqi missiles and other short-range rockets, artillery, and mortars. Unfortunately, our division's counterfire radar systems could not help us at the compound. We were too far forward. All we could do was continue mission. If we stayed here long, we would need to dig in and build fortifications.

Bushmaster found chemical defense equipment during one of its many searches throughout the compound. The Iraqis were clearly prepared for chemical warfare. It was not inconceivable to believe that the Iraqis would deploy chemical weapons on their own soil. The Iraqi leaders probably assumed that we would not deploy our own WMD in Iraq, especially with our own soldiers operating throughout the country. We would not want to put our fellow soldiers at risk. Our findings in the compound deepened my concerns about the potential to fight through contaminated areas. If the Iraqis were desperate, they might use chemical weapons, especially if their own soldiers had the means and the training to protect themselves.

The compound was critically important to Saddam's military and its logistics infrastructure. Because of its isolation and its sand-colored camouflaged rooftops, the regime clearly did not want this facility placed on the coalition's target list. Seventy-seven Iraqi soldiers, including the Iraqi general, were taken prisoner during Bushmaster's attack. It was the largest mass surrender of uniformed Iraqi soldiers during the division's march up. A big win. Most of the Iraqis captured claimed that they disliked Saddam Hussein and supported America and the coalition. They told interrogators that shortly before the war, Saddam Hussein told his soldiers that if they surrendered to us, we would execute them on the spot. Their fears were quickly put down after a couple of days. We abide by the laws of land warfare. We treat prisoners of war humanely, as we would want to be treated if our soldiers suffered the same fate.

We seized thousands of weapons and munitions at this site, ranging in size from assault rifles to antiaircraft artillery. Bushmaster and supporting coalition assets spent the next two days systematically destroying the cache using C-4 plastic explosives. Bushmaster guarded this site and the enemy prisoners of war long enough for a special exploitation team to conduct a more detailed search of the compound for the presence of nuclear, biological, or chemical weapons. We heard later that no signs of any such weapons or residue were found at the site.

Task Force 2-7 climbing the An Najaf escarpment, March 23, 2003. Courtesy of Task Force 2-7 History.
Source: Bill Thompson.

As soon as I felt the compound was completely secure, I ordered the rest of my shrinking task force to continue its onward movement to Objective Raiders. Rage was still separated from us, perhaps still securing Al Kindr in the south for all I knew. Bushmaster would stay at the compound to continue to destroy the captured weapons, process prisoners, and prevent a reoccupation of the compound by the Iraqi military. At the time, I did not have a good sense for how long Bushmaster would remain apart from the task force. It could have been hours, days, or weeks.

From the compound, Objective Raiders was only a ten-kilometer hike north, but the task force would need to conduct the march piecemeal with its lead elements traveling in total darkness. The TOC, scouts, and mortars would occupy Raiders initially, then Knight shortly thereafter. Bushmaster and Rage would trickle in over the next few days.

I was concerned because for this movement to Raiders, the task force would not operate in strength, with units scattered well outside supporting distance of one another. We were a mere fraction of what we were a few days ago, back in Kuwait. Regardless of our current composition, we were now in hostile territory, with Iraq's most professional military forces operating and defending this region of the country. It had been days since our last intelligence update on the Republican Guard. I had no idea if they repositioned since we crossed into Iraq. We just seized their primary logistics compound—I would have to guess that would trigger some sort of reaction or counteraction by the Republican Guard's main force. Once again, we would become the coalition's lead element, but we would operate in the blind. We would only know where the Republican Guard was if we bumped into them.

If the Republican Guard knew where we were and how vulnerable we were the night we began occupying Objective Raiders, they could have destroyed us if they tried. I recounted countless historical examples where the stronger side lost because it was dispersed and vulnerable: Lee's army in Chancellorsville beat the Union Army at twice its numbers, Alexander the Great did the same to the Persians in Gaugamela. The list went on and on. Task Force 2-7 was literally all over the map, and my soldiers and leaders were physically exhausted. Some of us hadn't slept in days and were not at peak fighting strength. Every thought, every word, and every step was a struggle at this point. If we did not suffer the same fate this night as the Union Army in 1863 or the Persians two millennia prior, it would be because of luck.

The TOC, along with my scout platoon, were the first to arrive and occupy Raiders around 2100 on March 23. During their occupation, they encountered six unarmed Republican Guard officers and quickly took them prisoner. They found a lot of hidden cash during their search of the Iraqis. We deduced that these Iraqis were likely stationed at the compound Bushmaster attacked only a few hours prior—judging by the time, distance, and direction the Iraqis must have traveled on foot.

The mortar platoon arrived later, around 2200 hours. They were slightly delayed by the darkness and disorientation caused by several Iraqi villages along their route—villages so small they were invisible on maps. The mortar platoon was equipped with several trucks, ideal for transporting prisoners. So I ordered the mortar platoon to load the Iraqi prisoners on their trucks and transport them to the prisoner collection point under construction back at the weapon's compound. A mortar carrier escorted the truck to the compound for the added protection. The mission took most of the night—rest and recuperation would be out of the question for those tired crews driving back and forth that night.

Knight was ordered to clear Objective Spartan, 2nd Brigade's Objective paralleling Raiders. They made contact with several fleeing Iraqi soldiers. Even though the Iraqis wore uniforms and carried weapons, Knight chose not to shoot them in the back. The ROE allowed them to shoot, but instead Knight showed them mercy. They deployed their tanks to try to force their surrender. They were like cowboys trying to round up a few stray cows from the rest of the herd. This became a team roping exercise, of sorts.

The Iraqi soldiers at Objective Spartan kept running to avoid capture, weapons still in hand and clearly visible to the tank crews. Right before the order to fire was given, the 1st Platoon Leader, First Lieutenant Gundrum, suggested to turn their headlights on. It was a clever idea because it became obvious the Iraqis running away did not know they could be seen as clear as day on our thermal sights. Once the lights turned on, the Iraqis quickly dropped their weapons and stripped off their uniforms in almost a single, fluid motion. When Knight took them prisoner, they looked relieved, almost glad they were under our care and out of the fight. They appeared happy once they realized they would survive this war.

Knight arrived at Objective Raiders around 2330 and established a perimeter east of the TOC. The Task Force 2-7 forces at Raiders that night conducted a very hasty priority of work. They did quick maintenance checks, cleaned weapons, dug hasty fighting positions, and then went to sleep. With Knight now in the perimeter, most of the soldiers could rest. A few tanks with crews up and on alert would be sufficient protection. We were all exhausted. We knew we would stay here a minimum of twenty-four hours. This was to be the first real break after a very long trip. We could execute more detailed preparations in the morning.

More than three days passed since our task force crossed the border into Iraq. Task Force 2-7's lead elements at Raiders were on the coalition's front line, only seventy-five miles from Baghdad. The rest of the task force was strung out all over south-central Iraq. Due to unexpected enemy contact during the march up, we fell just short of the planned goal of 2.5 days to Objective Raiders. The remainder of the task force would catch up to us at Raiders over the next twenty-four hours.

At this point, the greatest risk wasn't the enemy—it was success. At NTC, no plan survived first contact, but in Iraq we were still largely on our original plan. Units were intact, resistance was fierce in spots but quickly crushed or bypassed. Yet speed brought its own dangers: fuel, ammo, and logistics lagged as we pushed forward. Good tempo mattered more than raw speed, and uncertainty haunted me at Objective Raiders. I didn't really know if or when resupply would arrive. I didn't know for sure what we needed to do here, how long we might stay, and how our missions might change. So I rehearsed every move, pulled in commanders, and leaned hard on my war council. The best leaders know they don't know everything; rather, they ask questions, listen, and adapt. Every horrible incident at Raiders forced me to do exactly that—ask better questions, listen harder, and generate better ideas to adapt to changing conditions.

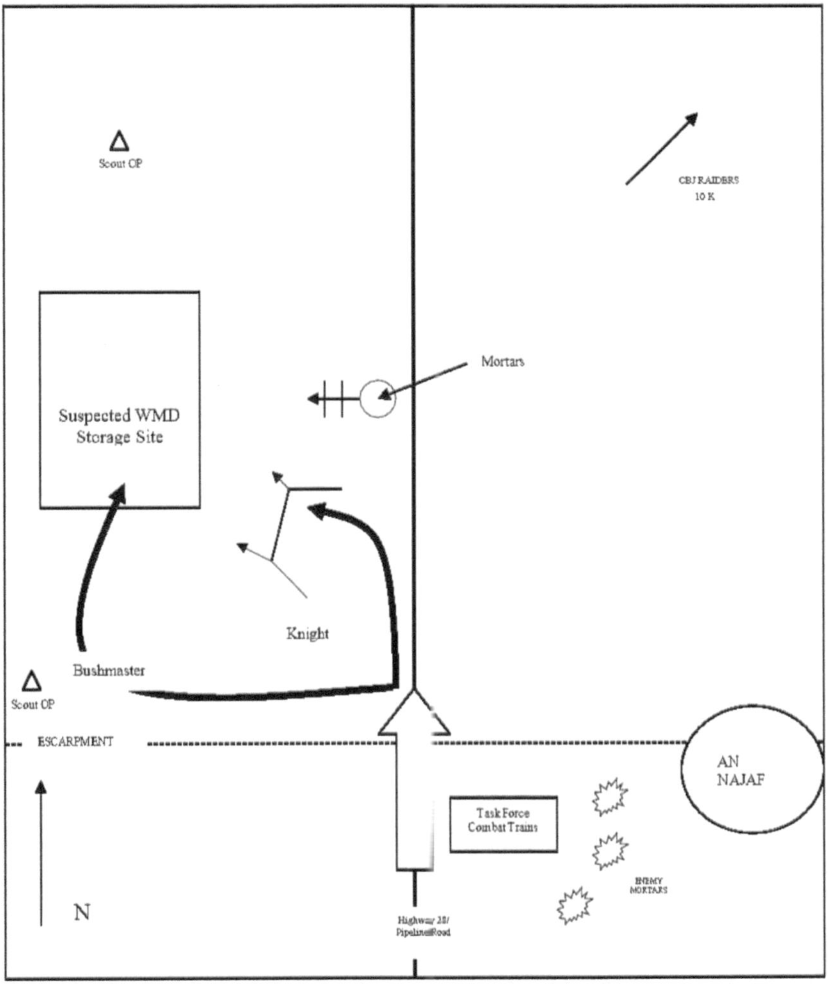

Task Force 2-7 assault on suspected WMD compound north of the An Najaf escarpment, March 23, 2003.
Source: Author's image.

OBJECTIVE RAIDERS

"If the enemy is to be coerced, you must put him in a situation that is even more unpleasant than the sacrifice you call on him to make. The hardships of the situation must not be merely transient—at least not in appearance. Otherwise, the enemy would not give in, but would wait for things to improve."

—Carl von Clausewitz, On War *(1832)*

Objective Raiders was our only deliberately planned long pause throughout the entire march to Baghdad. It was important for the brigade to remain at Raiders for several reasons—to allow our logistics assets to catch up and reestablish contact with forward units, to provide time to rest and reset prior to our final push to Baghdad, and to degrade the Medina Republican Guard Division with artillery, air, and helicopter gunships prior to our attack. A key goal was to degrade the Medina's artillery, inhibiting their ability to shoot chemical munitions at us as we drove north, through the Karbala Gap chokepoint. Meanwhile, tired Task Force 2-7 soldiers would seize a well-deserved rest and wait impatiently for the word to attack north.

The missions never stopped at Raiders, they only slowed and were more limited in their scope and scale. An Najaf became a hotbed of enemy resistance, and due to our proximity to the city, we had no choice but to take aggressive action to protect ourselves while awaiting the order to continue our attack north. So instead of sitting and waiting, we acted. The best defense is a good offense.

Around 0600 on March 24, the early morning sunlight reflected off the many villages and onion fields surrounding our perimeter. Our position at Raiders looked great at night, but in daylight it looked untenable. We were too close to populated areas and we were not alone. With his eyes now fully focused in the early morning light, Captain Lee looked around quizzically at the many farmers to his direct front. They returned the look. Lee wondered, would they be friendly? Indifferent? Shia or Sunni? Bedouin? It just didn't feel right. Where were the women and children? Lee wondered. Why hadn't all the noise from our tanks scared them off last night? How were they simply going about their business as if we weren't here?

The huts looked like dirt mounds through our night vision goggles and thermals the night prior. People actually lived there. Our goal during the march up was to keep the civilians at a safe distance. We would not allow them to distract us and interfere with combat operations. The civilians and any concerns of theirs could be addressed later, after the fall of the regime.

Captain Lee felt uneasy about being so close to the Iraqis. He repositioned his tanks to better defend against the potential enemy threat looming in the villages surrounding his perimeter. He erred on the side of caution and ordered his company to relocate to the TOC and secure a perimeter around it. The TOC was at least two hundred meters from the nearest village.

The skeleton crew who secured Objective Raiders the night prior had just woken up and were conducting personal hygiene, the typical morning ritual of brushing teeth, cleaning, and shaving their faces. As Knight refined its position within the battalion's perimeter, a loud voice interrupted the silence over the command radio net. "Able 6, this is Knight 6, one of my loaders has just been shot in the head by a sniper." A scout section and a Bradley section from Knight identified the source of the sniper fire located in straw house only two hundred meters away. They bounded forward to get closer to the village. The scouts deployed along the western edge of the village and unleashed a massive volley of .50 caliber and 40mm grenade machine gun fire to reduce the straw house to dust, killing the sniper and two spotters inside.

First Lieutenant Johnson identified muzzle flashes in the opposite end of the village and could hear the PINGPINGPING of bullets ricocheting off his Bradley. The enemy's fire originated from within a flock of sheep, with the snipers interspersed between the sheep and concealed by wool blankets. Shrewd and clever, these professional killers were as determined as they were prepared to fight. Bursts from Johnson's 25mm chain gun would neutralize the threat. Johnson's infantry then dismounted and cleared every building, hut, and farm within small arms range of Objective Raiders.

Indications from the enemy's uniforms and equipment were that they were either SRG or Republican Guard soldiers. They could have been soldiers who had retreated from the weapons compound the day prior. Or they learned about what happened in the compound and came from somewhere else. Given their stealth, speed, and preparation, I deduced that these combatants were professionals. Within only a few hours, they infiltrated to within a couple hundred yards from us, unseen by our advanced night vision technologies. They were probably part of a Republican Guard or SRG reconnaissance element, sent to gather intelligence on us or to disrupt our operations. We were getting closer to the bigger battles, and this incident proved it.

The sniper's victim was Specialist Gregory Sanders, and he would leave behind a new wife and baby daughter. He was the first death in the entire 3rd Infantry Division in Iraq. Knight 6 Captain Jimmy Lee rallied his tankers to try to save Specialist Sanders, performing several life-saving measures to no avail. The medics had not yet arrived with the rest of the task force, and at the time, were attending to several vehicle maintenance issues. Specialist Sanders's wound was too severe, and this was the worst place at the worst time to get shot.

We never thought we would lose one of our own. It was going to be in someone else's unit, not mine. My executive officer, Major Cooney, made the point in a meeting that night: "We were naïve to think that we could waltz right into this country and they would just give up." He was right, back in Kuwait we were planning for the worst but were also hoping for the best. No amount of preparation or training can prepare a unit psychologically or emotionally to cope with death. Back at NTC, the battles were bloodless, and we faked death. We went through the motions, rehearsing the procedures to transport dead and wounded. We rehearsed how to regroup and reconsolidate platoons, companies, and battalions after we took simulated casualties. But this was not the same.

A unit at NTC learns how to deal with death only in an administrative and logistical sense. NTC staff bring simulated casualties back to life between missions. We got conditioned to this reboot every mission. It was seamless; the dead and wounded soldiers left but then they returned to fight again another day. In real combat, death is permanent and soldiers struggle with the loss while doing their best to focus on the mission at the same time. I believe this is why it took some of the younger soldiers a few days to process this information and to absorb the shock of losing one of their fellow soldiers.

We all hoped that this conflict in Iraq was going to be easy. I hoped for a speedy victory. Since the breach into Iraq, we either shot at the enemy, were shot at by the enemy, or we shot at each other. Four engagements so far, and until now, we took no losses. Objective Raiders put down any hope that our mission in Iraq was going to be easy. Before this war is won, we will kill more, and we will take more losses. We were mortal, the enemy's bullets are just as lethal as ours. Major Cooney's statement was a reality check . . . we had to stay on our toes. While we were at Raiders, the Iraqis adapted their tactics and postured for a bigger fight.

It took a few days for the initial shock of Sanders's death to settle in, forcing us to confront the harsh reality—we were now in a real war. And just as easily as death had claimed this soldier, it could just as easily come for any one of us in the task force. Captain Lee handled this loss extremely well. He was a caring, compassionate leader. While displaying a subdued remorse for his loss, he still exuded all the confidence necessary to keep his soldiers motivated and remain focused on the mission. As a result, his soldiers rallied around him like they would a big brother, or even a father.

Because of the shooting, I ordered my PSYOPS team to drive to each surrounding village while broadcasting a message ordering the civilians to leave their homes and not to interfere with coalition operations. My intent was for the civilians to relocate to a friend or family member's house elsewhere for as long as we occupied Objective Raiders. We would take all necessary measures to protect ourselves. The ROE was simplified because of the incident: any Iraqi carrying a weapon could be treated as a combatant and subsequently eliminated.

I summed up my intent to my commanders shortly after the incident:

> Any people who have weapons or are seen running away with weapons, you have my orders: Kill them. Kill them. We need to protect ourselves. Remain vigilant. If you're in this situation, don't call me and tell me what you see, tell me what you've killed . . . you have my fire command.

Every morning following the incident and after our battlefield update brief, elements within my task force swept the surrounding villages to ensure that civilians or enemy combatants had not reoccupied them. We had four villages to our direct front, all within a kilometer east of our perimeter. Clearing these villages every morning became a ritual, a battle drill. The entire clearing process took about two hours. None of the patrols uncovered a reemergence of the enemy or civilian noncombatants. The bad guys kept their distance, for now. Patrols only ran into the same ugly stray dogs, donkey, and chicken. If nothing else, the patrols kept us busy, and the soldiers out of trouble. We settled into a routine at Raiders.

Our detailed searches of the homes would produce some clues about the culture of the people inhabiting the area. Each of the four villages was occupied by a single family—an extended family boarding elders, aunts, uncles, and cousins. Each of the families was Shiite, with every bedroom displaying a large picture of their popular Ayatollah. Throughout one of the searches, a soldier discovered what looked like a passport. On the cover was a picture of a woman with her printed name labeled underneath. Inside the jacket was a picture of what appeared to be her husband with his name and signature underneath it. Comprising the body of the passport was about fifty pages, each identical in their format and content. Every page had three columns, one for time, the other for destination, and the last requiring a signature. One of our soldiers with Middle Eastern heritage revealed what this was. It was essentially a permission slip. A woman from the family was not free to travel by herself without her husband's written permission.

This was not America, and as valuable the NTC experience was for my task force, it did not prepare us for this unfamiliar culture. We could shoot well, but we could not speak the language or recognize any of the typical patterns of Iraqi life. This cultural gap set us back in the early days of the Iraq war. It took years to recover, if we ever did.

The radio transmission about the sniper incident was the first traffic Rage's company commander, Captain Rob Smith, heard on the battalion command radio net in days. He was close, well within FM communications range by now. His 130-man company remained at Al Kindr for eighteen hours with no relief. He was supposed to be relieved by a follow-on unit. Like a caged animal, Rage company stayed anchored to the problem town while quietly observing over a dozen coalition convoys pass through them. Traffic eventually thinned out. With no guidance or ability to communicate with his commanders, along with an overwhelming desire to get back into the fight, Captain Smith took the initiative and resumed his company's advance.

Nicknamed the "Miracle Mile," his company drove 150 miles for thirty-four hours with almost no break. "We were like a pack of wolves," Smith joked with his fellow commanders. He weaved his company around and through traffic congestion caused by division and corps support units littering the desert highways. Rage refused to leave a single soldier behind, including the unlucky press reporter encountered at Al Kindr and a fuel truck left behind by a National Guard supply convoy north of As Samawah. They stopped for only a few hours here and there to borrow fuel from other units along the route and to also give the drivers an opportunity to rest before they could complete the trek north.

Smith believed the long drive and their ability to overcome the challenges together, as a team, made his company stronger—they now, more than ever, had the closeness and the determination to carry them through the remainder of the war. They had the initiative. Hearing Captain Smith's voice on the radio was a relief to us all. The entire Task Force 2-7 family would soon be reunited.

Late in the day, my brigade assigned my task force a new mission to block the southern approaches along Highway 9 near Objective Raiders. This four-lane highway connected Karbala in the north to An Najaf in the south. It intersected with other major roads and farm roads that connected to Baghdad and other population centers across the country. Highway 9 was a potential avenue of approach for the enemy—a major causeway the enemy could use to attack and to transport soldiers and equipment from the north to contested towns and cities in the south.

At this point in the campaign, An Najaf and As Samawah were considered hotbeds of enemy activity. The coalition needed to choke off these cities from reinforcements, or else it would never establish an effective supply line for its forces attacking north to Baghdad. A prolonged fight in these two cities meant a stalled campaign. We could not allow that to happen.

Other battalion task forces to the southeast of us isolated An Najaf in an attempt to contain the enemy activity to the confines of the city. Our sister units at An Najaf had to prevent the enemy in the city from influencing or interfering with our future attack on the Republican Guard and our follow-on operations in Baghdad. As other units contained An Najaf—looking inward—my job was to watch their back. My role was to look outward—preventing reinforcements from flooding into An Najaf from the north. We would destroy any combat formation transiting into our engagement area. But we would also leave Highway 9 open for civilian traffic. At this point in the war, we still wanted to create the least disruption to normal Iraqi life—innocent people still needed to eat, go to school, exercise their religion, and work. So we established a checkpoint to search all personnel and civilian vehicles moving south along Highway 9. We questioned all military-aged men for intelligence. Anyone posing a threat was detained for further interrogation.

This was our first significant opportunity to collect intelligence from the local populous. Not all Iraqis would be inclined to share. They may not reveal precise locations of Iraqi combatants, but we could learn a lot from their appearance, their belongings, and through discussions about their current living conditions. Establishing a pattern of life could help us later when we transit through other cities and certainly when or if we conduct an offensive inside Baghdad. Noncombatants were everywhere.

We had to know what "normal" looked like so we could more easily spot the "abnormal," including indicators of enemy presence. This would help us target combatants and avoid collateral damage. It would improve our lethality and survivability. The Highway 9 blocking mission was suitable for a platoon. Different Bradley and tank platoons in the task force took shifts, rotating the duty. At the time, the area was quiet and permissive. Relieving platoons in place here was easy, and it was also necessary. I wanted to keep the soldiers sharp and focused while at the blocking position. I also wanted to ensure every soldier had adequate time to rest while we were at Objective Raiders. Once we pushed north again, it could be days before we would sleep again.

I gave the blocking mission priority of effort for my task force. This meant that all resources I could bring to bear to support and help the blocking platoon were at its disposal. My mortars were in direct support. I sent out the scout platoon to screen their flanks, to provide them with early warning of an enemy attack. I gave this mission the priority for planning—which meant I would drive my staff to continue to collect, gather, and process intelligence to bolster the blocking mission. Whatever it took. We were on the front lines, and anything could happen here.

I drove the scout platoon hard while we were at Objective Raiders. "Scouts out" once again—never a moment's rest for the scouts. Although they were outside the perimeter, I knew First Lieutenant Gleason would find creative ways to ensure his troopers were fed and rested. I drove them even harder at NTC, so I knew they could handle the high operational tempo. They executed zone and area reconnaissance missions in support of the blocking position, directing their long-range optics at likely enemy avenues of approach in the north and possible infiltration routes to the east of the blocking position.

The mortar platoon directed their guns on a preplanned target called "priority target pink." Pink was a target located approximately six hundred meters north of the blocking position. Its purpose was to defeat a potential enemy ground assault on the blocking position. Apparently, the terrain north of the blocking position afforded the enemy with cover and concealment—ideal for a ground assault. Terrain to the east, west, and south comprised flat and open desert. The blocking platoons could easily see and target anything moving from those directions. But in the north, combatants on the ground could move to within RPG range of the Bradley or tank platoon almost completely unobserved. This preplanned mortar target mitigated this risk. The mortars could unload dozens of high-explosive rounds within seconds to break up any attack from the north.

Whatever scout reconnaissance mission or mortar fire could not address, Bulldog's engineers filled the gap by creating obstacles along the roads leading into the position. Their work limited the enemy's mobility while turning the blocking position into an impenetrable fortress. If the Iraqis damaged the blocking position, it would not be because the position was not well engineered. The Bradleys and tanks enjoyed as much protection as Bulldog could provide. The blocking mission lasted for nearly the entire time we were at Raiders, from March 24 to 31.

I ordered Knight to dispatch a platoon to be the first to occupy and establish the Highway 9 blocking position. Only minutes after their departure from Objective Raiders, Captain Jimmy Lee reported, "There are men with possible RPGs running and hiding in ditches. There appear to be women with them." It was after sunset, and the silhouettes were nearly indistinguishable between combatant or noncombatant.

From Jimmy Lee's perspective, the occupation into the blocking position became a hasty attack, of sorts. They would need to occupy the position by force. Knight observed combatants in the distance manning mortar positions and maneuvering along a dry canal paralleling Highway 9. Knight reported an endless stream of RPGs flowing from a small village nearby. It appeared that women and children were deliberately posted between us and them to serve as human shields or as a distraction.

In response, Captain Lee deployed most of his company to pacify the threat at the blocking position. His platoons charged to the highway and set up a defensive perimeter, with Bradleys facing north and tanks facing south. Combatants charged the blocking position from both directions using machine gun–mounted trucks. They were blown to bits as soon as Knight identified them as hostile targets. Noncombatants were avoided. The Iraqis then resorted to irregular hit-and-run tactics once their direct approach failed. After a few hours of resisting, the enemy fighters disengaged to a more tenable location east of the blocking position. They regrouped and started massing for continued attacks on the blocking position.

A truck approached the blocking position ferrying a squad of enemy combatants to their new fighting positions in the east. Knight quickly countered with massed fire from their tanks and from artillery delivered by 1-41 Field Artillery Battalion. After about twelve hours of repelling enemy assaults, Knight reported the blocking position secure. The enemy would not attack the blocking position in force again, but they would modify their tactics.

Knight's success at the blocking position initiated a weeklong game of cat and mouse, a game that we could not win yet had no choice but to play. Once the position went quiet, Knight disengaged most of his company except one platoon. Bulldog then showed up with its engineering assets once again. The engineers reinforced the blocking position with obstacles, digging ditches, building berms, and improving survivability by digging in "hull-down" fighting positions for the platoons' Bradleys and tanks. These fighting positions reduced their exposure, cutting the vehicles' tall silhouettes in half. Enemy RPGs would have a more difficult time finding their intended targets now. All Knight, Rage, and Bushmaster platoons would make themselves a hard target for whatever the Iraqis chose to throw at them.

By this point, the soldiers were running on fumes. The adrenaline that carried us through the breach and the drive north had worn off. Now it was just grit. You could see it in their eyes—red-rimmed, sunburned, and tired. They didn't complain. They dug in, checked their sectors, and waited. Some wrote letters. Some just stared into the distance. We all knew the fight wasn't over, but for a few hours, we could breathe. That mattered.

We were told that we would remain at Objective Raiders between twenty-four and thirty-six hours. Leaders conducted their final precombat checks and inspections and went over the scheme of maneuver for the upcoming fight with the Republican Guard's 14th Mech at Objective Hannah. Task Force 2-7 soldiers paid close attention and asked plenty of questions. They knew they needed to know every aspect of the plan in the event they became separated from their unit or if their leader was killed, captured, or separated. They would have to soldier on and complete the mission no matter the circumstances.

When the French general Napoleon Bonaparte completed a plan of attack on one of his many enemies, he would brief it one on one to a junior soldier in his Army. If the young soldier failed to comprehend the substance of the plan and was unable to brief the basic concepts of the plan back to Bonaparte, then Bonaparte would create a new plan, one that all under his command could understand and execute. Our task force had created a simple plan. Each company would occupy a predetermined position to shoot and kill the enemy at Objective Hannah. The scout platoon would observe suspected enemy strongpoints and provide real-time intelligence directly to the company commanders—they would act as their eyes and ears. The mortar platoon's mission was very basic: occupy two planned mortar firing positions and be prepared to fire quickly on targets of opportunity—fleeting targets too fast for air or artillery or softer targets better suited for mortar fire. Every soldier in the task force knew the plan down to the smallest detail.

Twenty-four to thirty-six hours came and went. We received word that it would be another twenty-four to thirty-six hours, at the earliest, before we would make our move on Objective Hannah. Many combat veterans would describe a combat environment as hours upon hours of sheer boredom marked by seconds or minutes of fear and excitement. My young and inexperienced soldiers were beginning to believe it. Aside from mission prep and the blocking mission, there was nothing to do. As far as mission preparations go, most soldiers had already reached the point of diminishing returns by day three at Objective Raiders. The mission was briefed, wargamed, rehearsed, and studied at length. Everyone was prepared. Leaders attempted to keep soldiers busy between rotations at the blocking position.

Soldiers and leaders filled the time by improving their fighting positions at Raiders—digging deeper holes, filling sandbags, and fortifying positions with overhead protection. Some did physical fitness activities—pushups, situps, and jumping jacks inside of their foxholes. Card games and dominos were popular too, easy to do inside tight spaces. A mechanized unit like Task Force 2-7 could always find something broken to fix. So soldiers fixed things and conducted preventative maintenance checks and services—over and over again. To many soldiers, it felt like being in a prison—no freedom, bad weather, bad food, no food, dehydration, boredom, and total isolation. The impact on my soldiers was nearly as bad as anything the enemy could do to us. In fact, it was so bad that most of my soldiers actually looked forward to more fighting.

"We are our own worst enemy," I always used to tell my company commanders. On the evening of March 27, this proved to be true. JSTARS reported columns of enemy tanks moving south through the Karbala Gap and were on a collision course with the blocking position along Highway 9. I dispatched Rage Company to investigate and intercept this threat, if it proved to be true.

Rage deployed their 2nd Platoon, under First Lieutenant Gallo, and their attached tank platoon, under First Lieutenant Sigler. Captain Rob Smith led his two platoons north to a screen line only a few kilometers from the Karbala Gap. This gap of terrain adjacent to the city of Karbala was a narrow corridor we would soon pass through to push north to the Republican Guard at Objective Hannah, and then onward to Baghdad. Captain Smith left his remaining 1st platoon back at the Highway 9 blocking position to prepare to defend themselves against a potential attack from the north. This blocking position might serve as a good fallback position if Rob was overwhelmed and had to withdraw his force from the north.

Captain Smith's movement took them north and then they swung east, hoping to strike the column along their flank if presented with the opportunity. It was always wisest to hit the enemy where they are weakest—in this case, on its flank. Through the blowing sand and the dark of night, Rob identified what appeared to be headlights. "Able 6, this is Rage 6, I am observing headlights . . . I am standing by to engage as soon as I identify." It was a tense moment, potentially our first major armor-on-armor engagement in the war.

Captain Smith continued to advance; he had to get closer to discriminate the target before engaging. Just as we were bracing ourselves for combat, Rob diffused the situation, "Able 6, this is Rage 6, disregard, those lights are only streetlights from Karbala." If the tanks identified by JSTARS did exist, they tucked into the city where Rage could not see and where Rage was unable to go. It started to feel crazy to me that our tactical intelligence was so bad at this point in the war. The coalition had total command of the sky and we were on the front line. Perhaps the battlefield conditions were evolving too rapidly for the intelligence to keep pace. In any event, I started to feel like we were on our own.

Rage disengaged from Karbala and moved back to Objective Raiders. On its way back, one of Rage's Bradleys drove headfirst into a deep hole in the ground—we estimated at least sixty feet. It was a cistern used for irrigation, like many others littering the Iraqi desert along the Tigris-Euphrates River valley. The hole was extremely difficult to see, especially while driving at night. It offered no warning. Our maps did not show much detail in the rural areas.

Imagine the effect of a thirty-ton anvil being dropped off a five-story building—the impact would rock the earth like an explosion from a five-hundred-pound bomb. At least half a dozen infantrymen rode in the Bradley, and I predicted that there would be few survivors. Upon my arrival to the scene moments after the accident, I learned that they were all still alive, with most of the crew escaping serious wounds. One of the soldiers even managed to climb out of the hole all by himself just seconds after the fall, with no help from the surface and while still suffering from the initial shock of the accident.

In total, six soldiers were injured, with injuries ranging from bumps and bruises to head trauma, broken bones, and internal bleeding. While waiting impatiently for the medevac helicopter, the Bradley impact claimed one life, Sergeant Roderic Solomon. This incident was an accident, a result of driving during severely limited visibility. Right before it happened, a desert wind produced a wall of sand in every direction. The crescent moon's light was unable to penetrate, rendering the Bradley crew's visibility ineffective. We were in a foreign land with rudimentary and incomplete maps—uncharted, random obstacles and death traps littered the countryside everywhere. These conditions were suboptimal and, unfortunately, ideal for such an accident. If we made it to the end of this war without another incident like this one, it would be largely a result of good luck.

First Lieutenant Delgado and his medical platoon quickly arrived at the scene and went into action. This was the first instance where they ever had to react to a real-life mass trauma situation. It was to become their baptism by fire. Multiple casualties emerged from the hole. The medics quickly set up their aid station, a battle drill they had repeated at NTC many times before. It was polished at this point. The Bradleys and tanks on the scene quickly surrounded the injured and turned their headlights on as an effort to aid in the treatment of the wounded. The most critically wounded soldier was Sergeant Solomon. His wounds were severe, and his body's defense and self-preservation mechanisms eventually gave up, ceasing the functions of both his heart and lungs.

The medics took turns performing CPR on Sergeant Solomon for an hour and forty minutes while waiting for the helicopter that could transport him to a field hospital back at Objective Rams. This was well beyond the "golden hour," precious time to get an injured or wounded soldier to a higher level of care. Sergeant Solomon needed medical equipment my medical platoon did not have.

Each medic, including First Lieutenant Delgado, took turns on the CPR, and each quit and handed off to another medic only at the point of complete physical exhaustion. Sergeant Solomon eventually loaded the helicopter and flew off into the dark horizon, unfortunately still without a pulse. We heard the disheartening news the next day that the doctors at the field hospital were unable to revive him. Sergeant Solomon, thirty-two, from Fayetteville, North Carolina, was irreplaceable . . . every soldier was. He would leave behind three children.

Our task force medics took this loss hard. They lost a fellow soldier under their own care. Good medics like ours take losses like this one personally, and they never forget the names and faces of the soldiers they treat. After every incident, they reevaluate what happened and determine what they can do better next time. Saved lives are how they measure their success. They captured critical lessons learned from this unfortunate incident, and they would apply them later during our fight north to Baghdad.

Just as we were getting over the shock of the incident, we had another one. The next day, around 0900 hours on the morning of March 28, a new soldier from the mortar platoon shot himself in the leg with a 9mm pistol round. He was a replacement soldier, assigned to the task force mortar platoon the day prior. He was fresh out of basic training, as green as they come. He came to us along with dozens of other replacements, officially labeled "augmentees." The coalition moved them north with the supply convoys. They were unexpected. They were not even permanently assigned to my unit; they were only here on a temporary basis. After the war, they would return somewhere else. It was unspoken, but I guessed the coalition expected more of us to die at this point in the war, and we would need these augmentees to return to full fighting strength.

Witnesses to the shooting claimed that the soldier was perched on top of his mortar carrier cleaning his assigned M16 rifle when the incident happened. He spotted a 9mm pistol resting on top of the vehicle and chose to grab it. The soldier picked up the pistol and proceeded to teach himself how to use it. Unfamiliar with its proper handling procedures, he discharged a round directly through his leg, just above his knee. Miraculously, the bullet struck no major arteries, bones, or ligaments, and he returned to duty in good health in just under one hour. The battalion surgeon could not believe this soldier's luck. He didn't require evacuation or even narcotics to numb the pain, just two Motrin a day to take the edge off.

An investigation into the discharge revealed that a round was not chambered before the replacement soldier grabbed the pistol. The weapon's owner left it on the deck of the mortar carrier to relieve himself. Some believed that the wound was self-inflicted—a young and scared soldier overcome by fear of the unknown. The soldier claimed it was merely an accident. I took him at his word and nothing further was ever spoken about the incident. We had more important things to focus on.

Remember the adage, "trouble always comes in threes"? On the morning of March 29, it did. Tragedy struck as Rage and Knight conducted a relief in place at the Highway 9 blocking position. A taxicab painted in typical white and orange slowly approached the roadblock while disregarding our warning signs written in Arabic. Moments prior, an elderly Iraqi man approached the blocking position in a bus and claimed that his ankle was injured. He was quickly removed, and the bus was subsequently searched. Knight's four-man fire team approached the suspicious taxicab and removed its driver. It was routine at this point: two soldiers provided overwatch and security, while the other two worked with the driver to open all the vehicle's doors and interior compartments. This was a drill performed many times before in training and during peacekeeping operations in Kosovo or Bosnia. The driver claimed, in English, that he was sent to pick up the injured man from the bus. That did not make much sense.

Over one hundred pounds of C-4 plastic explosives were wired to the trunk of the car. Opening the trunk triggered the massive explosion that followed, creating a mushroom cloud of destruction and enveloping all four soldiers as well as the Iraqi bus and taxi drivers nearby. They were all killed instantly by the blast. Among the fallen were Sergeant Eugene Williams, twenty-four, of Highland, New York; Specialist Michael Curtin, twenty-three, of South Plains, New Jersey; Private First Class Diego Rincon, nineteen, of Conyers, Georgia; and Private Michael Creighton Weldon, twenty, of Conyers, Georgia.

Without hesitation, First Lieutenant Johnson secured the civilians off the bus, organized the treatment and evacuation of the casualties, and prepared his soldiers for an attack. Sporadic enemy rifle fire from the east followed the explosion—the car bomb may have been the trigger for a larger enemy action. Johnson directed Rage's 1st Platoon, under First Lieutenant Horn, to race north of the blocking position to seal off the highway from additional traffic. Johnson performed exceptionally well amid all the chaos following the car bomb. His actions contributed calm, and his swift response prevented any further escalation or loss of life. He would later be awarded the Bronze Star for his actions.

The following day, I committed Bushmaster to the blocking mission. They had been relieved by another unit at the weapons compound a day prior and had just consolidated with the remainder of the task force at Raiders. Bushmaster stepped up force protection measures and pushed patrols out to over a kilometer east of the blocking position. Engineers from Bulldog built a six-foot berm on both sides of Highway 9. We put up an offensive-style defense, pushing patrols deeper and deeper into enemy territory to root them out. At the same time, we dug in at the blocking position. We went from a soft approach to forcibly rerouting oncoming traffic with warning shots. We effectively shut down Highway 9. Any vehicle that chose to disregard the posted warning signs and our warning shots would be destroyed.

The day after the car bombing, members of Knight Company were tasked with the gruesome and unfortunate mission of searching for and collecting our fallen soldiers' remains. They had to sift through the carnage as best they could to find their buddies. The remains would be sent back to the states for a proper burial. I could think of nothing worse than to gather the remains of one of my buddies. It was morbid and sad, but at least it was a way we could honor the fallen and their families. When they were done, they gathered up the Iraqi bodies and buried those not claimed by local family in an open field nearby.

The deaths hit everyone hard, especially those in command. It shook me. I wasn't expecting it. I wondered if we would see more bombings and did not know what this would mean for our mission, the ROE, or my soldiers. I wasn't sure how to protect my unit or how to reassure my soldiers they were going to be okay. In the twenty-one-day march to Baghdad, no other single event would create so much fear, doubt, and uncertainty. I had to wrap my head around this quickly and come up with a plan to rally my troops and adjust my tactics accordingly. It was important that Task Force 2-7 soldiers regained confidence and that they knew that I and the other leaders had their backs.

Captain Lee was a cautious and compassionate company commander, always going to great lengths to see to the safety of his men. This event was unforeseeable—at the time, it was unpreventable as well. Although attached to Captain Lee's Knight Company, the soldiers' parent company was Rage, under Captain Smith. Smith claims that the incident focused him in a whole new way. He told our embedded reporters, "The fear of failure, the fear of death is gone." "This was an attack against a family member. This was personal . . . we are motivated."

Despite this horrible incident, Captain Rob Smith managed to rally his troops and provide them with the motivation they would need to carry them through the remainder of the war. Rage would become one of the most aggressive and lethal infantry companies in the division. Like Knight, Rage would look up to their commander like a big brother. Rob was up to the task. Days following the incident, the squad leader of the four fallen, Staff Sergeant Ulster, announced to Smith that he intended to reenlist for four more years. He, like the rest of Rage Company, had much to fight for.

We heard later while listening to a radio broadcast that the Iraqi driver was a member of the Republican Guard and was decorated posthumously by Saddam Hussein. One of the Iraqi vice presidents claimed that acts like the car bombing would become "routine military policy" and "we will use any means to kill our enemy in our land and we will follow the enemy into its land." He concluded with, "This is just the beginning. You'll hear more pleasant news later." "I am sure that the day will come when a single martyrdom operation will kill five thousand enemies."

The car bomb was a gut punch. We all felt like we had just lost one of our own family. It hurt. Initially, we all felt numb, mentally paralyzed from the loss of these men. Some of the soldiers in the task force wanted revenge, others broke down emotionally. Some soldiers disappeared into a mental black hole. It was a leader's job to keep the soldiers focused on the mission. All we could do was reassure them that we wouldn't let this happen again and that our time to get back into the fight was just around the corner. The most difficult element for us to cope with was the overwhelming feeling of powerlessness. Our buddies are dead and we can't do anything about it. It was a challenge to express our feelings or deal with those emotions because we had no means to decompress here. All we could do was sit at Raiders and wait for the word to move again. Raiders was now worse than prison. Our only reprieve would come from continuing our attack north.

Dealing with the waiting and the anticipation was a challenge. Until this tragedy occurred, we all felt a false sense of security while in this defensive posture. In combat, you can't curl up into a ball and hope the bad guys won't get you. The enemy grew smarter and bolder with every passing day we were at Objective Raiders. It was a wakeup call for us. We soon realized that the safest we would ever feel was when we went back on the move again—there we could be the masters of our own destiny. The offense would protect the force and reduce our vulnerability to the enemy. Most importantly, transitioning to the offense would be the only way we could regain the initiative and bring this war to its conclusion.

The chaplain, Captain Jerry Seig, made his rounds to each of the companies the following day to offer the soldiers some words of encouragement. He was good at it. He was approachable to every soldier, from the new private fresh out of basic training to the senior officer. The chaplain had a talent for bringing the hard feelings to the surface and then making sense of them all. The net result was usually a more focused and better-prepared soldier. It helped—a good chaplain like Jerry can be a combat multiplier and can help a unit overcome adversity and hardship whenever the going got tough. In fact, Jerry was a godsend. He helped me through the tough moments. He would jump into my Bradley, close the hatch, and give me unfiltered advice about the soldiers. He always knew what they needed. And I always valued his advice.

Jerry approached me later that same day and asked me about a memorial service for all our fallen soldiers since the start of the war. After some discussion, we came to the agreement that the service would have to wait until after the war was over, or at least after the major fighting stopped. To reflect on death and loss now would bring the soldiers still fighting into a different place mentally. They would need all their concentration on the mission right now—it would be difficult to bring them back to the place they needed to be before we continued our attack north. Whenever death or the prospect of death was involved, it was always a difficult decision. I knew we would eventually honor our soldiers and their sacrifice. We could honor them after our mission had been accomplished, perhaps in the heart of Baghdad in the new Iraq—that would be an ideal setting to illustrate that their sacrifice was not in vain. It would help close a difficult chapter.

I visited my soldiers soon after the car bombing. Command Sergeant Major Fox and I walked among them, explained what happened, and helped them process it. The fallen were temporarily placed in Rage First Sergeant Moore's vehicle; Moore was struggling, and so were we. Words failed me—I just put an arm around him. In moments like this, presence matters. Treating our fallen with dignity matters. I made rounds to nearly every company and platoon. It helped them, and me. Staying close to my soldiers kept me focused on what I could control and lifted me up when the weight felt unbearable.

Amid the chaos, we fought to keep morale alive. Each morning began with the Cottonbaler Song and then our embedded reporters "Scoop 6" provided news from home, drawing soldiers together for a moment of normalcy. Humor and connection in the form of chess games between missions, commanders visiting squads, and other small rituals reminded us we were still human. Twenty years later, at our reunion, those moments came up again. They mattered too.

The rest of our time at Objective Raiders through March 31 we spent enduring the most unpleasant and challenging climatic conditions known to man. We lived through three straight days of sandstorms, brought about by anomalous wind patterns known as *shamals*. A few meteorological conditions needed to be present to create monster sandstorms in Iraq, including days of persistent northwesterly wind (shamals), bone dry desert soil, hot air at the surface with cooler air above, and low pressure. When all these conditions combine, you will see mother nature at her very worst. That is what we saw and lived through. The late March 2003 sandstorms were a phenomenon in size, scale, and duration unseen in a generation. From commercial satellite pictures, dust cover could be seen over Jordan, Saudi Arabia, Iraq, Egypt, and the Red Sea. It was nicknamed "The Mother of All Sandstorms."

These unforgiving sandstorms make the earth resemble the planet Mars, or hell. The sand found its way into our vehicles, weapons, eyes, teeth, and even into the air we desperately tried to breathe. Completely exposed as we were, simple and important tasks like sleeping and eating were difficult. At times, it felt like breathing through a straw. It even rained a few times, but the rain did nothing to break the wall of sand. Instead it simply turned the sheet of sand on our vehicles and equipment into a thick layer of clay-like mud. Cleaning it was almost an impossible task. The Iraqi leadership capitalized on our misfortune by claiming that the sandstorms were a sign from God. The regime attempted to rally support for their cause by playing to the population's religious fervor. It was a good use of propaganda, but it did not make a difference.

The weather conditions slowed us down but would not succeed in halting our operations in and around Objective Raiders. Slow is not an exaggeration. It took us over an hour to drive merely one hundred meters, from one spot to the next. To drive in these conditions while staying on track required good navigation skills and a strong sense of direction. Even with GPS or our Blue Force Tracking systems, it was not uncommon for us to overshoot our destination or to drive around in circles until we found it. But these navigation aids work best when you are in constant motion, and that was a real challenge when you could not see more than a few feet in front of you. Our movements were all start and stop. It was the only way to move safely and avoid an accident. And we were all still spooked from the Bradley accident that claimed one of our soldiers a few days prior.

The sandstorm favored the enemy. It slowed our logistics flowing up from the south, forcing us to ration what we had. It inhibited our ability to collect intelligence on the Republican Guard at our next objective. Additionally, it made us more vulnerable in our present position at Objective Raiders. The only way to find the enemy during the sandstorm would be if we crashed into them, literally. Our operations were limited and much less aggressive—they had to be, for our own safety and protection. I did not want to lose another soldier to an accident. Everything we did, even simple tasks, were harder and took longer. We moved like sloths. Everything devolved into frustration. Eventually, demoralization and fatigue set in. *Shamal* became a four-letter word at Objective Raiders.

The Air Force and Navy took advantage of the brief periods of clear visibility and bombarded targets of opportunity along Highway 9 and within the Karbala Gap. On one occasion, an Air Force B-52 Bomber targeted a fuel tanker traveling south through the gap. Intelligence believed it contained chemical agents the Iraqis intended to release into the air before we crossed through the Karbala Gap. The B-52's ordnance was so powerful, we could observe the explosion's smoke plume from over twenty kilometers away. The plume morphed into a mushroom shape—typical for an explosion triggered by such powerful ordnance.

Due to the current wind patterns at the time, Objective Raiders was located downwind of the B-52's bombing mission. Within thirty minutes, black smoke from the bombs and from the secondary explosions sailed past our defensive positions on Raiders. As a precaution, the division ordered us to maximize our defensive posture. We escalated to "MOPP-4" prior to the strike. Our FOX chemical reconnaissance team, along with a Bradley escort, deployed approximately ten kilometers north of Raiders toward the Karbala Gap. Their mission was to provide the rest of us at Objective Raiders with early warning if chemical agents were in the air.

If the FOX system gave us enough of a warning, we could displace east or west and attempt to avoid contamination. The alternative was to simply remain in place, endure exposure, and then conduct a deliberate decontamination process after the chemical agents dissipated. If the FOX detected chemical agents, my preferred course would be to move and avoid them. Decontamination is a laborious and time-consuming process that would likely delay our attack north. It would keep us here at Raiders longer—I was growing tired of this place. Moreover, I still didn't know if the coalition could even resupply us with fresh personal protective equipment. After exposure and decontamination, we couldn't continue to use the same protective garments. I was reluctant to jettison what we had.

The advanced chemical detection systems on the FOX vehicle can detect and discriminate between the presence of both persistent and nonpersistent chemical agents. Persistent chemical agents usually come in the form of a liquid or jelly and thrive in the earth for a period of twenty-four hours or longer. Nonpersistent chemical agents remain in the air as a vapor for only a brief period of less than twenty-four hours—usually under thirty minutes. For over two hours, Task Force 2-7 Infantry remained in MOPP-4, waiting eagerly for the "all clear" from higher headquarters.

Operating while wearing full protective gear is a miserable experience, to say the least. A soldier's performance gradually diminishes while wearing this cumbersome gear, dulling all his senses along with his ability and his will to fight. Imagine the intensifying heat generated by your insulated body as it desperately tries to cool its elevated temperature down with perspiration. Beads of sweat cascade down your forehead like a waterfall, stinging your eyes and blurring your vision, while you remain powerless to stop it. Your ability to see and engage enemy targets becomes exponentially more difficult. Protected by an airtight facemask, you cannot wipe your eyes free of the grime and sweat. Instead you blink uncontrollably or simply keep your eyes closed and hope that the whole experience will end soon.

The handicap of a lack of sight is compounded by a lack of air—the psychological impact of breathing through a mask will trick your brain into thinking that the lungs are not taking in enough air, causing you to breathe deeper and deeper, eventually making you lightheaded and prohibiting you from moving around very much because if you do move, this would require even more oxygen. Every move subconsciously prompts deeper breathing. The gloves and the boots dull your sense of touch, your galosh-type boots causing you to tend to trip over your own two feet while walking or running, with the gloves disrupting your basic ability to work with your hands—performing simple tasks like fixing vehicles, pumping gas, firing your weapon, or simply picking up objects off the ground.

Add the physical handicap to the fear, anxiety, and adrenaline building just prior to becoming engulfed by enough chemical agents to wipe out an entire American city. The shaking hands and knees, the dry mouth, and the rapid heartbeat all add to the uncomfortable effects of the experience. You hope that you will not have to fight. We trained for this last year—many hours in MOPP-4. No outfit was better trained or more ready to fight in MOPP-4 than Task Force 2-7 Infantry. Unfortunately, no amount of training or preparation can make it easy or feel anything other than uncomfortable and scary.

We in the Army refer to this experience as the "suck factor." Exposure to chemical or biological agents was truly the worst-case scenario. Nevertheless, we were trained and ready for such a contingency, and every soldier in the task force knew what to expect. We drilled on it repeatedly back at Fort Stewart during the hot and extremely humid summer months and later at NTC in California. Every mission, the NTC staff would repeatedly hit us with tear gas and force us into MOPP-4. They threw tear gas inside our command posts and hit us while we were sleeping, driving, and sweeping our objectives. They hit us while we were winning and while we were losing to the OPFOR. We were programmed and conditioned to it.

Iraq in MOPP-4 would be no different than training, from a physical standpoint. We had already learned our own capabilities and limitations while operating in MOPP-4 during training missions, and consequently we made the necessary adjustments to compensate here, in actual combat. With all our training and experience at this point, I am confident we could have remained in this degraded posture for ten times as long and still possess the ability to accomplish our mission. It would have been hard, but we could have done it.

We refused to surrender to the uncomfortable fatigue. Rather, we maintained a heightened security posture along the perimeter. We were in a more vulnerable position now, and a coordinated attack at that time could have been untenable for us if we were not prepared. Those soldiers not on alert elected to sleep, one of the few things a soldier can do well while handicapped in MOPP-4. Initially, we all thought the truck contained chemical weapons, but I eventually breathed a big sigh of relief when we received the long awaited "all clear" from brigade headquarters. Fortunately, no chemical agents were detected. The enduring prospect of chemical attack certainly kept us all on our toes.

Shortly after the all clear, we heard intelligence that Qusay Hussein, Saddam's son and head of the Republican Guard, deployed a brigade of tanks and armored personnel carriers south along Highway 9. The assessment suggested this move was an attempt to reinforce Iraqi forces defending An Najaf and threaten our division's eastern flank and rear. This armored column consisted primarily of the Hammurabi Division. It deployed from Baghdad's outer ring defense. Obviously, the Iraqis were unaware that our military had continuous observation on their ground forces from the air. On the eastern side of the Euphrates, our 3-7 CAV Squadron fixed the Iraqis in place and in the open long enough for our air power to scramble and drop enough bombs to neutralize the threat. The Iraqi column disappeared.

For this one and only brief period of the war, Iraqi leadership completely ignored those hard-learned lessons about American air supremacy from Desert Storm 1991. This is what coalition war planners were hoping for as a best-case scenario: to draw the Iraqi military out into the open. If the Iraqi military massed its forces to fight a conventional battle, they could be quickly targeted and destroyed from the air and other means. Every time the Iraqis exposed themselves, our coalition massed its own forces against them—air, artillery, and ground forces. I wasn't sure if this signaled a change in Iraqi tactics or strategy.

Perhaps if the Iraqis believed that if they had a tactical advantage to mass their forces for limited periods, they would seize the opportunity. From their perspective, we were stalled at Objective Raiders for days. Its irregular forces and debilitating weather conditions had been chipping away at us piece by piece. If I was an Iraqi commander, I might think I had a tactical advantage in this instance. However, if this Iraqi column signaled a broader strategy shift—massing all Iraqi forces for a sustained offensive action—that would have been a big mistake for them. It would have been a game changer for us.

It was possible the Iraqi military believed they had the gained the initiative—that they had coalition forces on the ropes. "Baghdad Bob," the Iraqi information minister, was doing a good job spinning lies and propaganda about our disposition and our success along the march up. He was so good, his generals and Saddam's own sons probably believed the minister's tall tales about our misfortune at the hands of the Iraqi resisters.

Later in the day, I heard BDA through my ETAC that B1 Bombers destroyed about half of the Iraqi brigade enroute to An Najaf. The other half was destroyed after they turned around and retreated north, back to Baghdad. Based off the Air Force's BDA, military planners could craft a whole new strategy—lure them to us, draw them out into the open, then kill them with airpower. However, one would also have to assume that the Iraqis learned from this mistake and would not send any more of their forces into the slaughterhouse.

This would be one less Iraqi brigade we would need to contend with after our attack on the Medina Division at Objective Hannah and the SRG at the airport. It would help even the odds. At this point in the war, it was difficult to compare Iraqi combat power to ours. On paper, we were still greatly outnumbered. But on the ground, it was difficult to determine what whole Iraqi units still remained, which ones disaggregated into smaller fighting units, and which ones simply dissolved. And the presence of irregular forces complicated all our assessments.

It would hinder our intelligence gathering and targeting if the Iraqis chose not to mass their forces but instead adopt a disaggregated approach. The lack of real-time intelligence coupled with the Iraqis' evolving tactics meant we would be moving and fighting blind. We were trained for this situation, called a "movement to contact." However, it was always better to know where the enemy was and what it was doing before first contact.

We spent the rest of our time at Objective Raiders defending the blocking position against small enemy probing attacks and enemy gun trucks (technical trucks) attempting to bypass and penetrate the blocking position on Highway 9. Toward the end of our stay at Raiders, our task force received sporadic and inaccurate enemy mortar fire, which was quickly answered by hails of friendly counterfire—compliments of the 1-41 Field Artillery Battalion. In total, we killed twelve enemy dismounts and destroyed one technical truck and two taxicabs attempting to penetrate our blocking position.

Task Force 2-7 accomplished its mission at Raiders: the enemy did not get through the blocking position. We succeeded in preventing the Iraqis from using Highway 9 as an avenue to reinforce An Najaf. Six of our Cottonbaler soldiers would make the ultimate sacrifice for this mission. Their efforts were not in vain, and they will never be forgotten. No other single location or mission during this war would see more fallen Task Force 2-7 soldiers than at Objective Raiders. It was a cursed place and it demonstrated all the risks and pitfalls of remaining static in enemy territory for too long.

Shortly after occupying Objective Raiders, our task force received an additional task within the brigade's attack plan. We were now responsible for containing the enemy inside Karbala city. By holding the enemy in the city, we would act as a shield for the brigade as it moved north through the Karbala Gap and into their final assault positions short of Objectives Hannah and Peach. My task force's plan was simple: each company and the scout and mortar platoons were to occupy a series of firing positions along the gap. We would occupy them sequentially and each move would be orchestrated by myself or my operations officer, Major Rod Coffey. My intent was to maximize the standoff range of our weapon systems to keep the enemy at a distance, and from inhibiting my brigade's movement through the gap.

Karbala is a popular Shia holy site, where religious believers all over the Middle East make pilgrimages every year. This was a very popular celebration among the Shia Muslims until Saddam Hussein took power in 1979 and quickly succeeded in suppressing religious expression. The city is one of the largest and most densely inhabited in Iraq, with the population upward of five hundred thousand.

Intelligence believed that irregular militia and up to a battalion of Medina Division soldiers defended Karbala. Our intelligence deduced that most irregular forces would focus their attention more on controlling the population and preventing an uprising while the regular Army or Republican Guard oriented on our coalition forces. Allowing the coalition to penetrate into the city's borders could have a serious psychological impact on the civilian population as well as the Iraqi military effort. Prior to the war, Saddam put down a potential uprising there while it was still in its infancy—killing a religious cleric along with scores of innocent civilians as collateral damage.

We received intelligence that the Karbala residents were on the verge of another uprising and the mere sight of our American tanks and troops might serve as a flashpoint. If we were spotted during our Karbala Gap crossing, the citizens might take this opportunity to overpower the military and paramilitary forces occupying their city. We had to be prepared to react to festive civilians attempting to approach our formations—possibly to thank us for their liberation and to celebrate our arrival. Or they could approach us to ask for our assistance. In any event, we had to keep the civilians at a distance. The enemy was everywhere, and after the car bomb incident, I could not afford to trust the Iraqis yet, regardless of their good intentions. Although unlikely, it was also still possible that the regular Iraqi Army forces would capitulate. If that happened, we could get bogged down for days dealing with a capitulated Iraqi Army unit. I wanted to get through the gap as quickly as we could. I didn't want to deal with the civilians or a capitulating army.

I subdivided Karbala into six tactical objectives. Shortly before our attack through the Karbala Gap, we received detailed imagery of the city. My staff pinpointed target reference points over the top of actual existing structures like water towers or power lines, for example. These objectives and target reference points were drawn on graphical overlays and were distributed to each of the companies and the mortar and scout platoons. The graphics allowed for ease in command and control and would enable us to mass our forces and direct our fires against targets of opportunity throughout the city.

Objectives Marino, Unitas, and Garcia were in the southern outskirts of Karbala. They were objectives because they were mountainous rock formations that favored potential Iraqi defenders. The rocks offered both cover and concealment. The enemy could occupy these formations and disrupt our advance with dismounted antitank weapons or snipers. They were well within range of our approach through the gap and could easily hit us on our flank or rear as we moved north. I tasked my scouts with the mission to recon and overwatch the three rock formations while the rest of the task force detoured to the west. If the scouts encountered the enemy, they could either attempt to neutralize the threat themselves or ask Bushmaster for additional firepower to finish the job.

Three separate objectives would require the majority of our focus and attention. Arrayed from south to north: Objectives Favre, Theisman, and Starr. The objectives divided Karbala equally into thirds. Each company would orient on each objective as they drove through the gap. It was a good plan. We would execute it as soon as the weather conditions were favorable for the attack.

Prior to our advance north, we received numerous intelligence reports from different sources operating in and around the Karbala Gap. This intelligence suggested that irregular militia was actively rehearsing the defense of the city. One of their preferred methods included taking potshots at the advancing coalition column in the gap from Karbala's adjacent roads and alleyways—between the densely packed buildings and structures of the city. They would only need to expose themselves for a few seconds, take a shot, then retreat deep into the city. They could use these tactics to slow our advance and cause our formation to bottleneck inside of the gap. This intelligence report indicated to me that the enemy would not commit to a full ground attack in the gap. Nevertheless, the move north would not be without operational risk or danger. The most dangerous enemy course would be to hit us with chemical agents if we stalled or bottlenecked in the gap.

Given the recent intel, it appeared that the Iraqis did not expect the coalition's lead elements to attack into the city. I think it was obvious to them, at this point, that we were gunning for Baghdad. Like the southern battles, the enemy in Karbala might attempt to draw us into another city fight. It was a possibility. They could try to bait us into the city with their hit-and-run tactics—causing us to split our forces as we had done previously, and then proceed to destroy us piecemeal. We didn't need another Bakara Market with tanks. We could not deplete our forces and equipment before our bigger fight north, with the SRG and Republican Guard forces. And we needed to preserve sufficient combat power for Baghdad. I always tried to fight with simple rules: number one, don't go where the enemy wants you to go, and number two, don't do what the enemy wants you to do.

The enemy's firepower inside Karbala was not trivial. Air defense weapons, artillery employed in the direct-fire mode, and infantry fighting vehicles occupied defensive positions in and around the city. Most of these weapons could shoot at least four kilometers with accuracy—the Karbala Gap was well within effective range. The ZSU-23-4, nicknamed "Zeus," can fire up to one thousand rounds of 23mm ammunition in less than a minute. We were about to drive straight through the middle of its kill zone. Many of those Iraqi weapon systems were hidden in or near mosques, schools, and hospitals, making it hard for us to shoot first or return fire.

If we destroyed Iraq's major weapon systems, intelligence suggested the Iraqis could resort to desperate, asymmetrical measures to blunt our advance through the gap. Aside from the chemical threat, Iraqis could use hang gliders to drop hand grenades on us from the air. That was an actual intelligence assessment. Additionally, the Iraqis could charge our columns with civilian trucks laden with explosives. Intelligence reported Iraqi irregular forces rehearsed this drill several times during the days preceding our advance. We were prepared for any contingency.

Speed through the gap would be key to our success. Our survivability required us to keep all Iraqis from getting too close to us. We would remain disciplined, adhering to the ROE requiring positive identification of threats before we could engage. Questionable targets would be warned before they were targeted. Compounding the typical dangers of driving through a prepared enemy ambush in his own backyard, the Karbala Gap was the one spot on the map that we believed, beyond a reasonable doubt, that we *would* be attacked by chemical agents. Biological agents like anthrax or smallpox were possible—we were given compulsory inoculations back at Fort Stewart and Kuwait for a reason.

The Iraqis could employ unconventional weapons in the gap using a variety of methods: preregistered artillery loaded with chemical warhead payloads, surface explosions designed to spread chemical agents or "dirty" nonnuclear yield radiation, aerosol delivery of chemical or biological agents from the ground or air, or liquid agents simply dumped into the same ground we would need to transit. We were even told to watch for small radio-controlled aircraft transporting small chemical weapon payloads. Our intelligence professionals had no shortage of imagination.

We upgraded from MOPP-1 to MOPP-2 to prepare for the nuclear, biological, and chemical threats. If we detected any agents in the gap, we could escalate to MOPP-4 within seconds. Additionally, our medics issued powerful antibiotics as a prophylaxis.

We were ready to cross the gap. After a leader's brief detailing the plan from the gap crossing through the attack on Objective Hannah, I offered these words to my commanders:

> The amount of people that we've lost, Solomon, Sanders, Rincon, Williams, Creighton, Curtin, that made us even stronger. What's gonna make us even stronger to the next step, or the next level, that's each other, the ones that are right here. We all depend on each other.
>
> All of the cross talk, all of the situational awareness, before we put Rage coming down, assaulting, we will kill three, four, five times as many enemy as we expect him to kill. These support by fire positions are very important. All of those condition setters that we spoke about before. As we're on this objective here, Hannah, we're looking across the river. We're looking on those avenues of approach that the CAS is actually looking at, and were talking to the Forward Air Controllers and controlling it ourselves, in order to protect us from the up close and personal fight.
>
> I have no doubt that we are going to be successful, absolutely no doubt. Talk to your soldiers and tell them what they are doing is right. We are fighting for each other. Focus on killing the enemy. Look to your left; look to your right. Remember, we all depend on each other. We are not animals. We're soldiers and we are leaders. We will do well and we will take care of our own. We will accomplish this mission and finish this guy once and for all. As for the Republican Guard, God help them. God help them.
>
> We're here, willing and able. And that's our motto, "willing and able." All volunteers, all of us collectively put together for a purpose. One in purpose. Each and every one of us brings something to the plate here. Artillery, CAS, fires, tanks, infantry, medics. But one purpose: that's to kill the enemy and to take care of each other.

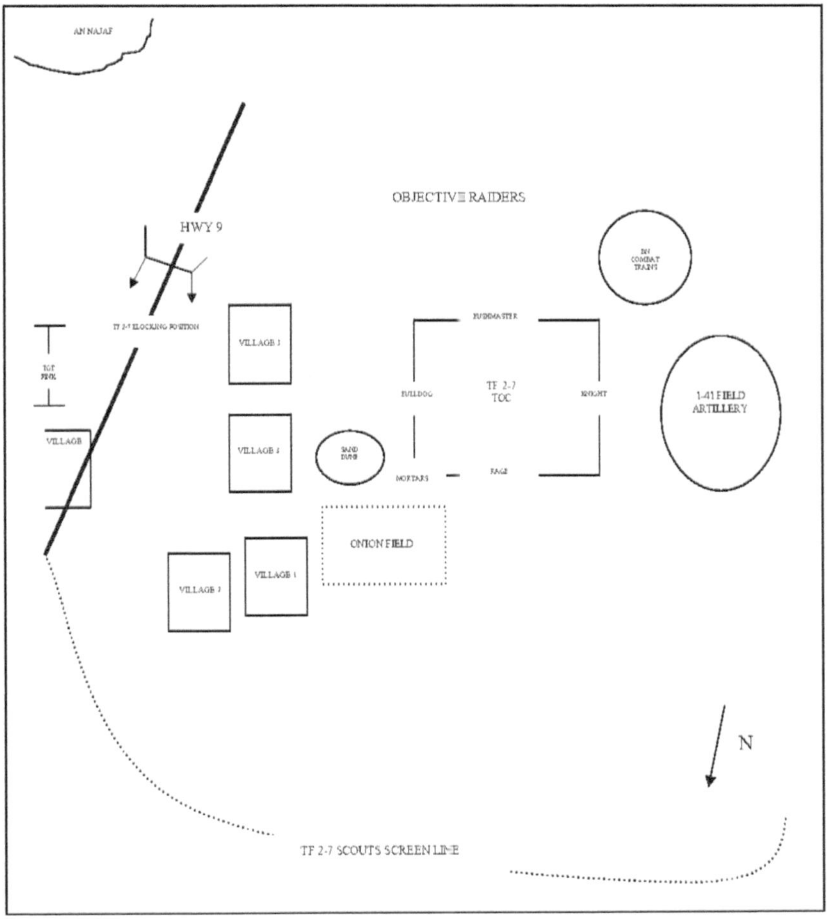

Task Force 2-7 at Objective Raiders, March 24–31, 2003.
Source: Author's image.

KARBALA GAP

"May God have mercy upon my enemies, because I won't."

—Attributed to General George S. Patton Jr.

Just as Hannibal forced his army and elephants through a narrow, dangerous corridor to strike at Rome unexpectedly, the 3rd Infantry Division took on the risk of the Karbala Gap to bypass stronger defenses elsewhere and to maintain momentum on the approach to Baghdad. Both movements relied on shock, audacity, and endurance.

The Karbala Gap is nothing more than a narrow passageway with dimensions of about ten kilometers in length and five kilometers in width, making a large, mechanized maneuver nearly impossible. It is sandwiched between a very large reservoir to the west and the city of Karbala, straddling the gap to the east. It was a natural chokepoint that we in the task force referred to as a "Fatal Funnel," "Engagement Area," or "Kill Zone." The exit of the funnel was marked by an irrigation canal, jetting out from the reservoir and extending east to the outskirts of the city.

The Karbala Gap was a funnel the enemy prepared to defend. Its characteristics closely resemble that of the Fulda Gap in Germany. The Fulda Gap was the primary focus of our defense of West Germany during the Cold War. Artillery, infantry, tanks, and airpower focused most of their attention on defending this key piece of terrain. The Soviet Army had inferior technology but certainly had us beat in sheer numbers. We were outnumbered at least three to one. We had to confine those forces to a tight space to slow them down and to deny them an opportunity to mass their forces against ours. We could bottleneck their formation and then hit them hard with our artillery and airpower. Using the terrain to our advantage could even the odds. Now the tables were turned on us.

As risky as driving through the Karbala Gap was, it was still a much more viable solution than transiting narrower approaches in the east between Karbala and the Euphrates River—maneuver would be even more impossible there in the built-up areas and within the marshlands lining the Euphrates. We could avoid Karbala altogether by swinging far to the west in the open desert. It was a contingency option—but not a great one. It would add days to our mission and I do not think our logistics would be able to keep up. They were already bottlenecked in the south and were stretched thin. At this point in the campaign, I altered any optimistic assumption my staff made about logistics—I figured it was going to take longer to get what we needed, we would get less than what we needed, or both would come true. Changing the plan and making it more difficult for resupply to reach my formation would be a recipe for failure. We could get stuck out there to the west, and we would become vulnerable.

Shock and awe would be our division's strategy at Karbala—speed, massed firepower, good communication, and synchronization of all our assets would be key to our success. My task force would lead for the division. As the first to make contact with the enemy in Karbala, we would take the first hits, drawing enemy fire to protect the rest of my brigade behind us. After we softened the enemy in Karbala, the division's 2nd and 3rd Brigades would race north through the city using Highway 9. They were also prepared to swing west through the gap, depending on the enemy situation in the city and the conditions inside the gap.

Getting the task force through the gap would meet resistance in two forms: the enemy and the terrain. We had high confidence the enemy would disrupt our passage from start to finish. Most of the terrain in the gap did not look very intimidating, but by now I knew that our maps would not tell us the whole story. We would likely encounter natural and manmade obstacles that would impede our movement and break up our formation.

On the far side of the gap crossing in the north lay two narrow passage corridors; one was a one-lane bridge located in the north-center of the gap and the other crossing point was situated in the northwest—it appeared to be a small dam lined with a road on top. Depicted on our maps as an earthen dam, it was actually manmade, constructed from concrete and stone. We received a few images of the dam back in Kuwait. The dam bordered Lake Razzazza, the reservoir to the west of the Karbala Gap. We believed the Iraqis might blow the dam to mire our advancing column inside the gap with a flood of wet sand and mud. If the Iraqis blew the dam or the bridge, the entire task force would have to backtrack and detour through the heart of the city. That would be the only way to break through Karbala and get to Objective Hannah if we were to adhere to our timetable. These two crossing points were so critical to the coalition's advance that special operations teams were inserted nearby, tasked with observing enemy activities there before we launched our attack.

By the time we reached the Karbala Gap, the campaign's logic had narrowed to a single truth: Baghdad was within reach, but only if momentum held. Division needed speed more than perfection. My task force was positioned to move fast, accept risk, and exploit collapse if it came. Failure here wouldn't just delay the attack—it would give the enemy time to regroup, reinforce, and harden the approaches to the capital.

On the morning of April 1, 2003, we uncoiled out of Objective Raiders and moved out with Rage Company in the lead, and with the mortar platoon tucked into the apex of their formation. We relocated to a forward area just southwest of the Karbala Gap, labeled Assault Position Able Fury—our last covered and concealed position short of the gap, just outside the range of Iraqi guns defending the city. Here we would wait and make final preparations for our attack, to be launched during the predawn hours of April 2.

Our simple move out of Raiders began a chain of events leading to the fall of the regime. Of course, we didn't know it at the time. It kicked off several straight days of no sleep, hunger, physical exertion, mental and emotional fatigue, and personal loss. Soldiers and leaders would reach their breaking point in the next few days. And Task Force 2-7 with all its combat power would reach its culminating point—the point in time and space at which a force can no longer continue the attack, according to military doctrine. The Iraqi military would break into pieces, never to recover.

Our movement to Assault Position Able Fury took approximately two hours and was uneventful. We only contended with the desert sand smacking our faces and permeating every critical nut and bolt inside our vehicles and weapons. Upon arrival, we immediately began our priorities of work, and we concluded with a final key leader's rehearsal over the radio. Commanders, staff, and special platoon leaders discussed where they needed to be and what they would do once they got there. Before we departed for Karbala, higher headquarters ordered each soldier to begin taking their antibiotics as a prophylactic against malaria and biological agents like anthrax.

The anticipation, eagerness, and fear of the unknown were building to a crescendo.

The city of Karbala lay directly in front of us. It was just to our north. Like As Samawah, the city was illuminated by the many lights lining the streets and alleyways, and from a distance it was a beautiful sight to see. Over six thousand years old, the city was ancient. A close neighbor to Babylon. The Islamic Prophet Muhammad's grandson fought and died here. Now the city resembled any other in America—from a distance and at night of course. It looked peaceful. Unfortunately, Karbala would serve as yet another gauntlet we would have to fight through before we could reach our prize, the Republican Guard, then soon after Saddam International Airport and Baghdad.

I detached my scout platoon from the task force around midnight and ordered them to conduct a route reconnaissance from our assault position to the mouth of the gap. I needed to know what was up there. The intelligence I had was getting stale, days old now, and could no longer be trusted. I had to ensure our plan was still feasible and executable given the current enemy disposition inside the city. The Iraqis could alter our course of action if they chose to reinforce their defenses with obstacles or armor. If they blew the dam or dispersed biological or chemical agents, everything about our plan would change. I would rather know that now and from a distance than while we were inside the gap in the morning. Being stuck in the gap and changing plans on the fly was the worst outcome I was trying to avoid.

For three hours, the entire scout platoon sat there alone and isolated with their eyes trained on the city, battling the irresistible urge to fall asleep. We would precede our attack with massive preparations of artillery and rockets on preplanned targets in and around the city of Karbala. Ba'ath Party Headquarters, along with other command and control sites and known troop concentrations, were targeted for destruction.

The Iraqis knew we were coming, but they did not know exactly when we were coming—until now. The artillery preparation negated our element of surprise. But it didn't really matter. The division wanted to hit the enemy and keep hitting the enemy until all three of its brigades made it safely past Karbala. It needed a weakened and depleted enemy at Karbala to break through to its objectives in the north. The artillery would do most of the work initially, then my task force would engage any visible targets in the city. Last, 2nd and 3rd Brigades would clear any remaining resistance as it charged north through the city. If the artillery decapitated any Iraqi military or civilian leadership in the city, regular or irregular forces could crumble, and the civilian population could seize control—a best-case scenario.

The artillery preparations preceded our advance by about one hour. At 0300, the task force began to move out—the wails from our Bradleys and the whines from our tanks were masked by the BANGS and the BOOMS from the artillery barrage now taking a heavy toll on the enemy positions in and around the city.

As a precaution, the task force moved in two separate columns, both moving astride one another along the prescribed route, Route Bruins. All combat elements traveled in the east while shielding my combat support trains, and engineer company traveling in the far west alongside the lake. Task Force 3-7 Infantry, commanded by Lieutenant Colonel Jack Kammerer, escorted my combat trains and engineers in the west and provided them with the protection needed to move safely through the gap. He also guarded the rest of 1st Brigade's administrative, maintenance, and logistical assets including those under my headquarters company commanded by Captain Mike Nixon.

In the east, Knight led the charge through the gap with the forward aid station and Rage following closely behind. Bushmaster protected the rear of the column. The mortar platoon moved abreast of Knight, just west of its column. Cutthroat, the brigade's reconnaissance troop, paralleled the mortar platoon farther to the west. Commanded by Captain Hancock, my higher headquarters placed his troop under my operational control for the duration of our attack through the Karbala Gap. Their mission was to screen our vulnerable western flank spanning our entire passage through the gap. Although the troop reported to me, I gave them the autonomy to do their job. I was glad to have an extra set of eyes and ears. We would need real-time intelligence on the ground.

Shortly after Knight entered the gap, the scouts repositioned to take the lead for the task force. The scouts made first contact with the enemy within only a few moments after taking the lead. Scout Platoon Leader First Lieutenant Gleason jumped on the radio: "Able 6, this is Sabre 1, I am engaging two squads of infantry drinking tea in a trench about eight hundred meters ahead." THUMPTHUMPTHUMPTHUMP!!! A stream of 40mm grenades entered the enemy trench along pipeline road. The Iraqis were dead before they even knew what was going on. Moments later, "Able 6, this is Sabre 1, I am observing three men in civilian clothes lighting a fire and are flailing their arms and pointing at us. I believe they are signaling the enemy. They have weapons. . . . I am going to engage." KAKAKAKAK. A few bursts of machine gun fire eliminated the threat.

Each company began to occupy their assigned firing positions and leapfrogged as necessary along the gap. Their displacements were brilliantly timed and triggered by my operations officer, Major Rod Coffey. The mortar platoon occupied their assigned firing positions to the immediate west of the Bradley and tank companies, hand-railing Bushmaster's movement for most of the way. Surprisingly, there was only scattered enemy resistance. It appeared the enemy's redoubts inside the gap were merely an early warning to a main force occupying positions deeper into the city.

Knight encountered a blue van parked in the middle of Highway 28 within the gap. It just sat there lifeless and against a backdrop of nothingness, totally out of place. Fearing another car bomb, Captain Lee ordered a .50 caliber round to be placed inside the chassis. Within seconds, major secondary explosions ignited and could be seen for miles. Astounded by what we saw next, two Iraqi soldiers, still alive and unharmed, jumped out of the burning van brandishing AK-47s while attempting to charge Knight's column! They were quickly cut down by multiple bursts of machine gun fire from Lee's 2nd Platoon at the head of his column.

It became clear the Iraqis had no intention of blocking our advance through the gap but instead made repeated attempts to draw us into the city. It was a challenge to traverse around and through the farms, irrigation ditches, berms, and villages located within the gap. We moved with a strong sense of compassion for the Iraqi civilians, exhausting all efforts to avoid driving directly through their crops and livestock. The mortar platoon split their formation on three separate occasions while negotiating the many variations in terrain. We were also concerned about another accident—nobody wanted to get stuck or drive into another hole in the ground. Our maps offered no great detail, making optimum route planning difficult. We thought the gap would mainly comprise flat sand and desert terrain, but we were sorely mistaken. Parts of the gap were pure labyrinth. At times, if felt like driving through a corn maze. It was especially difficult moving through this complicated landscape with limited visibility.

Just as the first light crept over the horizon, an Iraqi suicide truck charged toward our task force. It barely made it one hundred meters before one of Knight's tanks blew it to bits. Any doubts that the truck was friendly were put down after massive secondary explosions were observed.

The enemy inside Karbala avoided a direct confrontation. Antiaircraft artillery pieces, to include ZSU 23-4s, BMPs, and tanks, were playing cat and mouse with us. They would poke their heads out and harass our formation by taking a few potshots, then duck back into their hide positions behind the buildings and in the tight alleyways bordering the city.

Scouts observed groups of civilians loitering along the western outskirts of the city, and we did not know if they were placed there as human shields for the Iraqi armor. Their behavior was quizzical—they looked very calm, with some men even smoking cigarettes. Yet they just stood there as if it was their job. Maybe they were just curious onlookers, or perhaps they would be friendly and help us—ready to welcome us into their city. In any event, they didn't pose a threat to us, so we left them alone but kept a watchful eye on them for the time being.

Enemy forces in Karbala selected fighting positions near mosques and other sensitive sites. The Iraqis probably believed we would not target them given their proximity. They did not know that when one of these sites is used for military purposes, the site then becomes a legitimate military target. My battalion fire support officer, Captain Jason Happe, did a skillful job coordinating air support with artillery—using the air to pinpoint the most dangerous targets while minimizing any collateral damage to surrounding sensitive sites and civilian noncombatants. The air and artillery would work in concert with one another—engaging specific targets with tailored munitions to achieve a desired effect. Together they destroyed several armored vehicles while minimizing damage to nearby structures.

While exiting the gap around 0700, Bushmaster and Knight encountered several Iraqi dismounted infantrymen seeking cover in a trench network adjoining two machine gun bunkers. A few bursts of 25mm high-explosive ammunition reduced the bunker to rubble and killed or wounded nearly all enemy defenders inside the trenches. There was no time to confirm KIA; we had to push through the gap quickly to make way for follow-on forces and to posture ourselves for our main attack north to Objective Hannah. Speed was essential if we were to achieve the element of surprise there.

After our brigade passed through the gap to our west, we were subsequently relieved in place by Task Force 1-30 Infantry of the 3rd Brigade. They would cordon the city from the west to cover the rest of the division's passage through the city.

Our overall confirmed BDA from the Karbala Gap totaled two civilian suicide trucks, two D30 artillery pieces, and one ZSU 23-4. At least sixteen Iraqi soldiers were killed during our passage. There were an unknown number of armored vehicles destroyed by our air and artillery fire deep in the city. We took fifty-four Iraqi uniformed and nonuniformed soldiers prisoner. We accomplished our mission—all the division's supporting formations made it past Karbala without major losses or delays. Even though my task force played the punching bag role, we did not suffer a single casualty or loss of equipment in the gap.

We neutralized the hard targets inside Karbala. The enemy in Karbala would not mount another attack against our armored formations again. But the enemy would not remain idle. In less than twenty-four hours, they would regroup to harass our supply lines. Our logistics remained vulnerable and at risk. Our task force would need every ounce of fuel, every bullet, and every swallow of food and water to sustain our attack on the Republican Guard and beyond. Conducting operations in and around Baghdad would require a steady stream of supplies. Consequently, it became necessary to deploy the 101st Airborne Division to secure the city and eliminate any residual threats to coalition forces.

Driving through the Karbala Gap felt like threading a needle in the dark. Every soldier knew what this place could be—a trap, a funnel, a final stand. But no one said it out loud. Instead they checked their gear again, tightened their chin straps, and stared straight ahead. Some whispered prayers. Others just gripped the handles inside their Bradleys a little tighter. We didn't know for sure what was waiting for us in the gap or on the other side. We assumed the worst. I was glad to be on the other side now. Despite the uncertainty about the next steps, at least we were one step closer to Baghdad.

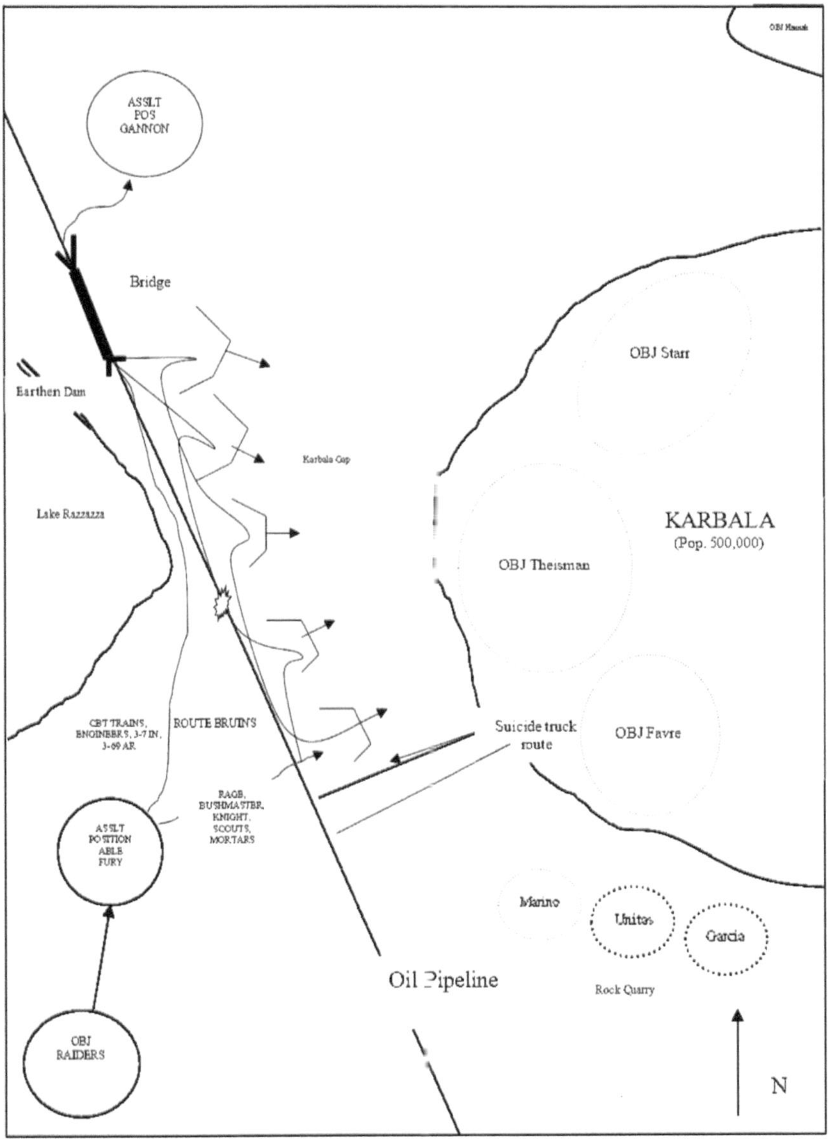

Task Force 2-7 Karbala Gap crossing, April 2, 2003.
Source: Author's image.

EVENT 6

Objective Hannah, the "Longest Night"

"There is only one tactical principle which is not subject to change. It is to use the means at hand to inflict the maximum amount of wound, death, and destruction on the enemy in the minimum amount of time."

—General George S. Patton Jr., quoted in The Patton Papers, *Vol. 2, ed. Martin Blumenson (1972)*

Our task force succeeded in containing the enemy within Karbala and providing the rest of the brigade with unhindered movement through the gap. By looking at a map, any military tactician could deduce that this was the perfect place to stop or at least slow our armored advance. A few well-placed weapon systems, mines, chemical agents, or flooding our route by blowing up the dam would have bottlenecked our task force in the gap. It could have forced us west into the open desert, delaying our attack on the Republican Guard and stretching our supply lines. It could have forced us east into the city where we would have clogged the routes and taken losses.

If I was on the other side, I would have focused most of my combat power at Karbala. The fact that Karbala was much easier than anticipated led me to believe that not only were Iraqi tactics flawed, but their entire strategy was also flawed. If they had a strategy, it buckled quickly under our coalition's shock and awe strategy—breaking the Iraqis' ability and will to fight. They were no longer influencing the terms or tempo of our operations. We clearly had the initiative now. Therefore it was important for Task Force 2-7 to maintain its momentum.

An Iraqi chemical or biological attack targeting the Karbala Gap never materialized. It was a big sigh of relief. I believed that if we didn't get hit with these agents while inside the gap, we most likely wouldn't get hit at all. Saddam would not likely use WMD north of Karbala, around his Sunni Arab populations—this population comprised his power base, and they legitimized his rule. Now beyond the gap, I could put those fears behind me and continue to focus solely on closing with and destroying the Republican Guard on Objective Hannah.

Passing through the gap, Task Force 2-7 once again became the vanguard for the division until we occupied Assault Position Gannon at 1300 on April 2. This was our last covered and concealed position west of Objective Hannah. Our plan required us to remain at Gannon for only a short period, affording us only enough time to refuel and regroup prior to our assault on the Republican Guard's 14th Mechanized Brigade. However, due to our speed and success within the gap, I thought we might stay here longer. I thought my brigade and division would need some time to ensure all their critical pieces were set for the attack.

We remained at Gannon for about an hour while we impatiently awaited the order to advance. I had heard through intelligence channels that the Republican Guard forces were now in a state of disarray from the constant aerial bombardments and from the multipronged advance of coalition forces. The enemy did not know where or how to mass his forces. Our actions and our movements were unpredictable. Conversely, the enemy's actions became extremely predictable. Now in a frenzied state, enemy forces attempted to disengage and reposition to any place where they could find refuge from the coalition's unrelenting air power and long-range artillery.

Fighting the enemy both deep and close simultaneously is not a new tactic. It was crafted during the Cold War as an effort to counter Soviet echelonment tactics—sending waves of reinforcements into the fray of battle as an effort to break our forces down both physically and psychologically until we would eventually crack. The tactic of engaging enemy forces throughout the depth of the battlefield with combined arms was titled "AirLand Battle Doctrine." Cutting-edge doctrine in the late 1970s, General Donn Starry designed ALBD for the vastly outnumbered American forces along the Fulda Gap in West Germany. The goal was to change not only the fighting capability but the perception of our forces as a mere speed bump along the Soviet's road to Western Europe. ALBD allowed the United States to bolster its deterrence in Europe, turning the tide of the Cold War in our favor.

After the Soviet Union's collapse, many military theorists and practitioners believed ALBD was obsolete in twenty-first-century warfare. They were wrong. Engaging the enemy everywhere—throughout the depth of the battlefield—was exactly what we did in Iraq in early April 2003. We synchronized airpower with artillery and maneuver. And once we resumed our attack through Karbala, we never stopped until Baghdad fell about a week later. We kept the Iraqis guessing. We kept them paralyzed while we chipped away at their defenses. By the time the Iraqis figured out where we were and what we were trying to do, it was too late for them. They could not organize a meaningful reaction that could make a difference. Apparently, coalition forces created so much chaos and confusion for the Iraqis that the deteriorating effects reverberated across the entire Iraqi military. I believe our division's push through Karbala created a domino effect. It was the beginning of the end for the Iraqi resistance. We would see this play out soon, at Objective Hannah—the outcome clearly evident on Iraq's main fighting force.

I adopted two courses of action for our attack on the 14th Mechanized Brigade at Objective Hannah. One was focused northwest of Al Musayyib and the other was focused to the city's southwest. We would execute our "Hannah North" course of action in the event that the 14th Mech defended within the vicinity of their barracks, northwest of Al Musayyib. We believed they would only defend here if they did not have sufficient time and intelligence to properly deploy elsewhere, probably farther south.

We would execute our "Hannah South" plan if the 14th Mech had enough time and opportunity to mobilize and deploy forces to defensive positions south and southwest of their barracks, just west of Al Musayyib. If they could leverage this opportunity, we believed they were more likely to defend from Hannah South because the city of Al Musayyib served as a natural obstacle, very capable of blocking the Highway 9 Bridge over the Euphrates River. We believed the 14th Mech recognized the significance of the bridge and would shape their entire defense around it.

While we were still in Kuwait, my staff officers recommended destroying the bridge to isolate and contain the 14th Mech. This would give us a tactical advantage—allowing us to fix or eliminate the enemy more effectively on the western side of the Euphrates. It would prevent their escape to the east across the Euphrates and it would prevent Iraqi reinforcements flowing in from east to west. Additionally, if we trapped the 14th Mech there, we could prevent them from reinforcing their comrades at Objective Peach, virtually ensuring my brigade's success.

From a tactical standpoint, demolishing the bridge made sense. But strategically, it posed serious risks. It would restrict crossing options for the coalition's follow-on logistics and combat forces and could even hinder our own brigade if their attack stalled or if the Iraqis destroyed the bridge at Objective Peach. My commander needed an alternative route—and the Highway 9 Bridge was the only viable option.

Beyond military considerations, the bridge held significance for post-war recovery. The coalition and the Iraqi people would need it intact to restore governance and revive commerce. Destroying such critical infrastructure would complicate and prolong reconstruction. The country could fracture, descend into chaos, and force us to stay longer to pick up the pieces. Commanders must see the bigger picture.

I envisioned the 14th Mechanized Division establishing a two-tiered defensive posture: one line positioned forward, west of the city, and a second line east within the city itself, anchored by the Euphrates River as a natural backstop. I also anticipated a small mobile reserve force positioned east of the river, poised to launch a counterattack across the Euphrates once our forces breached their initial defenses.

We assessed that the 14th Mech would likely consider the Highway 9 Bridge our division's primary crossing point—and therefore our main objective. From that position, we could advance directly to Baghdad. Highway 9 offered a high-speed avenue of approach, making it strategically significant.

I determined that the enemy's defensive posture was my priority intelligence requirement (PIR). I directed my scout platoon to exhaust every available method to pinpoint where and how the enemy was positioned across the terrain. Whatever they uncovered, I was ready to act decisively. We would take the fight to the enemy, wherever and however it decided to make its stand.

We expected the enemy on Objective Hannah South to consist of three mechanized infantry battalions, along with one tank company in reserve. Based off our intelligence gathered, I subdivided Objective Hannah South into four objectives: Objectives Stabler, Namath, Plunkett, and Bradshaw. Objectives Stabler and Namath each consisted of two enemy mechanized infantry companies and were in the southwest portion of Objective Hannah South. Objective Bradshaw consisted of three mechanized infantry companies located in the southeast portion of Hannah South. Objective Plunkett was defended by two tank companies occupying the northeast portion of Objective Hannah South.

Bushmaster's job was to pin down the enemy at Objective Stabler long enough for Knight to move in and destroy them there and then destroy enemy forces at Objective Namath. At the same time, Rage would keep the enemy occupied at Objective Bradshaw long enough for Knight to finish them off once it departed Stabler and Namath.

I designated Knight the "decisive operation," or the "main effort," with the other two companies as "shaping operations." Rage and Bushmaster would shape, or create, the conditions favorable for Knight to accomplish its mission. Additionally, Rage had a "be prepared to" mission to destroy enemy forces on Objective Plunkett. Objective Plunkett for my battalion task force was a "be prepared to" mission. The objective was the enemy force itself, not the specific terrain that they were defending. Depending on how the enemy was arrayed on the battlefield, Plunkett may have been located farther north, within Task Force 2-69 Armor's sector, and thus out of bounds for Task Force 2-7.

The "Hannah North" plan was similar to the Hannah South plan, but it excluded Objectives Stabler and Namath. We would instead focus all our combat power on Bradshaw and Plunket. Decisive and shaping roles between my companies would be the same—Knight with all its firepower would still be the decisive operation, and the other companies would support Knight. I needed to put Knight's tanks in the best position possible to kill the enemy.

An intelligence update prior to our attack confirmed some of our initial planning assessments. An artillery battery from the Medina's 2nd Armor Brigade and another from the 14th Mech were moving out of their hide positions and were repositioning south to firing positions just north of Karbala, within the vicinity of Al Musayyib. About a company of enemy tanks were also repositioning from Iskandariyah to the west side of the river, also within the vicinity of Al Musayyib. I believed my enemy was in the process of making their final defensive preparations. Assuming the intelligence reporting was accurate, I deduced that the Iraqis believed we would attempt to cross the Highway 9 Bridge and then turn on Highway 8 as our main axis north, to Baghdad. It looked like we would execute our Hannah South plan. First I would need some eyes forward to confirm the intelligence before I could decide on the right course of action.

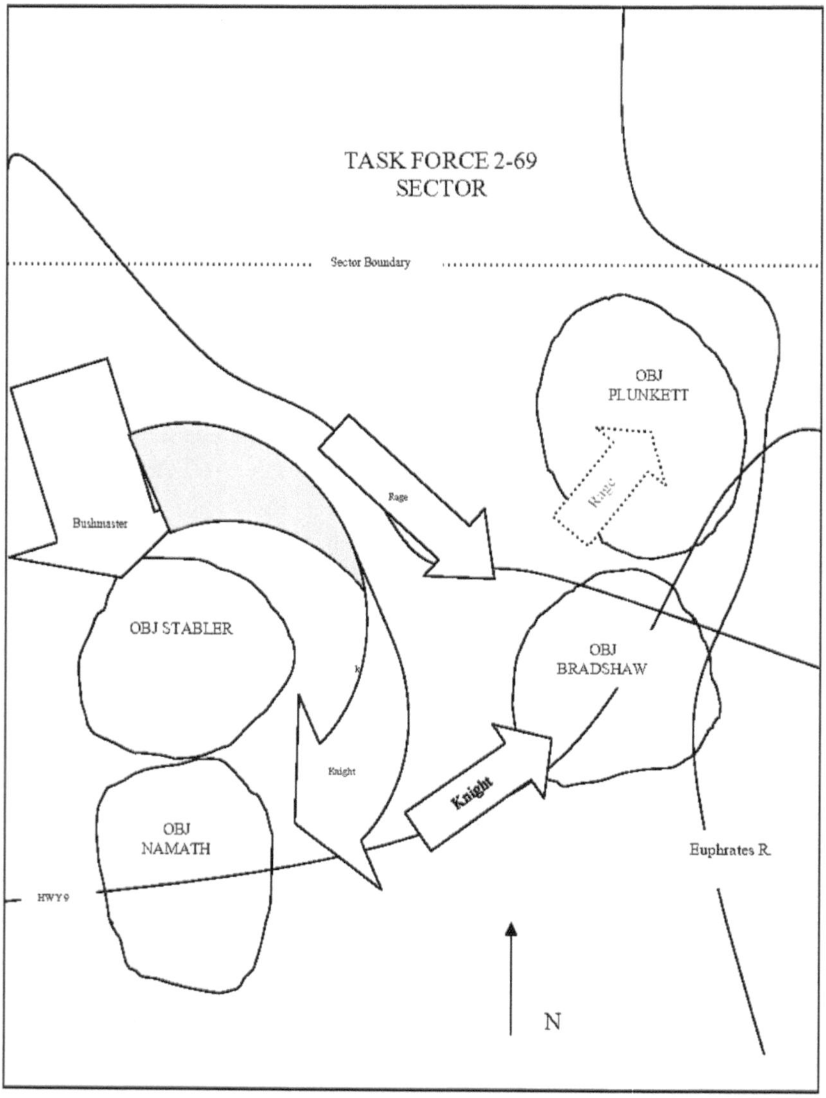

Task Force 2-7 battle plan for Objective Hannah South.
Source: Author's image.

Around 1400 on April 2, we began our advance. The scouts led the task force followed by Bushmaster, mortars, Knight, and Rage. The combat trains and Bulldog were in trail. Because of the need for speed and due to the restricted terrain, our task force traveled in a tight, staggered column formation. The route took us directly through the center of the

Medina Division's primary live-fire training area. The Medina trained here primarily in the summer months. We could see scores of unexploded artillery shells and rockets along the route. The drivers were briefed about the route's complexities and dangers back in Kuwait. The rule of thumb was, "If God didn't put it there, don't drive over it." Early into the march, an AH-64 Apache platoon, call sign "Shock," was placed under my operational control and in direct support of my mission on Objective Hannah. They could provide the eyes forward I needed to help me decide on a specific course action—Hannah North or Hannah South.

APACHE PLATOON LEADER: "Able 6, this is Shock 6, over."

LIEUTENANT COLONEL RUTTER: "Shock 6, this is Able 6, glad to have you with us." "Are you continuous?" "How much time do you have on station?"

APACHE PLATOON LEADER: "Able 6, this is Shock 6, we have enough to make a few passes over Hannah."

LIEUTENANT COLONEL RUTTER: "Shock 6, this is Able 6, need you to work Objective Plunkett."

APACHE PLATOON LEADER: "Able 6, this is Shock 6, roger, out."

About ten minutes passed until the Apache platoon informed us of the situation on Hannah.

APACHE PLATOON LEADER: "Able 6, this is Shock 6, we identified a convoy of military vehicles moving north of Karbala, we'd like to engage."

MAJOR COFFEY: "Shock 6, this is Able 3, negative, that is Panther, Task Force 2-69, they are friendly, over."

The radio went silent. The Apache platoon did not respond. The operations officer queried over the battalion command net.

MAJOR COFFEY: "Any Shock element, this is Able 3, over."

His call was repeated several times, and each time it went unanswered. The only thing I could think was, "Oh my God, they are lighting up an entire friendly battalion." The Task Force 2-69 commander, Lieutenant Colonel Jeffrey "JR" Sanderson, or "Panther 6," was a friend of mine. I couldn't bear the thought of a potential fratricide incident.

APACHE PLATOON LEADER: "Able 6, this is Shock 6."

MAJOR COFFEY: "Shock 6, this is Able 3, did you copy my last transmission about Panther?"

APACHE PLATOON LEADER: "Roger, sir."

MAJOR COFFEY: "The reason I ask is because you tend not to respond, over."

APACHE PLATOON LEADER: "Able 3, this is Shock 6, we passed over Plunkett and were taking heavy fire, sir." (Responding in a condescending tone.)

LIEUTENANT COLONEL RUTTER: "Shock 6, this is Able 6, limit your support to armed reconnaissance over Hannah and provide us with some on-site intel before we begin our attack, any support you can provide would be appreciated."

I did not want the Apaches to get shot down in enemy territory. I could not get the images from *Black Hawk Down* out of my head—we could not have a repeat of the Battle of Mogadishu 1993. We would have to splinter our forces to recover the downed helicopters, and it would jeopardize our primary mission. Instead of attacking the enemy, we would be doing more securing and defending. Objective Hannah would morph into something else, and it would make us all vulnerable.

The Apaches could serve as my eyes forward of the task force. At this point, I just wanted them to observe and report, from a distance and from higher altitudes. Apache pilots have amazing flying skills and are incredibly brave—but those were qualities I no longer required. If they went charging into the teeth of the enemy again, they would become a liability to me. And it seemed like they had little awareness of other friendly forces operating nearby—there would be no fratricide on my watch. Not here, not now.

Instead of giving the Apaches carte blanche to operate freely in my battlespace, I would keep them on a tight leash. The birds could help me make an informed decision on a proper course of action for Hannah. Hannah North or Hannah South, it really didn't matter. I knew we would be able to find and kill the enemy wherever it was hiding. Our concept of operation was simple enough to pivot to any geographical area. If we had to pick up and move to establish contact with the enemy, so be it.

My ETAC recommended we seize the opportunity and conduct a hasty, or "informal JAAT," on to the targets identified by the Apaches. An acronym for joint air attack team, this tactic is designed to attack hard targets with several types of munitions and to force the enemy to react to multiple forms of contact simultaneously—a difficult thing to do for a well-trained unit. It is a combination designed to keep the enemy target off balance and suppressed while overwhelming it with a knockout punch. In this case, the artillery fire would work in concert with the Apache's guns and missiles, and air force bombs delivered from high in the sky would deliver the fatal blow. We used similar tactics on Command Outpost Bravo during our breach into Iraq two weeks earlier. We trained on JAATs several times back at Fort Stewart. We knew how to do this, but it was always hard. It would be even harder on the fly and in the fog of war.

I considered it for a moment but quickly dismissed the idea. It would take some time for the artillery to be ready to shoot. They were on the move and were not prioritized to support my task force at this phase in the battle. And it would take more than a few minutes to relocate the Apaches over the target area while deconflicting the airspace—we would need to ensure the Apaches were not going to get shot at by our own artillery in flight. It would take several people looking at maps and talking to each other over the radio—precious time and opportunities for miscommunication.

We needed to maintain our speed and tempo. We were now within closing distance to our objectives and would need those air and artillery assets focused on close support to my companies in contact. A good suggestion it was, but it was not feasible here given the circumstances. I hated turning down good ideas. But in this moment, we needed speed and simplicity—we did not need slow and complex. A JAAT was fancy, and we didn't need fancy. Besides, I believed the enemy was already off balance since Karbala. This was the time to hit them hard and fast on the ground. I needed my armor and infantry to hit them like a wrecking ball.

About two minutes later, after the JAAT discussion, the Apache platoon leader reported that his birds were low on fuel and had to return to their forward arm and refuel point, or FARP. I requested their return after their refuel was complete and received assurances from the platoon leader that they would. I never heard from the Apaches again. The Apaches could have been more useful if we had more joint planning and rehearsals together before our attack. Instead they showed up to my battlespace unprepared and low on gas.

We began our deployment into the attack around the same time the Apaches left for their FARP. I quickly decided to execute the Hannah South course of action, without Objective Namath. Rage and Bushmaster would attack the 14th Mech from north to south, with Rage's main assault along a two-lane highway leading into the city from northwest to southeast. I hoped this would result in the rapid envelopment of the 14th Mech's northern flank and effectively collapse its front line of defense. Knight would attack from west to east and penetrate Hannah's primary defenses, deep inside the city, and all the way to the Highway 9 Bridge.

We would hit the enemy from two directions, using Knight to deliver the knockout punch.

The movement onto Hannah was described by a staff Officer in Task Force 2-7:

> As we approached Hannah, the terrain created a natural funnel into Al Musayyib. The feeling of being funneled into an enemy engagement area didn't sit well with me. Our approach took us through an open field of sand, with rows of palmetto trees enveloping us from two sides. It was now hot, dusty, and generally miserable—perfect conditions for an armored assault. The dust accumulated on our bodies along the drive to Objective Hannah now turned into a layer of mud by the sweat beading through our charcoal-lined chemical suits. Those fortunate enough to keep a towel nearby could quickly absorb the sweat streaming down their faces, each salty drop capable of burning one's eyes to near blindness. The sunlight was so intense it contributed to the blindness. It was literally impossible to see. Luckily, the sun was generally at our backs and in the enemy's face. It was about to set and soon we would fight a pitched battle in the dark, up close and personal.

As we crossed Phase Line Yukon, ten kilometers west of Objective Hannah South, the task force deployed into its attack formations. The scout platoon lunged forward of the task force and deployed into a "moving screen" formation. Just like Civil War–era cavalry, this line of mounted skirmishers was intended to provide my main force with intelligence on the composition of the enemy and their whereabouts prior to first contact. I needed eyes forward of the task force—the scouts could see what I couldn't see. The side that could get their forces into position first and employ superior firepower against the other would win.

The fight just ahead was what we had been drilling on for the last six months. All our planning and preparations were about to be put to the ultimate test. The task force could not be more ready for the fight ahead of them, and the soldiers' confidence was as high as it has ever been. Confidence backed by readiness is an intangible combat multiplier that could offset the enemy's home turf advantages or its superior numbers.

Our attack's success or failure hinged on our ability to remain flexible and to stay focused on the enemy. Killing the enemy, or at least holding the enemy in place, was the sole object of our mission on Objective Hannah. If our enemy knew how to defend his own backyard, we would be in for a real fight. Based off our previous encounters with the enemy, this was an unknowable. But these were Republican Guardsmen. They had numerical superiority, and they knew how to fight. Many of its leaders had combat experience. My hope was that they did not know what, where, or when to fight. If they were fighting blind, we would definitely have the advantage. Maybe we could surprise them and catch them off guard. All our questions would be answered soon. The 14th Mech would answer them for us.

As we rapidly closed the distance to Al Musayyib, squads of dismounted infantry ambushed the lead elements of the task force. RPGs flew inches past Captain Smith's face. Smith's company retaliated with massed fire from their Bradleys. Small units were attacking us, less than a company in size. The enemy fighters used conventional tactics and operated in compact yet capable formations. They used coordinated fire and maneuver. It was clear to me that this was professional military, not the same disorganized irregulars we encountered in the south. The resistance was calculated and methodical. But one thing did not make much sense to me: it appeared like they had deliberately abandoned their combat vehicles prior to our arrival and made the choice to fight on foot instead. I wasn't sure why they would not try to get their armor into the fight first; as the defender, they could have taken us by surprise and inflicted more damage using their tanks and other heavy weapons.

I had assumed, at this point in the fight, that we would have spotted enemy tanks or personnel carriers dug in and concealed by the surrounding earth, like Desert Storm 1991. The Iraqis could have been saving them for later, perhaps hiding them in the city. I was concerned about the possibility that we were being lured into an enemy engagement area—the enemy's heavy weapons and artillery could mass its fires here to inflict maximum destruction on our vulnerable forces flowing in. If the task force got caught in a prepared enemy engagement area, it would be difficult to fight through it. We would take losses, losing the initiative, and potentially lose the mission. If the enemy set obstacles and mines, the engagement area would be like a bear trap.

Fortunately, the enemy was disaggregated at Hannah and, as a result, unable to effectively mass their fires against us. They were just trying to harass our column along our flanks in an attempt to slow us down. My staff thought that this might only be a disruption force. Perhaps another main line of defense extended farther east, in or around Al Musayyib. Perhaps the enemy's infantry was attempting to lure us into the city—to bait us into a city reinforced with obstacles, mines, armor, and artillery—all tied in together to block our approach at the Highway 9 Bridge. It was a good staff assessment—we had to proceed cautiously.

Most of the scattered resistance we countered with heavy Bradley and tank fire, complemented by volleys of massed artillery. At one point in the engagement, there was so much artillery impacting around us, on all sides, that it was difficult to decipher friendly from enemy fire. None of the artillery impacted directly on top of us, so I assumed that it must have all been friendly.

When we made contact with the enemy on Objective Hannah, our task force had two batteries of six 155mm howitzers from 1-10 Field Artillery in direct support to our mission. After the first few volleys, the task force advanced so rapidly that it outpaced much of the supporting artillery fire. More than half a dozen missions were canceled due to the proximity of friendly forces to the enemy target. My mortars could not stop and set up their own guns fast enough—it takes minutes to lay in the mortars, but by then our lead elements were already out of range.

While pushing the task force forward along the highway to Al Musayyib, the trail vehicle in the formation reported an advancing civilian truck. It was a white Blazer, the same make and model of the suicide truck we destroyed in the Karbala Gap.

Captain Paul recounts this experience:

I told my trail squad to ensure the vehicle keeps its distance. I didn't want a repeat of the car bomb incident at Objective Raiders.

> SERGEANT MARSH: "Thunder 6, this is Thunder 4, the vehicle is getting closer, and is not stopping."
>
> CAPTAIN PAUL: "Thunder 4, this is Thunder 6, fire a warning shot, over."
>
> SERGEANT MARSH: "Thunder 6, this is Thunder 4, my .50 Cal is jammed."
>
> CAPTAIN PAUL: "Use your M-16."
>
> SERGEANT MARSH: "Thunder 6, this is Thunder 4, my M-16 is jammed."
>
> CAPTAIN PAUL: "Thunder 3, this is Thunder 6, help out Thunder 4, fire a warning shot, if that doesn't work, try to disable the vehicle."
>
> SERGEANT MARSH: "Thunder 6, this is Thunder 4, we turned the vehicle away."

Apparently, all weapons in the squad jammed except the driver's 9mm pistol. When the civilian truck closed to within twenty-five feet of his track, the squad's driver opened his driver's hatch, pulled out his 9mm pistol, and proceeded to launch five rounds into the engine block of the truck.

I think the occupants in the truck got the idea. The platoon's weapons collected some sand and dust since we departed Assault Position Gannon less than an hour ago. The desert can be more dangerous than the enemy.

The advance through the outskirts of Al Musayyib was surreal. As we pushed through pockets of enemy resistance along Highway 9, I found myself unexpectedly captivated by the elegant Middle Eastern–style mansions lining the road. Their beauty stood in stark contrast to the chaos unfolding all around us. I figured many of these homes belonged to privileged Ba'ath Party families—perhaps even officers of the 14th Mechanized Brigade. In Iraq's rigid socioeconomic hierarchy, Republican Guard officers typically enjoyed a middle to upper-class lifestyle, while professionals like scientists, doctors, and lawyers often lived more modestly.

Each mansion was immaculately maintained, surrounded by lush landscaping that seemed untouched by war. Many were still occupied. The surrounding properties featured small farms with cows, sheep, and even horses. None of us expected to see such scenes here—not in the middle of a combat zone. These glimpses of domestic life reminded us of home. It was hard not to imagine our own families, our own neighborhoods, and how jarring it would be to see tanks and Bradleys rolling through our front yards.

For a moment, the war felt distant. Then, as we passed one particularly upscale home, I saw a woman calmly milking her cow in the front yard. She seemed completely indifferent—or perhaps resigned—to the gunfire echoing around her. That image stayed with me. It was a haunting reminder of how life persists, even in the shadow of war.

Our rapid advance toward Al Musayyib came to a screeching halt once Rage made enemy contact within the vicinity of Objective Bradshaw. An Iraqi RPG team was dug into a berm on the flank—it took half of Rage's Bradleys to pick the fortified berm apart and neutralize the position. The rest of the column stopped and assumed a herringbone formation, triggering each vehicle to face toward the flanks of the road with every vehicle alternating in its orientation.

Rage continued to advance and it engaged dozens of abandoned artillery pieces lining the road. It looked like the Iraqis abandoned their artillery just moments before their advance. It felt like now we were chasing ghosts. Artillery shells were prepped and ready to be loaded up and fired. There were signs the Iraqis were camped out near the guns for some time. It appeared that the 14th Mech had begun their preplanned withdrawal to the east—to the city or perhaps across the Euphrates River to another line of defense.

While almost completely immersed in the decorative surroundings, my soldiers and junior leaders had to make life or death decisions. We were operating in the Iraqi heartland with civilians still going about their daily lives. Yet we still had a job to do. The mortar platoon and nearly every unit within my task force would grapple with these difficult decisions in the fog of war. Anecdotes like the mortar platoon's encounter with its "man in black" would play out time and again all over Objective Bradshaw.

Captain Paul's perspective on the "man in black" encounter:

> My mortar platoon noticed a moving object in its peripheral vision. Almost in slow motion on a picture screen, a black clad figure was moving against a backdrop of yellow grass only fifty to one hundred meters to the left of the column. Further investigation with binoculars revealed an enemy soldier. Had he remained still, he would never have been seen. While outfitted in full Saddam Fedayeen garb, dressed in a black jumpsuit and leather combat boots, it was still unclear his intentions. Civilians didn't dress in all black with leather combat boots. Typically, Iraqi Army officers wore brown leather combat boots and the irregular militiamen wore all black. He looked like a ninja and moved like a ninja, only we could see him. Ninjas were supposed to be invisible.
>
> His movement paralleled our column and was directed toward our opposite direction of travel. He did not move any closer or farther away from us and it looked like he was concealing a weapon of some sort underneath his belly. I deduced that his intentions were to infiltrate behind the column to snipe at us from the rear or get in close to the trail vehicle and detonate a suicide vest. He was not moving away from us. He was not trying to escape danger—he was repositioning for some sort of tactical advantage.
>
> During the microseconds following my assessment, I received a call from one of my squad leaders. "Thunder 6, this is Thunder 3, there is an enemy to your left, only fifty meters from your track." He saw the same thing as I did, but from a different angle. "Sir, he's got a weapon," my driver yelled at me. *"Kift, Kift!!"* I yelled in the most elementary Arabic tongue, hoping this order to stop would reveal not only that we saw him but also a desire for him to stop crawling, stand up, and surrender. I yelled at the top of my lungs, again and again. "Does he honestly think we still can't see him?" my driver asked. I shook my head, confused and in disbelief. Even if he just stood up, admitted defeat, and walked away in the opposite direction, I would let him go. I kept yelling and eventually gained his attention, making eye contact for an instant. I then raised my arms as a demonstration of how to surrender. The Iraqi

> was undeterred by my words and actions. So he kept crawling, looking for a better position to do something . . . and I had no idea what that was. This Fedayeen fighter was on some sort of mission. "Thunder 3, this is Thunder 6, do you see a weapon." "Roger, Thunder 6." "Then what are you waiting for, engage," I ordered. POP, POP. Two 5.56mm rounds from his squad leader's M16 rifle hit the "man in black" in his chest. Any plans he had to harm my platoon or the rest of the task force behind me were thwarted.

This was typical of the tough life or death decisions junior officers had to make while engaging Iraqi forces in close combat throughout the campaign. Most of the engagements were conducted in and around populated areas, with enemy fighters interspersed within the local civilian populations. In many cases, soldiers had to make split-second decisions, decisions that could alter the course of the battle, and decisions that would stay with them for the rest of their lives.

While Bushmaster and Rage were clearing out enemy resistance around the northeast portion of Objective Bradshaw, Knight began their attack in the southwest portion, near Highway 9. They stumbled upon what the commander, Captain Lee, described as a museum of combat vehicles and artillery pieces parked in a large parking lot. It was not a defensive position but rather an assembly area or hide position. On Lee's thermal sights, many of the targets appeared hot. The Iraqi artillery tubes were glowing on the thermals, indicating that they had recently been fired. Despite all the quiet, there was an enemy presence in that parking lot. Knight proceeded to engage each vehicle and artillery piece that presented a heat signature and engaged the ammunition and personnel bunkers encompassing the parking area.

As Captain Lee's tanks opened fire on the enemy's tanks, armored personnel carriers, and artillery pieces, his attached Bradley platoon engaged scores of dismounted infantry seeking shelter in a nearby wooded area. The enemy was caught off guard and their lack of security led to their demise. It was a turkey shoot, as soldiers described it. But after a few minutes, the Iraqis responded with volumes of accurate artillery fire. The enemy was either trying to reinforce its forces operating west of the Euphrates River or it intended to use the artillery to cover its withdrawal east of the river. In any event, Knight had to move. That would be difficult given the narrow roads, surrounding farms, and impassable marshlands everywhere. Knight buttoned up and adjusted as best they could to survive the enemy's barrage.

Luckily, Knight suffered no casualties or significant damage to its vehicles or equipment.

Most enemy contact was in the south, in Knight's sector. That was where most of the action was now. But that was exactly what I wanted—Knight Company was my decisive operation and my main effort wielding most of my task force's firepower. The combat reporting and intelligence suggested the enemy was making their stand there. The resistance was scattered, but it was also 360 degrees. The Republican Guard forces at Objective Hannah did not constrain themselves to fighting from lines and from contiguous areas. This meant that we had to keep our heads on a swivel. The enemy could be along our flanks or our rear area. Fighting from all directions would present us with greater operational risk, but as long as we could keep the Iraqis tied up at Hannah, we could accomplish our mission. In a supporting role, I could not allow the Iraqis to reposition north to threaten the rest of my brigade at Objective Peach.

I ordered the entire task force to quickly converge on Objectives Plunkett and Bradshaw. All my task force's combat power would now focus on these two objectives. Bushmaster oriented its Bradleys on Objective Plunkett, near the 14th Mechanized Brigade's barracks. Captain Szymanski ordered his infantry to dismount and clear the compound. The Bradleys could not advance more than a few hundred meters from the barracks due to the soft, wet terrain that lay in front of them. As a result, they had to make the assault on foot. Risky yet necessary, clearing out the compound was the only way our task force might achieve a decisive outcome. Bushmaster cleared the Iraqi barracks and its headquarters with relative ease. The facilities were completely sterile—absolutely no military footprint was left behind by the Iraqis. They were gone without a trace.

While Bushmaster consolidated their positions in the north, Rage and Knight continued to advance deeper into Objective Bradshaw in a two-pronged pincer move, with Rage from the north and Knight from the west. Bushmaster would contain any remaining enemy presence on Plunkett to the north. This could provide Rage and Knight the time and space to maneuver on Objective Bradshaw without any interference from Plunkett. If all my companies occupied defensible positions at Bradshaw and Plunkett, it would allow us to fix the enemy here in this space. The enemy would be unable to move north, south, or west of Objective Hannah. If we could also be in position to cover the Highway 9 Bridge in Al Musayyib, the enemy would be unable to move east too.

Major Coffey and I pushed Knight as far and as fast as we could. I felt we had the initiative. To maintain it, we needed Knight as far east as the enemy and the terrain would allow. I ordered Knight to set up a blocking position adjacent to the city. I wanted good observation on the Highway 9 Bridge and the east side of the Euphrates—this move would prevent the Iraqis' escape east of the river and it could also provide us with early warning in the event of an Iraqi counterattack. If Knight had good line of site with the bridge, it would stop a counterattack cold in its tracks. Knight would need to deploy its tanks and Bradleys with some breadth and depth to create an effective engagement area At the time, the bridge still had strategic importance, like Remagen or Arnhem bridges in World War II. The Iraqis' Highway 9 Bridge was decisive terrain, and we had to control it as best we could. Getting there and finding an ideal spot to set up would be our challenge.

I told Captain Lee to avoid getting sucked too deep into the city. Due to all the abandoned equipment, I believed the 14th Mech may have collapsed their outer defenses and retreated into the city to set up ambushes and employ hit-and-run tactics like we saw in Al Kindr, As Samawah, and Karbala. Knight's tanks and Bradleys would be vulnerable in the narrow streets and alleyways. It would be a perfect killing ground for the enemy. We would be fighting on his terms, not ours. I assessed that was what the Iraqis wanted us to do, and prudence compelled us to not do what they wanted us to do. Rather, we needed to fight the enemy on our own terms. I hoped that we could fix the enemy in place from a safe distance, preferably outside the city boundary. If we went deep inside the city, the enemy could fix us instead.

Knight treated Al Musayyib like a death trap and made a painstaking effort to avoid driving directly through it. Instead it traced the outskirts of the enemy-held city to occupy positions of advantage nearby. Captain Lee did not want to relive the same experience of As Samawah only a week earlier. Jimmy wanted to avoid another "Bakara Market with tanks." So their route around the city took them on unimproved roads and through large patches of mud—the ground was saturated by the Euphrates River nearby. We were in the middle of the fertile crescent after all.

While maneuvering through a highway overpass near the city, Knight encountered massed RPG fire from a nearby bunker complex. It was a perfect ambush position. It offered ideal observation as well as good cover and concealment. It resembled a World War II–style pillbox connected to an elaborate tunnel system running underneath Highway 9. Captain Lee dispatched his infantry platoon to clear out the complex. All four Bradleys deployed on line and suppressed the bunker complex with their 25mm armor-piercing and high-explosive cannon fire. The platoon then dismounted its infantry to conduct a ground assault. Led by First Lieutenant Johnson and Staff Sergeant Ulster, they maneuvered in stealth to the rear of the complex. They lobbed six grenades into the bunker and then they stormed in. The infantrymen discharged full magazines from their rifles, sweeping left to right, eliminating anything still moving after the 25mm cannon fire and the hand grenades. Eight Iraqi soldiers lay dead. First Lieutenant Johnson's platoon searched the rest of the complex and found maps, uniforms, and ammunition.

While Staff Sergeant Ulster focused his attention on the bunker search, First Lieutenant Johnson observed small blue wooden boxes lining the roads around the city. Johnson could only guess what they were until he observed the first of many explosions from a distance. The explosion rocked the earth. Aside from the car bomb at Objective Raiders, this was our first encounter with improvised explosive devices (IEDs) in Iraq, and it would not be our last. The Iraqis were using IEDs instead of conventional mines to block our advance. In April 2003, IEDs were rudimentary and easy to spot, but they would grow in stealth and sophistication as the war went on.

Four tanks and three M88 tracked recovery vehicles from Knight became mired in a large patch of mud adjacent to the road while attempting to bypass the city on the way to its blocking position. It was a large strip of marshland at the foot of the city. It was like a moat encompassing a medieval castle. Knight continued to charge through part of it, believing it could find better ground on the other side. But it was like quicksand, and Knight had few good options. The best way out of the marsh would have funneled Knight directly into the city—where they were trying not to go. Knight was surrounded by thick palm grove in the north and wet marshy sludge in the south. The east offered better ground, but it would lead them directly into the city. Knight was vulnerable in its present position. Not only could they not maneuver here, but they were also now within enemy weapons' range from within the city. And the city afforded the enemy a bit of elevation and clear fields of fire relative to Knight's position. In other words, the Iraqis held the high ground and the tactical advantage.

Two of Knight's tanks became completely stuck after about fifty meters into the marsh. Two additional tanks became bogged down moments later, after attempting to recover the other two. Then the M88 recovery vehicles sprang into action. Unfortunately, they fared no better than the tanks. They too became mired in the marsh and needed saving. I told Knight to stop; everything they tried just made their situation worse. Things were getting out of control. One-third of my only tank company was now dead in the water at the outer rim of the city, and it would get dark soon.

This enemy grew bolder at night, as we quickly learned at Al Kindr and later at Objective Raiders. This was not only the worst time, but it was also the worst place for Knight to camp out. The Iraqis would certainly take advantage of the situation. They were growing more adept at exploiting our vulnerabilities.

Predictably, the enemy capitalized on our misfortune and rapidly concentrated its forces on Knight as soon as they realized what had happened. Using the palm forest to our immediate north, the enemy infiltrated unobserved to within hand grenade throwing range of Knight's tanks. Iraqi AK-47 and RPG fire bounced off the tanks and Bradleys congregating at the recovery site. It caused some confusion, but fortunately it resulted in no casualties or significant damage to our vehicles or equipment.

First Lieutenant Johnson deployed his platoon on a line and advanced cautiously through the same marsh the heavier tanks and recovery vehicles attempted to cross only moments earlier. Their Bradleys being only half the weight of a tank, Johnson believed the risk was worth taking. The four Bradleys crept past the mired tanks and engaged the enemy to the east in the city and to the north inside the palm forest. The platoon would act as a shield for the tanks until they could be recovered. Johnson's infantry dismounted and patrolled the adjacent wooded areas to flush the enemy out of its hide positions. Johnson's three infantry squads rotated the patrol every hour throughout the night. The two squads not on patrol provided local security for the Bradleys and tanks in the marsh. There would not be much rest for them that night. This night belonged to the infantry. They had to own it or else Task Force 2-7 soldiers would die.

Before dark, artillery and mortar fire splashed down within two hundred meters of Knight's position. Captain Lee requested counter-fire support, but the request was denied. The artillery trailing my task force relocated to Objective Peach hours earlier and were now out of range. Peach was the brigade's main effort and the support its artillery and counterfire radars could provide it was critical to its success. But Knight was now a sitting duck. The Apaches could have helped here in this moment, but they were long gone. We were on our own. The enemy's artillery and mortar fire would not waiver until the following day.

Rage responded to Knight's desperate situation. When Captain Smith learned what had happened, he charged his company to Knight's position while destroying pockets of Iraqi infantry and abandoned artillery pieces along the route. Upon their arrival, Rage immediately tied their defenses in with Knight as best they could, while also being careful not to mire its own tanks and Bradleys in the mud. Both companies expanded the defensive perimeter, securing the mired vehicles as best they could. This whole affair reminded me of the movie *Blackhawk Down*. Only we weren't rescuing downed helicopters in a city, we were rescuing downed tanks.

Upon arrival, Captain Smith quickly ordered his dismounted infantry squads to conduct aggressive patrolling through the wooded areas surrounding the position. They would not be sitting ducks here and allow the enemy to pick them off one at a time. It was an attempt to remain on the offensive and to keep the enemy off balance. Like Knight Company, Rage's infantry needed to own the night and create a blanket of security around the Bradleys and tanks.

Rage's infantry squads yielded considerable success while patrolling through the woods. The enemy deployed small teams to harass Rage and Knight between 2200 and 0200 in the morning. It offered no respite. The Iraqi teams were equipped with sniper rifles, RPGs, and machine guns—capabilities that could have hurt us if they got close enough. Fortunately, Rage and Knight's infantry patrols would not allow that to happen. They thwarted every attempt the Iraqis made to infiltrate the marsh.

Captain Rob Smith reassured the tank company commander, Captain Lee, that he would not be left alone out there. "Knight 6, this is Rage 6, I'm not going anywhere buddy." Captain Smith's actions exemplified the true spirit of our task force, to help our fellow soldiers in need and to continue to make sacrifices for one another no matter what the cost. At Objective Hannah, I saw teamwork at its best.

Dubbed the "Longest Night" by members of the task force, this night would be the longest in either of the two company commanders' lives. Both companies fended off enemy probing attacks all evening and well into the morning. The level of resistance would not relent for most of the night—sleep, rest, or food were out of the question. Miraculously, not a single Task Force 2-7 soldier was killed or wounded that night.

First Lieutenant Johnson, in the Bradley nearest the city, could see billowing dirt inside the city and could hear the unmistakable clank and roar of enemy armor echoing through the city streets and alleyways. There was a force of some weight in the city, perhaps up to a company in size. Maybe they thought they had the initiative and could take advantage of our situation while we were stuck in the marsh. Despite the obvious signs, Johnson could not spot a single tank or BMP. The Iraqis were either attempting to retreat, counterattack, or dig in for a defense of the city. It was not clear the intentions. But it was another threat that we might have to contend with nonetheless.

The mortar platoon was collocated with Bushmaster, about four kilometers to the northwest of Rage and Knight. I positioned both of them there to block the main avenue leading to Rage and Knight—to protect them from an enemy counterattack in their rear. The mortar platoon occupied a firing position with their guns trained east, toward the city of Al Musayyib. Captain Paul made repeated requests to help, but there was not much the mortar platoon could do. Apparently, Rage and Knight were surrounded by tall buildings and did not have observation greater than one hundred meters. Paul could not fire his mortars that close to friendly troops unless it was a dire emergency and approved by the senior commander on the ground. And firing other munitions there, like illumination, would help the enemy more than us.

During the night, two of Bulldog's AVLBs managed to pull out one of the M88 recovery vehicles and two tanks stuck in the mud. Using the same hydraulic system to lay the bridge, the AVLBs managed to pull the tracks on to dry enough ground to free themselves from the marsh. The remaining tanks were in the earth too deep for Bulldog to grab hold, and even if they could, the resistance would probably bust the AVLB's hydraulics. We could not take the risk. I might need the bridge later, somewhere between here and Baghdad. I commended Bulldog for its field expedient, unorthodox recovery methods. Whatever works. But it had its limits, and now we needed more powerful recovery assets to finish the job.

My task force's TOC had called brigade, informed them of the situation, and requested Bulldozer support. The Army's new D-9 dozers fielded by our corps engineers could do the job. They were monsters in size and strength. The dozers were so effective, they were intended to quickly build airfields and construct logistics support areas along the march to Baghdad. At the time, they were working in the south, in the 101st and 82nd Airborne's sectors near An Najaf. It would take some time for the dozers to detach and make the fifty-kilometer march north. Traveling at a mere ten miles per hour, the earliest they could arrive was the next day. We would have to dig in for a long and unforgettable night. The rest of the brigade had already seized Objective Peach and were awaiting our arrival to consolidate and resume the attack north to Saddam International Airport—Objective Lions. Time was not on our side.

Knight's tanks were settled in the mud quite a bit, with the tracks themselves completely immersed in a stranglehold of mud. We continued to wait for the D-9 dozers, until we could wait no longer. The enemy situation became too untenable as the sun crested the horizon. That is often when surprise enemy attacks happen—in Iraq and throughout history. We gave up on the dozers and deployed the AVLBs once again, as a Hail Mary. This time even more cautiously than the last time. I owned the risk. Slowly but surely, the AVLBs were able to pull the remaining tanks out of the mud one by one. The recovery operation concluded around 1230 hours. It was constantly impeded by enemy small arms and mortar fire.

As the recovery got closer to the end, we could tell that the Iraqis were massing their forces in the city. Perhaps they read the situation as a fleeting opportunity to counterattack us while we were still vulnerable. I led a small force toward the Highway 9 Bridge as an attempt to draw the enemy's attention away from the recovery effort and to disrupt any plans to attack us in force. The feint worked—the enemy stopped harassing the recovery effort and started to harass us at the bridge instead. No Iraqi counterattack in force would materialize.

Knight 6, Captain Jimmy Lee's perspective on the "Longest Night":

> On April 2, 2003, after fighting north through the Karbala Gap, our task force was directed to attack east to Objective Hannah on the western side of Al Musayyib, the location of the 14th Brigade of the Medina Division, to protect the 3rd Infantry Division's attack north. We cleared east to the edge of Musayyib, stopping on the western edge of the town. The brigade tasked 2-7 to establish a blocking position on the south side of town to protect elements of 3rd Brigade who were attacking through the city of Karbala to our south. Able 3 subsequently tasked my company with the mission. While we were in our camps in Kuwait, I met with the geospatial engineers regarding the soil composition in the Euphrates River Valley area and learned that near the river, the soil would most likely not support our sixty-eight-ton tanks.
>
> When Able 3 tasked me with the blocking position, he further noted that a constraint is I cannot drive through the town of Musayyib to get there. I stated the only other option was going through the clearing next to the hard ball road we were on and tanks could easily become mired. After a quick exchange of me protesting, I finally relented, and we began to move out. I had the Mech IN Platoon (Outlaws) lead since the BFVs were lighter and less likely to mire down in the soil. We were only about two hundred meters into the field when my tank mired. I called Able 3 and reported one tank stuck and he replied on the radio, "are you going to let one tank getting stuck stop you from doing your job?" Simultaneously, while he was replying on the Task Force net, I received calls of three additional tanks being

stuck. I replied to Able 3 I have four tanks stuck and am now going into recovery operations.

I deployed the Outlaw platoon to establish a position between the four tanks and the town of Musayyib to protect the company during recovery operations and had the remaining tanks stay near or on the hardball to avoid also miring down. Shortly afterward, an Iraqi man with a white flag led a large group of women and children across the field away from the town. At that time, we knew things were about to get sporty. We spotted pickup trucks driving into the town from the north with Iraqi men. It wasn't long before the small arms, RPG, and heavy gun fire began. The Outlaw platoon performed remarkably, repelling the enemy attacks. First Lieutenant Johnson was regularly adjusting his positions, continuously maneuvering the squads to defeat the enemy and protect the company.

Once the firing stopped, the first sergeant got an M88 in to recover the tanks and the M88 also mired down. At this point, there were no recovery vehicles available and the sun was setting. After the town's evening prayer concluded, we were once again attacked. The infantry platoon continued to repel the attack and tanks returning fire only when the infantry platoon was not within the tanks' surface danger zone (SDZ). The attacks came in waves throughout the night. Meanwhile there were tank loaders and drivers on the ground with shovels digging to free their tanks and get back into the fight. The company first sergeant exhausted himself trying to identify recovery assets for the company throughout the night.

The next morning, 2-7 was directed to head north and join the brigade and assault across Objective Peach and on to the airport. The company was left alone, no radar coverage, and vulnerable of being isolated by the enemy. We were told dozers were on the way, but we were not certain when they would arrive. The company first sergeant (Knight 7) asked the task force engineer platoon to remain and assist with recovery, and they eagerly obliged. The AVLBs dropped their bridges behind the company's position at a safe distance and came forward to recover our tanks. The AVLBs daisy chained their two AVLBs (M60 chassis) together with tow ropes. They then hooked up to a tank and counted "1 . . . 2 . . . 3 . . . go!" and both vehicles would floor it along with the tank and they successfully recovered a tank. We were ecstatic but the enthusiasm was quickly overcome by yet another enemy attack that morning. Yet again the Outlaw Platoon kept the enemy at bay while the engineers continued to recover the tanks and M88. My tank was the last one recovered but the track came off during the process.

The engineers dragged my tank to the hardball road. At that point the enemy attack incorporated mortars that were impacting

> behind my tank on the hardball road while we were out walking the track back onto the tank. The rounds were slowly getting closer as we hurried to get the track back on. Once the track was finally back on and the company was organized, we immediately moved to link up with the battalion just before its attack across Objective Peach and on to the airport. In fact, I missed the orders brief and received a quick overview of the mission. Due to limited time, I had to issue the company order over the radio as we moved to Objective Peach.

In total, thirty-one enemy combatants were confirmed KIA. That was what we could see. The "Longest Night" was dark, confusing, and we probably were not keeping an accurate count of how many Iraqi fighters we killed. Our focus was on survival and winning. Perhaps hundreds of fighters may have been killed by our massed artillery early on in the fight. We destroyed the equipment we could see—anything of military value to the Iraqis. Two enemy tanks, two BMPs, gun trucks, and countless artillery pieces were destroyed on Objective Hannah.

The outcome at Hannah validated that Iraq in 2003 would be a different kind of war. It seemed like the enemy was everywhere and nowhere at the same time. We were fighting ghosts. How can we win at fighting ghosts? How would we know we were winning? It wasn't by measuring body counts and damaged equipment. We would have to adapt to this new kind of war—quickly. If Hannah was a tactical success, was it contributing to a strategic victory for the coalition? So many questions my staff and I were grappling with on little sleep, hungry bellies, dehydration, and little time to pause and reflect between missions.

As I looked down at my map board, I could see my route pointing north to Saddam International Airport and Baghdad. We would need to figure it out quickly. We could keep moving, shooting, and killing, but eventually we would need to seize and hold ground. If we captured and held the airport or even Baghdad itself, I wondered whether the Iraqis would fight on. And if they did, I wondered what would come next—all of my plans stopped at Baghdad. I had hoped that would be enough to defeat the Iraqi military and bring the regime to heel.

Despite the fighting and our success at Hannah, I was puzzled. This was too easy. What happened to the massed formations of tanks and BMPs we expected to encounter on Objective Hannah? "Where was the tough 14th Mech?" A few prisoner interrogations revealed that the Iraqis mounting their defense on Objective Hannah were a mix of the 14th Mech and other Republican Guard units, Regular Army, and irregular militia forces. Some of their forces repositioned to Karbala when word spread that we were passing through the gap and others withdrew to Baghdad to bolster the inner-ring defenses there. The forces remaining were left in place to delay and to disrupt our advance. The Iraqis' strategy defaulted to a hasty defense in depth—fighting and then withdrawing from one prepared position to the next.

The air campaign was a proven success here at Hannah. Our heavy bombers destroyed many of the enemy's tanks and artillery before we even arrived. The effects from the coalition's shock and awe campaign took their toll on the Iraqis and the effects on Objective Hannah were plain to see. This not only had a physical effect but also a psychological impact on the enemy's disposition and will to fight. Prisoners reported that many soldiers felt that further resistance against the coalition was futile and consequently dropped their uniforms, abandoned their vehicles, and went home.

The few Iraqi fighters that remained at Hannah had no command, control, or communications worthy of mounting any significant defense. Their combat power was shattered and in a state of confusion. At most, they were able to mass up to an infantry company's worth of combat power against us. The enemy was unable to synchronize their available armor, artillery, and infantry. We faced all three at Hannah, but it was uncoordinated and choppy, easy for us to evade or counter. By the time we arrived, I don't think that the Iraqis even tried to synchronize or mass all their combat power. It likely reflected the cumulative effects of coalition pressure and internal breakdowns, shaping the fight's dynamic and outcome. The fighters that remained at Hannah to fight us threw what they could at us to harass our formation and to slow us down. They were a mix of irregulars, professional diehards, and unlucky conscripts just doing their duty. The unfortunate few who stayed to fight were killed, captured, or sent running for their lives.

Objective Hannah showed me how vital momentum is. Every move and decision fed a rhythm we fought to keep. The enemy bent but didn't break; terrain was harsh, resistance stubborn, yet, for the most part, we could impose our will. At Hannah, we had momentum, lost it, then regained it. What mattered most wasn't chaos or brute force but coordination. Scouts, gunners, infantry, engineers—all of them played their part, and did it better than the Iraqis. Success rarely comes from fanfare or one heroic act; success is pressing forward, inch by inch, until the enemy has nothing left.

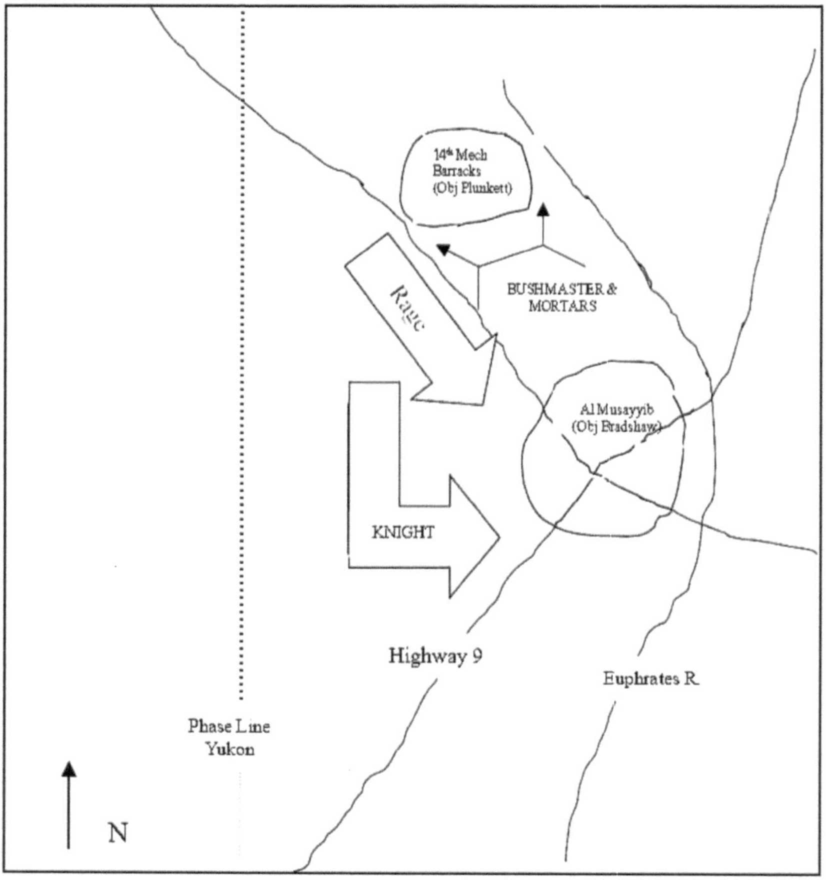

Task Force 2-7 actions at Objective Hannah, afternoon of April 2, 2003.
Source: Author's image.

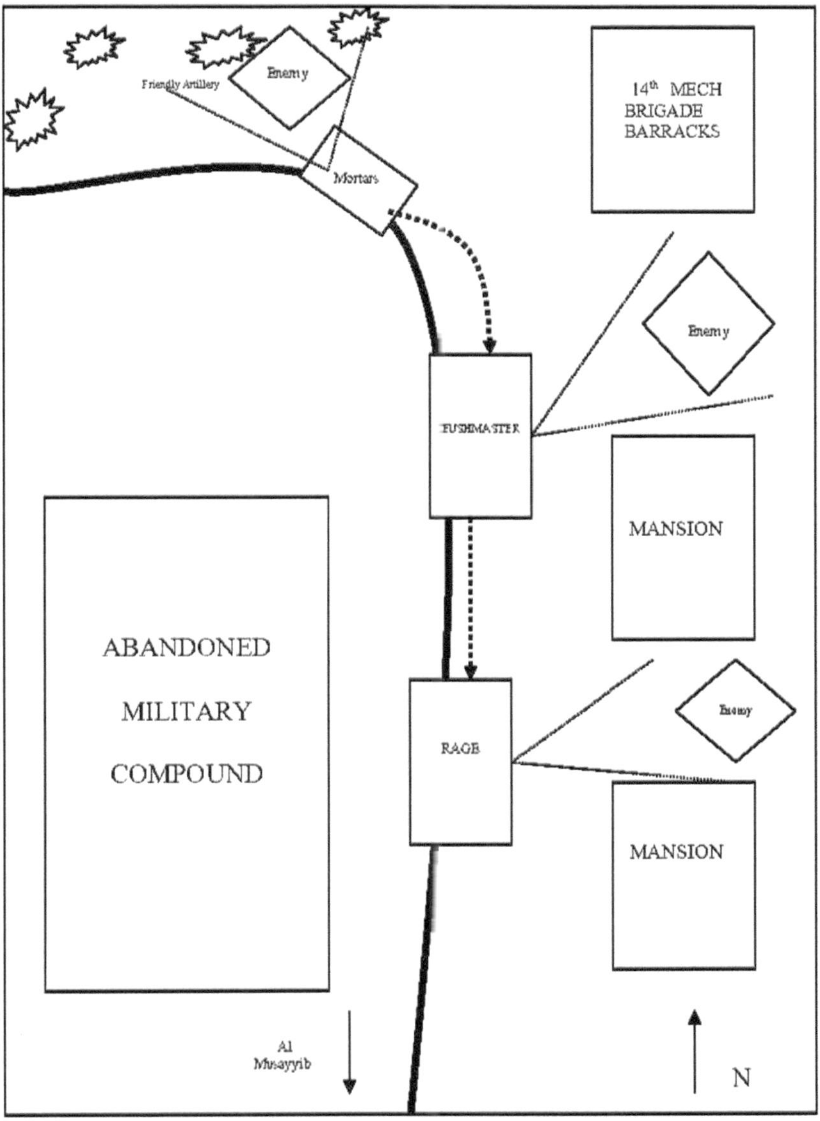

Task Force 2-7 detailed actions at Objective Hannah, April 2, 2003.
Source: Author's image.

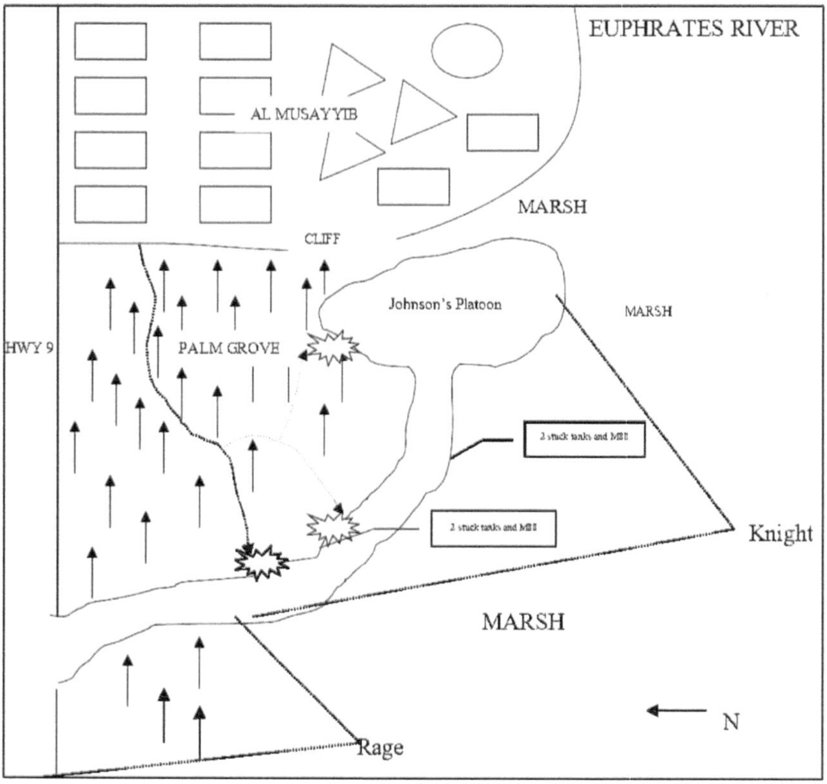

Task Force 2-7 actions at Objective Hannah, April 2–3, 2003, called the "Longest Night" with mired armored vehicles outside of Al Musayyib.
Source: Author's image.

EVENT 7

Objective Lions, the Battle for Saddam International Airport

"In front of us lay Berlin, and to our right a forest clearing, now a chaos of jumbled tanks, cars, armored cars, trucks, special vehicles and ambulances. They had uprooted hundreds of trees, probably in an attempt to turn round and escape. In this black, charred confusion of steel, timber, guns, cases and papers, a bloody mess of mutilated corpses lay strewn along the clearing as far as the eye could see. . . . Then I noticed a host of wounded men lying on greatcoats and blankets or leaning against tree trunks; some of them bandaged and others covered in blood, with no one to tend to them."

—Konstantin Simonov, Soviet war correspondent, April 1945, collected in The Road to Berlin *(1963)*

Saddam International Airport's construction was completed in 1987. It was designed and constructed by a French consortium at a cost of 900 million US dollars. It is situated in the outskirts of southwestern Baghdad and about fifteen kilometers from center city. It has a large, rectangular silhouette and is partitioned with half of the facility owned and operated by the Iraqi Air Force and the other by the government's commercial airliner, Iraqi Airways. Each half owned and operated its own runway. The civilian half has three passenger terminals capable of accommodating over seven million passengers per year. Nondomestic flights ceased in 1991 as a result of the UN-imposed no-fly zone and did not resume operations until 2000.

A thick, concrete wall encompasses the airport boundary and stands roughly eight feet tall. Myriad vegetation and attractive landscaping not native to the Middle East surrounded the airport. Palm trees lined the roads, creating a natural archway into the airport. Cultivated grass and treated plants and flowers surrounded the airport walls. In stark contrast to the landscape's vibrant colors, all of the buildings and structures contained within the airport walls are a bleak, light shade of brown.

Soon the airport would be under our control. For a fight of this scale, I did not like the lack of a detailed plan and coordination. At NTC, a brigade attack would take at least twenty-four to forty-eight hours to plan and prepare. Now we would launch our attack with only a fraction of the prep time we had months earlier in the Mojave Desert. General Patton used to say that it was better to execute a not-so-perfect plan of attack violently than to wait for the perfect plan and the perfect set of conditions to begin the attack. Patton and others like him also believed that when an army had the initiative during the attack, it should keep on attacking.

Successful against a well-trained and better-equipped army half a century ago, Patton's tactics could certainly prove successful here. We had better equipment, and we had the momentum. The Iraqi military was in disarray. With less time to plan and rehearse complicated maneuvers, we had to adopt a simple concept of operation. And we would rely on individual skills and small unit leadership as key to our success.

Our campaign would culminate within the next couple of days. It had to—the soldiers were exhausted, and the equipment was breaking down. But the soldiers could now see the end. One more big push and that should be it. Task Force 2-7 soldiers would stay strong and motivated enough to carry them to the conclusion. The only way home now was through the airport . . . we were getting closer by the minute.

At approximately 1000 hours on April 3, the bulk of Task Force 2-7, minus Knight Company, were back on the road and began their march north to Objective Peach. Knight caught up to the rest of us on Peach a few hours later and then completed its refuel and mission preparation with its platoons in record time. In less than thirty minutes, all their equipment and weapons were ready to go and every soldier in the company knew exactly what they needed to do to accomplish the next mission.

Event 7, our final objective, was about to be reached. The next movement was no greater than twenty kilometers to our northwest. An easy movement a week ago, we would now drive without a moment's rest and after two days of continuous operations. The last thing I needed now was an accidental death or injury before the big fight ahead of us at the airport.

The scout platoon launched ahead of the task force to recon the route linking Objective Hannah to Objective Peach. As we quickly discovered, the route was littered with enemy dead. About every one hundred meters lay a dead Iraqi soldier, lining nearly the entire route to Objective Peach. It almost felt like we were back home driving on a typical Georgia highway weaving around armadillo carcasses littering the road, only this time the roadkill were human beings. It repulsed me to see wild dogs and swarms of flies feasting on the rotting dead. I hoped that the younger soldiers hadn't witnessed the same haunting scene as I had. Seeing something like that could never be unseen. There was no time to bury or consolidate these Iraqis. Follow-on units along with the Iraqis would perform this horrid task. Evidently, the remainder of our brigade and Task Force 2-69 Armor of the 3rd Brigade produced considerable damage along their way up to Objective Peach.

Due to the number of enemy remains we observed along the route, it was clear that the Iraqis did not want us to cross the Euphrates River. They put up a stubborn defense here. From the looks of the dead, they appeared to be wearing Republican Guard uniforms. The uniforms and boots were in good condition and most of the soldiers looked well groomed, all indicators of a professional and well-disciplined army—different from the ragtag forces we encountered in the south. These soldiers did not choose to run. Rather, they stood their ground and fought to the last man.

We were required to move into an attack position just west of Objective Peach while awaiting the order to cross the Euphrates River bridge. When we occupied the attack position, we immediately began tactical refueling operations and our priorities of work in preparation for our next move. An intelligence update reported the 17th Armored Brigade of the Hammurabi Division repositioned southwest of the airport as an attempt to block our advance. If the report was accurate, it could certainly affect our movement to the airport. We would need to break through a substantial enemy force before we could even get to the airport. We would have to fight for every inch of ground. I called in all company commanders and specialty platoon leaders to the TOC to be briefed on the updated plan of attack for the airport, Objective Lions.

Our brigade created a simple plan to seize the airport. Task Force 3-69 Armor would breach the airport's southwest corner, penetrating the eight-foot wall encompassing the airport. Then Task force 3-69 Armor and Task Force 3-7 Infantry would clear all the trenches, bunkers, hangars, and terminals inside of the airport. My unit, Task Force 2-7 Infantry, would skirt around the southern wall of the airport as quickly as possible and occupy a blocking position along the Highway 8 interchange, near the VIP entrance.

Task Force 2-7's mission was to block a potential enemy counterattack from the city. Highway 8 was a wide, high-speed avenue of approach—it was the most logical path enemy armor would take to try to retake the airport. Our blocking actions would protect Task Force's 3-7 Infantry and 3-69 Armor from the enemy. Task Force 3-7 and 3-69 were the brigade's decisive operation and my Task Force 2-7 was a shaping operation—a supporting mission. The entire operation would begin under the cover of darkness.

Task Force 2-7 would deploy into Objective Lions a little differently than it previously had on Objective Hannah. As a precaution, we would leave most of the task force's soft-skinned trucks behind, west of the Euphrates River. We needed to get to the airport quickly and could not slow down in the event the enemy targeted our lighter vehicles. Destroyed or disabled vehicles could block narrow passageways leading to the airport. And I did not have time to stop the attack to treat scores of wounded soldiers. My order primarily affected the supply trains and the medical platoon. Half of their fleet consisted of unprotected trucks. The medics protested the order. They predicted that the task force would sustain a significant number of casualties at the airport, so they wanted to deploy at full strength. They would have to do the best they could with what they had.

I made one exception to the order: I allowed Captain Paul to bring up his three trucks with his mortar platoon. The trucks themselves and the soldiers riding in them were necessary to accomplishing his mission. The trucks contained all the spare ammunition, and I knew I might need to shoot all the ammunition at the airport. The mortars needed to be forward with all their ammunition because the Euphrates was far out of mortar range from our airport blocking position on Highway 8.

The medics and each of the company's supporting assets would have to cross-load equipment and personnel into their armored vehicles. Essentially, they needed to cram as many soldiers and equipment they could into vehicles with enough armor protection to stop a bullet. It was hard to find the space. Critical supplies and personnel could not take the trip. Consequently, the supporting trains and medical platoon could only detach small sections to support the attack.

At the request of First Lieutenant Gleason, the scout platoon leader, the scout platoon would not lead the twenty-kilometer movement to the airport. The scouts operated in semiarmored HMMWVs, and the platoon leader thought it prudent to intermingle his platoon between the Bradley and tank companies to maximize their own protection. We were about to leap into unfamiliar enemy territory where we believed the enemy was making his last stand. Removing the scouts from the lead position was significant because the scouts were experts in land navigation and route reconnaissance. These critical skills were tested and proved their worth time and again throughout our three-hundred-mile journey from Kuwait. If the latest intelligence was correct, we would have to fight our way to the airport. Repositioning the scouts was a hard choice—I needed the scouts to provide early warning to our formation so it could deploy to the right place and time to fight and win. But I also did not want to lose my scouts. If they drove through a prepared enemy engagement area, that would be the end of my scouts. The risk was too great, so we adapted.

I did not want to make decisions based on a lack of information or poor intelligence. At this point in the war, the tactical intelligence was not accurate or timely. Making plans based entirely on assumptions could be dangerous. Our attack to the airport assumed that the Republican Guard would fight us along the way. Even though intelligence estimated the Guard at only 60 percent strength, it was likely they would still mount a defense. Consequently, our route between the Euphrates and the airport would be contested. My ability to resupply our fighting forces in the airport would not happen until the airport and the battlespace between the river and the airport was secure. Casualty evacuation by ground was also out of the question. We would have to treat our casualties forward and perhaps we could evac by air—they may have to wait a long time. These tactical choices meant that speed was imperative. We would need this fight to be over fast or else we would run out of bullets and gas and our soldiers would die from their wounds.

My task force plan called for aggressiveness and a relentless effort to remain on the offensive. Maintaining a static and passive posture at our blocking position would make us vulnerable to attack. We learned from our blocking position at Objective Raiders the risks and the consequences—the enemy would take advantage. It could attack us head on with their tanks or infantry, or it could hit us from a distance with mortars or artillery. If it was desperate, it could deploy suicide trucks or even chemical weapons. I did need to maintain a core defense, but most of my formation would remain on the move, attacking in different directions—keeping the enemy off balance and creating a blanket of security east of the airport. Hopefully we would not deplete all our supplies before we called our logistics forward.

We would begin our attack with Rage in the lead, followed by mortars, Bushmaster, Scouts, and Knight. When we arrived at our blocking position east of the airport proper, Rage would penetrate and clear the SRG compound south of Highway 8 and Bushmaster would do the same in the SRG compound north of the highway. The two SRG sites protected the airport's eastern flank and needed to be taken or destroyed. The side that could control the two compounds could control all the major approaches leading into the airport from the east. Due to the masonry works and redoubts at both compounds, the enemy could put up a stubborn defense there.

Knight would set conditions for Bushmaster and Rage. It had to open up the battlespace by pushing east to Baghdad along Highway 8. Knight's attack along Highway 8 would not only help Bushmaster and Rage, it would also threaten Baghdad. It could force the enemy to dig in and abandon any plans to counterattack the airport. Best case, it might also force the enemy to abandon the fight altogether. The Iraqis' will and ability to fight was already crumbling from our attack through Karbala. It might not take much to push the Iraqis to surrender or quit. Scouts, mortars, and engineers would maintain a static, defensive posture in the Highway 8 blocking position at a four-way intersection we referred to as the "Four Corners." My PSYOPS and smoke assets would join them. Medics would set up and treat any casualties inside this space. Armored supply and recovery vehicles would also sit inside of Four Corners. My team at Four Corners would form the nucleus of the Task Force 2-7 blocking position—our center of gravity.

My operations officer, Major Coffey, adjourned the mission briefing with this sobering observation: "Unless I'm reading the map incorrectly, it looks like Task Force 2-7 Infantry will be the first ground unit to enter Baghdad." Technically, he was correct. As depicted on our 1:100,000 scale maps we were issued back in Kuwait, the route into our blocking position took us through the southwestern boundary of the city. Knight would then push east into the city as far as they could go. We were about to become the first American ground force in history to enter Baghdad.

At 1500 hours, our task force moved out of our attack position and proceeded to cross the Euphrates River. Knight Company rejoined us at 1400 hours and we were now at full strength. About thirty uniformed enemy prisoners were under guard and lined up near the entrance of the bridge. They all looked exhausted, hungry, and resigned to their fate. They almost looked relieved—relieved that they did not have to die for a lost cause. These same Iraqi river defenders from the day prior would now watch our entire task force cross it unopposed. As I drove past and looked into their eyes, it was obvious to me that they knew the war was over. The outcome was inevitable. We weren't just crossing a river, we were turning a page in Iraq's history and its future would be very different from the past.

Over the past few days, I had spoken with Iraqi officers and senior NCOs who had surrendered. They were awed by our Bradleys and Abrams and surprised by our momentum. Like us, they worried about families and fellow soldiers. What struck me most was their pride—elite, professional soldiers who still gave up. That told me the dominos had fallen: Karbala, then Hannah and Peach. Our push through the Karbala Gap may have been the first, and Hannah and Peach sealed the war's fate. Victory was inevitable but not easy. Large Iraqi formations were gone, yet we would still face fierce resistance, especially from those with the most to lose.

One lane of the two-lane bridge in front of us was near impassable by vehicle traffic. The Iraqis defending Objective Peach the night prior managed to detonate a few of their explosives rigged to only one side of the bridge. Engineers were in the process of laying a makeshift pontoon bridge about one hundred meters north of here. In the meantime, our brigade had to use what was left of the Iraqi bridge, miraculously still standing. Time was not a luxury of ours at the time. Waiting for the perfect river crossing was not an option.

The bridge itself was a bottleneck of traffic, worse than rush hour in Manhattan. Vehicles mixed from other units were perched on the bridge, and their presence created a major obstacle to our movement. The myriad combat and support vehicles lining the bridge comprised a tossed salad of friendly units. Artillery, engineer, and even boat units from the division and corps contributed to the congestion. My operations officer, Major Coffey, dismounted from his Bradley and shepherded the task force across. We made it across the bridge after two hours of snaking around the scores of friendly vehicles. The sun was beginning to settle below the horizon. Our movement would be conducted in total darkness, and this time without the luxury of our headlights or the scouts leading the way.

We were the rear element in the brigade's order of march, trailing behind our brigade's 3-69 Armor, 3-7 Infantry, and 1-41 Field Artillery Battalions. Our attack on the airport was preceded by a one-hour preparation of rocket artillery and tactical air support. These fire support assets were given strict guidance not to target the runway or civilian aircraft. Both would be necessary after the war. The runway could allow the coalition to sustain itself with supplies and reinforcements and the civilian aircraft could help reinvigorate the Iraqi economy. After the sun went down, I could observe the light from the explosions in the airport as we made our approach. They were so brilliant, the explosions literally turned night into day.

Our movement took us through a few small towns. They were ghost towns—not a single pedestrian on the street, just a few young men driving trucks on secondary roads paralleling the two-lane highway we were transiting—perhaps reconnaissance soldiers obtaining intel on our location, size, and capabilities for their commanders in Baghdad. Their actions were curious but not hostile. Had we spotted a single weapon, the trucks would have been toast.

There were homes, other buildings, and structures along our route, but they were all quiet for now. We did not see any Iraqi soldiers there; in fact, we barely saw any Iraqis at all. These were suburbs, not tightly packed, built-up areas like As Samawah. The Iraqis would not have been able to mount the same type of stubborn defense here. But still, I expected some level of resistance. This was no gauntlet like our intel suggested it might be. I was beginning to question whether "Fortress Baghdad" was a myth. In any event, we needed to remain alert and not devolve into complacency.

We drove on single- and double-lane secondary roads composed of hard asphalt. The roads and how they were depicted on our maps were confusing to the navigator, and about five kilometers into the drive we made our first wrong turn, requiring the entire task force to turn around. Rather than reorient the entire task force, I ordered each individual vehicle to turn instead, creating a new task force order of march with Knight now in the lead followed by scouts, Bushmaster, mortars, and Rage. Approximately two kilometers after the reorganization of the task force's formation, we took another wrong turn and were compelled to change the order once again. The enemy did not need to attack us to disrupt our movement—we were our own worst enemy.

It was now getting dark, and the rest of the brigade was closing in on the airport. Lieutenant Colonel Rock Marcone and his Task Force 3-69 Armor were at the tip of the spear, and Lieutenant Colonel Jack Kammerer's Task Force 3-7 Infantry followed closely behind. My two battle buddies and their troopers would be fighting hard in the airport soon, and I knew they needed my help. I needed to move faster.

Bushmaster now led the march, followed by mortars, Knight, scouts, and Rage. Surprisingly, these suburbs still offered no enemy resistance. If I was on the Iraqi side, I could have done any number of simple things to stop our advance. A few mines, a couple of artillery missions, or any obstacle could have worked. The route was so tight and we were so disoriented, any form of contact would have been a game changer. But the Iraqis did not lay a single strand of barbed wire or dig a single ditch on any part of our route leading to the airport.

The door was wide open, and it was crazy to me. Either the Iraqi military still relied on these roads for their own mobility or they never really intended to mount a serious defense. The Iraqis may have assumed that we would never make it across the Euphrates—that they could beat us back or knock down its own bridges before we crossed. In any event, the drive to the airport was just spooky, especially given all our enemy encounters in the south. I am glad the enemy did not realize how vulnerable we were that night.

Aside from Iraqi soldiers, we had many enemies. The weather and the terrain would take its toll on us. The sun, on numerous occasions, served as one of our greatest adversaries. Nicknamed and endeared to many soldiers as "Bob," during combat operations, the sun can be your best friend or your worst enemy. Bob's heat worked against us while wearing our heavy chemical suits. His light reflected on our formation during the day and made our presence known to the enemy—most of our soldiers killed at this point were killed in broad daylight. Bob negates our technological advantages that we rely on while fighting at night. The sun could help us navigate the rest of the way to the airport, but it would make us vulnerable. We would be seen and targeted, and the heat would add to our physical exhaustion. Some of us had not eaten or slept in days. And while fighting in the heat in and around Baghdad, we would have to ration our water because our resupply was back at the Euphrates River. Like Objective Hannah, our attack on Objective Lions would be a very long day and we had no idea how or when it would end

Our movement picked up some momentum and about three to four kilometers into the march, the environment and its surrounding terrain had taken new form. The roads we were now traversing were composed of narrow corridors of dirt irrigation trails and causeways, leading from one onion farm to the next. These were farm roads. The semiurban scene transformed into a rural, agrarian-type setting, consisting of a few homes surrounded by acres of crops and livestock.

Along the march, we made minor enemy contact in the form of two- to four-man enemy ambushes and probes. I believed they were Republican Guard or SRG scouts, posted along our route as an early warning to their main force defending the airport. They were disciplined. They knew where to hide, how to engage, and when to disengage and displace. They created a zone of disruption—it appeared that the enemy attempted to prolong our movement by forcing us to divert resources away from our attack.

The enemy scouts would emerge from their hide positions long enough to shoot then disappear into the darkness. They could also gather and report good intelligence about us based on our reaction. The Iraqi command in the airport and in Baghdad could use this information to their advantage—assuming the Iraqis still had a functioning command and control structure in place.

The enemy's repeated attempts at disruption failed. They were too insignificant to make a difference. We continued our movement and fought through the enemy's harassing fire as quickly as we could. We returned fire on each of the confirmed and suspected enemy positions as we sped by along our route. When an enemy was spotted, the grid coordinates of the location were pinpointed and subsequently relayed to every element within the task force. Without stopping, each unit unloaded a few rounds of ammunition. We had to make haste because we were now behind schedule. The rest of the brigade had already entered the airport and were beginning to clear it. They were depending on us to protect their eastern flank from an Iraqi counterattack.

Along the route, our task force approached a narrow irrigation bridge, and at a glance it appeared incapable of supporting the weight of our vehicles. Bushmaster chanced it and crossed anyway. Unfortunately, their trail vehicle carrying their first sergeant, First Sergeant Wilson, along with all their medical and recovery assets became mired on the far side of the bridge, blocking the rest of us on the near side. Bushmaster's trail vehicle was stuck in the one spot that could totally obstruct the passage for the remainder of the task force. The advance of four companies plus attachments—several hundred soldiers, fourteen tanks, and thirty Bradleys—was ground to a complete halt. We were dead in the water.

While sitting here, with the task force halted at the foot of the bridge, I couldn't help but recount the shortcomings of World War II's Operation Market Garden. It was a bold plan that could have ended the war, if successful. There was only one problem—the route. It depended on trafficable routes with functioning bridges. Our plan had the same dependency, and now we were at a standstill.

While I was pondering our next course of action, the section sergeant from the mortar platoon, Sergeant Johnson, quickly developed a solution to the problem:

> SERGEANT JOHNSON: "Thunder 6, this is Thunder 5, I see an open field to our left and a trail leading into it. The task force can turn around there."

CAPTAIN PAUL: "Thunder 5, this is Thunder 6 roger, good work, thanks."

CAPTAIN PAUL: "Able 6, this is Thunder 6, there is an open field up here, we can turn the task force around here."

LIEUTENANT COLONEL RUTTER: "Thunder 6, this is Able 6, roger. Good work. Execute. Out."

CAPTAIN PAUL: "Thunder 5, this is Thunder 6, I need you to help me guide the task force around."

SERGEANT JOHNSON: "Thunder 6, this is Thunder 5, roger."

The progress was slow because it was dark and disorienting. Consequently, it took about two hours to completely reorient the task force. Sergeant Johnson went to ground and played traffic cop, directing every vehicle in the convoy onto the right path. One of his squads dismounted and helped shepherd and the task force around the field and back onto the road.

We observed three explosions to our northeast while guiding vehicles through the field. Each explosion developed into a mushroom cloud and effectively turned night into day. Anyone unfortunate to be wearing night vision goggles at the time was temporarily blinded by the blast, almost as bright as the desert sun.

I suspected that the explosions were either friendly bombs or enemy missiles. The light was so brilliant that it looked like the source could have been Daisy Cutters, twenty-thousand-pound aerosol bombs dropped by the Air Force. But after I thought about it, this theory did not make any sense. Why would we drop so much ordnance on the airport? We needed the airport intact after the war. If we broke it now, we would have to fix it later, and that would not be fast or easy. Then I thought that maybe the brigade encountered sizable resistance and needed the extra firepower. It wasn't clear what was happening at the airport by simply monitoring the radio traffic. We would discover days later that the explosions observed on this night were actually secondary explosions from three Iraqi Airways jumbo jets lining the tarmac of Saddam International Airport.

Bushmaster would remain on the far side of the bridge. They miraculously found a main road leading up to the airport. My operations officer, Major Rod Coffey, and I backtracked and proceeded to link up with the lead elements of Bushmaster's column. We quickly consolidated and continued the attack into the airport blocking position. We left the rest of the task force behind with my executive officer, Major Kevin Cooney, in charge. His mission was to turn the task force around as rapidly as possible and lead it to the airport blocking position. We would be there waiting for them.

Along the route, Bushmaster bumped into a field ambulance unit left behind from 2nd Brigade along with the 1-64 Armor Command Sergeant Major. For their own safety, they commandeered this unit, and their medical support proved vital during the initial seizure and the ensuing battle for Saddam International Airport the next day. Female soldiers were part of this unit.

What made this moment historic was that female medics—meant for rear-area care—would soon fight through chaos and treat wounded Task Force 2–7 soldiers at the very heart of the fiercest fighting. In 2003, regulations strictly prohibited female soldiers from serving in combat units below the brigade level—we would have to ask for forgiveness later.

At 0100 on April 4, Bushmaster occupied the task force blocking position after encountering only scattered enemy resistance along the way. During their occupation, the Air Force targeted several enemy tanks in and around the airport. At this point in the war, my brigade was the coalition's main effort; therefore our airpower was stacked several layers deep in the sky and in position to engage the enemy on the ground at a moment's notice. We didn't need to wait long for bombs to drop. Bushmaster could not see any signs of enemy armor but could certainly feel the effects from the bombs. They were loud and they shook the earth.

While rattled and shaken by the explosions, they discovered numerous weapons caches hidden in bunkers along Highway 8, leading into the airport. It was a strange thing for American soldiers to see. The American soldier is taught to never abandon their weapon or leave it unguarded. Perhaps the bad guys were close by. The Iraqis either abandoned the fight or we caught them by surprise. If they intended to fight and knew we were coming, they would not have left their bunkers unguarded or kept their weapons so far out of reach. These were supposed to be professional and loyal soldiers guarding the airport, so I deduced that we took them by surprise.

Around the same time, the rest of the task force under Major Cooney postured to continue its movement to the airport. About one hundred meters into the drive, one of Rage's tanks from First Lieutenant Sigler's platoon drifted into a drainage ditch lining the road. The tank blocked half the width of the road. As bad luck would have it, a mortar carrier threw one of its tracks only a few meters beyond the tank opposite the road, creating a serpentine-like obstacle inhibiting traffic.

As Captain Paul passed the tank, he received the unfortunate call from one of his squad leaders: "Thunder 6, this is Thunder 1, I just threw track." The only response he could utter out of his mouth was, "What do you mean you threw track." "I mean, I threw track," his squad leader responded. "You have five minutes to fix it." Paul was hoping that the track was still intact but simply disconnected from the support roller. All they would have to do is pry the treads back in with a tanker's bar. As Paul drove up to the vehicle, he learned that he would not be so lucky. The track was broken. The crew would have to do a complete fix job. Paul knew it would take time, but he was hoping for a miracle.

Five minutes came and went. They couldn't wait here any longer and delay the rest of the task force. "Thunder 1, this is Thunder 6, we've got to go. I will call the combat trains and try to get some mechanics up here to help you. If they don't show up, First Sergeant Wilson is back down the road one hundred meters. His track is stuck in the mud on the other side of the bridge. If you are left here and don't get help from the trains, call him on his company radio frequency. Don't try to catch up to us and drive by yourselves. There is enemy out here. If you can piggyback with the trains or another follow-on unit, do so. Meanwhile you must provide your own security here. Coordinate with Rage's tank next to you and work together. Do you understand, over." "Thunder 6, this is Thunder 1, roger."

Captain Paul did not want to leave these guys behind, but he knew the task force could not afford to leave an additional mortar carrier behind to guard the one that was stuck. We would need at least three of the four guns to support the task force. I could not count on getting the brigade's field artillery to prioritize my mission, and I also knew resupply would lag. Captain Paul knew they would be safe if the tank and First Sergeant Wilson were nearby. They were not alone. This squad was a competent and aggressive crew and had a lot of experience through training and now combat. Nevertheless, their platoon leader was still worried about them.

The task force was bottlenecked once again. Within the chokepoint, the larger tanks and Bradleys only had a few feet of clearance to maneuver through to get to the other side. It would take time for the remainder of the task force to snake around the two dead vehicles and reconsolidate on the far side of the obstacle.

The movement from Objective Peach to Lions was the ugliest movement my task force has ever made, in combat or in training. If we performed like this at NTC, we would have been made to perform the movement over again, from start to finish and as many times as necessary until we got it right. And after the first few failed attempts, the task force would probably have a new commander! Removing my scouts from the lead was a bad decision, and it led to the chaos and dysfunction that night.

Fortunately, the remainder of the movement was uneventful, but it was a challenge to stay awake and alert. The task force was going on three days with very little time for food and water and with practically no time for rest. I was taught in Army leadership schools that performance declines by 25 percent with every twenty-four hours of no sleep—we were now operating at little more than 25 percent effectiveness. Drivers were falling asleep at the wheel and on a few occasions were playing bumper cars with the vehicle in front of them every time they nodded off and the formation came to an abrupt halt. It was bumper cars the whole way to the airport. We probably did more damage to our own vehicles in one single movement than the enemy did to us throughout the entire march up.

Staff Sergeant Gains from the scout platoon now led the task force, with Knight, Rage, remaining scouts, and mortars following closely behind. The formation experienced a few breaks in contact—whereby vehicle commanders could not see the vehicle in front of them. This created some disruption and delay but was not significant. They managed to reestablish contact quickly every time. Land navigation was near impossible. Everything looked the same and it was completely dark, with minimal illumination provided by the crescent moon. Those vehicles equipped with either a global positioning system or Blue Force Tracker fared better than the others. As we got closer to the airport, we started to see brigade scouts posted at critical intersections directing traffic, ensuring our formation remained on the correct path.

The bulk of Task Force 2-7 reached the outskirts of the airport around 0500 and it was beginning to get light. They traveled on the one-lane road paralleling the southern wall of the airport. The trees lining both sides produced a natural low-hanging archway into our blocking position. It was surprisingly quiet. How could it be so quiet? No gunfire, no explosions. It was an eerie feeling. What happened to the SRG? Did they run at the mere sight of our tanks? Has the Iraqi military surrendered? These were the questions that were weighing on my mind at the time. It was a tenuous period—the side that could find and target the other first would gain the initiative. I felt like I was playing a game of hide and seek, with guns. The enemy was supposed to be here, but they weren't. And now I was concerned. I am not sure if we had the element of surprise or if they did.

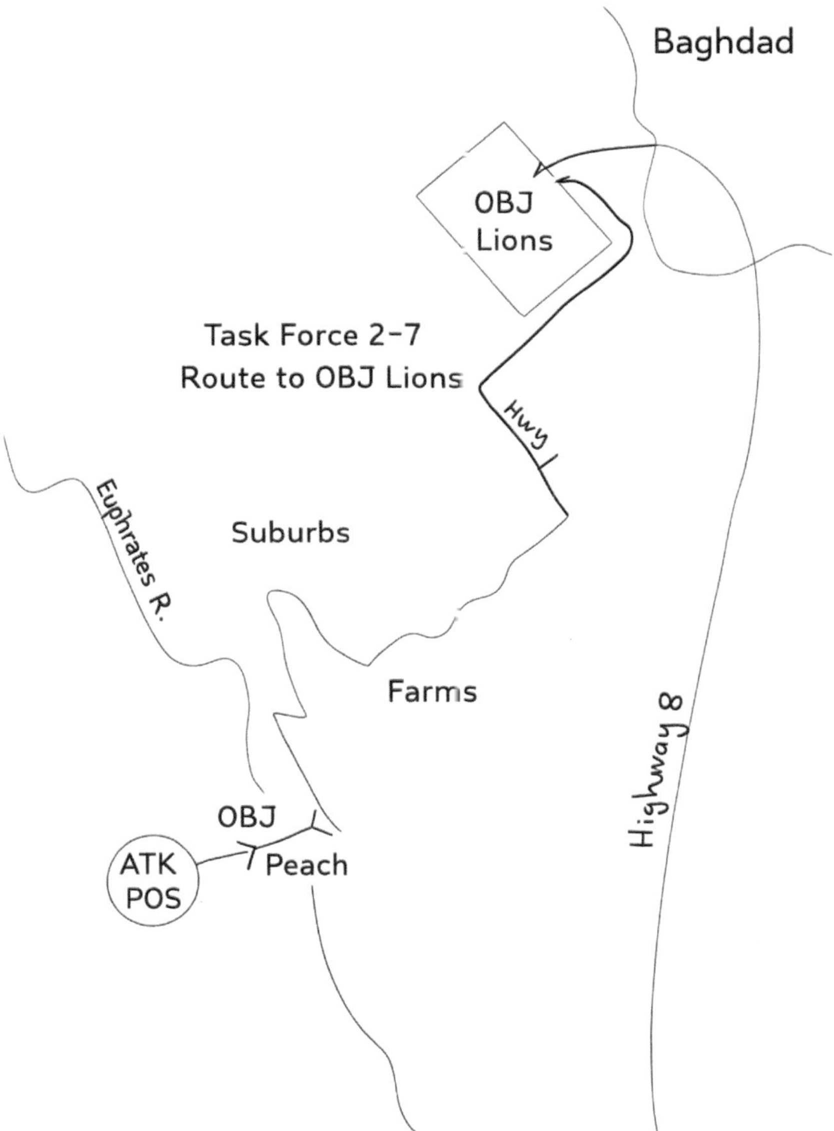

Movement from Objective Peach to Objective Lions, Saddam International Airport, April 3–4, 2003.
Source: Author's image.

The mortar platoon, under Captain Paul, was the last combat element in the task force to arrive. As the mortars closed into the blocking position around 0530, Bradleys and tanks of each company were preparing to conduct their attacks on to their respective SRG compounds. With the exception of the mortar platoon, the remainder of the task force would remain inside the Highway 8 interchange, identified as Four Corners. Each of the company's support elements, the scout platoon, medics, a Bushmaster-attached engineer platoon, and a PSYOPS team all occupied this densely packed space just east of the airport walls.

Captain Paul recognized the cramped conditions inside the Highway 8 interchange and asked my permission to set up his mortars elsewhere. I told Captain Paul that if he felt he could secure his platoon outside of Four Corners that it was okay for him to do so. I had to trust my leaders' best judgment and give each of them enough freedom to accomplish their missions. I was not a micromanager. Captain Paul found an open patch of ground about a kilometer south of the interchange, and it was large enough to properly set up his guns. Mortars typically required at least a football field to space out and set up correctly—they did not find anything close to that at Four Corners.

The mortar platoon pulled into their firing position and discovered scores of well-prepared bunkers and sandbagged guard towers surrounding them. Captain Paul ordered his platoon to "recon by fire" and place some well-aimed .50 caliber and 40mm grenade machine gun fire into each enemy fighting position. After they cleared the positions with fire, they dismounted and proceeded to visually and systematically clear each surrounding structure on foot. This was a precaution and was necessary for their own protection. Captain Paul did not want to take any chances. An enemy sniper or artillery observer could have caused significant damage to the platoon. The platoon was small and each mortarman played a critical role. With one of their gun crews left behind, the mortars were now only operating at 75 percent strength—they could not afford to lose a single soldier.

While searching a nearby office building, Captain Paul found a desk with an SRG beret and a general's uniform hanging up in a closet. In this desk, he found Polaroids of this general posed with Saddam Hussein. The mortar platoon also searched a nearby and recently vacated barracks building. The SRG soldiers lived well compared to those of the Iraqi Regular Army. They had clean showers, refrigerators packed with food, dry-cleaned uniforms hanging neatly in their large walk-in closets, and rolls of money in their desks. If these soldiers were treated so well by the regime, why were they not out here fighting to protect it?

A series of events began to unfold shortly after the powerful early morning sun—Bob— crested the horizon. Major Kevin Cooney, interpreting the silence as safety and security, walked away from the TOC and found a nearby patch of bushes, ideal cover to download three days' worth of processed MREs. His junior officers barked jokes and snapped photographs of him while squatting in the necessary but undignified position. Smiles turned to frowns when the first bullets and RPGs whipped past the XO, transforming a bad situation into a much, much worse situation. Dazed and still disrobed, Kevin managed to quickly bound back to seek cover in the TOC. This one comical yet serious event marked the turning point in our campaign west of the Euphrates. It was a seminal moment. The Iraqis would organize and fight back, hard—the sustained intensity of the fighting over the next week would be like nothing we had encountered up to this point in the war.

Minutes later, Rage and Bushmaster began their offensive operations on the northern and southern SRG compounds and began to make enemy contact. To our west, Task Force 3-69 and 3-7 Cavalry Squadron began to make enemy contact. Enemy tanks and infantry were mounting a hasty counterattack. It appeared that Iraqi soldiers were now directing their forces to fight on multiple fronts—fighting their way into and out of our lines at the same time. In fact, after initial contact, lines ceased to exist once the enemy's infantry cut us off from the rest of my brigade to our west. Parts of my task force were surrounded and outnumbered, and would have to fight in all directions.

Small arms fire erupted from every direction as the task force began to improve their positions throughout the blocking position. The fire reverberated with a high pitch—it was not friendly fire. The entire task force scanned their sectors. We stirred up a hornet's nest. The Iraqis counterattacked us on their own terms—waiting for daylight and initiating contact by first targeting our lightly armed and lightly armored units. The Iraqis took a run at my TOC first. That was smart, and it was something I would do if the tables were turned—take out the other side's command and control before expanding my attack across the depth of my enemy's formation. I just didn't know how in the world they were able to get that close, and out of nowhere. I needed to get the TOC some help, fast. At the same time, I couldn't neglect our main attacks to the east.

I ordered Knight to attack further east along Highway 8. Creeping east along the highway, the tank company engaged scores of Iraqi fighting positions paralleling the eastbound and westbound portions of the road. The tanks fired 120mm high-explosive rounds at the larger, fortified positions. The Bradleys engaged the smaller positions with 25mm armor-piercing ammunition to soften them up initially, then destroying them with three-round bursts of high-explosive ammunition—designed to explode upon contact.

Knight continued to advance east into the city, with their forces split between the eastbound and westbound portions of the highway. When Knight reached its limit of advance, First Lieutenant Johnson's infantry platoon dismounted and cleared the fighting positions the armor had just engaged. The clearing patrols included the wooded areas flanking the highway on both sides. Johnson's platoon uncovered body parts, uniforms, and maps in their search. One map depicted every Iraqi bunker in and around Baghdad.

Many questions remained unanswered about the enemy defending the airport on April 4, 2003. The night before, as we occupied our blocking position, we saw not a single guard tower manned along the airport wall, and every entry and exit point lay completely unguarded. Then the SRG appeared out of nowhere en masse, prepared and angry. Even now I cannot say whether their ferocity came from aggression or sheer desperation.

Interrogations after the battle revealed that our early morning activity caught the enemy completely off guard. They had no idea we were already inside their perimeter. The sounds of bombs and artillery the night before had masked the whine of our maneuvering Bradleys and tanks. The Iraqis assumed the blasts were just more of the air campaign hammering the city like the last two weeks of "shock and awe." Expecting an airborne drop or helicopter assault, they had oriented most of their weapons inward and upward—never outward. They did not anticipate an armored thrust straight into the airport.

The surprise was total. One Bushmaster soldier recalled watching an Iraqi step out of his bunker at dawn to relieve himself. Unarmed, unarmored, and unaware, he stood less than seventy-five meters away completely exposed, with an entire platoon of Bradleys already locked onto him.

Iraqi soldiers and airmen drove to work this morning as they would any other morning. They believed that we were bogged down in southern Iraq and were nowhere near Baghdad. Highway 8 was the most common route leading to and from the airport, and most of the Iraqi soldiers who owned vehicles were either Air Force or SRG officers. Knight positioned tanks astride all four lanes of the prominent highway.

When the darkness lifted, civilian cars began to flow in. For two hours, at least one car every ten minutes would drive down the westbound side of the road. It was obvious that they were unaware of our presence. Knight gave them ample opportunity to turn around and go back where they came from. The M1 tanks were in plain view along the road. First Knight would sit patiently for the incoming cars to close enough distance to see its tanks and turn away. If the Iraqis continued to advance, Knight would then escalate to firing warning shots over or around the car to force it off the highway.

It was impossible for us to know the Iraqi motorists' intentions the morning of April 4, 2003. We could not know if their intentions were hostile or not. We knew from Objective Raiders that the Iraqis would resort to suicide bombings as a weapon. Nothing the Iraqis did throughout the war seemed to make much sense. We attacked the airport and occupied Highway 8, and the Iraqis still chose to drive to the airport to work that morning. It was surreal. But eventually, that morning, the Iraqis in and around the airport were able to recalibrate and reorganize to fight us with everything they had at their disposal.

Since the war began, few Marine or Army units made significant contact with Iraqi T-72 main battle tanks. These Russian-made tanks were the showcase of the Republican Guard's armored forces—the most lethal, mobile, and survivable piece of equipment in their entire warfighting arsenal. Intelligence suggested that some of these systems were even retrofitted with new thermal optics, almost on par with that of our M1A1 main battle tanks. The Iraqis kept these tanks hidden and preserved for the final battle, the defense of their capital city. The tanks were to be used at their decisive place and time, when they absolutely needed them the most and when the coalition's unrelenting aerial bombardment finally lifted, enabling the tanks to move freely from one spot to the next. Intelligence estimated that two dozen T-72s would remain fully operational following the bombing campaign. Once the conditions were set, the T-72s would uncoil and spring from their hide positions, smashing into our lines with brute force.

My mortar platoon was the first Task Force 2-7 element to make contact with the elite Iraqi armor during the battle for Saddam International Airport. At Captain Matt Paul's request, they were out there isolated and out of sight from the rest of task force, set up on the extreme southern flank of the formation and at least a kilometer away from the nearest friendly tank or Bradley. And they were on their own, from a defense or security standpoint.

Matt wanted an ideal spot to emplace his guns. Ideally, the guns should be spread out a good distance to maximize the mortars' effects on the intended target. The most important thing any mortar platoon could do was occupy an ideal firing position to shoot from and to point the guns in the right direction, where enemy contact was expected. It needed to be close enough to the action to support the task force and range the enemy targets, but it also needed to be far enough away to avoid a direct exchange with the enemy. The mortar carrier that threw track the night prior was limping closer to the airport but still separated from the rest of the platoon the morning of April 4. So Matt knew he needed his three remaining guns in the best possible position to support the task force in the big fight ahead.

The tight spot within the Highway 8 interchange (Four Corners) would not meet Matt's needs. And due to the lack of enemy contact thus far, we all felt it was safe enough to start spreading out. Moreover, it was unwise to put too many critical assets in one place for too long. At one point in the morning of April 4, a sole Iraqi missile could have taken out over half of my task force's combat power at the Four Corners blocking position. Spreading out was a good idea. The mortar platoon was about to put all their skills to the test. Their survival would rely on teamwork, warrior spirit, and a whole lot of luck.

From the mortar firing position, Captain Matt Paul paired up with his base gun squad leader, Sergeant Jose Hernandez, and proceeded to pinpoint the source of enemy machine gun fire they could hear from a distance. Promoted to captain just prior to our deployment to Kuwait, Matt held down the job as my mortar platoon leader for over two years. He was about as trained and experienced as they come. He was also a critical thinker and a perfectionist—he never left well enough alone. He placed himself in personal danger here to not only benefit his men but to increase the effectiveness of his platoon and benefit the entire task force.

Captain Paul could hear the enemy fire but could not pinpoint the source or even estimate the precise direction or distance to it. The sound of gunfire seemed to originate from every direction. The airport's high walls created an echo. He wanted to assess the enemy situation and determine how best to improve the defensibility of his new firing position. He also wasn't sure if his guns needed to be repositioned and reoriented on a different direction of fire—the mortars needed to point to where the enemy gunfire was the loudest and most concentrated. While listening closely, he and Sergeant Hernandez combed the area around the firing position for signs of enemy presence and reconned likely enemy avenues of approach. This enabled them to identify ideal locations to position their observation posts and antiarmor weapons.

Captain Paul and Sergeant Hernandez patrolled for about one hour. Their survey of the surrounding area separated them from the rest of the platoon by over three hundred meters. They decided that as only a two-man buddy team, this was a little too far to be separated from the remainder of the platoon, especially while the task force was in contact with the enemy nearby. They proceeded to turn back and walk along the same road that they initially took into the position earlier this morning.

A minute into the walk back to the platoon, they heard the sound of a tank moving along the road behind them. They turned and spotted one of my M1 tanks heading in their direction. It was towing another tank. They decided to wave to the tank to ensure the gunner and tank commander knew they were friendly. They didn't want to fall victim to fratricide here; they made it too far in this war now to be killed by one of their own. As they approached, Captain Paul discovered that the tanks belonged to Rage Company. The lead tank was dispatched to a spot along the route approximately ten kilometers away to recover a mired tank left behind during the march up from Objective Peach. The tank commander's mission was to hook up his wingman's tank and tow it the rest of the way back to the airport. Staff Sergeant McDoogle, mounting his trusty Abrams identified as "B22," asked them where the blocking position was located, and the two on the ground properly directed him.

Less than a minute later and while walking alongside the road, they heard another rumble. It shook the earth, like an M1 Abrams would feel. They both nonchalantly turned and proceeded to wave to the trailing tanks, same as before. With their right hands in the air, they quickly discerned that these tanks were not of an American design. The long barrel, the dome-shaped turret, and the driver's V-shaped splashguard on the tank's forward hull clearly proved that they were not friendly. They were T-72s! Two T-72s were barreling down the road, less than seventy-five meters from where they were standing. Another T-72 traveled about two hundred meters behind the lead two. The two mortarmen were frozen and then confused when both Iraqi tank commanders smiled and cordially waved back at them.

What was going on here? Captain Paul questioned. Are they surrendering? Do they think we are surrendering? Do they think we are Iraqi soldiers? In any case, the two were not going to stay and find out the enemy tankers' intentions. Captain Paul looked at his squad leader and shouted,

"T-72s, T-72s!" "Oh shit!" Sergeant Hernandez properly replied. Nothing more had to be said. They quickly turned and darted back toward the platoon. Sergeant Hernandez ran to the right and Captain Paul to the left. KAKAKAK! The T-72 crewman began engaging them with a continuous volume of machine gun fire. ZINGZINGZING. The sounds of bullets flying past their heads compelled them to run in a zigzag pattern, making it difficult for the Iraqis to zero in on them. As a former Bradley commander, Matt knew how hard it was to engage small moving targets.

Captain Paul feared that he would be shot in the back and not make it the entire way back to the platoon. He sought cover in a small drainage ditch next to the airport's eight-foot wall. A two-foot-tall barrier nearby along with some tall grass provided Paul with limited cover and concealment from the tanks. He hoped that they didn't see him jump into the ditch. Sergeant Hernandez was fortunate to make it the entire distance back to the platoon in one piece. He was a fast runner. When asked by Sergeant First Class Broadwater what had happened, Sergeant Hernandez responded with a cold, blank stare. It looked like he had seen a ghost. KAKAKAK!

The mortar platoon could hear the staccato of 7.62mm bullets ricochet off the small two-foot wall that now protected Captain Paul from the tanks. He hoped that the Iraqis thought that they had killed him. Matt felt like the "man in black" must have felt back at Al Musayyib (Objective Hannah) right before he died. He hoped that they would not spare a 125mm round to finish him off. A tank shell could easily cut through the small barrier protecting Paul. He was now pinned down and had nowhere to go. He thought he might be able to jump over the eight-foot wall behind him but quickly dismissed that as an option. The tanks were no more than fifty meters away and their guns were trained directly at his location. Captain Paul could not make it over the wall in time. How could the tank crews possibly miss him?

Recognizing their untenable position, the mortar platoon broke contact and fled back to the Four Corners blocking position. They did what they were trained to do and reacted as they should have. It was textbook. If the mortars got entangled fighting the enemy head on, they could not do their job to provide fire support for the rest of the task force. The mortar platoon is supposed to know where the fighting is happening, then position itself in the best position possible to set up its guns—close enough to the action but in a covered and concealed location away from enemy fire or observation. Some enemy contact is acceptable and unavoidable, but under no circumstances is it optimal for mortar platoons to try to fight tank platoons.

Sergeant First Class Broadwater was a great mortar platoon sergeant. He was courageous, adaptable, and he always knew when to follow the NCO playbook. When the platoon arrived at the Four Corners blocking position, he took a headcount. Sergeant First Class Broadwater quickly discovered that his platoon leader, Captain Paul, was missing—perhaps still out there under fire. He promptly ordered the platoon back, intent on picking up his platoon leader and returning him to safety. It was incredibly risky for a mortar platoon to fight one tank, let alone three. Undaunted by the presence of this superior enemy force, the entire platoon willingly charged back into the teeth of the enemy.

While taking cover, Captain Paul remembered that he had his portable radio attached to his body armor. "Thunder 7, this is Thunder 6," Paul whispered to his platoon sergeant, Sergeant First Class Broadwater. He repeated several times with no response. What felt like hours but was only minutes later, Paul's platoon sergeant responded:

SERGEANT FIRST CLASS BROADWATER: "Captain Paul, are you there?"

CAPTAIN PAUL: "Roger, there are T-72s out here! Do you see them?"

SERGEANT FIRST CLASS BROADWATER: "No I don't see them, where are you at sir?"

Captain Paul began to think that maybe the T-72s were only a figment of his imagination and not actually out there trying to kill him. For a few seconds, he was in a state of denial. Then back to reality—his thoughts turned to his wife and unborn child back home. He looked down at a sonogram of his son, not knowing if he would live to see him be born. Not knowing for sure what his wife would end up naming him. The mortar platoon was unable to see the tanks through the trees lining the road. They had no idea how close they were. Captain Paul quickly responded, "I'm right here." Of course, Sergeant First Class Broadwater didn't know where "here" was.

SERGEANT FIRST CLASS BROADWATER: "Where?"

CAPTAIN PAUL: "Only one hundred meters in front of you, next to the wall. You need to go back to the blocking position and get an M1 up here. You need to leave."

SERGREANT FIRST CLASS BROADWATER: "We're not going to leave you behind, sir."

Sergeant First Class Broadwater prepared the platoon for a defense against the enemy tanks. They would make a stand and repel the tank's assault or die trying. The platoon placed their light antitank weapons into operation and their 120mm mortars into the direct-lay mode, orienting them onto the direction of the tanks. The gunners lined up their mortar sights along the road leading into the airport. It would take a direct hit to destroy a T-72 and a near miss to disable one, if they were lucky. Sergeant First Class Broadwater and Sergeant Johnson drove their trucks back and forth across the road in an attempt to draw the tanks' fire away from Captain Paul. With Paul's head in the dirt, all he could do was lay there and hope for support from the battalion.

BOOM! One of the T-72s fired a main gun round. Captain Paul's heart sank. "Sergeant First Class Broadwater, are you all right?" He did not respond. Paul thought that the T-72s finally acquired his platoon in their sights and were proceeding to destroy them in detail. All he could do was envision the faces of each soldier under his command. If he made it back alive, he would have to answer for their deaths. Paul would have to explain to their families how they died and that they died trying to rescue him, their platoon leader. After a few seconds, the silence was broken. "Sir, are you there?" It was Sergeant First Class Broadwater. Paul breathed a sigh of relief. They were all right. The tanks did not engage his platoon. They still could not see the mortar platoon through the trees lining the road, effectively blocking their view.

Word of enemy armor spread on the task force radio net. Bushmaster maintained one platoon south of Highway 8, near the overpass, and two platoons north of the Highway preparing to assault the northern SRG compound. Captain Szymanski quickly dispatched his southern platoon under Lieutenant Myslviwic, ordering them to intercept the Iraqi armor assaulting the airport. Myslviwic's Bradley poked its head out over the end of the overpass but could not locate the elusive Iraqi armor. The Bradley subsequently displaced to gain a better vantage point to identify and engage the T-72s. It was on the opposite side of the airport wall to Captain Paul, and it was not in direct radio contact with the mortar platoon. The Bradley was in the blind looking for a fight.

BOOM! One of the enemy tanks fired another round. This time, Captain Paul could feel the breeze. Within two minutes, the enemy tank fired a total of two main gun rounds over his head. Paul was not their intended target. The airport's overpass was located directly behind him, just over the eight-foot wall. Paul lay directly underneath the enemy tank's line of fire. The two rounds were directed at a FOX Chemical Reconnaissance

Vehicle and Bushmaster's Bradley driving exposed over the overpass. The first round missed the FOX vehicle and the second penetrated the Bradley's rear troop compartment. The force of the blast was so intense, all the hatches busted open, and the Bradley commander was blown completely out of the turret. Miraculously, he sustained no injuries, save an aching head and ringing ears.

With the Bradley's internal communications knocked out by the blast, the driver, Private First Class Kim, used quick thinking and acted under his own initiative by realigning the Bradley, throwing it in reverse, and backing down from the overpass as quickly as possible—before the T-72 could get off a second shot at it. Luckily, a T-72 used an automatic loading system that took about ten seconds between firing rounds—unlike the M1, where the muscles of a nineteen-year-old soldier could hurl a shell into the breech every two to three seconds.

Combat boots and personal equipment raining down from the overpass led observers on the ground to believe that they were blown off human beings. Within a few minutes, those fears were put to rest. These items were blown off the soldiers' bags strapped to the outside of the Bradley. Fortunately, all infantry soldiers in the rear troop compartment vacated the Bradley only seconds before impact. Call it fate. No friendlies were killed or injured from the enemy's tank fire, and the Bradley survived the blast and fought on for the rest of the battle, albeit in a severely degraded posture.

The T-72s began to advance closer to Captain Paul's hiding position. He knew they were close; he could hear the tank crewmen speak to each other and communicate fire commands to one another. The fact that they were speaking in Arabic put down any doubt that they might be friendly. They were yelling louder and louder, leading Captain Paul to believe that they were about to target him once again. Paul thought that they would either kill him or maybe try to take him prisoner. Captain Paul thought about all possible outcomes. Perhaps he would be executed on the spot, or maybe tortured first then executed. After targeting the Bradley moments prior, the tankers probably deduced that they were in for a bigger fight now. So they probably wouldn't even waste any time to take Paul prisoner—they would probably just shoot him from atop their tanks. They wouldn't even waste their time to dismount first before killing him.

Before the war, Captain Paul promised himself that he would not let himself be taken alive by the Iraqis. The Iraqis did not observe the laws of land warfare and the proper treatment of prisoners. Paul would go out fighting. At the very moment Paul resigned to his fate, suddenly, he heard the whine of a diesel-powered 1,500-horsepower engine. It was an M1 Abrams tank. It was Staff Sergeant McDoogle's B22, the same tank that passed by only moments earlier, still towing his wingman's tank. When he heard over his radio that enemy armor was engaging friendlies along the same road he had just traveled, he executed a quick 180-degree turn and raced into action.

The M1's movement into its firing position was the sweetest sound Paul had ever heard. His prayers and the prayers of the mortar platoon were answered. Sergeant First Class Broadwater didn't waste any time. He leaped onto the Abrams and directed it on to the T-72s while also pointing out Paul's location to Staff Sergeant McDoogle in order to reduce the risk of fratricide. While buried in the brush, Captain Paul could now hear the Iraqi tank crewmen shouting at the top of their lungs. They were frantic. They knew what was about to happen. It was now just a matter of time for the M1 to respond—BOOM!—the T-72's turret separated from the hull and like a rocket, launched over twenty feet into the air. The turret, along with the lifeless torsos of the former tank crew, landed only a few meters from Captain Paul's head. The impact felt like an earthquake, and now everything smelled like a barbeque. The second T-72 crew saw what happened to their wingman, quickly dismounted, and ran away as fast as they could. BOOM! BOOM! KAKAKAK! The second and third T-72s exploded into small, flaming pieces while a hail of fire from the M1's machine gun raked the Iraqi tank crewmen running for their lives.

Staff Sergeant McDoogle and his gunnery skills were unmatched. We would learn later that he made the engagements while firing his main gun in the manual mode—manipulating a wheel by hand to steer the turret and looking through his auxiliary sight to acquire and engage the targets. Staff Sergeant McDoogle and his World War II–era tank gunnery skills would allow the task force to gain the initiative and help win the day.

The impact of a main gun round smashing into a T-72 chassis sounded like glass shattering—like taking a crystal chandelier and dropping it from the roof of a three-story building. Secondary explosions ignited from the T-72's internal and external fuel tanks and stowed ammunition. Seconds later, through the crackling fire and explosions, Captain Paul heard the sound of one of his mortar carriers approaching. It was getting louder by the second. Somehow Paul could still hear. Sandwiched between friendly and enemy armor at less than one hundred meters between both, he should have been deaf after the three tanks fired their main guns. Between all three tanks, a total of five main gun rounds were fired, two 125mm rounds from the T-72 and three 120mm rounds from the M1 Abrams. The main gun blast concussion can be enough to swell the brain and even result in death if one is close enough. It must have been the adrenaline that protected him. Or he was just lucky.

The mortar carrier was sent forward to pick Paul up and return him to safety. His initial instinct was to leap up and run to the vehicle as quickly as he could. He thought that if he did that, he might be mistaken for one of the Iraqis and subsequently shot. Captain Paul was also concerned about the potential for additional enemy forces behind the three T-72s. Paul waited until the mortar carrier was within shouting distance from his position. When it was close enough, he got up and shouted "FRIENDLY!" He repeated it several times as he waved his hands in the air while darting to the rescue vehicle. Specialist Ball and his squad of warriors welcomed their platoon leader into their mortar carrier. While boarding, Paul could clearly see the look of determination and fearlessness in their eyes. Paul was going to make it, thanks to the courage and heroism of his men. Sergeant First Class Broadwater received the Bronze Star for his actions and leadership, undaunted by a superior enemy and overwhelming odds.

The soldiers of the Task Force 2-7 mortar platoon risked their lives for their platoon leader because that is exactly what they were trained to do—to never leave a fallen comrade behind. This principle is taught to the soldier from day one of basic training and is reinforced practically every day he or she continues to serve in the military. The training these soldiers received over the past year instilled confidence in their ability to kill and to survive on the battlefield. It enabled them to transcend the immediate danger and overcome any adversity or challenge that stood in their way. On this day, these soldiers embodied the same values they swore to uphold. Their unrelenting adherence to these values enabled a fellow soldier to live on and fight again another day.

By the time we arrived at the airport, we didn't expect to see enemy tank formations maneuvering for battle like we did on the morning of April 4. I thought it unlikely because we didn't make contact with any Iraqi armor along the march up from Objective Peach. We certainly did not expect to encounter these tanks from *behind* our formation. The mortar platoon's location, by chance, probably saved the task force blocking position from being surprised by the T-72s. Without the mortars in their way, the enemy tanks would have just kept driving right up to Four Corners, and at that time our Bradleys and tanks had vacated Four Corners to attack nearby objectives. Only one Bradley remained at Four Corners. The T-72s would have rolled up on my scouts, medics, and mechanics, and they would have been quickly overwhelmed. In one short encounter at Four Corners, I could have lost the ability to see, heal, and fix.

The chance encounter with the mortar position may have even had broader implications on our mission. If the T-72s were able to kill or force the withdrawal of my assets at Four Corners, the T-72s could have then turned to engage Knight, Rage, or Bushmaster from behind—they were all attacking in opposite directions. If the mortars hadn't delayed and disrupted their movement along the airport road, the enemy tanks would have had the time and opportunity to compromise my entire blocking position. I am confident we would have eventually neutralized the enemy tanks, but it would have been messy and the fog of war would have complicated our mission. And it would have happened at around the same time that the Iraqis' SRG infantrymen were regrouping and organizing a counterattack. The T-72s combined with the SRG infantrymen attacking us from the inside of our blocking position would have amounted to chaos for us.

The enemy tanks stopped moving after their initial engagement with Captain Paul and Sergeant Hernandez. They were probably surprised by the encounter with American troops there, in the eastern portion of the airport, or in the airport altogether. They could have been trying to envelop the rest of my brigade to the west—they had been here since last night. Maybe the T-72s did not know Task Force 2-7 now occupied the east and could have been using the approaches on our side of the airport to surprise the rest of my brigade along its flank. Rather than continuing their attack and charging through the resistance, like we would do, the Iraqi tankers just stopped. This was not too surprising. Junior Iraqi military leaders are not trained to take initiative, and they are not empowered to deviate from the plan. When conditions on the ground change, they cannot react in time. Their delay bought us the time we needed to react and refocus our combat power in and around the blocking position.

We thought the enemy did not have any fight left. We were wrong. Over two weeks into the war, we thought it possible that all Iraqi tanks would have been destroyed by our Air Force and Navy by now. Any remaining armor would be scattered, isolated, and disconnected from other assets like infantry or artillery. The enemy gets a vote. The Iraqis learned from Desert Storm 1991 and went to great lengths to hide their best tanks from our airpower until we got so close our airpower would be limited or ineffective. They hid beneath overpasses, underground, and inside of buildings. They were invisible from the sky. We must have driven right past them on our way up to the airport and into our blocking position. They were lurking everywhere. Luckily, they were either unwilling or unable to mass and maneuver more than a single tank platoon at a time, enabling us to destroy their armor piecemeal.

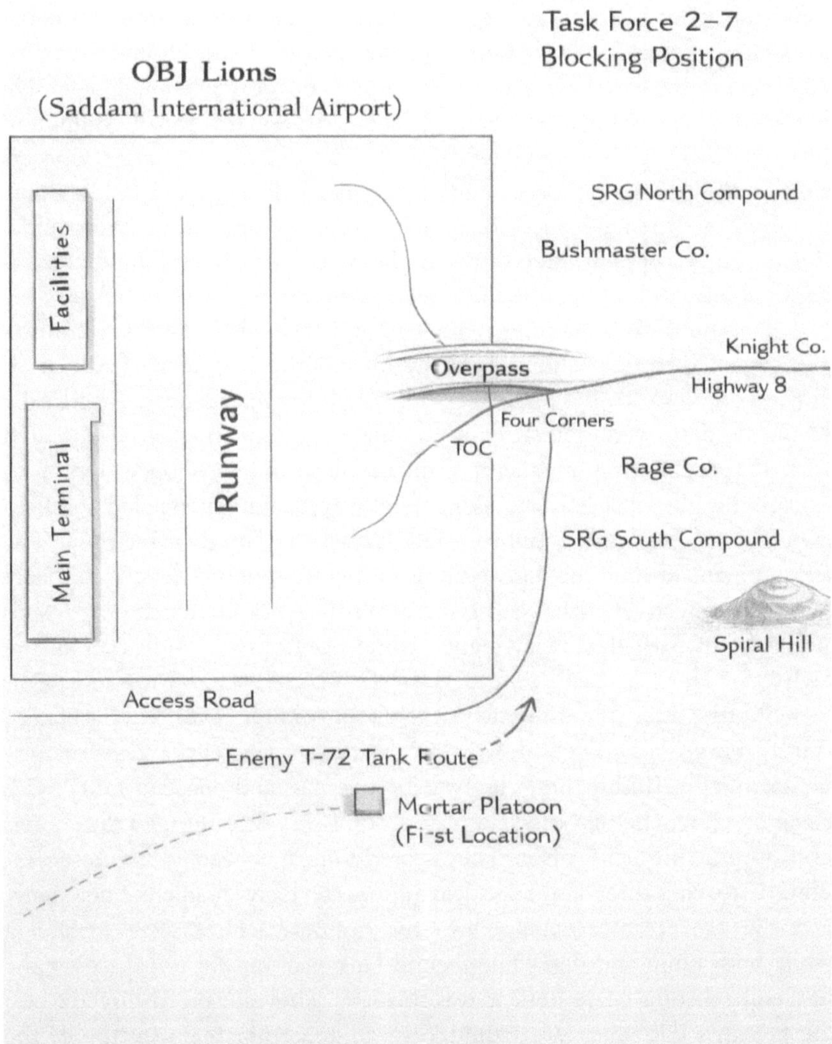

Task Force 2-7 actions at Objective Lions, Saddam. International Airport, April 4, 2003.
Source: Author's image.

By now, the task force was actively engaging the enemy in all directions. The fight was 360 degrees. Following their close encounter with Iraqi armor, the mortar platoon quickly displaced to Four Corners. Most of the larger tracks had moved out of the interchange, and this created just enough space for them to set up their guns there.

The heart of Four Corners rested the medical platoon, a PSYOPS team, the scout platoon, an engineer platoon, and each company's combat support vehicles. It was tight, but the mortar platoon found a way to squeeze in. Bushmaster's attached engineer platoon occupied defensive positions at the northeastern end of Four Corners, in a small compound adjacent to the airport's eight-foot wall. The engineers at Four Corners were in the process of constructing a prisoner collection and holding area for about a dozen prisoners Bushmaster rounded up during their initial attack. On the opposite side of the wall existed a small compound consisting of about ten buildings, including a mosque.

Outside of Four Corners, Bradleys and tanks from all three companies occupied battle positions at each corner of the task force's battle space directly on or astride the highway roads. Anything not identified as friendly would be destroyed. The Knight commander, Captain Lee, collaborated with the engineer commander, Captain Bliss, and developed a plan to expand Knight's battle space along Highway 8. Knight needed space to maneuver and clear fields of fire—360 degrees—to fire their big guns. The terrain in and around the highway was simply too tight for a tank company to operate effectively. Bliss set his bulldozers to work knocking down walls and rows of trees flanking Knight's battle positions on both sides of the highway.

Shortly after the mortar platoon's encounter with enemy tanks, Private First Class Joseph and Private Martinez, a Javelin antiarmor missile team from Bushmaster, climbed the overpass and engaged four T-72s creeping closely behind the lead platoon of T-72s that engaged the mortar platoon only moments prior. They scored four direct hits in quick succession, destroying three tanks and leaving one severely disabled. The enemy sent two tank platoons along this same causeway. They were advancing while both blind and deaf. The second tank platoon did not discover the first tank platoon's fate until it was too late. They advanced directly into the Javelin's kill zone. We would keep an antiarmor team on top of the overpass for the duration of the battle. They had a perfect vantage point and field of fire. They were not seen, yet they could engage tanks kilometers away.

The Javelin missile made its debut appearance during the battle for Saddam International Airport on April 4. The Javelin was a new antiarmor weapon system, fielded by the Army in the late 1990s and into the early 2000s. It replaced the Desert Storm–era Dragon missile, with marked improvements in range, accuracy, lethality, and the survivability of the crew. Unlike its predecessor, the Javelin missile is not guided by an electrical wire and does not need to be terminally guided onto the target like the older Dragon. Rather, a gunner could quickly jettison the missile tube and displace after he fired the missile, allowing him to seek cover from any return fire. Our antiarmor crews conducted a crash course on the new weapon just prior to our deployment. It proved to be worth its weight in gold. The Javelin and how we employed it were a real combat multiplier during our fight at Saddam International Airport. This fight was the Javelin's first T-72 kill in its history. It kept the Iraqis off balance, disrupting their counterattack, and it turned the tide of the battle in our favor.

After the T-72s were destroyed, Knight assumed control over the southern sector of the task force blocking position. Captain Steve Szymanski shifted his southern platoon to the north to support his company's attack into the northern SRG compound. As they prepared their breach into the compound wall, they took accurate mortar and RPG fire from within the compound. Sergeant Shall pulled a handful of his company's M203 gunners and formed a firing line. Together, resembling a line of medieval archers, they massed their fires and peppered each of the towers with enough 40mm grenades to quiet the enemy fire and set the conditions for the breach and ground assault.

The M203 grenades reduced several of the compound's towers and surrounding structures to rubble. Enemy forces inside either ran or were torn apart by shards of shrapnel—thousands of pieces in all directions. Once the enemy's guns fell silent, Bushmaster massed 25mm armor-piercing and high-explosive ammunition to soften the masonry citadel wall that lay directly in front of them. Two Bradleys led by Sergeant First Class Bost plowed through the wall with the dismounted infantry squads following closely behind. The move closely resembled a scene from an old World War II movie—where infantrymen huddled behind the large Sherman tanks, using the armored beasts as cover while moving deep into enemy-held territory.

The northern SRG compound was larger than Bushmaster had anticipated. Once they made it inside, the scale and complexity became obvious. This airport citadel was over two kilometers wide and roughly one kilometer deep. Inside contained over sixty buildings that all looked the same.

They served different functions but there were few distinguishing features from one building to the next. The buildings provided barracks and office space, armories and ammunition caches, and command post buildings. They all had to be cleared by Bushmaster's dismounted infantrymen. They needed to deploy boots on the ground.

The initial breach and assaulting force deployed into the compound deep enough to establish an effective foothold. Private French was the only soldier wounded in the assault. He was quickly evacuated to the aid station posted at Four Corners on the Highway 8 interchange. Follow-on Bushmaster forces flooded through the breach and began to systematically clear each of the buildings using five dismounted infantry squads and two platoon's worth of Bradleys providing close fire support. The clearing process was deliberate and exhausting to Bushmaster's soldiers. It was a building-by-building, room-to-room fight.

Captain Szymanski and his junior leaders commanded the assault into the compound very skillfully, controlling the overall tempo of the clearing mission by leap-frogging infantry squads onto each of the buildings. This provided his soldiers with a short breather before their assault on the next building. An unknown number of Iraqis were killed and over fifty were observed retreating north. Once enemy contact in the compound subsided, Bushmaster could focus its attention on conducting a detailed search for intelligence. It found enemy maps and written orders. Bushmaster also found stockpiles of ammunition, indicating that the SRG had a large force as well as the capacity to fight on for extended periods.

I recommended Steve for the Silver Star for his exceptional leadership under fire. He moved across the battlefield with purpose, maintaining flexibility in the face of an unpredictable and rapidly shifting fight. His ability to assess the situation and adapt in real time allowed him to maneuver his company with precision, ultimately leading them to decisively defeat a larger, entrenched enemy force.

Bushmaster began their attack around the same time as Rage in the south. Rage sized up the walled compound that lay directly in front of them, less than a kilometer to the south of Highway 8 and to the east of the airport. Captain Smith was forward with his company, straddled by a tank section to his north and his 2nd Platoon under Staff Sergeant Weisner. Weisner took over the platoon a few days prior, after his platoon leader became wounded after his Bradley fell into the cistern back at Objective Raiders. As a junior NCO, this was a big responsibility. He performed well at Objective Hannah and was doing well now at Objective Lions. I joked with him weeks later that for all his accomplishments, I would award him a battlefield commission to second lieutenant—to most career NCOs like Staff Sergeant Weisner, this equaled a demotion.

Rage was poised to strike the compound from the southwest. Captain Rob Smith identified one of the metal gates as a potential entry point and began maneuvering his company toward it. But as his soldiers crept forward, their movement stirred up a hornet's nest.

Almost instantly, rocket-propelled grenades poured from within the compound—so many that, as Smith later described, they seemed to "block out the sun." Fortunately, most of the rockets sailed high and failed to find their targets, but the volume of fire pinned Rage down before they could reach the gate. Smith pulled his force back roughly a hundred meters and called for air support. Moments later, two five-hundred-pound bombs struck the tallest building in the compound, believed to be the source of the heaviest fire. When the explosions subsided, the RPG barrage fell silent.

Seizing the opportunity, Rage advanced again, this time unopposed. After breaching the gate, Smith ordered his Bradley platoon to bound forward by section, clearing the compound along a two-pronged axis. Buildings that showed resistance were first suppressed with massed 25mm fire from the Bradleys, then systematically cleared by three dismounted infantry squads. Once an objective was secured, the squads remounted, advanced, and repeated the process, grinding through the compound with precision. By the time the fight ended near noon, Rage had destroyed roughly a platoon of SRG infantry and taken eight more prisoner.

After only a few minutes into their attacks, the company commanders' contact reports began to flood the battalion command net. Despite the shock of their close encounter with Iraqi armor, Captain Paul and his mortars wasted no time in seeking out a suitable spot to emplace their guns within the Four Corner intersection. Each of the mortar carriers drove over the guardrail lining the highway and set up their guns against the airport wall. It was extremely tight, but it had to do. Within minutes, my task force's fire support officer called the mortar platoon for support.

CAPTAIN HAPPE: "Thunder 6, this is Able 30, are your guns up."

CAPTAIN PAUL: "Able 30, this is Thunder 6, roger, we're up and ready to receive fire missions."

CAPTAIN HAPPE: "Roger, stand by."

Captain Happe directed the mortars onto a large building within Rage's assigned SRG compound. This building was hit previously by a five-hundred-pound bomb, dropped by an F-18 providing us with close air support. My FSO attempted to echelon the intensity of fire onto this building before Rage conducted their final assault into it. The ETAC directed another bomb onto the target building only minutes prior and the Air Force controller, Tech Sergeant Smith, politely jested with the mortar platoon leader, "We saved the basement for yah sir!!"

The mortars fired twenty rounds of high-explosive ammunition. The mission was "danger close"—extremely close to Rage's frontline troops. The mortar platoon leader told Captain Smith to button up his company before he could fire. Each round was set with a delayed fuse, designed to explode after it penetrated its target. The shell-fuse combination was ideal for bunker busting and for demolishing buildings. There would be nothing left of the building by the time Rage closed in on it. After all mortar rounds were reported "complete," my operations officer and I left Four Corners with the final assault force moving into the southern SRG compound.

My operations officer Rod Coffey and I insisted on being at the forefront of the action. Leading from the front was our style, and it worked well. We couldn't issue our commanders relevant orders and effectively maneuver the task force if we didn't have an appreciation for the enemy and the terrain they were fighting in. We had to be there to experience it for ourselves—to smell the smells, see the sights, and hear the sounds of the battlefield.

Over the next three hours, from 0900 to 1200 hours, all three companies were decisively engaged with the enemy. Rage and Bushmaster were engaging infantry strongholds located within both the northern and southern SRG compounds. Knight had its hands full to the east on Highway 8. And my TOC and supporting units were still playing defense against pockets of enemy resistance in and around Four Corners.

The Rage commander, Captain Rob Smith, dispatched an infantry squad from 1st Platoon to conduct a reconnaissance patrol of the company's next objective. Rob wanted intel on the location so he could deploy his company in the most optimal way. The squad would confirm or deny the presence of enemy forces in the vicinity of their next position. If there was a presence, the squad would pinpoint its composition and disposition. Their objective was located a kilometer south of the Highway 8 interchange, near the mortar platoon's first contact point with enemy T-72 tanks. This mission could prevent a surprise RPG attack, or another attack by enemy T-72s.

While searching and clearing the area, the squad leader, Staff Sergeant Robin, heard the sound of at least two tanks approaching. Robin notified his platoon leader while preparing an antiarmor ambush. He quickly deployed his men online in concealed positions—an ambush drill he conducted hundreds of times before. He set up his machine gun and antitank weapons, including his Javelin missile team. Robin kept his eyes trained on the causeway. When the T-72s were within closing distance, Robin could see the two tanks, with the lead tank commander's silhouette half exposed out of the turret. "This is too easy," the squad leader thought to himself. Did the Iraqi think that just because he was standing in a tank, *he* was also bulletproof? Robin rose up from his firing line and stood toe-to-toe with the tank. It was a showdown. He took aim, placing the Iraqi officer dead in his crosshairs, like lining up a trophy eight-point buck for the perfect shot. Robin knew he would only have one chance at success. If he missed, his Javelin might not be able to do the job on both tanks in time for at least one of them to return fire and annihilate his squad. It would take a few minutes before reinforcements from the rest of his platoon could arrive . . . precious minutes he didn't have.

Most of Robin's fingers on his right hand, including his trigger finger, were broken during a minor accident in his Bradley a few days prior. He had done a good job ignoring the discomfort in front of his men. But he felt no pain now. He was completely focused. POP! Sergeant Robin was credited for killing the Iraqi tank commander with his M-4 carbine rifle, mounting his own personal hunting scope brought with him from home. One shot from his rifle, fired over two hundred meters away, impacted center mass on this Iraqi tanker and sent him buckling lifelessly to the floor of his turret. The tank and its wingman froze instantly in place, sitting completely motionless while figuring out what happened and what to do next. Leaderless and ill-trained to deal with combat contingencies like making contact or taking a hit, they just sat there like the T-72s knocked out earlier in the morning. Meanwhile, upon hearing the reports, Captain Smith ordered more forces into the area to counterattack and roll up the enemy tanks stalled on the causeway.

After the initial engagement, Rage's 1st Platoon, under First Lieutenant Horn, was dispatched to Sergeant Robin's location, about a kilometer south of the tank's blocking position, and near the mortar platoon's former location southeast of the airport. Captain Smith brought up his tank section, under Staff Sergeant McDoogle, and ordered it to set up a blocking position to repel the enemy armor, attacking down the same path as before.

Staff Sergeant Robin linked up with Horn and pointed out the location of the tanks and the fact that they were still dazed and confused and sitting helplessly on the road. First Lieutenant Horn pushed further south and swung east, hoping to strike the T-72s from the flank. If he could hit them from their blind side, their Bradleys had a better chance at survival, and the hope was that they could force the enemy tanks to fight from two directions—McDoogle and his two M1 tanks from the north, and Horn and his Bradleys on the flank, from the east.

Horn targeted the enemy tanks before McDoogle could get into a good position. The T-72s were still motionless, giving Horn and his wingman enough time to raise their TOW arm and get off two quick shots. In less than a minute, Horn attacked and destroyed each of the two T-72s with a well-placed TOW missile shot. After the kill, Horn's platoon expanded their hunt for any other errant T-72s lurking around the southeastern flank of the airport. Horn kept his platoon in the area for a little while and then collapsed back toward the southern SRG compound to help support his company's main attack.

Rage was making rapid progress in the southern SRG compound until they approached a large building housing over thirty defenders equipped with RPGs, heavy machine guns, and small arms. Captain Smith needed fire support before he could dismount his infantry and assault into the building. His company fire support chief, Staff Sergeant Sowell, requested mortar support. The building was approximately two hundred feet long, one hundred feet wide, and three stories high. It would be another "danger close" fire mission. Captain Smith informed the task force TOC of his intentions and accepted full risk and responsibility for the fire mission.

Within seconds, the mortar platoon processed Rage's fire mission, and twenty mortar rounds were airborne. The mission yielded considerable damage to both the building and the enemy combatants inside. Without a single adjusting round, all twenty rounds were on target. At the request of Staff Sergeant Sowell, another volley was repeated. By the time the last round impacted, over 75 percent of the building was demolished. The enemy guns within the building fell silent. There was now no need for Rage to clear the building—it was reduced to a pile of rubble.

Rage now had an effective foothold into the southern SRG compound. They had a clear path around the building and onward to the next stronghold within the citadel. Captain Smith and I could not believe our eyes. It was the first time either of us witnessed the full destructive power of our mortars. For the remainder of the battle we would keep their guns hot.

Enemy armor kept emerging from the same place as before, threatening Rage in the southern SRG compound and our Four Corners blocking position. The armor appeared from out of nowhere. We couldn't figure out where they were coming from, how they were getting here, or why they kept coming from that direction. The T-72s would appear only a few hundred meters away from us before we could identify and destroy them.

More often than not, on April 4, we were the ones caught off guard in the opening moments of each engagement. Where could the tanks be originating from? With CAS stacked directly overhead, how could our planes not spot them further out from the airport? And JSTARS? The picture from the air must have been just as confusing as the one on the ground. I knew what the fog of war looked like and felt like on the ground. I couldn't even imagine what our pilots flying above us were thinking.

Even though we were forced to react to enemy contact, we could counter quickly with overwhelming force. Despite all the confusion and the fog of war, our ETAC called in numerous air strikes—A-10 Warthogs made several strafing runs along the northern and southern SRG compounds, and they hit the enemy tank positions nearby. The Warthogs dropped four five-hundred-pound joint direct attack munitions, or JDAMS, within only one kilometer of Four Corners. They shook the earth. Our task force's aggressive actions and our ability to synchronize direct and indirect fires with maneuver shocked our enemy, collapsing their defenses along with their ability and will to fight.

The TOC was not immune to enemy harassment. While controlling the fight, staff officers and NCOs found themselves dodging bullets, mortar rounds, and missiles. Though isolated inside the airport walls, the TOC's position beneath the overpass provided a measure of protection, making it semitenable even under constant fire.

From their vantage point, officers in the TOC observed waves of Iraqi infantry massing less than a hundred meters away. The soldiers in the TOC could fight, but that was not their job. Their job was to orchestrate the entire battle and not get bogged down trading fire with the enemy. If they did that, it could hinder the entire task force and its ability to accomplish its mission. Intelligence reports would be overlooked, artillery and mortars would go silent, targets would be missed, fratricide might happen, wounded soldiers would wait longer for medevac, and reinforcements might not come to the right place to beat the enemy.

Recognizing the threat, Major Coffey, my operations officer, rushed back to the TOC and immediately began engaging targets of opportunity.

His Bradley's 25mm high-explosive rounds tore into several antitank guided missile and mortar teams attempting to take cover in nearby bunkers. His Bradley's machine gun fire subdued the enemy's infantry assaults. His firepower was accurate, and it was overwhelming. It eliminated the immediate danger to the TOC.

The surviving Iraqi infantry quickly withdrew and repositioned, seeking new targets and avoiding the fate of their comrades. By then it had become clear to the SRG that closing with American armor was a deadly mistake. Perhaps they were realizing that our armor wasn't made of wood after all. For the next hours and days, the SRG would keep probing, looking for targets it could engage and outmatch.

The airport devolved into a company, platoon, and squad fight. We had exhausted all our deliberate plans at this point. We were now writing the playbook as we went along. I had to trust my company commanders and their people would do the right thing. All I needed to do was point them in the right direction and then give them the support and resources they asked for. I delegated more than I ever had at the airport. My troops did not let me down.

The Task Force 2-7 companies' attacks produced considerable success. Any threat Rage, Bushmaster, or Knight encountered, they eliminated and then moved quickly to their next target. The tempo was good, and at the time, I felt we had the initiative. Four Corners was secure, all the Iraqi T-72s that emerged were destroyed, and my companies were charging through every one of their objectives.

During one patrol south of Four Corners, two Iraqi soldiers were found wounded after a brief firefight. They were subsequently evacuated to the aid station at Four Corners. Without hesitation, the medics immediately went to work to treat the Iraqis. Friend or foe, our medics had a job to do. Caring for people was their duty, and they did it well.

Both Iraqi casualties suffered from severe trauma from large-caliber gunshot wounds. One Iraqi soldier's right arm had been completely blown off. A thin piece of bone protruded from his shoulder, and it rotated in a circular pattern. The Iraqi was in such a state of shock, he didn't even realize that his arm had been severed. The other Iraqi lost both kneecaps. All that remained were gaps of flesh and blood where his knees once were. Both casualties had already bled out and there was nothing our medics could do.

The medics did the best they could, but despite their best efforts, both Iraqis died within twenty minutes. After an hour or so, the decaying bodies began to collect bugs of all sorts, and the smell resembled that of rotted cheese. Soldiers could not walk within fifty feet of the bodies without gagging. The entire blocking position at Four Corners smelled like death.

After the mortar platoon fired their last mission, they heard machine gun fire on the opposite side of the wall. The audibles did not resemble the deeper pitch defined by American ammunition. The task force's TOC told them that there weren't any friendly forces on the opposite side of the wall. First Sergeant Moore, from Rage Company, threw a hand grenade over the wall to neutralize anything on the other side. He got the enemy's attention. The first soldier at Four Corners to spot enemy on the other side of the wall was First Lieutenant Jesse Delgado, the medical platoon leader. He mounted a scout vehicle, pulling security with its .50 caliber machine gun to protect his medics—unusual to see a medic mounting a machine gun, but by this point, every action at Four Corners was life or death.

> FIRST LIEUTENANT DELGADO: "Matt, get your guys away from the wall, there is an Iraqi soldier on the roof."
>
> CAPTAIN PAUL: "Why aren't you firing that .50 cal.?"
>
> FIRST LIEUTENANT DELGADO: "Your guys are in the way."
>
> CAPTAIN PAUL: "No they're not, shoot over their heads. I'll order them to get down in their tracks."
>
> FIRST LIEUTENANT DELGADO: "No, it's too unsafe."

Mortar Platoon Leader Captain Paul's perspective on the battle for Four Corners:

> I didn't want to take my guns out of action in the event we received another fire mission. Notwithstanding, I didn't want to miss an opportunity to kill the enemy that threatened us, so I gave in. "Hold on, I'll move them." I moved the platoon back toward the center of Four Corners.
>
> By the time we moved, the Iraqi soldier was gone. POP! POP! Within seconds, we began to receive sporadic sniper fire. We couldn't pinpoint the source. It appeared to be originating from all directions. The enemy fire began just after the last patrol departed Four Corners for their patrol. They must have been observing us, and when we were at our weakest and most vulnerable, they initiated their attack. The enemy began with sniper probes, followed by an increasing volume of RPG

fire from trees and on rooftops within the compound. We received another fire mission, and going against my better judgment, we accepted it. We fired the mission while dodging enemy bullets. All we could do was scan our sectors for enemy. I surveyed Four Corners for covered and concealed positions to emplace my men and vehicles. I quickly discovered that such positions did not exist.

The entire Four Corners site was completely exposed, and one spot was as good as the next. We didn't see any enemy until Sergeant Norris pointed out an Iraqi sniper in a tree about fifty meters from the other side of the wall. "Son of a bitch, there's one of them in the trees," Sergeant Norris informed me. "What are you waiting for Sergeant Norris?" I asked. POP! With one shot from Sergeant Norris's M4 Carbine, the sniper fell from the tree and hit every branch on the way down. I ordered the platoon to recon by fire on the trees in the compound and to scan for signs of enemy in the trees to our flanks and rear. We had to protect ourselves, and I didn't want to take any chances. More enemy soldiers began to appear in the trees, on rooftops, and now in the guard towers overlooking Four Corners. I decided to suspend our mortar mission and focus on our own survivability. "Go out of action and orient your crew served weapons on the compound. Don't fire into the engineers, they are on our right flank." WHYZZZZZ. BOOOOM! KAKAKAKAK! The unmistakable whistle from another enemy RPG round was fired at the engineer platoon, marking the beginning of the enemy's main assault.

Most of the Iraqis assaulted through a hole in the wall previously breached by the engineers, to be used later to store enemy prisoners nabbed from the company patrols. Sergeant First Class Paul Smith, the engineer platoon sergeant, along with a Bradley from First Lieutenant Johnson's platoon, found themselves isolated inside the wall when they discovered scores of enemy infantry dug in surrounding trenches and mounting guard towers and surrounding trees. Sergeant First Class Smith was quoted while telling his driver that "we're in a world of hurt." This prediction was as ominous as it was true. They began taking heavy fire from enemy in a nearby guard tower and from infantry firing machine guns and RPGs from within well-protected fortifications inside the airport walls. After sustaining multiple hits from RPGs and low on ammunition, the Bradley was compelled to disengage, leaving Sergeant First Class Smith along with his engineer M113 mounting a .50 caliber machine gun behind to his fate.

Some of the enemy climbed over the wall in an effort to avoid the sustained rate of our .50 caliber machine gun fire. The engineer platoon fired all their weapons into the onslaught of advancing enemy directly in front of them. "There is over a hundred of them over the wall," we heard an engineer cry, bracing Four Corners for the inevitable clash of close combat. This was not good. We were not the ideal type of force to handle this situation. A Bradley company would have been much more suitable. We had no choice but to stay and fight.

I looked around and realized that we were all that stood in the way of the enemy and the integrity of the task force blocking position. I also discovered that with the battalion commander, operations officer, and all of the company commanders out on patrol, I was the senior ranking officer on the ground at the Four Corners intersection. I would be responsible for what happened or failed to happen here. If the enemy succeeded in penetrating Four Corners, the whole blocking position could be compromised. I ordered my platoon "weapons free" into the compound, but I emphasized that they need to be cognizant of the engineers to our right. This enabled them to shoot anything that did not identify itself as friendly on the other side of the wall. The engineers were difficult to see through the shrubbery and trees that separated our two platoons, and the last thing I wanted was a loss of life due to friendly fire. My .50 caliber machine guns and Mark-19 grenade machine guns began pumping rounds into the trees and into the structures that stood in front of us. I had Specialist Arni, a PSYOPS soldier equipped with an M203 40mm grenade launcher, fire over thirty rounds into the center of the compound. The PSYOPS detachment also played a message over their loudspeaker attempting to coerce the enemy into surrender. Unfortunately, surrender was not a consideration for these Iraqi soldiers. We even fired an AT-4 antitank missile into the narrow, glassless window of the guard tower used by the Iraqis.

Despite all of our firepower, the enemy's fire was increasing in volume, and it eventually rose to a crescendo. He was firing at us with AK-47s, heavy machine guns, and RPGs from all directions and from elevated positions in trees and roof tops. It was a coordinated attack. It was a professional display of determined soldiers fighting as hard as they could because that is exactly what they were trained to do. They quickly earned our respect. WHYZZZZ!!! An RPG round missed my command post vehicle by less than one foot. The Iraqis' aim was improving. For the mass of RPG rounds fired, to miss each of my mortar carriers and my five-ton truck all packed to the gills with high-explosive mortar rounds was nothing short of a miracle. A single mortar carrier carried over two thousand pounds of high-explosive ammunition. It would only take a single mortar round to cook off, igniting the other sixty-eight, packed side by side and adjacent to the vehicle's fuel tanks, to transform the airport interchange into a meteor-like crater the size of football field and send all eighty souls fighting for their lives there into oblivion. A stray bullet would be enough to blow the 7,500 pounds of explosives laden inside our five-ton truck, protected only by a one-eighth-inch thick rubber tarp.

The fire was everywhere. There was little in the way of cover or concealment. One spot was as good as the next. All anybody could do was hope and shoot back. It was only a matter of time before one of us ran out of luck. Even a cat only has nine lives. "MEDIC, MEDIC!" Two of my soldiers, Specialist Jacobs and Sergeant Hernandez both took RPG shrapnel to the face. The RPG round missed their vehicle and hit the wall in front of them. The backlash of shrapnel found its victims, two of my soldiers. They were both evacuated to our aid station within Four Corners. They would be okay. Casualties within four corners were mounting. Eventually, the level of casualties were more than our few medics could handle. "Matt, I need four of your combat lifesavers."

It was a catch-22 decision. If I released my soldiers to perform medical duties, I would have fewer to defend the blocking position, thus creating conditions favorable to the enemy and enabling him to produce more casualties for us to treat. The engineer platoon and my mortar platoon were effectively keeping the enemy at bay for now, so I decided to release four of my soldiers to the medics. Fortunately, over 90 percent of my platoon became certified as combat lifesavers before we deployed to Kuwait. Choosing four soldiers would not be difficult. "Jesse, you got 'em." I found four soldiers not actively firing their weapons and volunteered them to assist the medics. I also tried to find a more tenable position for the mortar carrier previously occupied by my two wounded soldiers. In the process of relocating, the vehicle threw its track. It was now out of the fight. By now, everyone in Four Corners was completely engaged in close combat with the enemy. They were no farther that twenty-five meters from our lines.

I contacted the operations officer, informed him of our situation, and requested additional support. "Thunder 6, this is Able 3, the other companies are on patrol and are in contact, do what you can with what you've got." In retrospect, I don't think I articulated the situation as clearly as I should have. I read the situation as of vital importance to the task force. The heart of the blocking position was under attack and was being defended by only an engineer and mortar platoon and a section from the scout platoon. If the blocking position was penetrated, the enemy could exploit that penetration by engaging friendly tanks and Bradleys from the flanks or rear, thereby rendering them completely ineffective from performing their mission, to block an enemy counterattack along Highway 8. While inside a tank or Bradley, it is difficult to defend against a 360-degree enemy on the ground. Moreover, all of the task force's supporting assets were in jeopardy: the scouts who could provide the task force with intelligence, the mortars with fire support, the mechanics who could repair the tanks and Bradleys, and the medics who could treat casualties. The task force needed this infrastructure intact while conducting sustained combat operations.

The Task Force Tactical Operations Center was only a mile down the road inside the airport. Following our withdrawal or our annihilation, they would be the enemy's next target. We had to stay and fight, and we had to win. I didn't have time to argue the point with the S-3, and at the time I assumed that the companies were in as much if not heavier contact than we were at Four Corners. Instead of diverting a patrol to support us, I grabbed a tank blocking Highway 8 and guided it into position overlooking the engineer platoon's sector. I told the tank crew not to fire until I pulled the engineer platoon back from their position. I told them to fire the main gun into the hole when the engineers were clear; I would ensure everyone at Four Corners was clear of the concussion blast. I quickly learned that getting the engineers out was as impossible as it was dangerous. KAKAKAKAK. They were exchanging fire with scores of Iraqi infantry and were sustaining casualties. If they turned their backs to the enemy now, they would sustain more. The safest thing for them to do now was to stay and fight. I kept the tank positioned behind the engineer platoon as a second line of defense. WHYZZZ, BOOM!! An RPG and an enemy mortar hit one of the engineer platoon's armored personnel carriers and all of the combustible materials on board were now on fire. Sergeant First Class Smith pulled his wounded soldier from the vehicle and evacuated him to First Sergeant Campbell, the Engineer Company first sergeant. With no regard for his personal safety, he remounted the damaged vehicle and proceeded to engage the assaulting enemy with its .50 caliber machine gun. After changing ammunition three times while firing over four hundred rounds into the waves of enemy infantry, Sergeant First Class Smith sustained a fatal wound to the back of his head, killing him instantly.

It was estimated that he personally killed or wounded between twenty and sixty-five enemy soldiers attempting to overwhelm the blocking position. After the war, he would be posthumously awarded the Medal of Honor for his courage and selflessness under fire. It was the first Medal of Honor awarded in the Global War on Terror.

The engineer first sergeant, First Sergeant Campbell, and Sergeant First Class Mulligan, the scout platoon sergeant, evacuated the engineer casualties. Knight's first sergeant, First Sergeant Rodriguez, and one of his company medics aided First Sergeant Campbell while evacuating Sergeant First Class Smith's body and then helped with the rest of the evacuation effort. During the evacuation procedures, they were forced to react to harassing enemy fire. First Sergeant Campbell silenced one of the Iraqi guard towers with a grenade and his M16. Sergeant First Class

Mulligan charged into the wall and laid down suppressive fire with his machine gun, cutting into the enemy ranks. They would both earn the Silver Star for their actions.

The medics were now treating over fifteen casualties, and there was now a lull in the enemy fire. My soldiers flocked to the aid station to do what they could to help their fallen buddies. It took all the effort I could muster to pull some of my soldiers from the aid station and send them back to the line. I knew that the medics needed help, and I knew that my soldiers wanted to do whatever they could. This brief respite notwithstanding, I knew the enemy was far from finished. He still had fight left in him. I didn't want him to see the large gap along our line. He could observe this weakness and exploit it. I maintained approximately 60 percent of the platoon to help hold the line with the other 40 percent helping the medics treat and evacuate the wounded.

The medical platoon leader handed me an air medevac request form already filled out. He had to clear a landing zone and did not have time to call and request the birds. Nor did I, but because there was a break in the enemy's assault, I helped him out and called battalion for the birds. Reluctantly, I jumped into my command post vehicle in the middle of the intersection, a huge target painted for enemy RPG gunners. I could hear the whistle of RPGs flying high over my vehicle. I was lucky they were aiming high. Our battalion always took great care of our wounded—it was a priority and I had to risk everything for them. It would take some time to get the medevac on site, but it would eventually get here.

I then improved the defensive position and walked to each of my soldiers along the line. I visited with Sergeant Hernandez to ensure that he would be okay. He was high on morphine when I got there, but I reassured him anyway that he would make it out of there alive. I took a second to catch my breath while discovering how hot it became. The powerful Middle Eastern sun caused temperatures to soar up to one hundred degrees. We were still wearing our nuclear, biological, and chemical suits. The suck factor was taking its toll. I didn't know how much longer we could sustain ourselves in this posture while engaging in close combat with the enemy. I was completely dehydrated. If the fighting continued any longer, I would request battalion for a downgraded posture.

The lull in enemy fire began to lure us into a false sense of security. KAKAKAK! The enemy launched another assault, but this time not as intense as the last. I repositioned a couple of my crew served weapons to gain a better field of fire on the attackers. The engineers would need the support after Sergeant First Class Smith went down. The enemy would only get a few steps before they were cut down by rifle and machine gun fire. I even pondered firing a few mortar rounds into the compound, but because I did not have a good feel for where all of the friendly patrols were located, I decided against it. The minimum range of the mortar was not very close, and I didn't know how deep the compound extended. For all I knew, the rounds could have landed beyond the compound and endangered a friendly unit. After about fifteen minutes into the assault, the enemy disengaged.

The physical assault ended but the RPG and sniper fire intensified. I counted over twenty-five RPG rounds that flew over my head. My mind processed all of this in slow motion. It was like a dream. I could follow the RPG round from its source to its destination and could even read the military specifications written on each of the rounds as they flew by. The Iraqis were aiming too high, and many of the rounds failed to explode upon impact. As we discovered later, some of the RPG rounds still had the safety pins installed. I think this particular volley of fire was nothing more than parting shots.

In the midst of this rain of enemy fire, I took notice of the medics and how they performed under fire. They were completely oblivious to the fact that they were in the open and defenseless. Medics are nicknamed "angels of mercy." They exist to help others, and Saint Luke, often considered the patron saint of the combat medics, was watching over them on this fateful day. Their focus on their patients and on their duties as medics never wavered for an instant. They treated casualties in a cool, calm, and collected manner and without hesitation or regard for their own personal safety. As they tied tourniquets or performed CPR they never flinched, even when RPGs sailed past their heads. It was the most admirable vision I had during this battle, and it was one I will never forget. In the midst of this rain of enemy fire, I also took notice of several female medics I was surprised to see, having only just learned they were scooped up along our march from 1st or 2nd Brigade's rear-area medical company.

The second most admirable vision was when Lieutenant Colonel Rutter appeared. Hearing my medevac request, he knew we were in serious contact and raced back in his Bradley. At Four Corners, he dismounted—ignoring the protection of his vehicle—to get a face-to-face update while RPGs soared overhead. Fearless and seemingly everywhere at once, his presence brought calm to the chaos. I heard the sound of two helicopters. We all looked up and saw a Blackhawk with the distinctive red cross painted on its nose along with an Apache Gunship circling above it as cover. "Able 8, this is Rescue 11, we're on station, awaiting your signal." "Rescue 11, this is Able 8, roger." "I got it, purple smoke." The Blackhawk was guided into the landing zone and at the last second aborted his landing. The pilot told the medical platoon leader that it was too tight. The pilot recommended he land in the middle of the traffic circle at Four Corners. We all scrambled as fast as we could, and, while under fire, cleared all our vehicles from the traffic circle. Five feet from his landing, he aborted again. Jesse was beginning to get frustrated. We were all frustrated. It took the bird over an hour to get here, now it was going to take him another hour just to land. Meanwhile, five of our critically wounded buddies were losing precious time. They weren't going to be able to hold on much longer.

The pilot then took the initiative on his own and landed directly in the middle of the compound the enemy just attacked us from. "Able 8, this is Rescue 11, I've landed in a good spot over the wall." If it wasn't so tragic, I would have thought it was humorous. Jesse promptly replied, "NEGATIVE, NEGATIVE. That is where the enemy is. There are over a hundred enemy in that compound!!!" With the speed of a lightning bolt, the helicopter reached about five hundred feet in under two seconds. The pilot finally found a suitable landing zone about two hundred meters east along Highway 8. Now we had to carry five soldiers over two hundred meters to be evacuated. The wounded soldiers were evacuated with no further incident.

First Lieutenant Jesse Delgado, the medical platoon leader, recounts of the battle for Four Corners:

The day began actually two nights before for most of us. We were pushing up north into Iraq faster than I had expected, which was good, maybe it would get us home that much faster. Able 6, Lieutenant Colonel Rutter, had given us the mission on how we were going to take the airport. All in all it was not a very complex plan, each battalion had its mission and sectors to cover, clean, and cut. After the briefing he pulled me aside and told me he was only going to allow me to bring two vehicles in the initial push into the airport, the rest would have to come up with the battalion field trains. I immediately knew which two vehicles and personnel I wanted to bring. Before I made my final decision, I decided I would discuss my decision with Staff Sergeant Holliday first.

When I got back to Alpha Company's area, where we were tagging along, I told Staff Sergeant Holliday what our limitations were, and he immediately got upset and said we needed all the assets we could get. I totally agreed with him, but it was already not my decision to make. By that point we had already taken several casualties, and my medics understood what it meant to be shorthanded. And we all knew we did not want to be in that situation again. Consulting with Sergeant

First Class Davis, my platoon sergeant, and Staff Sergeant Holliday, the treatment squad leader, we decided that we had to use the M577 (command post track) we had on loan from the Forward Support Battalion, and definitely the two docs; First Lieutenant Smith (Smitty) and Second Lieutenant McGinnis (Mac). Staff Sergeant Holliday chose which medics he would bring with the condition that there would be enough room for Staff Sergeant Stebbens, our S-1 guy. After we ironed out the little details I found First Sergeant Moore, Alpha Company's first sergeant, and found out exactly where he wanted me in his formation. They usually like to stick us all the way in the back, but for this particular mission we made sure there was at least one Bradley from Alpha Company covering our rear. That at least gave us a warm and fuzzy.

The huge battalion column began moving out; I have no idea what time it was, all I know is it was dark, not just dark but desert dark. An incredible darkness that I truly believe you cannot experience anywhere else but the deserts of the Middle East. The radios were very silent, not the usual chatter between the crews in the different vehicles; we all knew what we were going to do but maybe we didn't know what to expect, and that had everyone a bit apprehensive. It seemed like we had been driving forever. Around dusk we started crossing small towns, suburbs of Baghdad. The streets were only big enough for a single file of vehicles. The radio chatter began to pick up about bad feelings, nobody liked driving through those little areas, but it was ghostly quite. I could probably count on one hand the number of people I saw in those towns. We finally made it into our position just north of the airport. The sun hadn't fully come up yet and nothing was happening. We set up the aid station in the northern side of what we were calling Four Corners.

The sun had risen now, and nothing was happening. We decided now was as good a time as any to bust open an MRE and eat some breakfast. Some of the guys were taking the time to write a letter home; I was preoccupied with finding a Bradley to get some hot water for the cup of noodles I had. We started talking and BS'ing when we started hearing some sporadic gun fire here and there. Nobody seemed concerned. By this point everybody knew the difference between gunshots being fired at you, if they were close or not, and gunshots being shot in the distance. These were in the distance, no snap or zing. The few sporadic shots got a little heavier and heavier until the unmistakable sound of the Bradley main gun firing. Specialist Tunar came up to me and said, "Looks like someone is home after all, huh, sir" before he walked over to finish his breakfast. Not long after that I got a call telling me two casualties were being sent over to me, Iraqi casualties. I found out what kind of wounds they had and advised the docs of what they had coming in.

When we received the patients, they were in bad shape: one had his arm almost completely blown off and the other his legs. The first person to care for them was from another brigade, and it seemed they did nothing for them except pour some quick clot on the wounds to stop the bleeding. The docs got right to work on them, which was not easy; the stench of open burnt human flesh is something that you will not soon forget, and these two Iraqis were reeking of it. It nauseated everyone in the area. Smitty was determined to do what he could when the Iraqi with the blown-off arm went into shock and died not more than eight minutes after being brought to us. It seemed as if the other Iraqi had been stabilized when Mac went to look him over and the distinct sound of AK-47 fire came screaming at us. It was as if someone opened the gates of hell all of a sudden.

The AK fire was now followed by repeated RPG blast impacting in the trees above and around us. The fire was so intense we had to move our patient to protect him from being shot by his own people. The scout section that was with us was returning fire with their .50 cal., and my medics began returning fire as we were being actively engaged. At that point it was determined there was an active enemy force beyond a high wall that divided our sectors. First Sergeant Moore ran up to the wall and threw a grenade over it; it must have pissed them off because the volume of fire intensified. Staff Sergeant Holliday updated me on the situation with our Iraqi casualty and told me if he wasn't evac'd he was going to die. I immediately put together a nine-line medevac request and sent it up to higher. The request come back denied. I sent it again and it was denied again. That Iraqi died there with us. To this day I do not know if he was a soldier or a civilian that was in the wrong place at the wrong time.

Staff Sergeant Holliday placed our vehicles in a crescent to make a barrier between us and the incoming rounds. I am not exactly sure when the battalion mortars rolled into our location, but I was sure as hell happy to see them. For a while I was the only organic 2-7 officer in the area; now with the mortars in the area we had more guns and Captain Paul took charge of our defenses. It was not too long before they received a fire mission and started slinging shells downrange when somebody started yelling "MEDIC!" One of our mortars took a piece of shrapnel right between the eyes that knocked him on his butt. Before I could say a word Staff Sergeant Holliday and Sergeant Chapman were sprinting over to the mortars to see what they could do. The shrapnel was lodged right in the bridge of his nose, an inch left or right would have lost him an eye. Smitty took a look at it and pulled it out with a leatherman, stitched him up, and told him to get back to the gun line.

At that point Sergeant First Class Paul Smith, the engineer platoon sergeant ran by and slapped the backside of my Kevlar and yelled out, "Gotta go to work, sir!" I yelled back at him to watch his ass. The engineers were told to bring down the wall that was between us and the enemy. They punched a hole in the wall, and it was like putting your hand in the beehive and shaking it up. The fire that came from the other side of the wall was amazingly intense. The engineers were pinned down for the moment. Sergeant First Class Smith mounted a .50 cal. and started returning fire. He was able to cover his engineers long enough for them to reposition and take up better firing positions when he took a round in his neck that exited behind his ear. First Sergeant Campbell came hauling ass in his HMMWV with Sergeant First Class Smith. Lieutenant Mac immediately went to work on him trying to maintain the almost nonexistent vitals he had. I immediately put together a nine line when Bushmaster 7 brought us two more casualties.

As I tried to send the nine line I could reach no one. I had three of my battalions' soldiers who needed to be evac'd and I couldn't talk to anyone on the net. I was finally able to communicate with Able 3, Major Coffey, who told me he was en route to our location. I gave Captain Paul the nine line and he sent it up to higher. By the time higher responded with a request for more information I had four more casualties on the ground that needed evac. When Major Coffey arrived on the scene, I updated him with the new info, and he asked me for an update on the previous casualties. I went back to Staff Sergeant Holliday to get the info when we heard the snap of a round passing by us and the ping of the round hitting the guard rail behind us. We both looked at the guard rail in disbelief. He gave me the info I needed, and we went back to work. Able 3 got the nine line approved and told me it would be forty-five minutes. I looked over to my medics, and they had already been taking turns giving Sergeant First Class Smith CPR. They were exhausted. I knew they would keep working until they passed out, and one of them almost did; Specialist Green had been working so hard and furiously to treat as many of the patients he could he had an asthma attack in the middle of all the action and no one could find his inhaler. He was able to calm himself long enough to get back in the fight.

I knew at this point my boys were exhausted, so I made the call for all available combat lifesavers to report to me ASAP, and almost half the mortar platoon came running over to help. The whole platoon would have run over if Captain Paul wouldn't have stopped them and said he still needs them to do their job. He then gave me eight of his guys to help me out. It was a beautiful sight to see them all running over to help their fallen brothers. By the time the medevac bird showed up we had treated over fifteen patients. Unfortunately Sergeant First Class Smith died there that morning on April 4, 2003. My medics were full of emotion, questioning why they couldn't save him; they shed tears for him that day, as we had shed tears for our other brothers that we could not save throughout our ride up north to Baghdad.

It had only been a couple of hours at most, it wasn't even afternoon yet, but that one day felt like a lifetime. Whenever we talk about this war this is the day that will always come to mind.

First Sergeant Timothy Campbell's perspective on the battle for "Four Corners":

Early morning on April 3, 2003, as we were preparing to leave Objective Hannah for the final movement into Objective Lions, we discovered an abandoned yet functional BMP, and we decided to destroy it with explosives. When preparations of the explosives were complete and all but one squad had departed the area I was shot by a sniper, making me our first casualty in my company—unfortunately I would not be the last. After being treated by the 2-7 Infantry medics I was able to rejoin the movement north to Objective Lions at Saddam International Airport. After two days of little to no sleep the company reached Objective Lions at around 0600 on April 4.

The mission was to block the main approach to the city, which was Highway 8 entering the city from the east. The company quickly established a defensive perimeter linked in with Knight Company on the north side of the westbound lane. The position was located in a strand of trees within two hundred meters of the mortar platoon and the forward aid station. The position was in a medium area between the highway and cinder block walls about ten feet high. The mortars and the aid station were located in a cloverleaf intersection at the main entrance to the airport. Shortly after arriving different missions came in for various pieces of our engineer equipment and squad size elements. The equipment moved out to perform the missions ranging from clearing sectors of fire for Bradley Fighting Vehicles to create a crater in the highway with explosives. The rest of the company was doing personal hygiene and ate their breakfast. By 0800, we were reducing holes in the walls along the edge of the compound to gain access if needed and to provide clear areas for overwatch.

At around 0900, we were noticing that there was an increasing volume of ineffective fires hitting the trees above us. The sound of the rounds hitting the dry chaff in the trees sounded like rattling cellophane and then came the RPG projectiles whistling through the air with the sound of tearing paper. My driver, Private First Class Gerrie, brought out a small tape recorder that I had brought along for recording messages to send home but had never used. We were curious if the sounds we heard would be heard on the tape. After getting it working and realizing that it would, he placed it in the between the seats inside my truck and let it begin running at about 0950. For the next forty-five minutes it would be forgotten and left there recording about half of the battle that was developing in the compound less than three hundred yards away.

About 0930, the company was given the task to construct an enemy prisoner holding area. Sergeant First Class Paul Smith reported over the radio that he had an ideal spot that we could use that would have controlled entry and exit as well as a tower overlooking the area. I agreed that he had the best location and sent him one ACE to reduce an entrance hole into a closed courtyard. At the other end was a large metal gate that fenced off an open area and a large white tower about two hundred to three hundred yards to the north. An additional two squads of engineers were sent forth with their squad tracks to emplace wire for the holding area. After getting wire from the 1st Platoon's trailer, Sergeant Bermie pulled his track forward to provide local security for the soldiers working. At first, when he looked into the courtyard, he reported enemy soldiers maneuvering on the far side in the distance. As more and more appeared, he immediately engaged with the M2 .50 caliber machine gun. They were getting closer.

There were fifty to one hundred enemy soldiers reported either trying to escape the area or to deliberately attack our position. At that time, without our knowing, at least two enemy soldiers had occupied the tower overwatching the courtyard while firing rifles and RPGs and, I believed, directing the forces still located outside of the courtyard. At that time, the first radio report was made somewhere around ten o'clock by Sergeant First Class Roush. He reported that the holding site was under contact and had taken casualties. I dismounted my truck and instructed the remaining two squads to get ready to move then made my way to the point of contact.

At that time an enemy mortar struck the top of Sergeant Bermie's track. The explosion and shrapnel stuck him in the right arm and neck, leaving him unable to continue. Private Miller was hit in the neck and left hand. Staff Sergeant Christopher was also struck in the face and neck, taking him out of the fight as well. Staff Sergeant Christopher's wounds left him unable to function. Sergeant Bermie was unable to use his arm and was in mild state of shock from his wounds. Sergeant First Class Smith had moved quickly up to the gate and took charge of the engineers at that site. First he threw a hand grenade at a suspected enemy position, then grabbed an AT4 missile from one of the other dismounted engineers to fire at the tower three hundred yards away. He then returned to direct the medic on site stabilizing the casualties for transport to the forward aid station.

Meanwhile, the enemy soldiers used the time to gain momentum and occupy key locations outside the courtyard. While that was happening, I had just about made my way to the "B26" track to assess the situation when an RPG from the overwatching tower struck the track, sending soldiers' equipment in all directions. I felt the heat from the rocket and stopped for a moment to look at the track. I realized that there were probably casualties in the track, so I went to the back door. The door flung open before I got to it, but when I arrived, I couldn't believe my eyes: dazed yet uninjured soldiers began to pour out. Luckily, the warhead had been disrupted by the soldiers' gear on the outside of the vehicle and had not penetrated the track's weak armor. I made my way to the wall where I found three more engineers and Sergeant First Class Mulligan carrying an M240B (medium) machine gun. As I looked across the yard, I could see the casualties lying against the wall being treated by the medic. They looked to me to be in bad shape, and I knew that we had to get them out of the yard. I ran about one hundred yards to their location and spoke briefly to the medic about their status. I then gathered up four soldiers to carry Staff Sergeant Christopher on the stretcher.

Sergeant First Class Smith had been working feverishly to establish a hasty defense. Unknown to me was the amount of enemy activity outside of the courtyard. Smith quickly checked the .50 cal. and put it back into action. By now the enemy had taken up positions in ditches and along the wall. I spoke to Sergeant First Class Smith in the hatch and told him that the tower must be taken out. He realized the entire situation and also realized that the track was in a bad position to effectively engage. I then started back across the courtyard with the wounded soldiers back in front of the tower that was still occupied by the enemy. When I reached the far side, I instructed Sergeant First Class Roush to continue the evacuation to the forward aid station. I made a quick assessment of what was available to me and what was needed to take out the tower. I selected Private First Class Gerrie with his AR and Specialist Montana with his M16 and attached 40mm grenade launcher.

Meanwhile, Sergeant First Class Smith had tried to turn the track toting the trailer back to a suitable location to continue to defend our position. Unable to drive and to see out of the back of the track at the same time and with no one to direct him, he proceeded to call for help. Private First Class Stephens came to his aid and quickly backed the track into position. Sergeant First Class Smith then called for some additional soldiers to unhook the trailer while simultaneously placing the machine gun back into action. He instructed Private Segar to ready the ammo from inside of the APC while he started to place fire initially on the tower, then redirected his fire on the soldiers trying to climb the wall, and finally at a third position at the gate where enemy soldiers were trying to enter. Realizing that he had distracted the enemy soldiers in the tower, I then took Private First Class Gerrie and Specialist Montana to move to the flank of the tower to engage. I threw a smoke grenade and unintentionally lit the grass outside of the wall on fire. The smoke from the grenade and from the fire began to build and effectively blocked the enemy's point of view. We maneuvered along his blind side, working our way around the tower to where we could see the enemy soldiers though the glassless window. Twice I heard Sergeant First Class Smith call for another can of ammo while I was getting into position. Within the minimum arming range, we made the decision that we were too close to use the grenade launcher and instead used the rifles to engage and kill two enemy soldiers inside the tower.

Shortly after we stopped firing we realized that Sergeant First Class Smith was also not firing. I then went back to the entry point to see what had happened. At that time Private First Class Stephens was driving the track up to where I was standing and came to a halt. What I had yet to discover was that the track had just quit running and that Sergeant First Class Smith had been shot through the neck and through his head. When Private First Class Stephens came down from the drivers' hatch and told me that Sergeant First Class Smith had been shot. I went to the back door of the track and looked inside. He was lying there with his body folded back over his lower legs. His face had lost all color, and I felt then that he was dead. Because the track would no longer run, we decided to pull him from the vehicle and put him on a stretcher, then crossload him into his M998 HMMWV. After getting him on the stretcher, I checked his vital signs and realized he had no pulse and that he had an exit wound in the back of his head. We loaded him in the truck and started to the forward aid station, but about halfway there, the truck became stuck in a mud puddle, forcing us to carry him the rest of the way.

When I got to the aid station, I felt the medics should work on Sergeant First Class Smith immediately. At first, they were already working on the previous causalities. Once I got one of the medics working on Sergeant Bermie's arm to check Sergeant First Class Smith, several of them began their work trying to revive him, but with no result. I would spend the next hour going back to where the medics were to see if there was any change to his condition while we were waiting on the medevac helicopter. When the chopper finally arrived, Sergeant Bermie would refuse to get on the aircraft because of the limited space and would spend several more hours waiting to be evacuated to the rear by ground medevac.

The battle for Four Corners lasted from approximately 1000 to 1200 hours on April 4. To this day, the enemy's true intentions there remain uncertain, even after analyzing every available report and conducting countless interviews with participants.

At the time, we believed the SRG was attempting to fight its way out of its compounds, fearing the impending attacks by Bushmaster to the north and Rage to the south. During the battle, Sergeant First Class Broadwater discovered a tunnel system that would later shed light on the mystery. He noticed a large rectangular manhole cover in the middle of the interchange, cautiously lifted it, and peered inside. The tunnel was massive, plunging deep underground, with a ladder descending into darkness as far as the eye could see. As a precaution, Broadwater parked the tire of his five-ton truck directly over the cover. His instincts were rooted in lessons from senior NCOs who had trained him as a young private in the 1980s—veterans who had learned firsthand how the Viet Cong exploited tunnels in South Vietnam for infiltration, exfiltration, and storing munitions.

The discovery explained much of our confusion during the battle. At first contact, it was difficult to understand how the enemy could surround us so completely while avoiding detection from our patrols outside the interchange. How could they have maneuvered into position without harassment? After the war, we learned that the tunnel connected the northern SRG compound next to Four Corners with the southern SRG compound that Rage had assaulted earlier that morning. The system was far more elaborate than we had ever imagined. Enemy forces in the southern compound could have used it to escape American artillery and bombs—or to alert their comrades at Four Corners of our presence. We now believe that many of the surviving SRG used the tunnels to retreat. No American soldier at Four Corners recalls actually seeing a withdrawal; the enemy simply vanished underground, desperate to escape death and fight another day.

By definition, a counterattack is a preplanned operation requiring coordination between infantry, armor, and artillery. Some might characterize the enemy action on the morning of April 4 as just that. Two theories emerged.

The first theory views the enemy's action as a deliberate, coordinated counterattack. By infiltrating our lines through the tunnels, they could strike at the heart of our defensive position, forcing us to focus inward instead of outward. In the morning of April 4, Task Force 2-7 focused its attention outward, on Highway 8 east and our northern and southern flanks. Once the Iraqi infantrymen diverted our attention inward, their armor struck the southern flank of the blocking position. The Iraqis may have attempted to combine infiltration with armored envelopment—a one-two punch. Their ultimate goal could have been to destroy the task force outright or to inflict enough chaos and losses to force us to withdraw. Even battered and fractured, the Iraqis were still capable of performing such a coordinated counterattack. This level of resistance and orchestration would have been consistent with any disciplined, well-trained adversary operating under explicit orders to hold the airport at any cost.

The second more likely theory is that the SRG was reacting in desperation rather than executing a carefully coordinated plan. Maybe some of their specific moves on us were random, chance, or improvised on the fly. Inside the airport, up to two brigades of SRG infantry were being isolated and squeezed by my sister units, Task Force 3-7 Infantry and 3-69 Armor. On the morning of April 4, they may have been fighting to break out of the airport and escape into the city. The enemy tanks striking our southern flank could have been responding to a cry for help, attempting to punch a hole in our defenses large enough to relieve their embattled comrades. If so, the "coordination" was limited to a simple trigger: the tanks moved when the infantry's situation became untenable.

What remains indisputable is that the enemy armor failed to mass or synchronize their assault, and their artillery was ineffective during the so-called counterattack. They may have assumed their tanks were superior to ours, or that we were only lightly armed paratroopers holding the airport. This is plausible, given the shattered state of their command and control system. For all they knew, the 3rd Infantry Division was still fighting in An Nasiriyah. The daily briefings by "Baghdad Bob" only reinforced this delusion. If the regime had told its soldiers the truth—that they faced an American mechanized infantry brigade—the risk of mass desertion might have rivaled the risk of defeat.

The cost of the battle was heavy for us as well. Many were wounded, including several key leaders. We lost one great American, Sergeant First Class Smith. He was a fifteen-year veteran, husband, and father. He was a hero who made the ultimate sacrifice. His loss was more than any of us could accept. He became a Medal of Honor recipient for his actions on April 4, the first to be awarded in the broader Global War on Terror. Unfortunately, he would not live to receive the award. His family accepted the medal on his behalf exactly two years later.

All the soldiers at Four Corners fought with determination. I watched quiet, introverted soldiers transform in the chaos, fighting with the ferocity of Audie Murphy. Yet when the firing stopped, many of those same soldiers curled back into themselves, emotionally spent. Combat affects every soldier differently. Some performed as expected, others surprised us. The sights, sounds, and smells left their mark on each of us in unique ways.

One truth was undeniable: things had changed. Many of our young soldiers—some not old enough to buy a beer or even cast a vote—were now hardened combat veterans. They had aged years in a matter of hours. By the end, I could see it in their eyes—the unmistakable, steely gaze of soldiers who had been tested in battle.

Every good battalion task force needs a strong brigade commander, and we had that in 1st Brigade. Colonel Will Grimsley, Raider 6, exemplified calm and steady leadership amid rapidly changing situations. His patient, reassuring voice over the radio steadied all task force commanders. What set Grimsley apart was his instinct for when to intervene and when to let subordinate leaders lead. At Objective Lions, he trusted me to fight my battle while he enabled us—coordinating artillery, close air support, and ensuring critical resources arrived exactly when and where needed. Even during heavy engagement, his swift shifts of fires and intelligence proved decisive without micromanaging. His leadership struck the perfect balance by empowering leaders while ensuring no one fought alone. He was key in the next phase of the airport battle, the Iraqi counterattack.

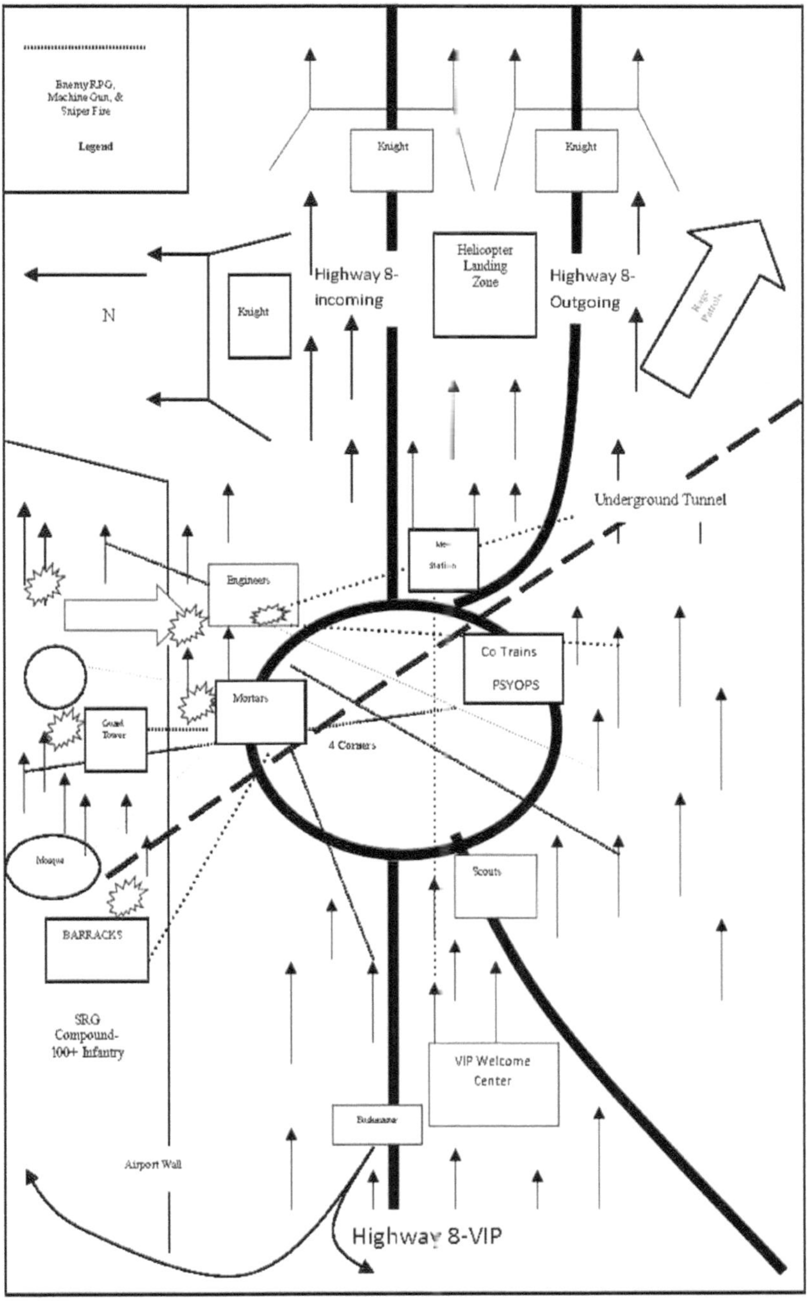

Task Force 2-7 actions at Objective Lions, Saddam International Airport, "Battle for Four Corners," April 4, 2003.
Source: Author's image.

Captain Paul and his mortar platoon shooting mortars at Four Corners during the battle at Objective Lions, Saddam International Airport, April 4, 2003. Courtesy of Task Force 2-7 History.
Source: Bill Thompson.

THE COUNTERATTACK

"Do not forget your dogs of war, your big guns, which are the most-to-be respected arguments of the rights of kings."

—Frederick the Great, Instructions for His Generals (1747)

Following the engagement at Four Corners, I ordered the mortars, medics, engineers, and scouts to reposition inside the airport walls near the Task Force TOC, still tucked beneath the overpass. Meanwhile, Bushmaster cleared the enemy compound adjacent to Four Corners, capturing twelve Iraqi soldiers. On the far side of the wall, they counted between sixty and eighty-five enemy bodies. We estimated at least as many wounded, and likely more dead carried off by their comrades. These were elite Iraqi troops, and they would not have left their fallen behind if they had the chance to remove them.

Our own losses that day were sobering—sixteen wounded and one killed as a result of the fighting on April 4. One casualty is too many. Seventeen was almost unbearable.

Because of those losses, we were forced to conduct a consolidation and reorganization. In the civilian world, this might be called a corporate reshuffle or downsizing. The difference, of course, is stark: in combat, soldiers don't get laid off, they get wounded or killed. We play for keeps. On that day, leaders throughout the task force were either killed or wounded. Their subordinates wasted no time stepping forward, assuming the duties and responsibilities of those above them. This is exactly what Task Force 2-7 soldiers were trained to do, and it happened automatically without hesitation or reservation.

One example of this situational leadership was Sergeant Hernandez and his mortar squad. Hernandez, one of the sixteen wounded, took RPG shrapnel to the skull but continued leading his men until the medevac arrived. His gunner, Private First Class Jacobs—himself wounded and bandaged, but not as badly as his sergeant—took charge of the squad and led with distinction for the remainder of the war. At nineteen, a junior private with less than a year in service suddenly found himself commanding four peers, each with about as much time in uniform as he had, while also responsible for one of only four mortars in the battalion task force. It was a staggering amount of responsibility for such a young, inexperienced soldier. He rose to the challenge, as did many others like him.

Shortly after our repositioning, we received an order to downgrade MOPP posture from Level 2 to 0, allowing us to shed our boots and protective overgarments for the rest of the war. The relief was immediate. I felt forty pounds lighter, as if I could run like the wind and leap over mountains in a single bound. Our combat effectiveness nearly doubled simply by getting out of those cursed suits. The enemy couldn't have known it, but we were suddenly faster, sharper, and ready to fight with renewed energy. The timing was perfect because the April Iraqi heat reared its ugly head on April 4, and it became unbearable as the day dragged on. If the heavy fighting continued, I am convinced we would have eventually lost soldiers to heat injuries. The order to shed our protective suits could not have come at a more opportune time.

As we packed away our chemical gear into already overstuffed vehicles, an important message came down from my brigade headquarters. Saddam himself had publicly ordered his forces to retake the airport at 1500 hours. Some believed the Iraqis were finished, that the order was nothing more than bluster. I wasn't willing to take that chance. Saddam and his regime could not afford to lose the airport, and I knew they would try to take it back. Whether it was an empty threat or a genuine order, we would be prepared. We were ready for whatever came next.

In 1815, 7th Infantry Regiment soldiers earned the nickname "Cottonbalers" by holding their ground behind bales of cotton during the battle of New Orleans. They didn't flinch, didn't break, and didn't give an inch. Nearly two centuries later, Task Force 2-7 Infantry would be asked to do the same. After seizing Saddam International Airport, we knew the enemy wasn't finished. They would come back hard, and we would need to hold firm. No retreat, no reset, and no second chances. This time, there were no cotton bales. But we had armor, grit, and the will to stand our ground.

Iraqi offensive doctrine dictated that ground forces must first isolate and encircle their objective. Once surrounded, the enemy would be softened with bombardment from the air, artillery, rockets, and at times chemical agents. These were the tactics the Iraqis employed during the Iran-Iraq War and in suppressing Kurdish uprisings in the north. Typically, they would besiege a city or town with infantry and armor, pound it with fire until resistance weakened, and then unleash an armored shock force to punch through like a bullet through warm Jell-O. The penetration would be exploited by waves of infantry, tasked with completing the destruction and seizing control.

The Iraqi counterattack would likely draw on Russian (Soviet) military doctrine. At the time, the Russian model remained the backbone of Iraq's military structure, especially in its approach to conventional warfare and strategic planning. Many of the Iraqi generals were trained in Russian military academies, where they absorbed Russian operational art, staff procedures, and command philosophy. It created a generation of Iraqi leaders steeped in Russian-style thinking. However, Iraq was not Russia—the Iraqis did not have the same combat power or will to fight. Moreover, the airport battle would reveal the fundamental flaws in the Russian model.

In a foolhardy effort, the Iraqi Army now sought to employ this conventional doctrine in their attempt to retake the airport. I believed Saddam Hussein would try to move heaven and earth to reclaim it. He understood that the loss of the airport marked the beginning of the end for his regime. Our capture of that ground was both a strategic and psychological victory, and Saddam knew it. However, the Iraqi's rigid command structure, lack of air cover, and struggle for real-time adaptability should leave them vulnerable to our precision strikes and rapid maneuver warfare.

Despite our advantages, I assumed the worst—that every committed Iraqi soldier, along with every reluctant conscript pressed forward at gunpoint by the Fedayeen, would join the counterattack. They may try to offset their qualitative flaws with quantity—relying on sheer numbers. Their advance, I feared, would be preceded by a colossal artillery barrage concentrated on our exposed positions inside the airport walls. With central Baghdad only a few kilometers away, hundreds of concealed artillery pieces in the city were easily within range to blanket us in fire.

I also expected massive civilian formations, including women and children, driven ahead as human shields to precede the attack. It was an evil yet shrewd tactic, one the regime had not hesitated to use before at smaller scales. Such methods could blunt the effectiveness of our weapons, preventing us from massing fires and forcing us into impossible moral and tactical dilemmas.

At 1500, I envisioned thousands pouring out of the city. Iraqi infantry, armor, and civilians would work in concert to overwhelm our small task force. Every tank, rifle, and cannon we possessed would be required to hold our ground. Even the loss of a single M1 Abrams tank could be paraded as a propaganda victory for the Iraqis. Pitted against large numbers of Iraqi combatants, we would shoot until we ran out of ammunition. Resupply would not be quick or easy. It may sound crazy, but I was even thinking we might need to fix bayonets like the 20th Maine at Little Round Top, Gettysburg, in the Civil War. We could also steal weapons and munitions from the Iraqi dead if we had to. Assuming we still had gas, we could use our tanks and Bradleys to ram the enemy, like the ancient Greek navy did against the Persian fleet over two thousand years ago. Or we would have to scatter and fight on as guerrillas like the US Army in the Philippines at the start of World War II. In any event, retreat or surrender was no option.

Our task force stood between the airport and Baghdad itself. We were the front line, the only line preventing the regime from reclaiming this critical ground. If there was ever terrain to be held at all costs, this was it. We concentrated our combat power on blocking the eastern approaches into the airport. Until then, our primary focus had been the destruction of the enemy. Now their destruction was secondary to holding the airport—the regime's namesake, and the symbolic heart of Saddam's crumbling power. Holding the airport and denying the Iraqis the ability to retake it would bring the coalition one step closer to strategic victory and the regime's collapse.

At 1430, Task Force 2-7 countermanded Saddam Hussein's order to retake the airport. One of the first actions I took was to crater both sides of Highway 8, denying the road to Iraqi armor. Additionally, we directed air strikes against other likely enemy avenues of approach along the eastern portion of the airfield. The earth shook with the BOOMs of F-18s dropping five-hundred-pound bombs and the BRRRPs of A-10s unleashing their 30mm Gatling guns. It was a powerful statement to the Iraqis: "If you want to take this airport back, it isn't going to be a cakewalk."

In doctrinal terms, we conducted a counterpreparation of the battlefield—disrupting the enemy's momentum and synchronization before his attack. In practical terms, it was a show of force, a demonstration of our overwhelming firepower. I believe it had the desired effect.

Beginning around 1600, the Iraqi Army attempted to encircle and isolate the airport with elements of the Hammurabi Republican Guard Division to the north and west and SRG forces to the east and south.

Our brigade's northern and western flanks were covered by the division's Cavalry Squadron, 3-7 Cavalry, which kept the Hammurabi at bay with Bradley and tank fire, supported by OH-58 Kiowa Warriors conducting armed reconnaissance deep into enemy lines. Our northern and western flanks were secure.

That afternoon, the SRG regrouped. Many of their dead had likely been replaced with reinforcements from Republican Guard or militia units deeper in the city. Several enemy tank platoons supported by BMP armored personnel carriers attempted to penetrate the southeastern wall of the airport. Each BMP and tank drove directly into our newly established kill zone. They were destroyed by A-10 Warthogs and 155mm howitzers supporting my task force. Most Iraqis never fired a shot. Those vehicles that survived the initial gauntlet were quickly dispatched by my Javelins, Bradleys, and M1 tanks, which had the enemy's exposed flank squarely in their sights.

There were many reasons behind the Iraqi counterattack's failure. Most importantly, they did not set the proper conditions before committing their armor. No obscuration smoke, no effective artillery or air support, poor or nonexistent infantry-armor synchronization, and a complete lack of communication between units—all of these were ingredients in their recipe for destruction. Unable to mass forces or coordinate fires, the Iraqi armor had no chance of breaking our defensive lines.

The Iraqis quickly realized that large-scale movements of infantry and armor would only draw devastating air and artillery strikes before they could get close to the airport. Instead they shifted tactics, attempting to infiltrate our lines with small, squad-sized patrols moving through tunnels and trench networks that funneled into the airfield. Their effort became a piecemeal attempt to dislodge us from within rather than overwhelm us from outside.

For the next two days, we worked to keep the enemy off balance by denying them the ability to reposition or concentrate their forces. What we couldn't cover with air or artillery, we patrolled with armor and infantry on the ground. My companies sent out continuous patrols and set ambushes throughout their sectors, often catching the enemy by surprise. These measures prevented the Iraqis from creating favorable conditions for a coordinated attack against us.

The philosophy I adopted for the defense was simple: "The best defense is an aggressive offense." I would not sit still and wait for the enemy to attack us on their terms. We took the fight to them, retaining the tactical initiative. Our aggressive patrolling, combined with precise air and artillery support, kept the enemy disorganized and prevented them from massing for an effective counterattack.

But the enemy always gets a vote. They could adapt and change tactics at will. By this point, the SRG, or what now likely included a mix of Republican Guard and irregular forces, could not muster enough combat power to penetrate our lines or breach the airport walls. Instead they relied on small unit infiltrations, slipping through gaps in our perimeter. Their goal was to remain hidden as long as possible before striking, forcing us to fight in multiple directions at once and creating enough chaos to drive us out of the airport. Despite their efforts, these tactics failed as decisively as their larger assaults.

The enemy was in a state of shock and disorganization under the weight of our aggressive actions. Our offensive-style defense worked. The only resistance they could muster came in the form of probing attacks with rifle fire, ATGMs, and the occasional attempt to direct mortar and artillery fire from hidden observation points. By then, we had positioned our own observers atop the overpass and inside the airport control tower, giving us excellent visibility. We neutralized their spotters with five-hundred-pound JDAM strikes and aerial strafing runs. Overhead, Air Force assets stacked five layers deep provided continuous close air support. Whatever the aircraft didn't destroy, we finished with mortars and artillery.

Before dark, each company dispatched squad and platoon-sized ambush patrols to cover likely infiltration routes into the airport. Every road, trail, and ditch was covered. The enemy was not going to get through.

Around 1700 on April 4, the task force's combat support trains arrived into the airport. This was a surprise to us. How did they get up here? Who told them to move up here from the Euphrates? I know it wasn't me. The airport was not completely secured yet. Did they know that? The combat trains consisted of mainly soft-skinned vehicles with a few M88 armored recovery vehicles mounting .50 caliber machine guns. In total, a very limited amount of firepower and protection. If they ran into an enemy tank, the results would have been catastrophic. The combat trains set up between the mortar platoon and the TOC. The battalion maintenance officer, Captain Dave Johnston, approached Captain Paul:

> CAPTAIN JOHNSTON: "Hey Matt, I spotted what looks like an unexploded mortar round up near the wall on our way in. I want to send a UXO report, can you or one of your guys classify it for me?"

CAPTAIN PAUL: "Sure no problem Hey Dave, by any chance did you run into any bad guys along the way up here?"

CAPTAIN JOHNSTON: "We were ambushed by dismounted infantry and armor. We passed a T-72 a few kilometers back. Luckily his gun tube was pointing the other direction and it was sandwiched between two trees. He couldn't back up and reorient in time to engage us."

CAPTAIN PAUL: "Dave, you are one lucky bastard."

He *was* lucky. In a highly underreported action of our campaign, my task force's combat trains ran through a gauntlet of their own. Only in an interview with the battalion's logistics officer, Captain Scott Knight, were the dangers and complexities of the drive revealed. It would be over a year before the tales of these unsung heroes of the war could finally be told.

Acting under minimal guidance, and with virtually no communications with my TOC, the combat trains elements composed of support, maintenance, and medical platoon soldiers made a homicidal and—some would argue—suicidal dash from the Euphrates River to the airport in an attempt to provide my combat units with much-needed fuel and water.

An entire convoy composed of mainly trucks and other soft-skinned vehicles managed to drive twenty-five kilometers through several enemy ambushes prepared by about two hundred dismounted infantry, a dozen technical trucks, and between ten and twenty armored vehicles. Along their route, they picked up Bushmaster's first sergeant and support vehicles and the disabled mortar carrier.

Bushmaster's first sergeant, First Sergeant Wilson, helped organize and lead the trains through the enemy's meat grinder en route to the airport. He helped direct the fire and maneuver of the convoy and personally engaged over fifty Iraqi infantry. His initiative and leadership under fire earned him the Silver Star. Captain Knight commented that the first sergeant's acts were indeed brave but may have been a bit too much. He stated, "Although the first sergeant wanted to stay in the gauntlet to try and kill everyone—I convinced him that not everyone was so equipped and leaving fifty-thousand-pound fuelers in the middle of a kill zone was not a good thing." Support convoys are taught to fight through the ambush by continuing to shoot and move until contact with the enemy force has been broken. But with the first sergeant on board, the suicidal dash became a homicidal dash—and the enemy would pay dearly for their audacity to attack this "vulnerable" supply column.

Rather than shoot up to the airport in a retreat-like dash, the combat trains made numerous stops to recover lost vehicles stuck in the mud along the route. This was the brigade's "trail of breadcrumbs." Captain Knight recounts, "We stopped short of Highway 1, while my truck and an M88 recovery vehicle tried digging an M1 out all night to the sound of sporadic gunfire. By morning we'd got it out, but because it tipped on its right side, all of the tension and track were broke." The mechanics patched up the sixty-ton beast as best they could.

It was now light, and the trains could not use the cover of darkness to mask their movement along the open and exposed Highway 1 interstate—the road was lined with trees and embankments flanking both sides, ideal for enemy ambush. During the final push up the highway, their formation's movement was advertised by the slow and unmistakably loud rumble of the M88 tracked recovery vehicles and the accompanying M577 command post vehicles—also slow, and decorated with large whip antennas, making a delicious target for any enemy armed with an RPG.

The combat trains responded to repeated enemy harassment from both sides of the large four-lane interstate. Hundreds of RPGs and enemy bullets crisscrossed the formation but miraculously were aimed too high to have a significant effect on the movement. Iraqi gun trucks made suicidal attempts to ram the flanks of the column. They were laid to waste by .50 caliber machine gun fire from Captain Knight's gunner, Private First Class Greer, and assistant S-1, First Lieutenant Gendron.

During the gauntlet, one of Captain Knight's passengers, Specialist Garcia, sat calmly in the HMMWV, juxtaposed against the turbulent situation surrounding him. He cradled his M16 in his hands as if it was a suitcase and as if he was in a limousine being taxied to the airport on a business trip. Captain Knight took a brief pause from shouting commands into his radio's hand mic and firing his rifle into the enemy redoubts along the route and noticed his soldier relaxing in the back seat. Knight asked, "What the fuck . . . do you see the flashes?" "Sort of, by the buildings . . . which building?" Garcia countered. Captain Knight promptly replied, "Pick a building and shoot at it . . . they're all shooting at us!"

Enemy T-72s were positioned along the route, but fortunately with their backs turned toward the formation, to the north. They were lying in wait for the rest of the division to advance north along the tight country roads leading into the airport. Perhaps it was an attempt at ambush, but they were in the wrong spot looking in the wrong direction. They were either unable or unwilling to reposition and reorient to engage the combat trains, much to the train's good luck. Perhaps the enemy did not believe that we would have the audacity to simply drive up to their capital along their most popular highway interstate. Notwithstanding, the luck of the trains ran out a few times—it was only a matter of time for a few of the enemy's rounds to find their desired targets. The trains stopped a few times to reorganize—the medics and the support platoon leader, First Lieutenant Oliver, worked feverishly to treat wounded and cross-level crewmen after a vehicle became disabled or destroyed by the enemy fusillade.

In one instance, the mortar squad now attached to the combat trains provided added firepower to the convoy and the gunner, Private First Class Aldrin, was recommended for the Bronze Star for his actions during one of the many ambushes along the route. The Mark-19 grenade machine gun mounted on the mortar carrier succumbed to the desert dust and jammed at the most inopportune time. The enemy launched one of its many ambushes, this time incorporating human wave assaults. With the enemy in closing distance and now massing for the kill, Sergeant Marsh put the entire weight of his body behind cocking the large bolt on the grenade launcher. His efforts proved futile. Marsh's crewman, Private First Class Aldrin, couldn't remain patient and wait any longer. In a single motion, Aldrin, very respectfully, tossed his smaller squad leader aside and pulled the cocking mechanism while employing every muscle in his body, dislodging the misfired round and chambering a new one to commence the mauling of each of the neatly formed ranks of his enemy's formation. He neutralized an entire platoon of enemy infantry with his automatic grenade launcher, allowing other elements of the convoy to drive through the ambush unmolested.

It was an amazing feat what this small, underprotected column of support soldiers was able to accomplish. With limited firepower and fragmented units, they inflicted substantial carnage against the enemy with minimal damage or losses. The convoy only lost two vehicles and sustained two noncritical casualties during the march up. It was estimated that they defeated a force equivalent to an entire enemy battalion. They fought through more resistance than the rest of the task force during its march to the airport. Moreover, the trains were able to fight through enemy contact without getting lost or turned around once. And if that weren't enough, they recovered about half a dozen stuck or broken down vehicles along the route while they were in contact and under fire.

The trains' soldiers were both resilient and lucky. One of their trucks even had an unexploded RPG round lodged in its chassis. This is as lucky as it gets. When your number is up, your number is up. Over a dozen medals were awarded for individual acts of valor performed during the combat train's homicidal (suicidal) dash to Saddam International Airport.

On a Cold War battlefield, doctrine stipulates that support soldiers should almost never be directly engaged by frontline enemy forces. This clash of forces truly illustrated the contemporary, post/911 battlefield and paved the way for new conventional Army wisdom—how the Army trains, equips, and fights on the modern battlefield. Every soldier is a rifleman first, regardless of his or her military occupational specialty.

It is still unclear to me what the enemy's plans or intentions were on April 4 following Saddam's order to counterattack. Studying history and doctrine and reflecting on my own past experience in training and combat, it's possible that our isolated engagements within the battlespace—wedged between the Euphrates River and the southwestern outskirts of Baghdad—were part of a larger effort to envelop our brigade. The attack on the supply column may have been intended to sever our lifeline and cut us off from the rest of the division to the south and east. This theory is plausible. The engagement occurred around the same time as the enemy's counterattack to the north, in and around the airport.

By April 3, most of the enemy's command-and-control systems had been destroyed. Any coordination across large Iraqi formations from that point forward was unlikely. I believe the enemy had originally been posted along the southern approaches to the airport to blunt or disrupt our attack somehow. They could have lain in wait in hide positions, allowing our combat formations to pass by, then triggered an ambush against our vulnerable supply columns. This seems more plausible than assuming a brilliantly coordinated counterattack in response to our assault on the airport. Similar actions occurred all over southern Iraq, but attributing that level of sophistication to our battered enemy and their inept leadership is probably giving them too much credit.

By early evening on April 4, enemy activity subsided, and the airport was reported secure. Embedded and Associated Press reporters immediately swarmed my battalion TOC looking for interviews. I confidently told them, "The Cottonbalers have taken the airport." The press also announced that the facility was renamed Baghdad International Airport. We later heard that this footage aired on all the major television and radio networks. Naturally, we wondered how our families back home would react. Would they be worried, proud, or relieved that the war was one step closer to ending?

That evening, we improved our positions. Despite their fatigue and personal losses, the soldiers' spirits were high. Many laughed and told jokes, reliving the tragically humorous moments of the day. This resilience was remarkable. We were approaching four days with little rest, food, or water. Yet the soldiers endured. Mental and physical stamina are just as critical to a soldier as strength or courage. That day, they had taken lives and suffered losses, but they still managed to transcend the conditions around them, continuing to fight as disciplined soldiers. They motivated one another and learned what it truly meant to fight for each other.

Knight Company, now responsible for nearly all the battlespace along Highway 8, including the southern SRG compound, set up their command post in a small barracks just west of SRG South. During the initial search of the building, they discovered a cache of food, some of it marked "UN Oil for Food Program." It was disheartening to realize the Iraqi military had hoarded food meant for starving civilians After months of eating nothing but MREs, First Lieutenant Carmody, Knight's stocky Italian XO, opened several containers of pasta and tomato sauce and cooked enough of this unexpected treasure to feed most of his company.

Meanwhile, soldiers not on patrol dug shallow fighting positions. The clay-like earth limited us to about two feet in depth. They dug as deep as possible because our 1-41 Field Artillery Battalion had not moved their Q36 and Q37 counterfire radars forward. The radars remained near the Euphrates with their soft-skinned vehicles. That left us dangerously exposed to enemy mortars, rockets, and artillery. All we could do was hope that the Iraqi gunners could not shoot straight. We had hoped that their fire either missed or that our holes were deep enough to protect us if they didn't.

After the holes were dug, Sergeant Norris from the mortar platoon walked over to investigate an unexploded mortar round. Minutes later, a loud BOOM shook us, followed by an explosion. At first, we thought Norris had accidentally detonated the round. The blast occurred less than fifty meters from him. However, the blast was actually caused by an enemy 152mm artillery round striking an eight-foot wall about one hundred meters away. A piece of shrapnel hit Norris's Kevlar helmet but didn't penetrate. He was crouched over the unexploded mortar round when the 152mm artillery shell impacted the wall; had he been standing, the shrapnel would likely have struck his torso. He was lucky.

We expected the enemy to follow with a massive barrage, so I instructed the task force to remain under cover inside their tracks or fighting positions. Iraqi doctrine suggested that after such a strike, they would attempt a large armored thrust against the airport walls. But the artillery salvo never came. Instead sporadic and inaccurate rounds landed inside and outside the airport, close enough to keep us on alert but too scattered to be effective.

We weren't content to sit passively while under fire. My staff and I decided to challenge the enemy to an artillery duel. There was one problem: 1-41 FA was critically low on "white bag" powder charges, needed for close-range fires. Earlier, it positioned one of its batteries an optimal distance away southwest of the airport, and it could have provided us with support. But after sustaining losses, they were forced to displace into the airport for added security and to regroup with the rest of their battalion. That meant that the enemy could get dangerously close to us, especially at night. Our only viable solution was to rely on the task force mortars. They were eager to get back into the fight, but their ammunition was limited to what they carried on their tracks, and resupply was three days and over one hundred kilometers away.

We huddled over the map and devised a plan. I tasked the mortar platoon with firing harassment and interdiction missions throughout the night. Their guns were laid on a nearby hilltop we nicknamed "Spiral Hill." On a topographic map, its contour lines formed a concentric spiral, standing alone on otherwise flat desert. I learned later it was called "Tall Raml" and was an ancient sand hill formed over centuries by human settlement and sediment accumulation. It rose about 190 feet from the ground level, only a few feet taller than "Little Round Top" in Gettysburg, Pennsylvania's Civil War battlefield. But at the time, I didn't know if the hill was a landfill, a bunker, or perhaps even a WMD site. Regardless, the hill overlooked the entire airport and lay less than two kilometers southeast of our position. From there, an enemy observer could easily adjust artillery onto any point inside the airport walls. Coincidentally, the Union Army had similar concerns about Little Round Top at Gettysburg 150 years prior.

Spiral Hill was key terrain. Doctrine would have required us to seize it, but the risks outweighed the benefits. A small force positioned there could be isolated and cut off, making resupply and evacuation nearly impossible. Instead we chose to deny it to the enemy with continuous mortar fire, making the hill an undesirable place to operate. That night, the mortar platoon fired six missions against the hill. In turn, the task force received only sporadic, ineffective artillery fire. We concluded the enemy was now firing blind, thanks to our efforts.

Meanwhile, the scout platoon's antiarmor team, led by Specialist Schmidtt, went into action, destroying two T-72s just two hundred meters beyond the airport's boundary wall. Both missiles found their mark. The scouts also dismounted one of their long-range acquisition systems (LRAS) and positioned it atop the overpass, giving them the ability to observe enemy movement miles beyond the airport and even deep into the city. With this advantage, Iraqi forces had no chance of closing within the maximum range of their weapons before we spotted them—and destroyed them with Javelins, close air support, or mortars. If our artillery could shoot targets without its white bag charges, we would get the artillery into the fight too.

Task Force 2-7 mortarman cleaning his mortar between fire missions during the battle of Objective Lions, Saddam International Airport, April 4, 2003.
Source: Author photo.

Task Force 2-7 Tactical Operations Center (TOC) commanding and controlling the Saddam International Airport battle at Objective Lions, April 4, 2003. Courtesy of Task Force 2-7 History.
Source: Bill Thompson.

On the morning of April 5, Task Force 1-64 Armor executed an attack along Highway 8. They attacked directly through the heart of Baghdad from the south, then swung west, into the airport. The purpose was to probe and to test the enemy's defenses in preparation for a final thrust into the city. In addition to the tactical advantages, the attack would have strategic implications as well. The Iraqi people were told that the international press reports about the airport being seized by the Americans were false and that we were nowhere near Baghdad. The sight of an American column of tanks and Bradleys would prove the Iraqi leadership wrong.

As an added benefit, the attack through the city succeeded in softening the city's fortifications. Many Iraqis defending redoubts along the main approaches into the city dropped their uniforms and ran. Task Force 1-64 Armor engaged scores of Iraqi defenders along Highway 8. To our tankers' advantage, the Iraqis posted along the highway were oriented west, toward the airport. Their backs and, most importantly, their guns were all pointing in the wrong direction. They thought Baghdad was a "rear" area, a safe haven. We had the element of surprise.

I charged Knight with receiving 1-64 Armor about three kilometers west of the airport along Highway 8 and then guiding them into our perimeter inside the airport walls. We didn't get much notice about 1-64 Armor's attack through the city, so Knight had to work quickly with Bulldog's engineering assets to fill in the craters in the road that we made the previous day.

While sitting there on the highway, Knight was harassed by small hunter-killer teams of Iraqi infantry, playing their usual game of cat and mouse. They attacked from the northern and southern SRG compounds. RPG shrapnel caught Sergeant First Class Deel, a Knight Company platoon sergeant, in the back of the neck, exploiting a small gap between his Kevlar helmet and his body armor. The tank pulled out of their firing position and darted back to the airport to evacuate Deel to the aid station inside the airport. His wingman and platoon leader, First Lieutenant DeArmas, followed him. DeArmas's tank was damaged and completely without radio communications; it had to play follow the leader with Platoon Sergeant Deel's tank.

Major Coffey observed Knight's withdrawal from the highway and to the observer, it appeared as though the tankers were retreating from enemy contact. He cornered Captain Lee inside the airport and the two engaged in a heated discussion about the episode. Initially, Coffey was unaware of the circumstances surrounding the incident, but after a fifteen-minute exchange of words, the two eventually came to a mutual understanding.

During the heated discussion between the two Officers, Sergeant First Class Deel was evacuated back to within the airport walls, to the aid station. Sergeant Cox, the tank's gunner, took charge of the tank while treating his boss and fighting through the enemy RPG gunners at the same time. Back at the aid station, First Lieutenant DeArmas ditched his disabled tank, took over Sergeant First Class Deel's place in his tank, and charged back into the fight—all in less than two minutes.

The majority of resistance Knight encountered along the highway originated from the southern SRG compound. The enemy backfilled part of the compound after Rage pulled out the night prior to secure the perimeter around the TOC and supporting assets inside the airport grounds. The enemy infiltrated the compound just before Knight took over—probably using the same underground tunnel system used by the enemy SRG forces the day prior. The enemy could move within the tunnel system to quickly displace from one position to the next while remaining undetected and to avoid being spotted from the air.

1-64 drove through a hornet's nest of enemy resistance in Baghdad. The Iraqis believed it to be their last stand. When 1-64's S-3 called our TOC over the radio and informed us of his arrival, he sounded like he had just seen a ghost—still very professional and concise, just an unusual vibration in the tone that signified the severity of the situation. Charging through all the fire, 1-64 lost only one tank along the route through the city. They suffered one casualty, and we made the call requesting a helicopter medevac.

Despite the incident with the two tanks, Knight did an excellent job receiving 1-64 and guiding them into position within the airport. The attack through the city was a huge success. Enemy casualties were estimated upward of over a thousand KIA. As a result of the attack into the city, the level of resistance in the airport begin to taper off. It was a turning point; the enemy had reached a culminating point in their ability to mount a counterattack.

We hypothesized that 1-64 Armor's attack through the city diverted some of the enemy's attention and resources away from the counterattack into the airport and subsequently refocused their efforts on defending their capital city. "Fortress Baghdad," as it came to be known, was not to be. 1-64 Armor pierced their defenses with relative ease, and this would quickly set the 3rd Infantry Division on a new course toward regime change.

The 1-64 Armor's attack through the city was later nicknamed the "Thunder Run." A fitting analogy, "Thunder Run" was a phrase coined by mechanized units while fighting in the jungles of Vietnam. At the time, the army positioned artillery throughout the country in what were called firebases and many of those bases were nicknamed "Thunder." The mechanized units were charged with clearing main supply routes between firebases in advance of large vehicle convoys. They would patrol their tanks and armored personnel carriers along these ambush-laden roads and trails at night while conducting armed reconnaissance. They massed their cannon and machine gun fire on all suspected enemy positions along the route. This technique was successful a generation ago, and, with great care and attention taken to prevent collateral damage, it would be successful once again.

On the afternoon of April 5, I ordered Knight to clear the southern SRG compound out one last time. The task force needed to eliminate the residual enemy presence in and around the airport. The blocking position would never be secure if the SRG compound remained intact as an enemy strongpoint or hide position. I knew we would be relieved by a battalion from the 101st Airborne, currently making a rapid advance north from Karbala. We needed to secure the surrounding area in preparation for their arrival. This was necessary to conduct a seamless and uncontested relief in place between our two forces. So we would finish the SRG off once and for all.

Preparatory fires from A-10 Warthogs and long-range artillery preceded their advance. The compound was isolated by two platoons of tanks and Bradleys before the infantry began their assault. Enemy resistance inside the compound was light. Every building inside was cleared by Knight. They began with 25mm and 120mm cannon fire to establish a breach, then the dismounted infantry charged through. The infantrymen used their Bradleys for cover while moving from one building to the next. They repeated this drill over two dozen times until every building was given the "all clear."

Two dismounted infantry squads cleared a large barracks building, a mission fit for an entire light infantry battalion. Fewer than twenty brave infantrymen from Knight would perform this taxing mission. Clearing multiple rooms and floors can get physically exhausting, fast. Almost the entire first floor was lined with thousands of rifles and RPGs. Knight consolidated all their C-4 plastic explosives and rigged everything they had to the first floor of the building comprising the Iraqi armory. The powerful explosion collapsed the entire first floor, immediately followed by the second and third stories above. The building was thoroughly reduced to a mushroom cloud of dust and debris. This demolition may have marked the end of resistance within the two SRG compounds. The Iraqis did not want to occupy a building that we could flatten with bombs from the air or with direct fire or explosives on the ground.

An Iraqi gun truck on top of Spiral Hill, overlooking the southern SRG compound, fired effective antiaircraft fire onto Knight's infantry as they were maneuvering from one building to the next. Just as they were getting pinned down, First Lieutenant Johnson deployed his Javelin against the truck, and within seconds the truck was in flaming pieces. In total, Knight defeated at least a platoon of SRG infantry in its attack. I ordered Knight to secure the compound for the night and prevent the SRG from once again reinforcing it. I could not allow the SRG to disrupt our relief in place with the 101st the next day.

During the mission, I received intelligence that enemy combatants had retreated farther north to a nearby residential area used for housing Air Force pilots and support personnel. Reports indicated that the civilian homes within the Baghdad suburb were being used as safe havens, using the civilians as hostages or human shields. I dispatched Knight to investigate. First Lieutenant Johnson dismounted with his infantry and began to knock on doors. The civilians appeared petrified, but it was unclear if they were more frightened by us or the Iraqis who may have threatened them earlier.

The suburb appeared to be clear of enemy combatants from what we could tell. It was hard to distinguish friend from foe at this point. We were on their home turf. For all we knew, enemy combatants could have simply dropped their weapons and uniforms and walked back to their homes, in the same neighborhood we were now searching. A few English speakers reported hostage takings had occurred the day prior, but the enemy cleared out that same night. Others played dumb, as if they didn't even realize that there was a war going on. I think they would have said anything to create confusion or to draw our attention elsewhere. They simply wanted us to go away.

We applied a simple formula to the rest of our airport battle: find the enemy with patrols and observation posts, then destroy it with massed artillery, mortar fire, and airpower. Our scouts maintained their vantage points atop the overpass and inside the flight control tower, calling in fire missions on everything from squad-sized patrols to tanks, armored personnel carriers, and trucks attempting to press against our lines. The mortar platoon alone fired more than twenty missions and expended over five hundred rounds between April 5 and 6.

One of their most remarkable missions came when the scouts spotted a BMP skirting the contours of Spiral Hill, trying to conceal its approach toward the airport wall. Javelins were out of range, Bradleys couldn't maneuver into position to fire TOWs, and artillery and CAS were tied up in the west supporting Task Force 3-69 Armor and 3-7 Infantry. With no other assets available, the mortars were our only option. They fired sixteen rounds—fifteen of which seemed to have little effect. But the sixteenth round struck home, piercing the turret and detonating inside the vehicle. The BMP erupted in flames and burned for hours, a testament to persistence, skill, and luck.

Roughly an hour later, the mortars scored again, annihilating over fifteen enemy soldiers huddled in a trench less than two kilometers from the eastern wall of the airport. The Iraqis had attempted to infiltrate using the terrain as cover and concealment. They tried to get close enough to render our long-range fires irrelevant. But the trench they occupied lacked overhead protection. When Rage Company's platoon sergeant, Sergeant First Class Erskine, called for fire, the mortars responded with twenty high-explosive rounds armed with proximity fuses. Each detonated several feet above the ground, raining lethal fragments into the trench. Not one of the Iraqis survived the initial volley.

Weeks later, we revisited the site. The scene was overwhelming: severed heads, limbs barely clinging to torsos, and uniforms of the SRG layered beneath civilian clothes. An Iraqi captain was identified among the formation—identifiable by his brown leather boots worn by officers and his burned rank insignia on his shoulders, barely recognizable. It was proof that, even so late in the campaign, some degree of small unit leadership remained. To this day, I find myself reflecting on those fifteen men. Their actions may have been futile, even reckless, but their courage and perhaps their loyalty to their country was undeniable.

History tells us that in war, artillery inflicts many casualties and a lot of destruction, and this battle was no exception. Our artillery would live up to its title as the "king of battle" during the Iraqi counterattack to retake the airport. Between artillery, mortars, and tactical air support, the results were decisive: three T-72s, two BMPs, two gun trucks, and more than fifty enemy infantrymen were destroyed. Whatever armor the Iraqis had left after the battle for Saddam International Airport was pulled back into the city, preparing for a final defense.

Denied the ability to strike en masse, the enemy shifted to smaller, desperate tactics—RPG and sniper teams working in twos and threes at the outer limits of their weapons' range. Time and again, they tried to establish positions on Spiral Hill, only to be driven off by our mortars and artillery. In one particularly brazen attempt, they placed snipers atop a construction crane near Saddam's Palace, just two kilometers away, overlooking the entire airport. Within an hour, our concentrated artillery and A-10 strafing runs eliminated the threat. Each attempt to find our weakness ended the same way—with heavy Iraqi losses and retreat into the city. Every block brought new danger, but by then fear had burned off. The Iraqis' actions became predictable, and our counteractions were more effective every time they engaged.

Iraqi infantry patrols continued probing for weaknesses, slipping toward what they believed were gaps in our defenses. But those gaps were deliberate, covered by hidden ambushes and overlapping fields of fire. These were our engagement areas, our kill zones. Each attempt ended the same way—with heavy losses for the Iraqis followed by a hasty retreat into the city.

By the end of the fight, the SRG was shattered. As a coherent fighting force, it no longer existed. Those who survived faced only two choices: disappear into the shadows or regroup in Baghdad's streets for one final, desperate stand.

Combat at Saddam International Airport was conducted at extremely close range. The intensity of the experience would serve as the climax of our journey to Baghdad. The enemy fired just as many bullets at us than we at him. Fortunately, our superior training, equipment, and warrior spirit prevailed. The emotional reaction of three days of close combat will never leave me—the roar of engines, the flash of tracer fire, and the unbreakable will of the soldiers beside me. It was described and characterized by many in the task force.

A young soldier from Task Force 2-7 Infantry described the combat experience the best:

> When the first enemy bullets and RPG's flew past my head, I felt like I was in a state of denial, like the experience wasn't actually happening to me . . . almost like I was watching this combat unfold on television. Once I accepted this experience as my own personal reality, denial evolved into fear and confusion. These emotions developed into the instinct of self-preservation. I wanted to jump into a hole and to curl up into a little ball. This impulse lasted for only a few seconds. After absorbing this initial denial and shock of close combat, my training and killer instincts kicked in. I sustained both over the course of the battle by fighting alongside my buddies to my left and right and by following my leaders who also placed themselves in harm's way . . . by leading from the front.

After prolonged exposure to the carnage of battle, the body and mind eventually reach a crossroads. A soldier either breaks under the strain or becomes numb. This numbness is both physical and mental, arriving when the adrenaline fades after the first rush of combat. It allows the soldier to steady himself, to focus on his duties with clarity and control. Instinctive fear of death diminishes, replaced by a cold detachment that enables him to fight and kill without hesitation, sometimes for hours on end. Many within the task force felt this numbness during our clash with the SRG at Saddam International Airport.

But once the fighting stops, the return to normalcy is anything but immediate. It is not as simple as flipping a switch. When the guns fell silent, many of my soldiers ran headlong into a wall of fatigue, hunger, rage, guilt, remorse, and disgust. Some grew physically sick. Others found that when fear did return, it struck even harder than before. Combat reminds every soldier of his own mortality. Once the unknown becomes known, the weight of it can crush a soldier's spirit. Keeping soldiers balanced and focused amid these swings was one of the greatest challenges for the task force's leaders, and it was never easy.

By the end of the battle, we estimated that more than one hundred Iraqi infantry had been killed and forty-five captured. On the battlefield, twelve T-72 tanks, four BMPs, three D-30 artillery pieces, five truck-mounted SA-2s, and three gun trucks were destroyed. Our own cost was heavy in its own way: Task Force 2-7 lost one brave soldier during the fight for Objective Lions. We treated countless wounded.

The fall of Saddam International Airport was more than a tactical victory. The Iraqis threw what they could at us. Days of trial and error, adapting their tactics and trying different ways to beat us back had failed. It was a devastating blow to the Iraqi defense, stripping away not only their physical strength but also their psychological will. It was a strategic success, the last big domino to fall before Baghdad. In hindsight, this was the moment the enemy stopped trying to blunt our division's main attack. Instead, the enemy reoriented more on the terrain now, where they could slow us down and hurt us the most. We were no longer simply pressing into Baghdad, we were pounding on the regime's front door.

Standing at the airport, I knew this was the next phase of the war. No plan would guide us now. We would fall back on our training. It felt like a new beginning—not just for us, but for Iraq. We knew the capital lay ahead, and with it, the reckoning. The road to Baghdad was open (sort of), but the future was uncertain. We had done our part. The end felt near.

BAGHDAD

The Battle for Highway 8

"Nine times of ten an army has been destroyed because its supply lines have been severed."

—General Douglas MacArthur, remarks to the Joint Chiefs of Staff, August 1950

On the afternoon of April 6, we were relieved from our positions by Task Force 3-187 Airborne Infantry Regiment of the 101st Airborne (air assault) Division, nicknamed the "Rakkasans." This Rakkasan battalion fell under Lieutenant Colonel Lee Fetterman. His brigade commander, Colonel Michael Linnington, and division commander, Major General David Petraeus—having commanded battles in southern Iraq since the start of the war—began to shift their gaze to north, to Baghdad and beyond. This was the inflection point for the 101st. All three leaders would distinguish themselves in Iraq, and in their careers after the Army.

That morning, before 3-187 arrived, my command sergeant major—ever the standard bearer—toured the battalion and ensured that all 2-7 soldiers shaved, cleaned, and put on fresh uniforms for the relief in place. He didn't want our soldiers to look whipped, tired, or beaten, even if they were. 1st Brigade and my Task Force 2-7 Infantry did an incredible thing at the airport—it beat the Iraqi Army and forced its retreat into Baghdad. We needed to look like winners now. A brief rest would come a little bit later.

The relief in place was smooth and without incident. It was quiet and largely uncontested. My soldiers gave the Rakkasans their foxholes and sectors of fire. Soldiers also traded food, tobacco products, and a few war stories. My leaders shared intelligence, pointing out the enemy hotspots and explaining the tactical challenges in the area. I chatted directly with the battalion commander, Lieutenant Colonel Lee Fetterman. It was important for the two of us—as fellow commanders—to achieve shared understanding of the enemy, the surrounding battlespace, and key terrain.

The Rakkasans had less firepower than we did, but it probably didn't matter at this point. By now the blocking mission morphed into a different kind of fight. When the Iraqi counterattack failed, it became less of a large-scale force-on-force fight between two armies and more of a scattered hit-and-run fight with the remaining Iraqi resistance in the area. It was still dangerous, but the character of this battle had changed considerably over the past couple of days. The Rakkasans looked sharp, professional, and determined; if the Iraqis continued to resist, they would do so at their own peril.

Command Sergeant Major Fox seized the opportunity and attempted to provide our task force with twenty-four hours of refit, rest, and recuperation. We hadn't slept in days, and Fox knew we would need to take these soldiers somewhere else very soon. The war was not over yet. He reconned a small lodging area on the west side of the airport. These were Iraqi SRG or Air Force barracks. Indications from looking at the barracks were that they hadn't been lived in for at least a month. All the furniture and floors were layered with a red/orange coat of sand and dust, probably left over from the shamal over a week ago. We didn't mind the mess. Our priorities were to shower, eat, then sleep. We had plenty of time to refit and resupply in the morning, or so we thought at the time.

Shortly after the entire task force began to power down, our PSYOPS detachment began driving up and down the street, nicknamed "Able Avenue," while playing the "Cottonbaler Song" over their loudspeakers. The soldiers of the task force cheered at the sound of it. Playing the song represented the long tradition of the regiment's steadfast courage in the face of the enemy. We played the regiment's song every morning over the radio, just before my battlefield update brief, or "Bub." Until now, most of the soldiers thought the song was a little corny and many failed to appreciate the history behind the words. Not today. At the airport, our task force certainly lived up to the regiment's finest traditions, and today the soldiers knew it. They embraced it.

The words came over the loudspeakers, scratchy and familiar, drifting down Able Avenue as the PSYOPS trucks rolled past. We heard it before, usually in the background, dismissed as a relic from another era. But this time was different. We were filthy, exhausted, and running on fumes after days of combat. As that old song echoed through the barracks, something shifted. No one laughed or rolled their eyes. For the first time, we understood it. It wasn't about Andrew Jackson or New Orleans, not really. It was standing your ground when everything in you wants to quit—stubbornness, refusing to break, holding the line with the outcome still in doubt. In that moment, we were living it. The Cottonbaler soldiers were nearly two centuries apart, but the spirit was the same. As the last notes faded into the Baghdad night, we felt it.

Although our disdain for the British has certainly waned over the ages, the song speaks to the regiment's spirit, its stubbornness on the battlefield. Now the British were our closest allies, fighting and dying alongside us in southern Iraq. That wouldn't have been possible without the 7th Regiment two centuries ago.

Soldiers spent the night taking showers and cleaning weapons and equipment. Some found time to write letters home, even though the mail system was down, and it would be days or even weeks before letters could flow back and forth again. It took their minds off the explosions and the loud BRRPs! from the A-10 strafing runs echoing in the distance. I fell asleep to the sound of fireworks and the flashes of light just a few miles away.

During the early morning hours of April 7, we awoke a clean and well-rested task force. Many of us all had at least eight hours of uninterrupted sleep for the first time in weeks. Luckily, the shower facilities had enough water to bathe most of the soldiers in the task force who wanted to clean off weeks' or months' worth of sand and grime. It was beginning to take its toll.

At 0800 hours, the staff held a planning session for a follow-on mission. The TOC was set up inside an SRG facility, perhaps a former headquarters or a training facility. The inside of the compound contained classrooms, barracks facilities consisting of open living quarters, a library of Iraqi field manuals graphically depicting the proper way to ambush and attack an American formation, an arms room containing hundreds of antique rifles and muskets, and even weight training facilities with a picture of an Iraqi version of Arnold Schwarzenegger displayed on a wall.

While the rest of the task force was enjoying their sleep, all night the staff huddled around a large 1:100,000 scale map of Baghdad and several pictures depicting nearly every street, alleyway, and building within the city. Major Coffey was an excellent planner. He always used to tell his staff that "time not spent planning was time wasted." He pushed his people to their limits. No doubt they were a better staff for it. They were up all night wargaming our next move, to attack one of Saddam's Presidential Palaces, a command center we called the "Iraqi Pentagon" building, and another SRG compound further to the east. We were to then posture ourselves for future operations deeper into the city. The time to attack was "on order," or "to be determined."

The staff looked like the walking dead—black bags under their bloodshot eyes with five o'clock shadow along their rough, sunburned faces, their normal body movements slowed and their speech severely slurred from a lack of sleep. They hadn't slept a full night for weeks now. The stamina of these unsung heroes helped win the war and saved many lives. They pushed themselves beyond the limits of human endurance. They never stopped thinking, always trying to improve the current mission while planning for the next.

At 0900 hours, the S-2, Captain Derrick Smits, noticed friendly icons appearing on their battle tracking computer screens in the middle of Baghdad. 2nd Brigade was in the middle of the city! Shortly after our discovery, we received a warning order to be prepared to attack into the city to secure their main supply route—their line of communication (LOC) running along Highway 8. Highway 8 was a major four-way intersection running from Saddam International Airport through central and southern Baghdad, and all the way down to southern Iraq. It appeared that 2nd Brigade had no intention of leaving this time. Baghdad's defenses would not be taken down one piece at a time, from the outside in. They would be taken with one rapid stroke, and they would be taken from the inside out.

As the only infantry task force within the 2nd Brigade of the 3rd Infantry Division, Task Force 3-15 Infantry was responsible for securing the brigade's LOC for its two armored task forces, Task Forces 1-64 and 4-64 Armor. Securing this critical artery for the brigade would enable the armored units to continue their attack throughout the city. Providing boots on the ground, Task Force 3-15 infantrymen were better suited than the tanks to seize and retain key terrain along the LOC. Their unique ability to deny the terrain to the enemy could provide the armor forces with unfettered movement to and from their assigned objectives within the city.

2nd Brigade's initial penetration into the city from the south was a success, but in quick succession, enemy forces from all sides began to counterattack. It became a hornet's nest. They were hit hard on their flanks by enemy armor from the Republican Guard and SRG infantry, Ba'ath Party militia, Saddam Fedayeen, and a sizeable force of foreign jihadists. They were taking casualties and were getting stretched thin as the lead elements pressed their attack into the northwestern quadrant of the city. Without the LOC adequately secured, their attack would stall, leaving the brigade isolated and cut off in the heart of the city.

I placed the task force on a REDCON 3 posture. This meant that we must be combat ready within fifteen minutes notice. Soon after, I was given the green light to go from my boss, Colonel Grimsley. I quickly ordered the task force to REDCON 1, ready to go within a moment's notice. We were to attack into the city and reinforce Task Force 3-15. Together we could effectively secure 2nd Brigade's LOC along Highway 8. For this battle, my task force would be placed under 2nd Brigade's operational control.

I gave the task force another fifteen minutes to uncoil from their rest positions and move out. It took time to pack up the cots, strap the bags to the vehicles, do the radio checks, and a whole host of other tasks required before we could properly begin movement. The only way home now was through Baghdad. There was not a moment to waste.

Commanders and platoon leaders quickly pulled their soldiers together and briefed them on the situation and our upcoming mission. Many of the soldiers were excited. They knew the war was about to be over. Some didn't want to go. Anyone could tell by looking at their facial expressions. Regardless of their personal misgivings, we were going.

The task force achieved REDCON 1 in less than five minutes, but it took another ten to snake out of the tight compounds and get lined up on the road. The soldiers were used to getting prepared for combat quickly. They had been practicing and had become proficient on this act of "getting ready to go" over the last two weeks. We also had countless reps and sets at NTC. Anything not mission critical would be left behind. On my way out of the airport, I saw more than a few half-empty trailers lining the exit.

I ordered to make haste as we crept out of the southwestern exit of the airport by 1200 hours. I pressed our movement as much as I could. All of us were traveling as fast as our cumbersome tracks and wheels could carry us. Our support vehicles could only move slowly and we had engines in the formation that were worn down and barely working now. Twenty miles per hour was probably fast for Task Force 2-7 at this point in the war. I wasn't about to leave anyone behind, stranded halfway between the airport and the city, in the enemy's backyard

We may have moved slower than I would have preferred, but nothing would stop our forward progression. We would need to quickly engage and bypass any enemy resistance along our route into the city. We did not have time to finish them off or seize ground. Other units behind us would perform the systematic mop-up along our route from the airport to the southern edge of the city.

Our route into Baghdad took us south of the airport, then due east to Highway 8. I positioned my scouts at the head of our column; I wouldn't make the mistake of positioning them anywhere else in my formation again. Staff Sergeant Dow and his scout section would lead the attack, followed by Rage, mortars, Knight, Bulldog, then Bushmaster, with the combat trains in trail. As we exited the airport, we received an addition to our convoy, our division commander traveling in his Bradley Fighting Vehicle. I assumed that he wanted to get into the city as quickly as possible. He probably wanted to ascertain whether the city could be taken or if he needed to call for reinforcements. Additionally, the power vacuum in the capital would have to be quickly replaced immediately following the regime's collapse. An authority figure would have to legitimize our presence and reestablish law and order.

We knew we must be close, for any division commander to be so close to the action was uncommon. His presence was a source of motivation. It was inspiring to see our division commander, Major General Buford C. Blunt III, join our formation as we were about to charge directly into the jaws of the enemy. Surely the regime was about to crack.

The entire movement into the city would take us twenty kilometers and about forty-five minutes—our last significant movement of the war. Luckily, most of my tanks and Bradleys made it over three hundred miles, traversing rough terrain, while operating within the most tumultuous climatic conditions, and without a single resupply of repair (spare) parts over the last twenty days. Nearly all my Bradleys and tanks had at least one maintenance deficiency—some major and some minor. A few Bradleys had broken TOW missile systems, some had main guns or machine guns that didn't work properly, and a few had hydraulic problems that the crews had to work around manually. One last push and we were home free.

At 1300 hours, we halted at the intersection of Highways 1 and 8, identified as "Objective Saints" by 2nd Brigade. Most of our supporting combat trains set up near the intersection and would remain here until we could assess the enemy situation in the city. The rest of the task force took a few moments to establish radio contact with 2nd Brigade's TOC. After receiving a brief situation report from TF 3-15, I dispatched my operations officer to make face-to-face coordinations with their unit defending Objective Curley, underneath a highway overpass intersecting Highways 5 and 8.

Major Coffey took a small detachment forward to make the initial link up and, in cooperation with Task Force 3-15, devised a simple plan to relieve it from its positions along Highway 8—from its southernmost objective about five kilometers north into the city—down to Objective

Saints, about five kilometers south of the city. The plan was immediately communicated to all the subordinate units within our task force and they each, in turn, acknowledged that they understood the plan and then confirmed their assigned locations to relieve the Task Force 3-15 units.

As soon as the plan was completed, Major Coffey gave us the green light to continue our movement north. When we reached the outskirts of the city along Highway 8, we carefully maneuvered through and around a minefield. Before our arrival, the two northern lanes of the four-lane highway were cut open for our passage. A daring "covert" breach preceded 2nd Brigade's armored advance into the city by a few hours. Dismounted sappers (engineers) executed the breach at 0330, conducted under the cover of darkness. On the other two lanes of the highway lay hundreds of antitank mines. All the mines rested on the surface of the road, and for some strange reason the Iraqis tried to conceal these mines by draping sand over top of them. I thought, "Did they think we wouldn't realize that these objects were actually mines and just drive over them?" I discovered later that most of the mines were dummies, their true identity concealed by the layer of sand.

Once we were clear of the minefield, we quickly penetrated the outer defenses of the city and raced north as fast as we could. There was a sign painted on a building adjacent to the highway at the edge of the city. It read:

USA: 2
IRAQ: 0

Obviously, 2nd Brigade has a sense of humor. It was humorous to see, but it was also motivating to the young soldiers who were about to engage in sustained urban warfare—for the first time in our entire campaign. Finally, we could dispel the myths circulating that US forces do not have the stomach or the skills for a city fight.

The charge into the city felt like I was on a rollercoaster ride. It was an adrenaline rush. I accompanied Rage in the lead. We engaged scores of bypassed redoubts and earthworks still occupied by enemy forces after 2nd Brigade's advance into the city.

Initially, the 2nd Brigade was not planning on staying in the city. It was to be the "Thunder Run Part II"—another violent probe into and out of the city. Clearly, the plans changed due to the initial success of 2nd Brigade's attack. But now, obvious enemy targets and other potential threats were appearing from everywhere. Every street, building, and car posed a danger to our task force. My gunner, Staff Sergeant Trombly, engaged a suicide truck advancing on the commanding general's Bradley from our eastern flank. A well-aimed burst of 25mm blew it to pieces. General Blount thanked us later for the assist. Trombly was always on alert and could see things the rest of us could not see.

The city looked like pure hell on earth. The sky hung a large and dark cloud over the city. Geysers of smoke were rising high into the sky from every direction, from all reaches into the city. I remember thinking to myself that if it rained, the raindrops would be black. Around the time of our attack, commercial satellite photos would illustrate a large smoke screen covering most of Baghdad. It was 1330 hours—the middle of the day—yet it was nearly as dark as night. There were explosions erupting directly in front of us and off to our flanks. We were driving into a storm of fire . . . straight into the bowels of hell.

The four-lane highway leading into and through the city comprised our new area of operation. Maneuver space for our armored vehicles was scarce. The highway was flanked on both sides by masonry walls and densely packed buildings no more than fifty meters from the highway's shoulders. Our options were severely limited. Not only could we not maneuver to the left or right without getting funneled into the city piecemeal, we were also exposed and in the open on the highway—a perfect target for enemy rockets and artillery.

Our plan was simple: shoot up Highway 8 north to connect with 2nd Brigade, secure the highway, then fan out and create a blanket of security around the LOC. The plan would require all our combat assets including Bradleys, tanks, and infantrymen's boots on the ground.

Throughout our push up Highway 8, we bypassed many disabled antiaircraft artillery and larger 152mm field artillery pieces oriented south on the highway—the working end of the guns trained on any tank or Bradley that would attempt to penetrate Saddam's capital city from the south. Burning technical trucks and Fedayeen dead littered the highway's shoulders like roadkill. I could see that most of the buildings flanking the highway had bullet holes in them, and I could look down anywhere and see pools of shattered glass. We were now in the belly of the beast.

Task Force 3-15 had quite a pitched battle underway along Highway 8. While decisively engaged with the enemy in a 360-degree fight, a relief in place by our two forces would not be easy. We would have to literally break through the enemy before we could relieve them from their positions. We knew that they were taking casualties, but we didn't know how heavy the numbers. I had hoped we weren't driving straight into a bloodbath.

Task Force 3-15 Infantry, call sign "China," had three objectives along Highway 8. They were ordered to seize three major intersections along Highway 8—Larry, Curley, and Moe. Their primary task was to secure and expand the LOC for the remainder of 2nd Brigade. The LOC was their lifeline—the only feasible route to ferry in fuel and ammunition while ferrying out casualties and damaged vehicles in need of repair. 2nd Brigade's forces attacking north, east, and west of the highway could not sustain their attack without it. However, the main highway and surrounding city were simply too vast and the enemy too many for just one task force to secure. The brigade needed our assistance in securing it. If we could secure the LOC around Objectives Larry, Curley, and Moe, China could redirect parts of its formation to other segments of the highway and continue the attack elsewhere throughout the city. Once my task force was set, China could reinforce 2nd Brigade's armored task force attacks, destroy enemy strongpoints, and seize key terrain, facilities, and structures.

Task Force 2-7's lead elements were finally within visual range of Objective Curley around 1330 hours. While on the move and traveling north along Highway 8, Rage encountered significant enemy resistance originating from a large five-story building overlooking the highway. The opportunistic enemy used this building as a means to isolate 2nd Brigade and sever their LOC. My fire support officer, Captain Happe, directed three artillery volleys into the building with no success. My ETAC reported to have close air support on station, and they were armed with five-hundred-pound JDAMS, GPS-guided bombs. The first bomb released missed the building by about ten meters. The pilot told us that the grid coordinates we sent him were inaccurate. It would take the pilot fifteen minutes to realign himself for another release. This time the ETAC requested that Rage mark the target. I wasted no time and announced, "Standby, I'm going to mark the target with a TOW." The explosion from the impacting TOW missile provided enough of a signature for the pilots circling at ten thousand feet to identify where to drop. The aircraft dropped another bomb and it finally found its mark, collapsing the building and eliminating all enemy resistance inside.

At approximately the same time as the CAS mission, Major Coffey concluded his coordinations with Task Force 3-15 as the rest of the task force postured itself into defensive positions along Highway 8. Bushmaster was set in their position first, followed by Knight then Rage. Each individual vehicle pulled off the road into a herringbone formation. The scout platoon identified and cleared a suitable location to house the TOC. The Task Force mortars positioned their guns within Bushmaster's sector, along the eastern embankment topped by railroad tracks running parallel to the highway. They oriented their cannons north but would need the flexibility to reorient east or west depending on the enemy situation.

Surprisingly, the relief in place between the two task forces unfolded smoothly and according to plan. The tempo of the handover between vehicles and units was relatively seamless—something that could have passed for a textbook training event at Fort Stewart, Georgia, or even at the NTC at Fort Irwin, California. A relief in place, even under the best conditions, carried the potential for disaster. Luckily, no soldier in either task force died during the relief in place—either from accident, fratricide, or enemy fire. It wasn't flawless, but in a city now gripped by chaos, perfection was never an option. But the enemy took advantage, and unfortunately our good luck ran out around 1345 hours just as the last elements of my task force were adjusting to their new sectors of fire along the highway.

"Able 6, this is Able 3 Golf, Able 3 is hit!" Major Coffey's gunner, Sergeant Steiner, called out over the radio. "He was hit by an RPG."

Moments earlier, Major Coffey had dismounted from his Bradley to conduct face-to-face coordination with Task Force 3-15 Infantry at Objective Curley. He was only a few feet from his vehicle when an RPG slammed into a nearby HMMWV, sending twelve pieces of shrapnel into his right leg. Almost immediately, additional RPGs struck Curley, two of them impacting against Coffey's own Bradley.

Despite his injuries, Coffey stubbornly pressed on, continuing to coordinate the relief in place and refusing to accept the fact that he was wounded. His Bradley crewman, Specialist Cook, dismounted and sprinted toward him. On the way, Cook spotted four enemy fighters with RPGs less than fifty meters away, exposed in the open. Without hesitation, he dropped to a firing position and delivered four well-aimed shots from his M16, killing three of the attackers before they could launch another volley. With the immediate threat suppressed, Coffey and his crew remounted their battered Bradley and withdrew to the aid station near the TOC.

The defenders at Curley were surrounded, outnumbered, and totally exhausted. They were taking casualties. Still, 3-15 had fought like lions, with incredible grit and determination. They wouldn't quit whether we showed up or not. At the fiercest moment, Objective Curley was being flooded by swarms of irregular fighters who hurled themselves into withering fire from the intersection. Witnesses described it as suicide—enemy troops openly sacrificing themselves against a wall of return fire. Human wave attacks eventually took its toll on the defenders, and I was both proud and relieved that we arrived in time to help our brothers and turn the tide. Timing in combat is everything.

Meanwhile, our medics worked anxiously to treat Major Coffey's wounds. Frustrated with his uncooperative patient, they urged evacuation, but Coffey refused. He was still focused on the handoff and defense of the highway. After a brief three-way exchange over the radio between my wounded S-3, my medical platoon leader, and myself, I deferred to the medical experts and overruled him. Coffey was ordered evacuated to the ambulance exchange point (AXP) at the intersection of Highways 1 and 8.

At the AXP, around 1500 hours, Coffey managed to trick the doctor into believing his wounds were minor flesh injuries rather than a fractured leg. In a display not unlike a drunk driver attempting to walk a straight line for the police, he masked his pain long enough to pass the inspection. Minutes later, we spotted HQ33—Coffey's Bradley—rolling past us on the highway, followed by a radio transmission: "Guidons, this is Able 3. I am okay and I'm back in the fight."

We were stunned. Was this shock, stubbornness, or sheer willpower? What was a task force commander supposed to do? Stop him? Regardless, he carried on his duties as the task force's operations officer for the next four days before finally seeking further treatment. In addition to all the shrapnel wounds, an x-ray later also confirmed a fractured leg. I don't know how Rod was able to push past the pain for so long. For his actions, Major Coffey was awarded the Purple Heart and the Silver Star. It wasn't ego or vanity, he was simply a warrior who didn't want to let anyone down. Rod would die a hero fifteen years later. I would always remember him as a perfect mix of brave and intellectual—the best wingman a task force commander could ever ask for.

My engineer company, Bulldog, spent the evening demolishing walls that surrounded the highway as an effort to clear our fields of fire. I did not want to give the enemy an opportunity to infiltrate into our sectors and engage us unexpectedly. These walls afforded the enemy with cover and concealment. They enabled infiltrators to move unobserved, allowing them to engage, displace, and then reengage. We were not going to play the perpetual game of cat and mouse with our enemy tonight. We had our fill of those tactics back at Objectives Hannah and Raiders.

Around 1745, a Bulldog platoon sergeant, Staff Sergeant Lincoln Hollinsaid, immediately sprang into action to help neutralize the gathering threat along the neighborhood walls paralleling the highway. He connected his platoon's M113 armored personnel carriers (APCs) with his ACEs to provide localized security while they were busy knocking down the barriers.

An M1 tank section from Knight company and two Bradleys from Rage overwatched the engineer platoon, providing overhead security and security to their flanks as best they could. Staff Sergeant Hollinsaid was working with his third squad's M113, "B23," and the ACE, "B48," driven by Specialist Binter. Staff Sergeant Hollinsaid placed B23 into a hole that could observe the other side of wall. He then guided B48 about one hundred meters down the wall where a gate was. Staff Sergeant Hollinsaid peeked inside the gate to observe what was on the other side of the wall. He then ordered the ACE to push through the gate, which B48 did with relative ease.

Once the gate was knocked down, Staff Sergeant Hollinsaid walked into the hole to check the work. Enemy fighters on the opposite side of the wall were lying in wait. They engaged Staff Sergeant Hollinsaid from three different directions, with dismounted infantry in a trenchline, a BMP on the far side of the trench, and more infantry in a nearby building overlooking the trench. Staff Sergeant Hollinsaid was hit in the legs by an RPG round, and numerous pieces of flying shrapnel pierced the rest of his body. After the initial impact, Hollinsaid immediately fell lifeless to the ground. His war was over.

Bradleys from Rage opened fire into the hole, engaging the trenchline and BMP with controlled bursts of machine gun fire. Sergeant Papp's .50 caliber machine gun on B23 jammed and would not fire. He then grabbed an AT-4 antitank missile, from his M113 and ran toward the B48 ACE. Papp ran so fast toward the hole that his helmet flew off his head and hit the ground behind him. He was so focused now that he wouldn't even realize it was missing until after the engagement. He met up with First Sergeant Campbell and Sergeant Kelly, as they both took cover beside the ACE and exchanged a few rounds with the enemy in the nearby building. Specialist Binter lent Papp his M9 pistol so that he would have a weapon and could at least defend himself at close range after he fired the AT-4.

The enemy, positioned inside bunkers—now clearly visible—were pumping rounds furiously at the dazed engineers. The engineers were pinned down. There was no safe passage to retrieve Hollinsaid's body. A few attempts were made but were repulsed by accurate and massed RPG fire. A Rage tank platoon leader seized the initiative and rushed his M1 Abrams tank through the hole and into the blindside of the bunker. Enemy fighters attempted to counter the tank with dozens of RPGs but were now firing too high to affect the tank's assault. Meanwhile, First Sergeant Campbell and two of his soldiers saw the friendly tank spring into action and attempted to keep the enemy RPG gunners pinned down with small arms fire. The tank commander ordered his driver to drive over the bunker and stop, then pivot steer 360 degrees. All sixty tons succeeded in collapsing the bunker and killing the enemy fighters inside. Specialist Binter moved his ACE forward to where Staff Sergeant Hollinsaid laid on the ground. This provided cover for First Sergeant Campbell, Sergeant Kelly, and Sergeant Papp who then extracted Staff Sergeant Hollinsaid's body back to the near side of the wall. The engineers' courage and tenacity had no limits. They would never leave a fallen comrade behind on the battlefield.

Staff Sergeant Hollinsaid would not be left behind. The tank commander and engineers were decorated after the war for their valorous actions under fire. Staff Sergeant Hollinsaid's ultimate sacrifice potentially saved the lives of many in the task force—the determined enemy forces could have gnawed at our positions along the highway all night until we mobilized enough forces to root them out and neutralize them.

Staff Sergeant Hollinsaid's death affected the morale and chemistry of the task force because he had just replaced Sergeant First Class Paul Smith, the platoon sergeant killed only three days earlier while fighting in the airport. Who would want to step up and do the job now, after two back-to-back deaths . . . in less than a week of each other? The younger NCOs would have to fill the leadership void, whether they liked it or not.

Our engineers took a beating, but this neither stopped nor slowed their contributions to the task force. For days after Staff Sergeant Hollinsaid's death, engineers drove up and down the highway asking each of the companies what they needed in terms of engineer support. They worked around the clock digging fighting positions, building berms and breaching walls, all the while exposing themselves to enemy RPG and rifle fire. There were more than a few close calls.

Throughout the evening of April 7, Rage and Knight began to expand their sector east and west of Highway 8. It was an attempt to remain on the offensive—to safeguard our vulnerable flanks while retaining the initiative. They launched limited attacks into the roads and alleyways intersecting the LOC, constantly shooting while on the move. A quick and violent assault in, followed by a quick withdrawal out. Some Bradleys and tanks didn't even waste time turning around—drivers just threw their track in reverse and gunned it. Our intent was to launch enough armored stabs into the city blocks to pick apart the Iraqi defenses a piece at a time, keeping them off balance until they break. Like the enemy did to us back at Hannah and Raiders, we were playing our own form of cat and mouse, but we were playing with Bradleys and Abrams tanks—the most capable weapon systems in the world.

During one of Knight's initial probes into the city blocks, First Lieutenant Johnson repulsed the charge of an Iraqi suicide truck, creating secondary explosions that could have been seen and heard from anywhere in the city. He engaged scores of enemy fighters as they were scattering like a family of roaches when the lights go on—but many still managed to find a suitable hide position to sling RPGs and bullets at his platoon. One warhead found Johnson's Bradley but was detonated on his infantry squad's baggage strapped neatly on to the side, rocking the Bradley but leaving it completely undamaged by the blast. Amid all the chaos, Johnson missed a golden opportunity to engage two BMPs that managed to sneak around behind him during his Bradley section's egress back to the LOC—after their mad dash into the city blocks on their eastern flank. The BMPs would be dealt with later.

During a local patrol by Knight's headquarters tank section, they discovered a large cache of weapons and equipment near the aid station. A stockpile of night vision goggles was also found in the cache. The devices were tested and were found to be just as effective as our night vision goggles. I wondered why they were cached and not issued out to the many Iraqi fighters we already encountered since the war started. I wasn't sure if this find meant that the enemy we were fighting did or did not possess night vision capability. I told the task force to assume that the enemy had night vision and to take appropriate precautions. The sun was setting, and we would find out if the enemy could fight at night soon enough.

During one of Rage's clearing patrols, First Lieutenant Horn's 1st Platoon intercepted and destroyed four BMP armored personnel carriers attempting to counterattack the LOC along our eastern flank, via the Dora Expressway. The BMPs maneuvered as a platoon, making a clever attempt to occupy a battle position above us on an overpass—the intersection of Highway 8 and the Dora Expressway, dubbed Objective Curley.

Before the BMPs came into view near the overpass, Horn heard reports of enemy armor approaching from the east and he promptly reoriented and improved on his Bradley's new firing position, now situated to cut down the enemy before they could even take the opportunity to get into a suitable position and fire their first shot. Sensing what was happening, the Iraqi BMP platoon hesitated and exposed themselves piecemeal on the high ground overlooking Highway 8 from the east. First Lieutenant

Horn, consequently, picked them off one by one with a well-aimed burst of 25mm armor-piercing ammunition, each round placed carefully into the chassis, killing the crew instantly while igniting fuel and onboard ammunition. It was like shooting ducks in a pond. The Bradley gunnery skills of Horn's crew were superb. This was our last significant force-on-force engagement in our campaign.

The Iraqis quickly learned that their efforts to isolate the 2nd Brigade were effectively thwarted. Consequently, they displaced much of their resistance into the heart of the city, to defend strategic infrastructure and symbolic locations. Iraqi fighters holed up in Saddam's mansions, around statues, on bridges and intersections, and in government office buildings. Perhaps an equal number of Iraqis dropped their uniforms or black pajamas and blended into the civilian populous. Some of the defeated enemy went home to live in peace or to fight again another day.

Fighting in Baghdad was different. You weren't just scanning for muzzle flashes—you were scanning faces. A man with a shovel could be planting a tree or planting a mine. A kid on a rooftop could be waving or spotting for mortars. The line between combatant and civilian blurred fast. Every decision felt like a gamble. And every wrong call stayed with you.

Around 1800 hours, Colonel Perkins, the 2nd Brigade commander, deemed the LOC secure and suitable for traffic to flow into and out of the city. All four of the brigade's task forces began to evacuate their killed and wounded to the rear to be air lifted via helicopter pickup zone, located approximately ten kilometers south of the city. 2nd Brigade handed their casualties to us and we, in turn, evacuated them south to the pickup zone.

Captured prisoners would be interrogated then evacuated along with the friendly casualties. Highway 8 would get busy soon. Scores of combat and support vehicles would flow in both directions. Combat units needed to get casualties back, and support units needed to push supplies, ammunition, spare parts, and engineering assets forward. I hoped that someone was playing the role of traffic cop over the highway before it got so bogged down it became a big target.

Bradleys, Medic M113s, M88s, and supply trucks made dozens of trips up and down the LOC over the course of about four hours, from 1800 until about 2200 hours. It looked like rush hour traffic in New York City. There was a lot of activity going on, especially so because we were still engaged with pockets of enemy resistance on all fronts, up and down the highway until well into the night. It was hard for everybody to stay focused while so much was happening all at once.

Fearing for their lives, the civilians kept their distance. They knew the potential consequences if they approached us in this tense situation. As a precaution, our PSYOPS detachment drove up and down Highway 8 while broadcasting civilian noninterference messages.

Converted from Arabic to English:

> "ATTENTION, ATTENTION, ATTENTION
>
> DO NOT INTERFERE WITH COALITION OPERATIONS. YOUR INTERFERENCE COULD PLACE YOUR LIFE IN JEOPARDY.
>
> COALITION FORCES ARE CONDUCTING COMBAT OPERATIONS TO REMOVE YOUR REGIME FROM POWER AND PROVIDE THE PROUD PEOPLE OF IRAQ WITH FREEDOM AND PROSPERITY THAT HAD NOT EXISTED UNDER THE DICTATOR, SADDAM HUSSEIN."

The mood of the civilians was a blend of curious, excited, tired, and frightened.

From Bushmaster's position, they could observe enemy gun trucks driving around frantically in the distance while weaving in between buildings and through alleyways on the eastern side of the highway. They missed two opportunities to engage due to hundreds of civilians sandwiched between them and the trucks. The civilians were directly in the line of fire. By the time we fired a warning shot over the civilians' heads as an effort to disperse them, the enemy trucks had already disappeared.

Initially, I suspected that the civilians were being forced to congregate outside as human shields. After observing their behavior over the next three days, I discovered that this behavior was quite normal. Most Iraqi city dwellers did not enjoy the same amenities that we did back home. Most did not have air conditioners, televisions, video games, computers, or phones. Many do not have power in their homes twenty-four hours a day. So they would meet up outside. And they were very curious people. Curious and social. Gathering outside provided them with entertainment, socialization, news, and physical comfort. It was familiar, and it made them feel safe.

We would also discover later that the Baghdad residents were completely without power. They lost electricity just prior to 2nd Brigade's final incursion into the city. The civilians could have met on the street to seek assistance, or maybe they had nothing better to do or had nowhere else to go. These civilians were innocent, and we were fortunate to have exercised the prudence and control that we had. I knew the regime was days from collapse, and if we were to kill any civilians accidentally, it would have made it that much more difficult to win over the populous' hearts and minds later. The quicker we could pacify and befriend Iraq's people, the quicker we could all go home.

At 1900 hours on April 7, the neighborhood imam began the call to prayer in Bushmaster's sector. The call summoned believers to the mosque for prayer, news, guidance, and instruction. That night, the imam's voice echoed through the loudspeaker in an animated and impassioned speech. Though we could not understand the words, the tone made its purpose clear—it resembled a war cry. We believed he was rallying civilians to mount an attack against us along the highway. Without an Arabic speaker or interpreter with the task force at the time, we could not confirm his message; all we could do was guess.

The night of April 7 was the darkest since our breach into Iraq more than two weeks earlier. Black fire clouds from the day's battles thickened overhead, blotting out the moon and stars. Visibility dropped to almost nothing—a few meters at most—and our night vision goggles were nearly useless. I expected civilians to pour from the mosque with AK-47s and RPGs blazing. We suspected Saddam's loyalists would exploit mosques as safe havens, hiding weapons and ammunition inside. My soldiers remained on full alert, weapons trained and ready. Yet when the civilians filed out, they carried no arms and displayed no hostility. They simply returned home. The soldiers relaxed, and we treated the civilians as noncombatants.

That night, we discovered an important advantage: Iraqis did not stay outdoors after dark. Whether this was the result of fear, a curfew, cultural custom, or simple habit, it worked to our benefit. Like clockwork, after evening prayers, entire neighborhoods dispersed back into their homes. Likely they rested for the dawn prayer. For us, this pattern made it easier to distinguish civilians from combatants. We could suspect anyone found outside at night as a potential threat until proven otherwise. Once we confirmed weapons or hostile intent, we engaged swiftly.

As the night wore on, I realized a massive counterattack would not come. Civilians were not in play. Only a handful of fanatics in pajamas and a few remaining uniformed soldiers prowled in the dark, desperate to kill one of us before accepting the truth I already knew—Saddam Hussein was irrelevant, and the battle for Iraq had been won.

One of my chief concerns was enemy snipers. Baghdad offered infinite hiding places, and by the time we spotted one, it might be too late. Snipers could have been devastating, especially with our column exposed on Highway 8. The best defense against a sniper is another sniper, so I ordered all company snipers into elevated positions along the highway. Had the Iraqis employed skilled marksmen, our efforts could have been severely disrupted. We were fortunate they never did. Instead we endured harassing fire from small arms and light machine guns, sprayed wildly and without discipline. At night, enemy fighters silhouetted themselves on rooftops, oblivious to our thermal sights. Our thermals were effective at spotting targets like that. The Iraqis managed only one or two shots before we spotted them and cut them down with precision fire from Bradleys and tanks.

The first night along what came to be known as the "Highway of Death" tested our physical and psychological endurance. We had accumulated barely ten hours of sleep in the previous week. I ordered heightened security for the first twenty-four hours, though I knew few soldiers could have slept that night, no matter how hard they tried. Adrenaline ran high. Explosions echoed constantly—artillery, bombs, cruise missiles—all mixing with sporadic enemy gunfire that gave the illusion of a looming counterattack. The city reeked of burning charcoal, the air thick and suffocating. Minutes stretched into hours; hours dragged into days.

Iraqi fighters probed our positions throughout the night. They attempted to infiltrate Knight Company's sector by scaling the large masonry wall surrounding a nearby concrete plant. It became another game of cat and mouse. An engineer platoon, attached to Knight, worked to breach part of the wall to reduce the threat. While operating an ACE, its crew surprised an Iraqi fighter hiding on the far side. The enemy fled, and the ACE pursued, hoping to flush him into Knight's engagement area.

The Iraqi leapt over the wall, only to find himself fully exposed. Realizing his mistake, he tried to scramble back, but a Knight tank commander tracked him in thermal sights. After confirming with the engineers that no friendlies were beyond the wall, the commander fired a 120mm round. Anything smaller would have been ineffective. The round breached the wall, and fragments struck the ACE operator, Private First Class Jason Meyer, resulting in a fatal injury. Despite protective gear, certain vulnerabilities remained, and this incident was a stark reminder of those risks. Tragically, several of our task force's losses up to that point were due to similar fragment wounds.

This was our only fratricide incident of the war—a direct result of a communication breakdown. In the confusion of close nighttime engagements, critical information didn't reach the right people in time—resulting in the worst outcome. Throughout OIF, coalition forces suffered remarkably few friendly fire incidents compared to previous wars—a testament to improved training and technologies. But this loss underscored the ever-present risk. My engineers' fearlessness in the fog of war often saved the day for Task Force 2-7, but sometimes it resulted in unfortunate and irreversible consequences. Jason was a hero and will never be forgotten.

In the early morning hours of April 8, the Iraqi military organized for a counterattack from the eastern side of the Tigris River. They made several attempts to relieve pressure on their fighting forces on the western side. Bridges connecting both sides of Baghdad became decisive terrain—whichever side controlled the bridges would control Baghdad. Jumhuriyah Bridge, in particular, was a scene of pure carnage. Combat in Baghdad would remain fierce, with losses encountered on both sides. Until the Marines arrived to secure the east, the Iraqis would fight on. The enemy still fighting us in the west became emboldened. Resistance was fragmented at this point, but it was still intense.

Our day began with Bulldog Company attempting a casualty evacuation to the brigade's rear area at Objective Saints, the intersection of Highways 1 and 8. Along Highway 8, 2nd Squad, led by Platoon Sergeant First Class Roush, encountered another minefield laid directly on the highway. In the dark, enemy fighters had backfilled the same minefield cleared by 2nd Brigade the night prior. The Iraqis recognized the importance of Highway 8 to our survival and sought to cut our lifeline not with direct confrontation but with obstacles.

Staff Sergeant Harmon and Sergeant Smith dismounted from their M113 to inspect. Using night vision devices, they determined the mines were not armed and could simply be pushed aside. Still, doctrine demanded precautions. Their squad carefully cleared the highway and reopened the main supply route within the brigade's sector.

By morning, I issued orders to further secure the 2nd Brigade's LOC. The brigade's other task forces were still on the attack to our north and east. I knew it would exhaust its supplies quickly and would need the LOC as its lifeline. The built-up neighborhoods along Highway 8 posed a constant threat to convoys. Soft-skinned, unarmored supply vehicles were exposed and defenseless against RPGs and sniper fire. To protect them, we needed to blanket the flanks with security and remain on the offensive.

Each company was assigned a portion of Highway 8, covering roughly ten kilometers. The plan called for sequential expansion of sectors east and west, using armed reconnaissance patrols. We flooded the surrounding city blocks with tanks and Bradleys. We started to nickname these patrols "Thunder Runs." They were designed to locate and, when possible, destroy the enemy, but always with caution not to become decisively engaged.

Each company commander committed platoon-level patrols, backed by a quick reaction force on the highway. The rest of the company secured the LOC, ensuring resupply and casualty evacuation remained possible. The key to success was finesse: focused firepower, rapid maneuver, and overwhelming shock when contact was made. Instead of cat and mouse, combat in Baghdad now became more of a game of whack-a-mole.

Whenever possible, patrols remained mounted. Bradleys could withstand heavy fire and still protect the troops inside, but once infantry dismounted into the city, casualties were almost guaranteed. Given our tenuous evacuation routes, we avoided unnecessary exposure on the ground. Leaders would have to exercise prudence.

Our operating environment in Baghdad's southwestern tier resembled an upscale American neighborhood in some ways: primarily residential, with small shops interspersed. Nearby lay the Mansour District, an affluent Ba'athist enclave of large homes and apartments. Over the next few days, all three companies would patrol there. The area was "nonpermissive," meaning freedom of movement could not be assumed. Every alleyway, rooftop, and basement offered potential threats.

For the US Army, transitioning from defense to offense is always the goal. Offense wins battles and maintains initiative, forcing the enemy to react to us. In Baghdad, with threats on every flank, we could not afford passivity.

Task Force 2-7 mortarmen occupying fighting positions along Highway 8 to protect 3rd Infantry Division's LOC to seize control of Baghdad, April 8, 2003.
Source: Author photo.

From April 8 to 9, the task force executed a series of Thunder Runs. These initial patrols were quick thrusts into the city to gauge enemy strength.

On the morning of April 8, First Lieutenant Johnson of Knight Company surprised an Iraqi tank crew repairing a T-72 under camouflage netting. Three crewmen fled, but one manned the tank turret and swung the gun toward Johnson's patrol. The Bradley crew reacted instantly, launching a TOW missile from such a close distance it could barely arm itself before impact. The missile struck the tank and blew it apart.

That afternoon, Johnson's section encountered a frantic Iraqi woman waving them toward an alleyway. Investigating, they found a T-72 only one block away. The tank attempted to retreat but exposed its rear. The conditions were suboptimal for a TOW shot, so Johnson's gunner fired over twenty rounds of 25mm armor-piercing ammunition into the engine compartment, igniting fuel and ammunition. The turret launched twenty feet into the air, killing the crew instantly.

Meanwhile, Bushmaster patrolled south of the highway, destroying bunkers, filling trenches, and disabling artillery and rifles. On April 9, Knight identified a missile site west of Highway 8, while Bushmaster reported another to the east. Some missiles were fully fueled, even venting smoke. The previous day, 2nd Brigade's TOC had been struck by a missile; perhaps these sites were responsible. EOD teams later investigated for chemical or biological agents.

By April 9, the Thunder Runs had destroyed two T-72s, seven BMPs, eight BRDMs, two SA-2 missile systems, and two D-30 artillery pieces. Eighteen enemy fighters were confirmed killed and eight captured. These were all isolated engagements, where crew and soldier-level skills mattered the most. Countless hours on the gunnery ranges back at Fort Stewart paid off here. Every time a Bradley or tank platoon rolled out of the LOC to its next objective, the streets got quieter and quieter. More importantly, our free movement through Baghdad's streets showed the Iraqis that we controlled their city, whether or not that was fully true. Resistance tapered sharply. Most Iraqi soldiers were dead, captured, or hiding among civilians.

Prisoner interrogations revealed that foreign fighters—Syrian, Sudanese, Jordanian, Saudi, Egyptian, Palestinian, and Lebanese—had infiltrated Iraq to fight for "the Faith." Many charged our tanks with only AK-47s, embracing death as martyrdom. Their efforts were futile, but their fanaticism foreshadowed the insurgency to come.

The Marines occupied positions in eastern Baghdad on April 8 and 9, forcing organized Iraqi resistance there to crumble. With the Army firmly in control of the west and the Marines now in the east, the battle for

Baghdad was over. For many of us, this was "VI Day"—Victory in Iraq. Every war requires a symbol of triumph. On April 9, Marines across the Tigris provided one when they toppled Saddam's statue before cheering crowds. The image, broadcast worldwide, convinced people the regime had fallen. Perception became reality. April 10 was a new dawn.

With the city and government now in our hands, our posture toward civilians shifted. No longer could we assume every Iraqi approaching us had hostile intent. It was time to break the ice, explain our presence, and earn trust.

As explosions subsided, civilians began venturing out. They approached soldiers with cautious curiosity, asking questions in broken English: "Are you Americans?" "What state are you from?" "How long will you stay?" "Is Saddam dead?"

Once convinced of our good intentions, they turned to looting. The collapse of authority unleashed a frenzy. Government buildings were ransacked, then set ablaze. When those were stripped bare, mobs turned to businesses and private homes. Men, women, and children alike joined in. Some soldiers thought, "Good for them—this is their first taste of freedom." Others, like me, saw danger. The looting was a sign of deeper problems. If Iraqis could not cooperate to rebuild their country, the burden would fall entirely on us.

Looters fought over refrigerators, air conditioners, and generators. English-speaking Iraqis insisted they were not stealing—they were reclaiming what the regime owed them after decades of deprivation. But watching an eighty-year-old woman haul home an entire living room set strained credibility. My first impression of the Iraqi people was not favorable.

We wanted desperately to stop the looting, but our mission remained clear: protect the task force and destroy the enemy. With a thousand looters to every American soldier, intervention was impossible. We tried to persuade English speakers to return home, deployed smoke to disperse crowds, and warned that fighting continued and they were in danger. Nothing worked. At its peak, the looting dwarfed anything seen in postwar Germany. We never expected it; we assumed Iraqis would rush to rebuild, not tear down what remained.

On April 11, Task Force 2-7 Infantry was ordered out of Baghdad and back under 1st Brigade control. We moved along Highway 11, north of Baghdad International Airport (since renamed), clearing resistance and securing another LOC. We seized Baghdad University's School of Agriculture and

Veterinary Medicine, a Ba'athist radio station, Abu Ghraib Prison, and a Republican Guard training facility.

Attention then turned to Saddam's birthplace and power base, Tikrit—the northern point of the "Sunni Triangle." Intelligence believed his supporters would make a last stand there. For days, Air Force and Navy aircraft pounded the city. Reports suggested perhaps a brigade-sized force remained. Rumors spread that our division would advance ninety miles north to finish the job.

But on April 12, word arrived that a Marine reconnaissance battalion had already secured Tikrit. The defenders melted away without significant resistance. We remained in Baghdad.

In truth, remaining in Baghdad was for the best. The task force had reached its culminating point—a doctrinal term meaning our offensive momentum was spent. Vehicles and soldiers alike were worn down. Logistics lagged far behind. Spare parts, ammunition, food, and especially water were scarce. Soldiers were rationed to a single bottle of water per day, guarded like treasure in the one-hundred-degree heat.

Our mechanics performed miracles. Lacking spare parts, they improvised with tape, rope, and ingenuity. When necessary, they practiced "controlled substitution," or cannibalization—removing parts from one vehicle to keep another running. Despite these hardships, more than ninety-five percent of the fleet remained (somewhat) operational during the 350-mile march to Baghdad. The mechanics were our unsung heroes, keeping us in the fight. Behind us, the "loggies"—Army logisticians—rushed to establish secure supply lines from Kuwait to Baghdad. Once in place, we could refit and prepare for whatever came next.

By mid-April, overt looting subsided; there was little left to steal. Crime, however, flourished. Thousands of criminals released by Saddam before the war resumed their trade—robbery, murder, and rape. Cars vanished by the hundreds. Banks became prime targets for organized gangs.

Residual enemy elements also lingered. Former regime loyalists and foreign jihadists avoided direct contact but regrouped in secret, planning resistance. Political prisoners spared from execution began aiding coalition forces, providing intelligence on infrastructure and communities.

For us, the enemy as a maneuver force was finished. We made no major contact while holding Highway 11 except once. On our initial entry, Knight Company spotted a T-72 guarding Abu Ghraib prison. At over a kilometer, First Lieutenant Johnson's Bradley froze as the tank turret slewed toward him. His gunner scrambled to raise the TOW launcher.

Precious seconds ticked by, but the missile fired just in time, engulfing the tank in flames.

The effects of "shock and awe" were evident at Baghdad University's School of Agriculture. Bushmaster discovered more than a dozen destroyed or disabled Iraqi attack helicopters. The wreckage—likely Mi-35s or Mi-8s—lay scattered, barrels warped, and missiles still dangling from their pylons. These aircraft had terrorized Shia uprisings in 1991, but here they were as charred ruins.

The stark juxtaposition of a university serving as a military launch site was not lost on us. UNMOVIC inspectors had long suspected Iraq might retrofit helicopters with crop-spraying equipment for chemical or biological weapons delivery. Finding them here at the School of Agriculture only fueled unease. They had lab facilities that could have been used for nefarious purposes. The Iraqis mined the outskirts of the university, leading me to think that this was a sensitive site they did not want to surrender.

Elsewhere on campus, we found hundreds of abandoned antiaircraft weapons on rooftops and crates marked "Made in Russia, 2003." Instead of munitions, they contained spare machine parts—likely for BMPs or T-72s. Based on what we saw on the campus grounds, it appeared that Russia or a third party it trades with violated UN sanctions to help the Iraqis—either to make money, help an ally, kill Americans, some other purpose, or all of the above. Tank tracks scarred the surrounding fields, suggesting the grounds had served as a maintenance collection point.

Republican Guard uniforms littered the campus. A landscaper told us that Iraqi soldiers had shed them several days earlier, right after we seized Baghdad International Airport. Terrified, they had run home in civilian clothes.

University professors described how Saddam had walled off universities, hospitals, barracks, and government buildings, turning them into fortified instruments of control. "Big Brother" had been watching for over twenty years. Their questions focused first on water and electricity, then on when they could resume teaching. We had no answers. False hope would only damage trust, so we promised nothing we could not deliver. And at the moment, we could not deliver much.

The professors' patience was limited. Iraqis wanted instant solutions to their problems. With what little we had, we tried to help. Soldiers repaired a ruptured water pipe using a plastic MRE wrapper and zip ties, channeling water back into homes. Our medics set up an aid station, treating hundreds of civilians for preventable illnesses.

Iraqi families cautiously approached us with tea and bread, offered by children with shy smiles. The tea was strong, the bread some of the best we had ever tasted. After nearly two months of nothing but MREs, even small portions felt like a feast. We were careful not to overindulge. Our stomachs were not ready for local water, but we ate just enough to show respect. In return, we shared what we could: candy, bottled water, and items from our care packages.

Through these gestures, we earned respect. Iraqis are a proud people, eager to feel valued. We learned that one genuine act of benevolence was worth more than a thousand promises For a brief time, we bridged the gulf between occupier and local, proving we were human and shared their concerns.

Our short time along Highway 11 became a test of patience, ingenuity, and humanity. We continued to exchange food and pleasantries with the Iraqis. Forging ties with the locals was important in our transition from combat to stability operations. In the evenings, soldiers played soccer with local children. Every boy seemed to own a ball, and the games offered rare moments of laughter. Older boys lingered to talk, eager to hear stories from young American soldiers about girlfriends back home. With Iraq's demographics skewed with more male than female, the conversations carried a mix of amusement and longing.

These small exchanges mattered. They built trust. Iraqis wanted to see that we were human, that their problems mattered to us, and that our successes could also be theirs. We discovered that a single act of kindness could win over an entire neighborhood block. In those early days, we believed we were laying the foundation for peace. Unfortunately, our stay was brief. Just as we began forging connections, orders came to move once again—this time deeper into the heart of Baghdad.

Shortly after securing Highway 11, our two embedded journalists prepared to depart for Kuwait. With the regime collapsed, most reporters withdrew. Yet saying goodbye was harder than expected. Over three weeks, they had become part of the team, sharing the same dangers, braving the same bullets. They were fearless—willing to stand in a hail of gunfire for a story.

Carolyn Glick had proved her courage even before embedding with us. A dual US-Israeli citizen reporting for the *Chicago Sun-Times* and the

Jerusalem Post, she had navigated Kuwait's restrictions, which barred Israeli reporting. Using alternate credentials, she reached us despite legal and political obstacles. I once asked how she planned to leave without arrest. Half-joking, she told me, "You'd better seize Saddam International Airport and slip me on a plane." At the time, she could not have known that was exactly what we intended to do.

Throughout her time with us, Carolyn reported faithfully, never sensationalizing our hardships or losses. She told us that what we were doing in Iraq was right for America and for civilization. She reminded us that our National Anthem was born as a battle cry, and that America's freedom had always been secured through the will and might of its military.

Michael Corkery of the *Providence Journal* earned equal respect. He told us we would never be forgotten. We insisted it was simply our job, what we were trained and paid to do. But he had not been ordered into harm's way. He had chosen to endure the risks—chemical attack, death, dismemberment, and the unforgettable sights and smells of combat. For that, he too earned our respect.

By the time they left, both reporters had the full trust of the task force. In just twenty-one days, they had proven themselves professionals and teammates. Every soldier would have taken a bullet for either of them. Their job had been to report on the war. They may not have realized it then, but while the battles were ending, the harder war was only just beginning. The struggle for a free and democratic Iraq would rage on for years.

By mid-April 2003, Baghdad lay under our control. The city was battered, its government toppled, its military shattered. Yet victory brought new challenges: lawlessness, looting, and the seeds of insurgency. For every moment of connection with civilians—soccer games with children, shared bread and tea, small acts of goodwill—there were equal reminders of chaos: mobs stripping buildings bare, foreign jihadists flooding across borders, criminals released to prey on their own people.

We had fought through three hundred fifty miles, maintained over 95 percent of our fleet, and toppled a regime. We had endured endless nights, constant fire, and unimaginable fatigue. Yet as we prepared to push further into Baghdad, it was clear that winning the city was only half the battle. Holding it, and securing the peace that would follow, would be far more difficult.

Task Force 2-7 defense of Highway 8 LOC ir Baghdad, April 7–10, 2003.
Source: Author's image.

THE AFTERMATH

"It is my earnest hope—indeed the hope of all mankind—that from this solemn occasion a better world shall emerge out of the blood and carnage of the past, a world found upon faith and understanding, a world dedicated to the dignity of man and the fulfillment of his most cherished wish for freedom, tolerance, and justice."

—*General Douglas MacArthur, Japanese Surrender Ceremony, USS Missouri, September 2, 1945*

America gained possession of the Philippines, along with several other territories, following the war with Spain in 1898. That war was fought with relative ease, evidenced by casualty figures totaling fewer than four hundred dead and wounded. Yet the ensuing American occupation failed to understand or appreciate the fragile situation in the Philippines that had existed well before the war. The Filipinos desired independence—freedom from foreign rule of any kind, whether Spanish or American. They would not submit quietly to another outside power.

The nationalist movement, fueled in part by religious ideology among Muslim resistance groups, grew into armed resistance. Filipino discontent boiled over in 1899, hurling 120,000 American troops into a bloody guerrilla war. Though the conflict officially ended in 1902, sporadic violence continued for another decade. Early in the war, the Filipino Army proved no match for American ground forces in conventional battle, but they became formidable in small unit guerrilla tactics—hit-and-run attacks, sabotage, and terrorism. The death toll far exceeded that of the Spanish-American War just three years earlier. By the time the dust settled, more than four thousand Americans had been killed. It took the United States three long years to impose even a tenuous peace. Sound familiar?

The parallels to Iraq in 2003 were striking. Following Saddam Hussein's fall, Iraq too faced its own tenuous period, shaped by unique circumstances and challenges. Ethnic and religious groups vied for power, each fearing domination by the others—a paradox Iraqis had endured for thousands of years. Understanding and protecting the people, practicing sound politics, and forging constructive relationships with local leaders would prove critical to securing the peace.

Our military victory in Iraq was bittersweet. Few could have predicted the speed of the Iraqi Army's collapse. It was a coup de main—a sudden strike in which the perception of victory itself helped create the outcome. Our presence in Baghdad devastated not only the Iraqi military but also the citizens and leaders who had depended on the illusion of regime strength.

Saddam Hussein's true center of gravity was not his palaces, nor even his person, but the perception of his military's power. For decades, the Iraqi Army had crushed uprisings with an iron fist, leaving the people in quiet resignation to his rule. When American tanks and Bradleys moved freely through Baghdad, that illusion shattered. We struck directly at his center of gravity, and the remnants of his resistance bled out—not only in Baghdad but across the provinces. Days after Baghdad's fall, entire corps of regular soldiers, stripped of their uniforms and disguised in civilian clothes, streamed south along the highways, abandoning the battlefield. Once they believed the regime irrelevant, they simply walked away.

Some critics later claimed we won the war "too quickly." I reject that notion. Most of those so-called experts had never donned a uniform, never stared down the barrel of an AK-47. For those who have, the idea that combat should last longer than necessary is absurd. Enduring the threat of death and inflicting it is a burden that should be borne only as long as required. Future generations will study the evolution of postwar Iraq and judge for themselves.

The dust of combat settled quickly, leaving new questions: Do we stay or go home? We had taken the ground, but what would we do with it? How would we deal with prisoners of war? With the Iraqi people? We had won the battles but had we won the war? And had we achieved all our objectives?

For veterans of Desert Storm 1991, Panama, or Grenada, victory meant celebration: win the battle and go home. Iraq in 2003 was different. We would not be going home soon, and no ticker-tape parades awaited us. Our experience resembled that of our grandfathers after Germany's surrender in 1945. They had won the war but then had to secure the peace through occupation. The same soldiers who had lost comrades in combat were asked to help their former enemies rebuild.

Some civilians may insist "it isn't personal." But to the combat veteran, death is always personal. It always hits home. Task Force 2-7 soldiers were battling personal demons, including survivor's guilt and PTSD. A brief period of rest and reflection since the Baghdad fight would help some but the mental and emotional baggage would take its toll on many for years to come. Yet the mission continued now with no end in sight. Discipline was tested then, and again in Iraq, as we grieved our fallen while embracing the mission of securing a better future for the Iraqi people.

Following Saddam's fall, the coalition began the monumental task of rebuilding Iraq. Ironically, much of the country's ruin was not caused by our bombs but by decades of neglect, corruption, and the looting that followed the regime's collapse. Saddam had squandered the nation's resources on dozens of lavish palaces, furnished with imported opulence from Europe and the Middle East. Meanwhile, Iraq's infrastructure, including its electrical grid, water and sewage systems, schools, and streets, crumbled from disrepair.

The Office of Reconstruction and Humanitarian Assistance (ORHA) was established as the interim authority over Iraq's civil affairs. Soon its leadership shifted and the office was subsumed by the Coalition Provisional Authority (CPA). It took ORHA several weeks to realize that there were no functioning Iraqi institutions or credible leaders to partner with to restructure and provide humanitarian assistance—to fix what we broke during the war so we could quickly go home. ORHA faced significant structural and authority challenges during the initial post-conflict period.

The CPA entered the scene and changed everything. It had a broad mandate to take control over Iraq and implement a long-haul strategy to rebuild Iraq from the ground up. Coalition forces would work with the CPA but maintain a separate command structure with separate authorities. To make this postwar mission work required unity and cooperation between both organizations, even if they remained separate.

On April 20, 2003, Task Force 2-7 Infantry was ordered back into Baghdad to relieve Marines occupying two zones in the city center. Unlike the dramatic names of earlier objectives—Stabler, Namath—these zones were simply labeled 15 and 16. They lay between the Tigris River to the west and Sadr City to the east. Zone 15 encompassed the Old City, Baghdad's historic political, cultural, financial, and religious core. Its significance had endured for over a millennium, though as outsiders it would take us time to fully appreciate that.

Each zone spanned ten to fifteen blocks, made up of government high-rises, adjoining commercial sprawl, and clusters of modest homes three to five stories tall, all painted the same drab shade of desert brown.

Zone 15 was notorious. Intelligence warned it contained the highest concentration of criminals in Baghdad. Many criminals were released by Saddam just prior to the war to foment chaos. With no functioning police force, they moved freely, resuming lives of theft, rape, and murder. Worse still, the zone bordered Sadr City, a vast Shiite enclave long hostile to the regime. In the heart of the Sunni Triangle, I knew this Shiite district would not easily coexist with its neighbors. Ethnically aligned militias would be born soon. Friction was inevitable as Iraq struggled toward self-government. Mistakes here could be catastrophic.

Our second entry into Baghdad revealed a city changed. Fires from bombs and arson had been extinguished, but new odors filled the air. Piles of rotting garbage lined streets and alleys, uncollected, open, and baking under the rising summer sun. Baghdad smelled like a garbage dump, the stench overwhelming. It was a stark sign of the collapse of municipal services—and the enormity of the task before us.

Operating under new theater orders, coalition units were authorized to commandeer Iraqi government buildings as headquarters and garrisons. Private homes and businesses were to remain with the locals. Our task force took over a three-story government office building, still with electricity and even limited air conditioning. Surrounded by a masonry wall, it was easily defensible. Sandbagged windows and scattered MRE wrappers revealed the Marines had occupied it before us. Once they were relieved, many Marines redeployed south or even returned to their ships.

After a week of cleaning and repairs, the building became our TOC. Offices were assigned, rooms fitted with portable air conditioners, and before long, the interior resembled a college dormitory.

With our headquarters established, the task of rebuilding began. Each company was assigned a subsector within Zones 15 and 16, with missions ranging from reopening schools to capturing Ba'ath Party leaders and criminals. They operated in the very the heart and soul of Baghdad, the oldest part of the city predating the Middle Ages. They had to operate with care and caution.

Rage Company occupied Zone 16's northeastern sector along the Tigris, largely residential with schools and shops. Predominantly Sunni and relatively affluent, the area contrasted with Baghdad's ghettos. In Saddam's Iraq, the Sunnis were the "haves," while the Shia were the "have nots."

Knight Company's sector lay in Zone 16, between Rage to the north and Bushmaster to the west. Its neighborhoods were less developed, with a mixed population of Shia, Sunni, and a small but growing number of Kurds.

Bushmaster assumed responsibility for most of Zone 15—the largest and most violent of all. The scouts managed a small enclave next to Bushmaster in the same zone. Its landscape was dominated by government buildings, commercial businesses, and dense residential ghettos. Gunfire echoed nightly, as constant as background noise. It was the Wild West. Infantry strength was essential, and Bushmaster had more of it than any other company. The mortar platoon would help out when Bushmaster needed to surge troops on specific problems in trouble spots. Baghdad needed to be patrolled, criminals flushed out, and civilians reassured. Protection of people and property fell squarely on the shoulders of the grunt with his helmet, body armor, and M16 in hand. Boots on the ground was our greatest asset now.

Prior to the war, the Iraqi Ba'ath Party claimed 1.5 million members, with about fifty thousand "full" members truly running the country. The party permeated every major institution including schools, hospitals, utilities, ministries, law enforcement, and the military. Iraq resembled a medieval feudal system, each "fief" governed by a trusted loyalist of the regime. Prewar Iraq in 2003 showed the world what happens when one-party rule calcifies into total control—where the Ba'ath Party's absolute grip left a hollowed-out state, silenced its people, and set the stage for national ruin. They didn't get there overnight—it took fifty years to ruin the country. By April 2003, Iraq was so brittle, it broke.

With the collapse of Saddam's government, Iraq's intelligentsia—those who had administered the nation for decades—became fugitives. The CPA's de-Ba'athification policy outlawed the party and barred former high-ranking Ba'athists from serving in the new Iraq. It was considered a necessary measure, but it made rebuilding exponentially more difficult. We couldn't run their electrical grid or their oil industry for them. And the alternative, to stick around long enough to train and develop the expertise from scratch, would amount to a generational commitment. I never thought America and its political leaders would have the patience for that.

De-Ba'athification orders reached down to every unit. Our task force went to great lengths to identify senior party members, neutralize their influence, and dismantle their networks across schools, mosques, hospitals, and ministries in our sector. But finding them was no easy task. Human intelligence was the only way. A few brave Iraqis—patriots, in my view—stepped forward. Some became interpreters, bridging the cultural and linguistic divide without which our mission would have been impossible. Their courage far exceeded what most Americans could imagine; they risked their honor, families, homes, and lives every day.

Most civilians, however, feared reprisal and stayed silent. They knew who the Ba'athists were and where they hid, but the former regime's shadow government continued to intimidate and kill. Many tips we did receive proved false, often fabricated by rival clans hoping to use us as proxies in their feuds. This starkly contrasted with postwar Germany, where civilians—especially clergy—readily exposed hardcore Nazis, enabling the Allies to prosecute thousands within months. Iraq was different: the Ba'ath Party was too large, our forces too few, and the environment too unstable.

Ultimately, coalition efforts narrowed to the top fifty-five most-wanted regime figures. These individuals comprised Saddam's inner circle. To aid the hunt, soldiers were issued a deck of playing cards with each fugitive's face. The repetition served its purpose; patrols memorized those names and faces quickly.

Around the same period, the CPA disbanded the Iraqi military, leaving it up to us to rebuild it from scratch. Before the war, Iraq had over 400,000 active servicemen. They could not match our Army in direct combat, but they might have helped restore basic security and governance. Had efforts been made to recall some of them early on, many likely would have returned to service—and it could have made a difference. Based on numerous conversations with former Iraqi officers after the regime fell, I believe the old army could have been reconstituted far more quickly than what ultimately occurred.

It took over two hundred years to build the US military, and now—in addition to reestablishing governance, law and order, civil engineering, and searching for old regime leaders—we had to remake the Iraqi military in our own image. This would be no simple task and it would not happen quickly. Overnight hundreds of thousands of trained Iraqi soldiers were out of a job. In my view, the combination of de-Ba'athification and disbanding the military contributed significantly to the conditions that fueled the insurgency for years. The consequences were profound and costly.

Looking back, I wish more Americans understood the complexity of what we faced. Saddam was a brutal dictator, but his regime held Iraq together through its institutions. The Iraqi Army, as a major institution, and the looming threat from Iran helped maintain that balance. Disbanding the army fractured the country's ethnic fabric, and regional actors quickly seized the opportunity. In hindsight, a more precise approach might have served us better—but instead we chose a sweeping one, and the consequences were significant.

Beyond hunting Ba'athists, our daily mission was to secure and repair Iraq's fragile infrastructure. We guarded banks, gas stations, ammunition depots, and even Baghdad's only fire station. That station came under daily attack from diehards determined to burn the city faster than Iraqi firefighters could save it. It was part of a broader strategy: sabotage the infrastructure to break civilian faith in the coalition. Their war was not over—it had only shifted forms.

Nights in Baghdad became surreal At sunset, tracer fire laced the sky, mortar rounds illuminated the horizon, and explosions echoed across the city. Often the attacks had no clear target; they seemed designed to sow chaos and convince Iraqis that the coalition lacked control. From May to June 2003, we failed to recognize what was taking shape: the early stages of a coordinated insurgency. Intimidation of civilians, attacks on infrastructure, random chaos. This was all groundwork. We mistook it for mere lawlessness. In reality, former regime loyalists and foreign jihadists were organizing in plain sight, biding their time until they could strike us directly.

During reconstruction's first months, the Iraqi Police were still being screened and retrained. Those already in uniform could not carry firearms, restricted instead to directing traffic. A functional civil police force was essential to any nation's survival, but it was still far from ready.

In the meantime, we filled the void. Our soldiers conducted presence patrols, manned checkpoints, detained looters and curfew violators, and responded to crimes. But our authority was limited. Iraq's justice system had collapsed. There was no revised constitution, no vetted judges, no reliable prisons. Soldiers found it frustrating to detain offenders only to release them days later.

Some situations were morally wrenching. On one patrol, soldiers intervened when a man was beating his wife for protesting his abuse of their daughter. Under Saddam's government, such violence was legal. With no law yet in place to protect the woman, we could only hold the man briefly and release him. For young soldiers raised in small town America, this was bewildering. For commanders, it was a painful reminder of how long it would take to rebuild Iraq's institutions or to build new, better ones.

Alongside security, we sought to build trust. Soldiers engaged civic and religious leaders, helped displaced families, created community programs, and supported schools. Cultural missteps were inevitable, but the patience and discipline of our troops minimized conflict. Task Force 2-7 Infantry adapted quickly to what the Army defines as stability and support operations (SASO)—a mission that demanded fighting insurgents one moment and fostering trust the next.

On May 1, 2003, President Bush declared major combat operations over. For us, that meant gathering information on the city's needs including electricity, sewage, water, and garbage disposal and passing it up to brigade for action. Fire support officers who once targeted the enemy with artillery now became information officers, mapping out neighborhoods in need of repair. It was "nonlethal targeting" focused on finding what needed fixing rather than destroying.

Civil affairs teams became invaluable. Captain Bill Thompson and his team worked with us from March to June 2003, serving as our eyes and ears into Iraqi society. They recruited interpreters, vetted applicants for jobs, and even helped hire local security guards to relieve overstretched 2-7 companies. Nightly meetings brought together IO officers, civil affairs, PSYOPS, and operations staff to prioritize nonlethal targets for action. Every week showed progress—power restored, schools reopened, crime reduced. Progress was slow, but it was steady.

Early in the occupation, Baghdad faced a gasoline crisis. Under Saddam, fuel had been free but strictly rationed. After his fall, lines at the few operating stations stretched for miles. Black market sales thrived, with attendants often complicit. Our soldiers took over managing two stations—one in each zone—turning away can carriers, manning pumps, and posting heavy weapons as both deterrence and protection. Even so, drivers waited all day only to fill half a tank. It was a bitter irony: a nation sitting on vast oil reserves unable to fuel its own cars.

Life became a grind. Soldiers patrolled in 130-degree heat, wrapped in body armor. Days blurred together, dubbed "Groundhog Day" after the film. Combat stress teams circulated to treat depression and early cases of PTSD. Soldiers coped in different ways—exercise, movies, letters home, or cards played with the Iraqi "Most Wanted" deck. Leaders bore the added challenge of keeping young men away from drugs, alcohol, and forbidden relationships.

By late May 2003, the 1st Armored Division began relieving us in Baghdad. Through "right-seat" and "left-seat" rides, we handed over responsibilities, completing transfer by early June. Task Force 2-7 became a reserve force in and around Baghdad, to be used as the mission dictated and as conditions unfolded. The rest of my brigade shifted to Falluja—a Sunni stronghold and suspected insurgent base about thirty miles west of Baghdad. The city would soon become infamous as the epicenter of the insurgency, culminating in the bloody 2004 al-Fajr campaign.

Meanwhile, my task force redeployed its tanks and Bradleys to Kuwait for refit. We would not see them again; instead those vehicles went to follow-on units. Losing our armor stripped us of our most visible deterrent. HMMWVs and trucks replaced Bradleys and Abrams tanks. It was a transition the enemy noticed.

It was then, during convoy escort duty, that insurgents struck with new tactics. On Highway 8, a command-detonated IED killed Private First Class Jeremiah Smith and wounded three others. The attack marked a shift. No longer content with sabotage and intimidation, the insurgents moved to direct strikes including ambushes, IEDs, helicopter targeting, even assaults on police stations. For the first time since Vietnam, the US Army found itself locked in a grinding insurgency.

From June through September, attacks increased steadily, averaging one per day. Morale was tested as casualties mounted. Unlike the march north, where we had tanks and clear targets to shoot at, now every patrol, every food run, every bridge crossing carried the threat of sudden, unseen death. Soldiers no longer felt in control of their fate; the enemy held the initiative.

The strength of the US Army has always been adaptation. We adjusted quickly: varying patrol patterns, hardening targets, building trust with Iraqis, and launching offensive raids to keep insurgents off balance. Information from civilians became our most valuable tool, allowing us to snatch insurgents from their safe havens with speed and precision.

By July 2003, operations intensified threefold. By year's end, forty-seven of the top fifty-five regime figures had been killed or captured—including Saddam Hussein himself in December, a remarkable success by the 4th Infantry Division.

But the enemy shifted focus. When coalition forces became too hard a target, insurgents attacked NGOs, contractors, and even the United Nations headquarters in Baghdad, killing scores, including a senior UN envoy. Their message was clear: if they could not strike us, they would punish those rebuilding Iraq.

Stabilizing Iraq proved harder than defeating the Iraqi Army in battle. During the march north, the mission had been simple: find and kill the enemy. Now, within just a few city blocks, a single task force conducted combat operations, peacekeeping, and humanitarian aid—all at once. The Army later called this the "Three-Block War." Task Force 2-7 Infantry lived it daily for four months after Baghdad fell, until they finally received orders to return home.

In September 2003, Task Force 2-7 Infantry redeployed to Fort Stewart. Families and communities greeted us with warmth. It was a welcome that Vietnam veterans deserved but never received. It was a moment of pride, but also of unease. Iraq was still burning. Soldiers were dying every day. Our mission there was far from over.

Back home, they trained relentlessly, preparing for an inevitable return in 2005. The Army itself restructured, transforming brigades into self-sufficient, modular units designed for both conventional warfare and counterinsurgency. Battalions would operate as task forces much more frequently because of Army transformation. Leaders rotated out to recruiting or instructor roles, passing on hard-earned lessons to prepare the next generation for a fight unlike any the Army had formally trained for.

We had completed our mission, but the war in Iraq and the transformation of the Army itself had only just begun.

PARTING THOUGHTS

Iraq marked the last large-scale combat operation (LSCO) where the US Army relearned the unforgiving realities of logistics, armored warfare, and the unpredictable aftermath of battle. Task Force 2-7 Infantry did more than fight; they defined modern mechanized warfare with grit, trust, and adaptability, embodying the soul of the Army in every sleepless night, every sniper's shadow, and in every sacrifice. Their legacy is a beacon for future soldiers facing new threats around the globe. For me, this wasn't just history—it was personal.

Task Force 2-7 Infantry was made up of damn fine soldiers. Individuals from every corner of the country, every background, every ethnicity. We were given new technology just before the breach—and we used it effectively. The leaders, the staff, and the teamwork were exceptional. There were countless acts of valor, including one that earned the Medal of Honor. But what I'm proudest of is how we cared for each other. Young soldiers took this battalion task force to battle, and they took care of each other every step of the way. That's what I hope history remembers. That's what I hope their families remember.

That pride made the day I relinquished command all the more difficult. In June 2003, I handed over the colors of the 2nd Battalion 7th Infantry. I had known this day would come all along, but it was all too soon for me. As Major Kevin Cooney started the ceremony, I thought I would lose my composure. I thought repeatedly of the soldiers that had become a permanent part of my thoughts, guideposts and signal bearers. I thought of those that had been killed as I rubbed the ten stones that I had kept in my pocket as a memorial to their lives, a reminder of my mortality and their sacrifice.

As I shook hands with Lieutenant Colonel Todd Wood, the incoming commander, I felt certain that he was left with the absolute best and strongest infantry battalion that had ever marched. I would miss them and the single-minded drive of war. The farewell reception at the Baghdad Sheraton Hotel was bittersweet. Who would have imagined, a change of command ceremony on the grounds of the Iraqi's Martyr Monument, an area reminiscent to our Vietnam Memorial in Washington, DC? It seemed fitting and it felt right.

Many of my fellow commanders continued to pursue their careers in the military and to proudly serve the people of the United States of America; I chose to retire. Many, many people have asked me why. After being awarded the Silver Star and the Bronze Star for Valor, what greater honor could there be than to ascend to the rank of general? I had mulled this over for many months. The truth is, that after battalion command, the one-on-one connection with soldiers is broken. These relationships had provided sustenance for me during my entire career. The feeling of sheer determination and strength in the company of these soldiers could never be replaced.

When I looked out over the horizon on the concrete surface of the Martyrs Monument, I saw a future for Iraq, a clarity for the people of this beleaguered nation. I believed that my two tours in Iraq, during Desert Storm and Operation Iraqi Freedom, had given these people a new start, and I had completed my mission. It was time for me to tell the story of these great soldiers and ensure that for generations to come their deeds and sacrifices are never forgotten.

When America crossed into Iraq in 2003, Task Force 2-7 Infantry was at the tip of the spear. We carried more than rifles and rucksacks—we carried the weight of a nation's hopes, the burden of history, and the responsibility to act when called. The invasion changed Iraq, it changed the world, and it changed every one of us who marched north into uncertainty. Yet our legacy endures. Out of the desert came a generation of leaders forged in fire, who carried hard-earned lessons back into the Army, into our communities, and into the nation we swore to defend.

The world will long debate the war's consequences, but one truth is certain: when the moment arrived, Task Force 2-7 did its duty and performed honorably. Its *damn fine soldiers* left a mark not just on Iraq, but on history itself.

ABLE 6: NOTHING FURTHER. OUT.

Lieutenant Colonel Scott Rutter's last day in command of Task Force 2-7 Infantry. Courtesy of Task Force 2-7 History.
Source: Bill Thompson.

AWARDS AND MEDALS

Medal of Honor:	1
Soldiers Medal:	4
Silver Star:	12
Bronze Star with Valor:	27
Bronze Star:	69
Army Commendation Medal with Valor:	114
Army Commendation Medal:	947
Purple Heart:	19
Combat Infantryman Badge:	545
Combat Infantryman Badge 2nd Award:	21
Combat Medical Badge:	33
Combat Medical Badge 2nd Award:	1

Lieutenant Colonel (retired) Scott Rutter on his Bradley Fighting Vehicle, March 19, 2003. Courtesy of Task Force 2-7 History.
Source: Bill Thompson.

GLOSSARY OF TERMS

2-7 Infantry (2nd Battalion, 7th Infantry Regiment): The main US Army unit featured in the book; a mechanized infantry battalion known as the "Willing and Able" Battalion.

3rd Infantry Division (3ID/Marne Division): A heavy US Army division that led the ground assault to Baghdad in 2003.

A-10: US Air Force ground attack aircraft ("Warthog") designed to support troops by striking enemy targets close to friendly forces.

AAFES (Army and Air Force Exchange Service): Military-run retail stores that sell everyday goods to soldiers on bases and in deployed areas.

AAR (After Action Review): A structured discussion conducted after a mission or exercise to analyze what happened, why, and how to improve.

Abrams Tank (M1A1): The US Army's primary battle tank, combining heavy armor, speed, and powerful firepower.

ACE (Armored Combat Earthmover): A heavily armored bulldozer used by military engineers to clear obstacles and build fortifications.

ACR (Armored Cavalry Regiment): A heavily armored reconnaissance unit; at the National Training Center, the 11th ACR acts as the enemy force.

AH-64 Apache: A US Army attack helicopter designed to destroy armored vehicles and provide close air support.

AirLand Battle Doctrine (ALBD): A Cold War–era US Army strategy integrating air and ground forces to fight a layered, deep battlefield.

Al Qaeda: A transnational terrorist organization responsible for the September 11, 2001, attacks.

APC (Armored Personnel Carrier): An armored vehicle designed to transport infantry safely on the battlefield.

Assembly Area: A temporary location where military units gather to organize and prepare before combat operations.

AT-4: A portable, shoulder-fired antitank weapon.

BDA (Battle Damage Assessment): An estimate of the damage caused by an airstrike or attack.

BDU (Battle Dress Uniform): The standard US Army uniform worn during the period described in the book.

BFT/Blue Force Tracker (FBCB2): A satellite-based system that shows friendly units on a digital map to reduce friendly fire risk.

BMP: A Soviet-designed infantry fighting vehicle that carries troops and provides fire support.

Bradley Fighting Vehicle (M2/M2A2 ODS): An armored vehicle that carries infantry soldiers into battle while providing fire support.

BRDM: A Soviet armored scout car used for reconnaissance.

C2 (Command and Control): The exercise of authority and direction by a commander over assigned forces.

CAS (Close Air Support): Airpower used to directly assist troops engaged with enemy forces.

CASEVAC (Casualty Evacuation): Moving wounded personnel using whatever vehicle is available.

CENTCOM (US Central Command): The US military command responsible for operations in the Middle East.

Coalition Forces: Military forces from multiple allied nations fighting together.

COIN (Counterinsurgency): Military and political actions taken to defeat insurgency and address its root causes.

Combat Power: The total fighting strength of a unit, including people, equipment, training, and morale.

Cottonbalers: The historic nickname of the 7th Infantry Regiment, originating from the War of 1812.

CPA (Coalition Provisional Authority): The interim governing body established by coalition forces in Iraq after the 2003 invasion.

D30: A Soviet 122mm towed artillery piece.

Deuce and a Half: A nickname for a 2.5-ton military cargo truck originally designed in World War II.

EOD (Explosive Ordnance Disposal): Specialists trained to detect and safely remove or detonate unexploded bombs and mines.

ETAC (Enlisted Terminal Attack Controller): A soldier who coordinates close air support missions.

FARP (Forward Arm Refuel Point): A temporary location near the front lines where aircraft or vehicles can refuel.

FBCB2 (Force XXI Battle Command Brigade and Below): A digital system that tracks friendly and enemy forces on the battlefield.

FRG (Family Readiness Group): A support network for soldiers' families during deployments.

Global War on Terror (GWOT): The US campaign launched after 9/11 to combat terrorist organizations worldwide.

HMMWV: A high mobility multipurpose wheeled vehicle used for transport and combat support.

IED (Improvised Explosive Device): A homemade bomb often hidden along roads or in vehicles.

IFV (Infantry Fighting Vehicle): An armored vehicle designed to transport soldiers and fight alongside them.

Javelin: A man-portable, fire-and-forget antitank guided missile.

JSList (Joint Service Lightweight Integrated Suit Technology): A modern protective suit against nuclear, biological, and chemical threats.

Karbala Gap: A key geographic corridor south of Baghdad that coalition forces had to seize to reach the capital.

KIA (Killed in Action): A soldier who has died during combat.

LMTV (Light Medium Tactical Vehicle): A military truck used for transporting troops and cargo.

LOC (Line of Communication): Routes used to supply and communicate with frontline units.

Logistics: The systems that sustain military forces, including supply, transportation, maintenance, and medical care.

LRAS (Long Range Acquisition System): A thermal imaging device used for long-distance target detection.

M113: A widely used armored personnel carrier.

M1A1 Abrams: The main battle tank used by the US Army.

M2A2 Bradley (ODS): A variant of the Bradley infantry fighting vehicle upgraded after Desert Storm.

MDMP (Military Decision-Making Process): A formal planning process used by military staffs to analyze missions and develop plans.

MICLIC (Mine Clearing Line Charge): A rocket-propelled explosive used to clear minefields.

MOPP (Mission-Oriented Protective Posture): Levels of protective gear worn to defend against chemical, biological, or nuclear threats.

Mortar: A portable artillery piece that fires explosive shells in a high arc.

MOUT (Military Operations in Urban Terrain): Combat operations conducted in cities and built-up areas.

MRE (Meal, Ready-to-Eat): Prepackaged field rations for soldiers.

NTC (National Training Center): A US Army training facility in California for large-scale combat exercises.

Operation Iraqi Freedom (OIF): The 2003 US-led invasion of Iraq to remove Saddam Hussein's regime.

OPFOR (Opposing Force): A unit that simulates enemy forces during training.

OPTEMPO (Operational Tempo): The pace and intensity of military operations.

PIR (Priority Intelligence Requirement): The most important information a commander needs about the enemy.

PSYOPS (Psychological Operations): Military operations aimed at influencing the attitudes and behavior of enemy or civilian populations.

Q36/Q37: Counterfire radars used to detect and locate enemy artillery.

Rage, Bushmaster, Knight: Nicknames for infantry companies within the battalion.

ROE (Rules of Engagement): The rules that define when and how troops may use force.

RPG (Rocket Propelled Grenade): A shoulder-fired antitank weapon that launches explosive rockets.

RSOI (Reception, Staging, Onward Movement, and Integration): The process of preparing arriving units for combat in a war zone.

SA-2: A Soviet surface-to-air missile system.

SASO (Stability and Support Operations): Military operations aimed at maintaining or restoring order in a region.

Scout Platoon: A unit tasked with reconnaissance and gathering battlefield intelligence.

SDZ (Surface Danger Zone): The area around a weapon where friendly forces cannot be present during firing.

Shock and Awe: A military strategy focused on overwhelming the enemy with rapid, powerful attacks.

SRG (Special Republican Guard): Saddam Hussein's elite security force.

Task Force: A temporary, mission-specific military formation combining multiple unit types.

Technical Truck: A civilian vehicle modified with mounted weapons for combat.

Thermal Sights: Devices that detect heat signatures to identify targets.

TOC (Tactical Operations Center): The command post for controlling military operations.

TOW (Tube-launched, Optically tracked, Wire-guided missile): An antitank missile system.

Troop Leading Procedures (TLPs): A step-by-step method leaders use to plan and execute missions.

T-72: A Soviet-designed main battle tank used by Iraqi forces.

UN Resolution 1441: A United Nations resolution demanding Iraq comply with weapons inspections.

UXO (Unexploded Ordnance): Bombs or shells that have not detonated.

WMD (Weapons of Mass Destruction): Nuclear, chemical, or biological weapons capable of causing mass casualties.

XO (Executive Officer): The commander's deputy who assists with managing the unit.

ABOUT THE AUTHORS

LIEUTENANT COLONEL (RETIRED) SCOTT E. RUTTER

It was US Army Lieutenant Colonel Scott E. Rutter's unit that assaulted the Iraqi Special Republican Guard and secured the Baghdad International Airport in Operation Iraqi Freedom. For this daring maneuver, his unit was broadly recognized and Lieutenant Colonel Rutter was decorated with the Silver Star.

During Operation Desert Storm, then Captain Rutter commanded C Company, 2nd Battalion, 16th Infantry, "Rangers" in the 1st Infantry Division and was decorated with the Bronze Star for Valor in 1991. During Operation Iraqi Freedom, Lieutenant Colonel Rutter commanded the 2nd Battalion, 7th Infantry "Cottonbalers" in the 3rd Infantry Division and made the initial assault into Iraq all the way to Baghdad as part of the "Tip of the Spear."

Scott retired from the US Army after serving over twenty years. He served as a FOX News Channel war correspondent, then as senior director at BAE Systems leading a $500 million business area. He currently serves as founder and president of the Valor Network Inc. and as a member of the board of directors and treasurer for Tragedy Assistance Program for Survivors (TAPS).

Scott is a graduate of Campbell University (B.S. History) and holds an M.S. in Management from the University of Saint Mary. In 2010, he was awarded Distinguished Alumnus from Campbell University.

MATTHEW C. PAUL

Commissioned a second lieutenant in 1999, Matthew C. Paul served in several Infantry assignments including Operation Iraqi Freedom in 2003 with the 3rd Infantry Division and later the 101st Airborne Division (Air Assault). He earned multiple decorations for his combat service, including two Bronze Star awards.

He returned to Iraq in 2006, overseeing a large area of operations to ensure peace and stability, train the new Iraqi Security Forces, and conduct sustained counterinsurgency operations. Matthew Paul transitioned into the Army Acquisition Corps in 2009, deployed to Afghanistan in 2013 to equip the Army with next-generation drones, and was hand-picked to lead the Army's most consequential information technology projects over a decade.

He continues to serve the Army full time and works part time as an adjunct college professor teaching information science. Matt is a graduate of Rowan University (B.S.), holds an M.S. in management from Austin Peay State University, and earned a Master's in government information leadership from the National Defense University.

Throughout his career, Matt has been recognized for his leadership and dedication to modernizing Army systems and developing the next generation of military leaders. His combined experience in combat operations and technological innovation brings a unique perspective to the story of Task Force 2-7 Infantry.

www.ingramcontent.com/pod-product-compliance
Ingram Content Group UK Ltd.
Pitfield, Milton Keynes, MK11 3LW, UK
UKHW011948180826
8008IPUK00002B/26

9 781493 096992